AF607949

THE JUDICIAL ROLE IN A DIVERSE FEDERATION

Lessons from the Supreme Court of Canada

The Judicial Role in a Diverse Federation

Lessons from the Supreme Court of Canada

ROBERT SCHERTZER

UNIVERSITY OF TORONTO PRESS
Toronto Buffalo London

Toronto Buffalo London
www.utppublishing.com

ISBN 978-1-4875-0028-3

Library and Archives Canada Cataloguing in Publication

Schertzer, Robert, 1981–, author
The judicial role in a diverse federation : lessons from the Supreme Court of Canada / Robert Schertzer.

Includes bibliographical references and index.
ISBN 978-1-4875-0028-3 (cloth)

1. Canada. Supreme Court. 2. Federal government – Canada – Cases. I. Title.

KE4275.S34 2016 342.71'04 C2015-908026-6
KF4483.F4S34 2016

This book has been published with the help of a grant from the Federation for the Humanities and Social Sciences, through the Awards to Scholarly Publications Program, using funds provided by the Social Sciences and Humanities Research Council of Canada.

University of Toronto Press acknowledges the financial assistance to its publishing program of the Canada Council for the Arts and the Ontario Arts Council, an agency of the Government of Ontario.

Canada Council for the Arts | Conseil des Arts du Canada

Funded by the Government of Canada | Financé par le gouvernement du Canada

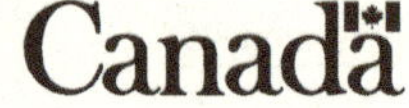

Contents

Part Two: The SCC's Federalism Jurisprudence, 1980 to 2010

Tables

Acknowledgments

This book would not have been possible without the support of my partner in all things. Bronwyn, it is dedicated to you.

I also owe a great deal to my doctoral supervisors, John Hutchinson and Martin Loughlin. Your guidance during my thesis, from which this book draws, was more than anyone could ask for.

There are many other people who have also contributed to this project. First and foremost is Eric Taylor Woods, who has been a constant source of motivation and constructive commentary. Grace Skogstad provided advice and in-depth comments that sharpened the analysis and writing: I am in her debt. A host of others have also commented on drafts along the way, and I would like to thank them, including John Breuilly, André Lecours, Brendan O'Learly, François Rocher, Stephen Tierney, and Stefan Wolff. The support offered by my colleagues and the Department of Political Science at the University of Toronto has been invaluable. Also, the team of energetic scholars at the Association for the Study of Ethnicity and Nationalism have played a major role in supporting me and shaping my thinking. Angela Pietrobon provided excellent indexing and proofreading services. The team at UTP have been truly amazing in all stages of the process getting this book to print.

The Social Sciences and Humanities Research Council, London School of Economics, and University of Toronto supported the research underpinning this book at various stages.

I would like to end by thanking my family for their unwavering support.

THE JUDICIAL ROLE IN A DIVERSE FEDERATION

Lessons from the Supreme Court of Canada

Introduction

The Topic

This book is about the management of diversity and conflict through federalism, and the role courts play in this process. It primarily focuses on an important case within the field of federal theory, Canada – investigating the work of its federal arbiter, the Supreme Court of Canada (SCC). While this is a study of Canada, it is consciously designed to engage with broader theory and policy. As such, Canada is treated as a particular type of case: a plurinational federation. The concept of plurinationality is a central element of the study. As I explain in detail below, a plurinational state is one where the national composition of the country is contested by different groups (i.e., one group argues a state is *uni*national with another group arguing it is *multi*national). This concept thus provides a distinction between the moniker of "multinational" (which implies the citizens of a state overwhelmingly accept that it is comprised of multiple, sealed national groups) and "plurinational" (which implies the very nature of the state's national composition is contested by various groups).[1] The motivation for classifying Canada as a plurinational federation is to facilitate the use of general theory to better understand the case and the work of its federal arbiter, while also informing analysis and reflection applicable to other similar cases (i.e., other plurinational federations).

The scope of the study is to investigate how diversity and conflict are managed in Canada through the federation and its federal arbiter. The

1 On plurinationality, see Keating (2001).

goal is to draw on this analysis to advance theory and policy in this area for Canada, and for other similar states. This book is thus both theoretical and empirical. It reflects on federalism as a means to manage diversity and conflict. This theoretical analysis provides the lens to interpret and assess the work of the SCC as federal arbiter. This empirical analysis, in turn, provides the base to reflect back on the wider theory and policy issues related to the use of federal systems to manage diversity and conflict.

While there have been many studies of how diversity and conflict are managed (both looking at Canada and beyond), this remains an important area of research. The twentieth century was marked by a significant rise of intra-state warfare and ethno-national conflict.[2] This phenomenon can be linked to the implementation of the doctrine of national self-determination in a system of states that are internally diverse.[3] In other words, a strong argument can be made that ethno-national diversity within a state increases instability and the probability of violent conflict.[4] And, even in diverse states where conflict does not manifest itself as violence, struggles for national self-determination inside and outside the political system can have significantly destabilizing effects on the association.

For many, federalism is one of the solutions to the problem of diversity and conflict. Federal systems tend to be seen as maintaining the territorial integrity of a state, while either placating or accommodating ethno-national groups.[5] In line with this viewpoint, there are those who promote federalism as a nation-building tool, as a way to divide

---

2 See Hewitt (2008) and Quinn (2008). Ethno-national conflicts involve at least one party linking their objectives and motivations to ethno-national identity. They are conflicts where "the primary fault line of confrontation is one of ethno-national distinctions"; see Wolff (2011: 162). As Stefan Wolff notes, these are "among the most intractable, violent and destructive forms of conflict."

3 The central driver of this conflict is thus the "problem of fit": more than 600 language groups and 5000 ethnic groups are housed in fewer than 200 states; see Gurr (1993).

4 For support of this view, see Montalvo and Reynal-Querol (2005); Gurr et al. (2008: 9); Toft (2003); Kaufmann (2011). On the other side, there are those who argue ethnic heterogeneity is not a predictor of civil war; see Fearon and Laitin (2003) and Laitin (2007).

5 Throughout the book I distinguish between the terms "federalism" (which refers to the ideology and principle of promoting federal systems of government) and "federation" (which refers to the system of government establishing shared and self-rule through institutional mechanisms); on this distinction, see King (1982).

ethno-national groups to create a sense of national unity.[6] As part of the post-1989 movement towards minority rights regimes in international society, federalism has been (increasingly) promoted as a means to grant ethno-national groups territorial autonomy.[7] What these two approaches share is an underlying assumption that federalism can *solve* ethno-national conflict by removing the *problem* of diversity through an institutional mechanism (that either assimilates diversity into a single national community or segregates national groups within a single state).

This shared characteristic of federal theory is problematic. It assumes that ethno-national conflict can be dealt with through fixed institutional mechanisms. Underlying this assumption is the view that once a federal system is in place conflict between groups will largely take place within that structure, not over the way a federation recognizes identity and distributes power and resources. In reality, conflict over the way the state recognizes national identities (or not) and accordingly distributes resources and power via a federal system (or not) continues over time. In other words, the main federal approaches to managing diversity and conflict fail to recognize fully that a federation is, at its base, a normative framework that is contested by those subject to the system.[8]

The view of federal institutions as sitting above contestation is linked to another problem with contemporary work in the area: the relatively under-examined role federal arbiters play in managing conflict over the distribution of power and resources via federal systems. While there is a strong lineage of work on Canada's federal arbiter (the SCC), this work has not been fully integrated into the comparative and

---

6 The objective of this approach is to design the sub-state jurisdictions so that they cut across ethno-national boundaries to break down these allegiances and to create a centripetal force that generates loyalty to the state; see Horowitz (2000: 597–600).

7 This approach uses a federal system to accommodate a territorially concentrated group's nationalist ambitions via self-government. For example, prominent scholars promote multinational federalism for Spain (Requejo 2005), Iraq (O'Leary 2005), and India (Tillin 2007), to name only a few cases. Will Kymlicka has been promoting multinational federalism for national minorities for some time (Kymlicka 2000), seeking to apply this aspect of his work to Eastern Europe (Kymlicka 2002, 2005), Africa (Kymlicka 2006), and Asia (Kymlicka 2007). For a review of the promotion of multinational federalism in conflict management, see Schertzer and Woods (2011).

8 As I explain in greater detail below, the complexity of recognizing identities and distributing resources and power via a federation means it is, at any given time, contested by one or another group subject to the system.

conflict-management literature: more often than not, the institution of the federal arbiter receives insufficient study in broader theory.[9] There are single case studies of the work of federal arbiters in various federal systems; but accounts that link such studies to wider debates and theories about the functioning of federal systems to manage diversity are not common. Where the institution is considered, it is assumed that the arbiter should act in an independent and objective manner (and be assessed against this benchmark). Generally, in theory and practice, the role of federal arbiter falls to the judiciary (and ultimately an apex court), which is supposed to be the neutral umpire within a federation, enforcing the rules of the game when parties conflict. The problem with this assumption is that neutrality and independence are difficult for a federal arbiter to achieve. A federal arbiter cannot retreat to neutral ground in exercising its duties – it is part of the very system being challenged. In other words, federal theorists generally fail to recognize that

---

9 I discuss the Canadian work on the SCC's role in the federation below, as well as the lack of integrating this work on the judicial role with wider federal theory. An example of the under-examined and under-theorized role of the federal arbiter can be found in Will Kymlicka's (1998) *Finding Our Way*, which provides prescriptions and recommendations to accommodate diversity through multiculturalism and multinational federalism in Canada. In this 220-page book, Kymlicka dedicates two paragraphs to the topic of the SCC, saying that Canada's federal arbiter guarantees representation for Québec as three of its nine justices must be from that province; see Kymlicka (1998: 114). There is no additional substantive reflection on the Court's role in the development of the federation or on the role it should play in managing diversity and conflict. This is also evident in the influential collected volume edited by Sujit Choudhry (2008a), *Constitutional Design for Divided Societies*, which provides an overview of the different issues and cases of seeking to accommodate or integrate diversity through constitutional arrangements. In this volume, there is no dedicated, in-depth, consideration of the role the courts play in these processes. Similarly, in an article that provides a comprehensive account of ethno-national conflict management theory, Stefan Wolff does note the role promoted for the judiciary among the main approaches; see Wolff (2011: 172). However, among these main approaches, the promoted role for the judiciary is simply "independent," with the only alteration (for the liberal consociationalist approach) being that it should also be "representative." Important for my point is that Wolff has to turn to personal correspondence with a liberal consociationalist (John McGarry) to make this distinction given the lack of work on the subject. Notable exceptions to this lack of reflection in the wider conflict-management scholarship are a recent study by McCrudden and O'Leary (2013), *Consociations and Courts*, which investigates the impact of recent European Court of Justice rulings on consociational democracy in a number of European states, as well as a chapter by Ran Hirschl (2013), "The Constitutional Jurisprudence of Federalism and the Theocratic Challenge," in *The Global Promise of Federalism*.

conflict over the distribution of power tends to manifest as conflict over the rules themselves (not the application of a rule).[10] The tendency to overlook this point is one of the reasons for the continued lack of in-depth theorization and study on the role of federal arbiters.

This study seeks to address some of these gaps in the work on federations. As I have already said, it does this by looking at how conflict manifests itself over the distribution of resources and power within a plurinational federation (Canada) and how its federal arbiter (the SCC) has managed this conflict. Building on this analysis, the book presents a federal model that accounts for this conflict, with a particular focus on the role of the federal arbiter. I am thus trying to advance theory and policy applicable to Canada and other similar cases.

I focus on Canada for three main reasons. First, as a plurinational federation, it represents a particular type of case. Examining this plurinational federation, where there has been long-running (political) conflict over national identity and the way identity is recognized and power and resources are distributed via the federation, facilitates analysis of these conflict dynamics and the way they are managed. This examination allows for future comparative analysis, and can inform theory and policy applicable to other similar cases.[11]

Second, Canada is a key case within the field of federal theory (and ethno-national conflict management). Canada holds this status not just because it is one of the oldest federations or because it is generally perceived as one of the first states to accommodate national diversity through territorial self-government. Its status as a key case stems from the fact that analysis of Canada plays an important role in the development of general theory and policy. Even a cursory glance at comparative federalism texts,[12]

10 Conflict over the federal system is akin to conflict over the way any normative framework recognizes identities and accordingly distributes power and resources. Such conflicts are not struggles *for* recognition, but rather, are struggles *over* the way norms recognize identities and distribute power; see Schertzer (2008: 108–7); Tully (2004: 87–8).

11 There are 26 states that have adopted (or are in the process of adopting) federal systems of government. These 26 states house over 40% of the world's population. However, not all of these states are plurinational (i.e., not all have widespread competing conceptions of the nature of the state's national composition). I discuss the applicability of my analysis and argument beyond Canada in the final chapter.

12 For example, see Hueglin and Fenna (2006); Burgess (2006); Erk (2008); Baier (2006).

or the work of those promoting territorial self-government in diverse states,[13] supports this point.

Third, Canada tends to be misunderstood. As I argue throughout the book, those analysing the case, and particularly those seeking to export a "Canadian model" of federation, generally fail to account for the contestation that takes place over the nature of national identity and the federal system itself. A comprehensive analysis of Canada can inform our understanding of these conflict dynamics and how they are managed, thus advancing the theory and policy that has been developed in relation to the Canadian case.

More generally, focusing on Canada and its federal arbiter helps to contextualize discussion, rather than remain aloft in theoretical reflection. It provides the empirical basis to examine conflict and its management. While violent conflict has generally been absent in Canada,[14] the state has been marked by sustained political conflict over the way national identities are recognized and the way power and resources are accordingly distributed via the federation. Over the last three decades, a significant amount of this conflict has tended to take place through, and been managed by, the judiciary (the state's federal arbiter). Canada thus provides an opportunity to look at how conflict manifests over national identity and the federation through well-formulated arguments presented by key social actors in the legal forum, and also how the SCC manages this conflict through the historical record of court decisions.

The Argument

The central question driving this study is how the SCC has managed conflict over national identity and the federation in Canada. Through a comprehensive examination of the Court's work as federal arbiter over

13 For a discussion of the important role Canada plays in the promotion of multinational federalism, see Schertzer and Woods (2011), and note 7 above.

14 The most notable exception is the series of bombings perpetrated by the nationalist group Front de libération du Québec (FLQ) throughout the 1960s and the related "October Crises" in 1970, when the FLQ kidnapped a high-ranking government official (Pierre Laporte) and a British trade commissioner (James Cross), subsequently killing the former. The Government of Canada responded by implementing the War Measures Act, suspending civil liberties and resulting in the arrest and detention of almost 500 individuals. Also noteworthy is the three-month armed standoff in 1990 at Oka between a Mohawk (Aboriginal) first nation group and the Canadian army. The conflict related to a blockade of land the Aboriginal group claimed as their territory.

the past thirty years, I argue that the SCC has managed this conflict in both problematic and beneficial ways. The key distinction between the former and the latter is the approach adopted by the Court. The problematic approach is where the SCC imposes a particular understanding of the federation through its decisions. The beneficial approach is where the Court recognizes that the federation is a process and an outcome of negotiation between the subscribers of legitimate competing perspectives. I argue that the second of these approaches, where the Court tends to adopt a broad role of facilitating this negotiation, is preferable because it can generate and maintain legitimacy for the federation and the way it manages conflict.

These two lines of analysis support the broader point of the book: federal arbiters play a critical role in the development of a federation and the maintenance of its legitimacy in diverse states. Federal theory and conflict management thus need to better account for this role when analysing the functioning of existing systems and when devising new systems. One of the central points I make throughout this book, then, is that a federal arbiter should be fulfilling its role with an explicit focus on generating legitimacy for the federal system. In a diverse state, I argue the judiciary can generate legitimacy by recognizing the inherently contested nature of the federal system and reinforcing its dynamic elements. And, in adopting such an approach, the judiciary can exercise its duties as federal arbiter in a way that facilitates ongoing negotiation between the different conflicting groups within an association when the courts are called upon to mediate a dispute.

This argument has a number of layers. It recognizes that conflict over the nature of national identity and a federation is an inherent part of politics in many states, particularly in Canada. The argument also accounts for the fact that the judiciary is often called upon to mediate disputes over the nature of the federation, and so the courts have an important role in managing this conflict. In addition, the assessment of the SCC's work as problematic or beneficial for the legitimacy of the federation draws from general theory about the way a federation and federal arbiters should manage diversity and conflict. Elaborating on each of these related points helps to further explain them and my main argument.

In Canada, conflict over national identity and the federation are part of political life. As a plurinational federation, Canada's politics is marked by conflicting views about the state as a *uni*national or *multi*national polity. While an oversimplification of the categories and location of these groups, anglophones outside Québec tend to argue Canada is uninational, while francophones inside Québec and Aboriginals tend to argue Canada is multinational. However, it is important to recognize the complexity of these debates. As Michael Keating's investigation of plurinational states argues, historical analysis and polling shows that within Québec the "evidence suggests ... that there is a core of separatist voters and a core of anti-nationalists (found almost entirely outside the Francophone community), but [also] a large number of Quebeckers who are looking for a third way between separatism and federalism."[15] These competing nationalisms within Québec are paired with a traditionally strong pan-Canadian nationalism in English Canada and an emerging acceptance of the Québécois as a nation with the wider polity.[16] Thus, there are substantial, organized groups that are often institutionalized through political parties that mobilize and conflict over the nature of nationality in Canada. At the same time, the nature of the federal system as a normative framework means the way it distributes power and resources is contested by one or another group subject to the association. The result in Canada and other plurinational federations is that competing views of national identity mix with associated views of the appropriate distribution of power and resources to create considerable conflict over the federation.

This conflict is exemplified and propelled by three competing perspectives on the actual and ideal nature of the federal system: the pan-Canadian, provincial-equality, and multinational visions.[17] These three "federal visions" represent divergent perspectives on the national composition of the country, with associated views about the way the federation should be organized to distribute powers and resources. As I explain below, the pan-Canadian, provincial-equality, and multinational models are linked to the broader approaches within federal theory of trimming, trading, or segregating away national diversity. However, these models are not just abstract theories; they are comprehensive accounts of what the federation is and ought to be that inform political mobilization. As a result of this mobilization by groups and the associated belief in the rightness of their particular perspective, the

15 Keating (2001: 93). For Keating's discussion of Canada as plurinational, see pp. 89–98.

16 For an overview of these conflicting nationalisms in Canada, see Woods (2012: 278–86).

17 See Rocher and Smith (2003).

Canadian federation has developed in such a way that the subscribers of each model can point to elements of the legal and institutional structure of the state to support their perspective. Each of these models thus stands as a legitimate perspective on the actual and ideal nature of the association.

The conflict driven by these competing perspectives plays out in many forums, from the political process, to the legal arena, to the social realm, and even outside politics as violence. For example, we see it in acrimonious intergovernmental relations, in court disputes, in the media, and in instances of politically motivated violence and clashes on the streets (the latter being rare in Canada). By far the most common manifestation of this conflict in Canada is through intergovernmental relations and also related court cases when intergovernmental negotiations break down or when private parties want to contest an order of government's constitutional jurisdiction to pass legislation. The tendency to call on the courts to mediate disputes has meant the development of the Canadian federation has been marked by important (apex) court decisions on how the division of powers between the orders of government is to be implemented. In this federalism jurisprudence, the SCC is generally forced to deliver its decision in the face of competing arguments about the very nature of the federation made by subscribers to the various federal models.[18]

This activity means the SCC plays a critical role in maintaining the legitimacy of the federation. The critical nature of this role stems from the importance of political legitimacy in diverse federations, as well as recognizing the unique nature of a court's work as a federal arbiter.

Legitimacy – the belief in, and acceptance of, the validity of a form of political association – is important in all polities, but particularly so in diverse states.[19] It is the loyalty those within an association feel towards the polity, as a legitimate association, that ultimately maintains

18 The dynamic of conflict in such court cases tends to be between the orders of government, with the federal government arguing for the pan-Canadian model, Québec and Aboriginal groups arguing for the multinational model, and other provinces (particularly the western ones) arguing for the provincial-equality model. However, as discussed in subsequent chapters, the dynamic of conflict can also be between a private citizen or organization (arguing from the position of a particular federal model) and an order of government (arguing from the position of a competing federal model).

19 I am drawing here from Max Weber's reflections on the basis of political legitimacy and its link to authority (Weber 1968: 31–8, 54).

its unity.[20] A perceived lack of legitimacy in the way a state distributes power through institutions (such as territorial autonomy) thus threatens the very survival of the system.[21] In other words, loyalty towards a federation (and a particular view of the way it recognizes identities and should distribute power) helps to maintain unity. Conflict over a federal system is principally about the definition of the political community and how the state ought accordingly to be governed and resources and power distributed. In diverse federations, then, the legitimacy of the association takes on a particularly pressing concern: loyalty to the system (and the set of principles that define that system) is important to offset the centrifugal demographic and institutional forces that abound.

The judiciary is a particularly important institution in generating and maintaining legitimacy in federal systems. When the institution is called upon to settle disputes or interpret and apply the constitution, it is playing a part in defining the nature of the political community and the way the state recognizes identities and distributes power. In Canada, the SCC's role in maintaining the legitimacy of the system is evident through its work as the federal arbiter. This aspect of the Court's work is not simply about applying rules, or deciding if one party is right and the other wrong. In its federalism jurisprudence, the Court is acting as the arbiter between parties holding, and arguing for, competing conceptions of what the federation is and ought to be.[22] When the Court makes a decision in such cases, it is acting as part of the federal system: it is one of the key mechanisms by which the federation manages conflict over the association and evolves in response to this conflict. In exercising this duty, the Court can generate (or erode) loyalty among the subscribers of the various perspectives to the way the federation manages conflict and to the resulting federal system. What the SCC says in a decision can either recognize or deny legitimacy to a particular party's perspective on the nature of the federation, thus directly and indirectly affecting the way the federation develops and

20 In other words, as I explain in chapter 1, legitimacy is important because it is the very basis of political authority and thus sovereignty. In this view, sovereignty is essentially the expression of political power, which is generated from the loyalty of the governed to their state and government; on this, see Loughlin (2003: ch. 5).

21 Loughlin (2003: 78–82).

22 These competing conceptions are generally informed by the three federal models discussed above.

also contributing to a group's political and material standing within the association.

This view of the importance of the SCC's role leads to the empirical question of how the Court actually exercises its duties and manages conflict. Looking at the Court's work as federal arbiter over the past thirty years reveals two distinct streams: one that has the potential to generate loyalty to the federation among the subscribers of the various federal models (by recognizing their perspective) and one that arguably erodes loyalty to the federation (by imposing a competing perspective).

Thinking about this argument raises issues about how one can demonstrate the Court's effect on the legitimacy of the federation and the loyalty groups feel towards the association. An empirical confirmation that SCC decisions affect the legitimacy of the federation by recognizing (or not recognizing) particular perspectives is beyond the scope of this study. Such empirical research is possible: one could, for example, investigate how attitudes towards the federation shift in response to particular decisions as indicated through instances of nationalist mobilization, the tone of public debate (in the media and in legislatures), and polling data. However, this line of inquiry requires the analysis here before it can be properly conducted. Studying how decisions affect the federation *necessarily* follows an assessment of what decisions to investigate, and what to look for (i.e., to have a sense of whether a particular decision is potentially problematic or not). The empirical aspect of my work here addresses these questions, which are important in their own right, while also providing a framework to facilitate later analysis of the SCC's role in generating or eroding the legitimacy of the association. At the same time, this study of the Court's federalism jurisprudence works from a set of assumptions – which are outlined and defended throughout the book – about how a federal arbiter can generate legitimacy in the way it manages conflict. I am making a case for why one stream of the SCC's federalism jurisprudence can be seen as problematic and another stream can be seen as beneficial. But, I do not claim to *prove* this point, empirically.

Returning to my argument, the analysis in subsequent chapters shows how the Court problematically imposes one federal model over others in a great deal of its federalism jurisprudence. The Court imposes particular perspectives by working from, and reinforcing, only one of the several federal models when making a decision. In such instances, the Court legitimizes a single federal model over alternative models by saying that it properly describes the federal system, while also aligning the federation with the privileged model through the decision outcome. For example, a decision that imposes the pan-Canadian model presents the federation as a centralized system that represents a pan-state nation, while asserting that this "fact" allows the central government to undertake a certain activity. This line of reasoning and the resulting outcome would be seen as an imposition by the subscribers of the multinational model, who view the federation as a decentralized and asymmetrical system that accommodates minority nations like the Québécois and Aboriginals. Through my subsequent comprehensive review of the Court's work, I show that this type of decision takes place in a significant percentage (57%) of the SCC's federalism jurisprudence.

In these imposing decisions, the Court fails to recognize and account for the competing conceptions of national identity and the federation in Canada. This failure is problematic because it has the potential to negatively affect the legitimacy of the federation by eroding the loyalty parties feel to the conflict-management process and its results. Those being imposed upon in a decision can perceive the process as unfair because they see the Court favouring a competing view of what the federation is and ought to be. Such imposing decisions reinforce the sense that some groups are political outsiders, alienating them from the conflict-management process and from the resulting federal system. Moreover, the approach adopted in these decisions arguably leads to non-optimal outcomes: they are based on partial understandings of the institutional and legal structure of the federation and so reach outcomes based on incorrect assumptions. In other words, the outcomes of imposing decisions would be stronger if they accounted for the plurality of perspectives on the nature of the federal system.

At the same time, in some circumstances, we can see the Court exercising its duties as federal arbiter in a way that can generate legitimacy for the conflict-management process and the resulting system. The potential for legitimacy generation is found in those decisions that draw from, and reinforce the legitimacy of, multiple federal models – or those that explicitly recognize that the federation is the process and outcome of negotiation between the subscribers of legitimate models. In such decisions, the Court rejects the overall approach of solving a conflict by enforcing a fixed set of rules that aligns with a particular understanding of the federation; rather, in these decisions, the Court embraces an inclusive understanding of the federation that incorporates elements of multiple federal models, while promoting the management of conflict through negotiation between the conflicting parties.

The archetypal example of a decision following this approach reaches an outcome that is positive to all the parties of a conflict (or has positive elements for all parties), with the outcome being based on a view that the federal system incorporates elements from all the federal models.[23] In such decisions, the Court may even go so far as to explicitly say that the federation is a contested normative system, which is the process and outcome of negotiation between the subscribers of legitimate and competing views about its nature.

This approach of recognizing and accounting for the parties' perspectives in arbitrating a conflict can engender loyalty to the process and outcome of conflict management, while also demonstrating that the federation is an inclusive system where all parties are stakeholders. Moreover, the Court's rejection of zero-sum outcomes allows subscribers of each federal model to find an aspect of the decision that supports their particular view of what the federation is and ought to be. Consequently, the subscribers of the various models are not alienated from the resulting federal system (they do not see it as inherently biased against their position); rather, they see the decision as reaffirming that elements of the federation reflect their view. Such an inclusive approach can show how the Court is subject to, and is affected by, the prevailing dynamics of the federal system, which can build loyalty to it as part of a fair and representative federal system. In other words, a federation can generate loyalty to the system and the way it manages conflict through a court *recognizing and accounting for* the conflicting views of national identity and the federation. Arguably, this recognition also leads to optimal outcomes in federalism jurisprudence because decisions are based upon a consideration of the various elements of the institutional and legal structures that have developed in response to this conflict.

It is the comprehensive account of the SCC's federalism jurisprudence over the past thirty years undertaken in subsequent chapters that brings into relief the divergent approaches of imposing particular federal models and recognizing the legitimacy of multiple models. This account also illuminates a number of important and related trends in the jurisprudence, which will be dealt with in more detail later. For example, my analysis shows an early tendency for the Court

23 As an example, such a view of the federation can highlight that it has both centralist and decentralist elements, while also allowing asymmetry between provinces, given the fact that Canada is at once a pan-state political community and one that incorporates multiple sub-state political communities, some of which identify as nations.

to impose the pan-Canadian model. It also shows an initial lack of support for the multinational model, which softens from the 1990s forward. The review also demonstrates that the Court makes a significant shift in its approach to conflict management with the *Secession Reference* in 1998.[24] In this case the SCC provides the exemplar of a decision that recognizes the legitimacy of multiple federal models, while also providing a picture of the federation as the process and outcome of negotiation. Taking into consideration the decision-making process and outcome of all federalism jurisprudence between 1980 and 2010, my analysis shows that this change of course is increasingly followed after the *Secession Reference*: from 1999 to 2010, 71 per cent of the SCC's decisions in its federalism jurisprudence adhere to the approach set forth in the *Secession Reference* of recognizing the legitimacy of multiple federal models.[25]

There is theoretical and practical value in noting and reflecting on these two streams of the SCC's federalism jurisprudence. Looking at the tendency to impose particular federal models, while the frequency of this type of decision is declining, the Court has still employed this problematic approach in a quarter of cases since 1998. And there is always the possibility the SCC will rely on an imposing decision method in future decisions. The SCC is a constantly changing institution, currently undergoing a period of transition with seven (of nine) justices appointed between 2006 and 2014.[26] At the same time, the Court will continue to play a critical role in shaping the federation and managing intergovernmental issues, as exemplified by its recent important decisions on proposed reforms to the Senate (the upper chamber of Parliament)[27] and on the appointment of SCC justices as representatives

---

24 *Reference re Secession of Quebec*, [1998] 2 S.C.R. 217.

25 Compare this to the fact that, when looking at the decisions in the federalism jurisprudence before the reference (from 1980–98), some 64% of decisions imposed a federal model. The framework used to review the Court's work and support this analysis is explained in detail in chapter 3.

26 Justice Rothstein, appointed during this period, retired in August 2015. He was succeeded by Justice Brown.

27 See *Reference re Senate Reform*, [2014] 1 S.C.R. 704. In this decision the SCC largely blocked the Government of Canada's ability to unilaterally make any significant changes to the composition of the Senate. In most areas where reforms were proposed by the central government (length of terms, electoral procedures) the Court stated that a substantial amount of provincial consent is required, and that abolition is only possible with unanimous federal-provincial consent.

from Québec.[28] Looking beyond Canada, and considering federalism's popularity as a means to manage diversity and conflict, broader federal theory can also benefit from reflection on this stream of the SCC's work. The tendency to impose a federal model demonstrates how a federal arbiter can exercise its duties in a way that can negatively affect the legitimacy of the system. Accordingly, the analysis in this book can inform theory and policy related to the federal arbiter's role in managing diversity and conflict in other similar cases to Canada's (i.e., other plurinational federations).

The subsequent chapters also demonstrate how a federal arbiter can fulfil its role in a way that generates legitimacy for the federal system. This analysis provides the elements of an approach and role for the federal arbiter that should be promoted for Canada (and, in certain respects, more generally). At the centre of this approach is an institutional model and theory of judicial review that calls on federal arbiters to recognize the validity of competing viewpoints on the nature of a diverse federation. In this regard, when asked to interpret the constitution and manage a conflict between the orders of government, courts should reinforce the dynamic nature of a federal system to the extent possible. Courts can achieve this objective in two related ways: pushing the orders of government to negotiate a mutually agreeable outcome through political processes; or, where this is not possible (which is not uncommon, given the inherently adversarial nature of conflict in court cases), reaching an outcome that rejects a zero-sum approach and reinforces the validity of the competing parties' perspectives on the nature of the federal system. In other words, federal arbiters should seek to *facilitate ongoing negotiation* between the conflicting orders of government and the continued use of political mechanisms to manage disputes, whenever possible, to help generate and maintain the legitimacy of a federal system.

---

28 In October 2013 Prime Minister Stephen Harper appointed Marc Nadon (from the Federal Court of Appeal) to the SCC (as a justice representing Québec, which is guaranteed by statute to have three justices represent the province of the nine available seats). In a March 2014 decision, the SCC blocked the appointment, essentially saying that since Nadon was a member of the Federal Court of Appeal (and not a sitting judge from Québec or a member of the Québec bar) he could not act as a representative for Québec; see *Reference re Supreme Court Act, ss. 5 and 6*, [2014] 1 S.C.R. 433.

We see this role exemplified in the *Secession Reference* and increasingly adopted in the decisions that follow this opinion in Canada. It is a role that recognizes there are multiple legitimate, if competing, conceptions of the national and federal character of the country. It accepts the objective of a federal arbiter is to manage conflict between those holding competing perspectives on the nature of the nation and the federation, not to solve it. And it appreciates that the Court does not sit above the conflict, but rather is part of the field of struggle and the system being challenged.

Situating the Argument

My main argument, and the layers of analysis underpinning it, draws from elements of constitutional theory, nationalism studies, federalism studies, and conflict-management theory.

From constitutional theory, I bring the above-noted appreciation of the critical role legitimacy plays in a political association. This perspective is based in particular on the work of Martin Loughlin and the argument that sovereignty is the expression of a political relationship.[29] Seeing sovereignty in this light illuminates the importance of maintaining the loyalty of those within an association to the way it is governed. My arguments also rest on a related view that constitutions are dynamic normative frameworks (rather than static legal documents).[30] My approach turns away from the more positivist accounts of constitutional theory and law, as well as work that views constitutions as primarily mechanisms to enshrine particular forms of liberal-rights regimes; instead, I draw on republican-inspired arguments, which stress that constitutions represent a nexus of politics and law, and that constitutionalism should be about protecting civic freedom within political associations and the promotion of political mechanisms to manage conflict.[31]

I also draw on three important developments within nationalism studies. First, I appreciate that nationalism is a dominant discourse of modern politics.[32] Nationalism plays a vital role in legitimizing political

29 See Loughlin (2003: chs. 1, 3).

30 See Tully (1995, 2000b, 2004).

31 See Tully (1995, 2004); Bellamy (1999, 2007); Petite (1997).

32 For an overview of the emergent importance of the principle of nationality from the nineteenth century, see Breuilly (2011); Mayall (1990).

power – it provides the necessary identity for the "people" that wield sovereign power.[33] Accordingly, legitimacy in a political association is inherently bound up with questions of national identity in the modern period.

Second, I follow the "ethno-symbolic" approach to understanding the phenomena of nations and nationalism, particularly the variant developed by John Hutchinson.[34] This approach seeks out the middle ground between those who argue that nations are discursive, elite constructions and those who argue that they are natural, real, and enduring groups.[35] Accordingly, I understand nations as imagined, and recognize that conflict between actors with competing views about the nature of the nation shapes their identity. At the same time, nations do exist, as defined by some combination of shared myths, symbols, language, practices, institutions, and political culture. The importance of these characteristics is the limit they impose on actors and elites to shape national identity.[36] I argue that this definition allows an understanding of the enduring and loyalty-generating nature of nations,[37] while also accounting for their contested and discursive nature.

This last point leads me to highlight the value of recognizing certain states as "plurinational." As noted above, the classification of plurinational builds on Keating's distinction between the categories of "uninational," "multinational," and "plurinational."[38] Plurinational states are marked by conflict between actors over the nature of the state's national identity, which is the case in states like Canada, the

33 Yack (2001).

34 See Hutchinson (2005) and Smith (2009). For a comprehensive review of the different streams within the field of nationalism studies – the modernist, primordialist, perennialist, and ethno-symbolist camps – which tend to diverge on the question of when nations emerged and the causal link between nations and nationalism, see Smith (1998).

35 These are the positions of the so-called modernist and primordialist camps. For an example of the former see Hobsbawm (1990); Anderson (1991); Breuilly (1993); and Brubaker (1996, 2004). For the latter see Geertz (1973); van den Berghe (1978, 1995); and Grosby (1994).

36 However, it is important to note the interplay between the debate over national identity and the more tangible aspects of national identity: as the limits on national identity frame the debate, so the debate over these characteristics shapes the understanding and nature of the nation. The definition of the nation put forth in the last three sentences mirrors that in Schertzer and Woods (2011).

37 In particular, the strong emotive force nations produce for those who identify with them (even pushing some to die in the name of their nation).

38 Keating (2001: 27; 2002: 361).

United Kingdom, and Spain (where pan-state nationalists and minority nationalists try to frame the state as uninational or multinational). The value of this perspective is that it allows for an understanding of the drivers and manifestation of conflict over nationality in states like Canada (conflict that also mixes with, and manifests itself as, conflict over the federation).[39]

Related to this view of national identity, I follow the line of scholarship that identifies federations as a type of normative system.[40] I argue that a federation is best understood as a system that arises out of conflict over the way identities are recognized and power is accordingly distributed via the governing norms, what James Tully terms an "intersubjective normative framework."[41] A federation is distinguished from other systems of rule in the way it constitutes multiple orders (or levels) of government within a state to which it distributes power and resources. Federal systems stand as one of the clearest examples of intersubjective normative frameworks, as they *explicitly* distribute power and resources in line with the way the identities of their constituent units are recognized.[42] Within federal studies, I also follow the practice of distinguishing between federalism (as an ideology) and federation (as a form of government).[43]

Finally, my work seeks to build on the stream of conflict-management theory that argues a nuanced understanding of nations and nationalism is of the utmost importance because one's view of national identity affects one's view of the preferred management approach.[44] For example, those who view national identity as a malleable elite construct tend to promote centripetal mechanisms that seek to resolve conflict by eliminating the offending ethno-national diversity (i.e., through assimilation),[45]

39 On the manifestations of conflict in such states, see Schertzer and Woods (2011: 197–203).

40 See Tully (2004); Schertzer (2008); Marchildon (2009); and also the foundational work in this area by Carl Friedrich (1968) and Preston King (1982).

41 See Tully (2004, 2001, 2000b).

42 On the link between recognition and distribution, see Tully (2000b: 469–71).

43 There has been considerable debate about the definition of these key terms: the key division is between those that argue federalism represents a normative position and those that argue it is a descriptive category. Watts (2008: 8–18) provides an overview of the positions and the key distinction between "federalism" and "federation" that was articulated by King (1982).

44 Woods, Schertzer, and Kaufmann (2011); Wolff (2011).

45 This position is well represented in the work of Donald Horowitz and his followers; see Horowitz (2000); Reilly (2001).

while those who view nationality as real and enduring tend to seek rigid institutional structures that accommodate this fact.[46] In contrast, this study applies an understanding of national identity that stakes out the middle ground between these two perspectives, along with a view that recognizes the contested nature of a federation. Accordingly, I am seeking here to advance conflict-management theory and policy by applying insights from the above three fields to the use of federal systems to manage ethno-national conflict.

As my analysis in subsequent chapters will demonstrate, the combination of insights from these four fields allows me to avoid some of the pitfalls of other studies that are based within one field, or that work from under-examined, and ultimately problematic, assumptions. For example, the above allows me to avoid drawing an overly bright line between law and politics when reflecting on the role of the judiciary as federal arbiter. As just discussed, it also allows me to see nations as more than mere elite constructs or real and fixed facts, while also rejecting the use of contested terms associated with particular positions in the debate over the nature of nationality in Canada to describe the state.[47] The above also allows me to discuss and promote federal systems as a means to manage conflict without seeing this as a panacea to solve conflict through the implementation of fixed institutional structures. Finally, drawing from the fields of constitutional law, nationalism, and federal studies allows me to approach the theory and practice of conflict management in a way that moves past the application of "cookie-cutter" solutions from the centripetalist or consociationalist handbooks.[48]

---

46 This view is exemplified by the above-noted Canada School of multinational federalists and the related liberal consociationalists that follow the work of Brendan O'Leary and John McGarry; see McGarry and O'Leary (1993, 2007, 2009).

47 This is one of the central reasons why it is so important to shift our descriptive terminology from that of "multinational" to "plurinational." As Brubaker argues, nations are a useful analytic category, but we need to avoid reifying them in our analysis of the phenomenon; see Brubaker (2004).

48 The view that successful conflict management requires a nuanced understanding of the theory of nations and nationalism, and a proper account of the context within a state, are part of Stefan Wolff's contribution to the field, including his argument that this approach tends to promote a mix of conflict management techniques, so-called complex power-sharing; see Wolff (2011, 2009).

The Structure of the Argument

I seek to answer the central question of this book through a series of chapters spanning both theoretical and empirical subjects over two broad sections.

The focus of the first section is federal theory and practice. The chapters look at the main approaches to managing diversity via a federal system and the associated roles for the federal arbiter (both in the Canadian context and more broadly). I also discuss the positive and negative elements of these approaches, while developing a contrasting and what I argue is a preferable federal model. This section thus establishes the analytical foundation for the main argument of the book, while providing the theoretical position that informs my empirical investigation of how the SCC actually manages conflict.

In line with these objectives, the first chapter looks at the promotion of federalism as a "solution" to the "problem" of ethno-national diversity. It starts by discussing the challenge ethno-national diversity presents to the legitimacy of a state, going on to look at the broad attempts to solve this problem by trimming, trading, or segregating away diversity through federal systems.[49] The chapter then discusses how these broader approaches are expressed in Canada as the pan-Canadian, provincial-equality, and multinational federal models. From this discussion I show how these federal models inform and drive conflict over national identity and the federation in Canada, and how each is a legitimate view of what this contested federation is and ought to be.

Building on an understanding of the Canadian federation as inherently contested, the second chapter argues that the federal arbiter is important in the development and maintenance of legitimacy for federal systems. It starts by elaborating on the contested nature of federations given their status as normative frameworks, while also making the point that conflict over the system is only exacerbated in plurinational states like Canada. From here, the chapter looks at the various forums through which this contestation unfolds, focusing on the federal arbiter (which in Canada is the judiciary and ultimately its apex court, the SCC). The chapter also examines how federal theory (both

49 Managing diversity through "trimming," "trading," or "segregation" are categories of analysis used by Richard Bellamy to investigate the main liberal approaches to the issue; see Bellamy (1999, 2000). I elaborate on these categories and apply them to the use of federal systems to manage diversity in the next chapter.

applicable to the Canadian case and more broadly) has generally presented the ideal role for the judiciary as a federal arbiter, arguing that the three roles most widely promoted for the courts (as umpire, branch of government, or guardian) are problematically linked to the broader approaches of trimming, trading, or segregating diversity. The chapter concludes by presenting an alternative federal model, one that accounts for the contested nature of a federation and promotes a role for the federal arbiter that seeks to facilitate negotiation between conflicting parties, which should help to generate and maintain legitimacy for the federal system.

This line of argument raises difficult questions about the extent to which federal arbiters can, and do, live up to the ideal of facilitating negotiation. The book thus transitions to an empirical investigation of related issues. The second half of the study provides an in-depth view of the SCC's federalism jurisprudence over the past thirty years, looking at the extent to which the Court's decisions draw from, and reinforce, the key federal models. This allows me to identify and discuss two streams of federalism jurisprudence: decisions that recognize and account for conflict over national identity and the federation, and those that do not. In my review of these two streams, the problems associated with the latter decisions are discussed, notably the potential negative effect they can have on the legitimacy of the federal system. At the same time, this review illuminates the key tenets and potential benefits of a federal arbiter exercising its role in a way that recognizes and accounts for contestation over the federation, particularly the potential for this line of jurisprudence to generate legitimacy for the federal system.

Chapter 3 explains my methodology: describing how I conduct my review of SCC decisions and defending the underlying premises of my analysis. It starts by addressing some of the central issues related to the scope of my work here (viz., why focus on the SCC and why look at decisions from 1980 to 2010). It then discusses the nuances of my investigation of SCC jurisprudence, presenting a framework that facilitates analysis of how the Court either does, or does not, recognize and account for the contestation over national identity and the federation in a single decision.

Chapter 4 argues that the *Secession Reference* represents the exemplar of a decision that recognizes and accounts for the conflicting views over national identity and the federation in Canada. It applies the framework introduced in chapter 3 to discuss how the depiction of the federation, the decision outcome and the self-selected role for the Court in the decision draw from, and reinforce, a view of federation as the process and outcome of negotiation between the subscribers of legitimate federal models. It also introduces some of the potential benefits of this approach by discussing the context and reasons why the Court made this turn in the face of a legitimacy crisis for the federation. This chapter advances the central argument of the book and the analysis in subsequent chapters in two ways: (1) it provides a detailed example of how I undertake my review of SCC federalism jurisprudence, which is particularly important given the high number of decisions covered in subsequent chapters; and (2) it provides an example (a benchmark) of a decision that accounts for the contested nature of the federation.

Chapter 5 turns to those SCC decisions that negatively affect the federation, explaining how they do this and elaborating on why they are problematic. It explains how 57 per cent of the Court's federalism jurisprudence over a thirty-year period fails to account for the contestation over the federation by imposing particular perspectives of what the federation is and ought to be. The chapter goes on to discuss how the Court, acting in this way, can negatively affect the loyalty parties feel towards the federation and the way it manages conflict.

The sixth chapter investigates those SCC decisions that account for the contestation over national identity and the federation. It looks at the stream of federalism jurisprudence that follows the lead of the *Secession Reference* by recognizing and reinforcing the federal system as the process and outcome of negotiation between the subscribers of legitimate federal models. The chapter demonstrates that the Court can actually undertake its role as federal arbiter in a way that potentially generates loyalty to the federation and the way it manages conflict. This discussion accentuates the positive implications of this approach, as well as how to promote this activity.

I conclude the book by reflecting and elaborating on some of the key points. In particular, I address some of the potential issues of applying my argument, while also discussing the extent to which my analysis can inform broader theory and policy development in the management of diversity and conflict.

PART ONE

The Theory and Practice of Managing Diversity via Federalism

Chapter One

The "Problem" of National Minorities and the "Solution" of Federalism

This chapter provides the context for the book, explaining how many see national diversity as a problem and how federalism is presented as a solution. I begin by looking at how nationalism, and its role in legitimizing political authority, problematizes national diversity. I then discuss the oft-proposed solution of federalism and the three main approaches federalists tend to promote to deal with national diversity. Turning to Canada, I illustrate how these broad approaches inform the three key perspectives on the nature and ideal direction for the Canadian federation – perspectives that both reflect and drive conflict over national identity and the federation. This line of discussion – tracing the problematization of national diversity, the way federal systems are proposed as a response, and how this plays out in Canada – lays the necessary theoretical and empirical groundwork to inform later analysis.

By starting with an appreciation of the way national diversity is understood and approached within federal theory, I am able to identify and address particular normative positions as I build my own approach to managing national diversity and the role the judiciary ought to play in plurinational federations like Canada. At the same time, I cannot discuss how the judiciary manages the conflict over national identity and the federation in Canada without first discussing the nature of that conflict. Nor can I make an argument about the preferable way to manage national diversity and the role the judiciary should play in the process without first discussing the nature of the problem and current approaches (both within the comparative scholarship and the work on Canada).

The "Problem" of National Minorities[1]

The view of national diversity as a "problem" is about legitimacy. No form of diversity challenges the legitimacy of a state more than national minorities.[2] They represent a particularly acute challenge to the very basis of political power in the modern period.[3] To understand this challenge, it is necessary to explain briefly the nature of sovereign power and the role national self-determination plays in legitimizing the popular variant of sovereignty.

The legal aspect of sovereignty is well developed and has been prominent in the literature since the time of Thomas Hobbes and the first international lawyers, Hugo Grotius and Emerich de Vattel. The notion of the king as the sovereign authority within a state, translated into the supremacy of singular governmental authority acting under the rule of law, is a recognizable equation. Few draw attention to the legal aspect of sovereignty more explicitly than international-relations scholars, with most arguing it represents the constitutive norm of international society and that a state's right to territorial integrity and non-intervention is based on its legal sovereignty.[4]

It is vital, however, to pull out the political core of sovereignty. As Martin Loughlin argues, "The authority invested in the institutional framework of government is founded on a political relationship."[5] In

1 The "problem" of national minorities has been identified by many; for example, see Macartney (1934); Claude (1955); Laponce (1960); Jackson Preece (1998, 2005).

2 I understand national minorities as *a named human population occupying a historic territory and sharing common myths and memories, a public culture, and perhaps common laws and customs for all members, but standing in an inferior relationship (numerically and/or substantively) to the rest of the population of a state and showing, if only implicitly, a sense of solidarity directed towards preserving or attaining autonomy to protect their national identity*. This draws from the definition of minorities put forth by Francesco Capotorti in the 1970s (in his UN study on the rights of persons belonging to ethnic, religious, and linguistic minorities) as well as from A. Smith (2003: 24–5) and Jackson Preece (1998: 28–9). National minorities are akin to Laponce's "minorities by will" (groups seeking autonomy), being distinguished from "minorities by force" (those seeking integration) (1960: 6).

3 On the particular problem presented by national minorities in modernity (as opposed to religious minorities, for example), see Jackson Preece (2005, esp. at 8–13).

4 This cornerstone of international law is evidenced in clauses stressing the territorial integrity of the state going back to the Peace of Augsburg in 1555, the Peace of Westphalia in 1648, and today with article 2 of the Charter of the United Nations; see Jackson (2003: chs. 7, 12).

5 Loughlin (2003: 82).

this light, sovereignty is "concerned not so much with [legal or administrative] competence but with capacity, not with [legal] authority but with power."[6] This proper understanding of sovereignty takes account of (1) the power to constitute, abolish, and alter government,[7] (2) the group that wields this power – "the people" as constituent power,[8] and (3) the way that power is generated. The generation of *public power*, as separate from material power or coercion,[9] is a central component of this understanding of sovereignty. When one realizes that public power is the institutionalization of political power,[10] which is generated from loyalty, allegiance, and the act of a group of people living together "for the purposes of action,"[11] it can be seen that sovereign authority in its legal institutional variant ultimately "rests on the allegiance of the people."[12] The link between the legal and the political aspect of sovereignty is thus illuminated: the legal authority of government is an expression of the political core of sovereignty, which in turn is an expression of public power and the constituent power of the people – all of which rests on the loyalty of the people to the association itself.[13]

The political nature of sovereignty points to the important role national self-determination plays in legitimizing a state. While the emergence of the state system through the sixteenth and seventeenth centuries was marked by the territorialization of political authority wrestled from the papacy, this power was still seen as generated from on high through dynastic rule embodied in the king.[14] It is the subsequent rise of national self-determination and nationalism in the eighteenth and nineteenth centuries that fundamentally altered perceptions of legitimate authority. National self-determination "shattered the homogenised world of shared values and assumptions," splitting international

6 Loughlin (2003: 85).

7 See Loughlin (2003: 85, 66–8); Lawson (1992: 47) (cited in Loughlin 2003).

8 See Loughlin (2003: 85, 61–4, 99–113); Sieyès (1963: 124–8).

9 Loughlin (2003: 76–9).

10 Loughlin (2003: 78).

11 Arendt (1973: 175). See also Arendt (1958: 200); Loughlin (2003: 77–82).

12 Loughlin (2003: 82).

13 See Loughlin (2003: 85).

14 Jackson (2005: 82–3); Osainder (1994: 27–8). The oft-cited signposts in this process are the Peace of Augsburg in 1555 and the Peace of Westphalia in 1648 and the role they played in solidifying the maxim *cuius regio, ejus religio* (whose realm, his religion). On this process also see Brown (2002: 23); Mann (1986, 1993); Teschke (1998); Wight (1977: 151–2); on the earlier stages of this variant of power, see Loughlin (2003: 74).

society into little more than the sum of its distinct (national) parts.[15] A state system based on the principle of *national* sovereignty did not come about overnight, and the fight against dynastic rule was arduous as the American and French Revolutions attest; yet, on a theoretical level, from the introduction of the concept of national self-determination, it became increasingly difficult to rule a people without proper reference to their role.

The doctrine of national self-determination has three components: (1) there are nations as empirical fact;[16] (2) the nation is the ultimate locus of political authority;[17] and (3) a subsequent normative argument that there must be congruence between the nation and the state.[18]

This doctrine traces its roots back to the early contractarian thinking of Hobbes, John Locke[19] and Jean-Jacques Rousseau,[20] to the work of Abbé Sieyès and, particularly, John Stuart Mill's influential concept that "the question of government ought to be decided by the governed."[21] This line of thought combined with the emerging discourse on the "fact" of nations provides the formula that free institutions demand "the boundaries of governments ... coincide with those of nationalities."[22] This simple equation of "one nation, one state" has been solidified as part of the basic syntax of modern politics.[23] As Ernest Gellner points out, nationalism, the overarching ideology of modern politics, "is a theory of political legitimacy, which requires that ethnic boundaries should not cut across political ones, and in particular, that ethnic boundaries within a given state – a contingency *already formally excluded by the principle* in its general formulation – should not separate the power-holders from the rest."[24]

15 Mayall (1990: 25).

16 See Breuilly (2011).

17 See Loughlin (2003: 85, 61–4, 99–113); Sieyès (1963: 124–8).

18 See Mill (1991: ch. 16); Tilly (1994: 133–4). It is often the last of these three components that is taken as the definition of national self-determination.

19 See Locke (1982: ch. 7, esp. at s. 89).

20 Notable here is Rousseau's concept that authority emanates from the collective of the people who together form a society. See Leerssen (2006: 82); Rousseau (1993: book 1, esp. at chs. 6–7); Benner (2012).

21 Mill (1991: ch. 16).

22 Ibid.; see Breuilly (2011) on the emerging discourse of the "fact" of nations in the nineteenth century.

23 On this idea combining with the notion that each state is sovereign, see Jackson (2005: 73; 2007: 310).

24 Gellner (1983: 1) (emphasis added).

This line of thought illuminates the important role nationalism and national self-determination play in legitimizing political power, as well as the challenge posed by national diversity. As Bernard Yack argues, popular sovereignty provides powerful grounds for legitimatizing authority, but contains a fundamental flaw with its inability to define "the people" that wield power.[25] The nation provides what is lacking in popular sovereignty: a sense of the pre-political basis of the community and the necessary separate identity from the one that is derived from the establishment of political authority.[26] This separate identity is necessary because "the people" (as a coherent body) must be able to survive the abolition of political authority to truly wield power, which is where ethno-national criteria are used to generate a sense of stable unity. It is this "sleight of hand" of nationalism – its ability to merge the concepts of the people and the nation[27] – that is central to understanding the tension created by ethno-national diversity in the modern state.

If legitimate political authority is understood as conferred only when there is congruence between the boundaries of "the people," "the nation," and "the state," any group that brings the congruence between these three conceptual categories into question is seen as a problem. Thus, if congruence between these three categories is seen as critical by those in control of a state (as they try to legitimate their authority) and those seeking their own state (to legitimate their actions and eventual rule), it is easy to see how the stress on congruence at the heart of national self-determination drives the problematization of national diversity and minorities. By drawing attention to the fact that congruence is a myth, or something not yet achieved, national minorities challenge the very fabric of legitimate political authority in their own state and beyond at a systemic level.[28]

The problematization of national minorities at a practical level begins with the transition from national self-determination as a theoretical concept to the doctrine dictating the activity of politics. One of the key ways this transition happens is through the "nationalization" of politics in the nineteenth century, as the national principle – that nations exist,

25 Yack (2001: 525). See also Jennings (1956: 56).

26 Yack (2001: 524–5).

27 Breuilly (1993: 390).

28 This disjuncture is what Jackson Preece terms the "national self-determination fudge"; it is because national minorities draw attention to the lack of congruence that they are so problematic, see Jackson Preece (1998: 29).

deserve, and require autonomy – shifts from the periphery to become the core of politics.[29] For example, we see

> after 1800, the frequency with which subject populations revolted in the name of their distinct nationalities – and especially the frequency with which previously acquiescent minorities demanded full independence – greatly increased. The proportion of all revolutionary situations [in Europe] that included a clear national component rose correspondingly, from a typical 30 percent before 1800 to a typical 50 percent thereafter.[30]

The emergent primacy of the doctrine of national self-determination is evidenced not only by its application in revolutionary movements (e.g., the "Spring of Nations" in 1848), but also by the adoption of the discourse by those that had the most to lose with its implementation: European dynastic empires. For example, in the late nineteenth century we see the tsarist government taking up policies of Russianization for non-Russian Slavs and the Habsburgs explicitly recognizing national distinctions.[31] This turn towards an essentialist view of the nature of the state (as necessarily being a nation-state) is crucial in understanding the problematization of national minorities in the modern period.

The point at which national self-determination becomes the primary way sovereign authority is legitimized in practice was President Woodrow Wilson's Fourteen Points at the end of the First World War.[32] This process – the solidification of the nation-state as the basic ideal of political organization and key to legitimate sovereign authority – reaches its peak as a global-level phenomenon with decolonization in the mid-twentieth century.

Despite this process of nationalizing political authority, there remains a significant gap between the discourse of national self-determination and its practical implementation.[33] In reality, despite being a pillar of

---

29 See Breuilly (2011).

30 Tilly (1994: 137).

31 Breuilly (2011).

32 The shift was ushered in with explicit recourse to the notion of *national* self-determination as the "primary consideration in the formation of new states in Central and Eastern Europe in the areas of the defeated or disintegrated Habsburg, Hohenzollern, Romanov, and Ottoman Empires"; see Jackson (2005: 87).

33 The argument that national self-determination has been revised with its implementation in international law is evident in most studies looking at the concept; see, for example, Mayall (1990); Cassese (2005); Crawford (2007); Emerson (1971); Jackson Preece (2005: 168–70); Archibugi (2003); Weller (2005).

post-1945 international law,[34] national self-determination as a right to form a state in international law has been applied narrowly and does not take ethnic, cultural, or linguistic divisions into consideration.[35] This restriction is exemplified by the accepted principle that the doctrine does not grant national minorities the right to form their own state.[36] Over the twentieth century a compromise has thus emerged: national self-determination is held up as the legitimating principle for sovereign authority, but it is a revised understanding of the doctrine, with the key being a juridical (as opposed to sociological) basis for state borders.[37] This revised doctrine represents the interests of maintaining order and the territorial integrity of states in the face of the perceived chaos caused by an explosion of new members to the international community and the related ethnic conflict that would stem from the application of the "pure" theory of national self-determination.

The rise of the doctrine of national self-determination, its revised implementation, and the tendency of states to jealously guard territorial integrity has resulted in the oft-cited "problem of fit": approximately 600 language groups and 5000 ethnic groups are housed in fewer than 200 states.[38] This paradox – the embodiment of the lack of congruence between "the people," "the nation," and "the state" – leads national

34 For instance, the "right" is enshrined in a number of the standard bearers of international law: Charter of the United Nations (articles 1 and 55); United Nations Covenant on Civil and Political Rights (article 1); United Nations Covenant on Economic, Social and Cultural Rights (article 1); United Nations General Assembly Declaration on Principles of International Law concerning Friendly Relations and Co-operation among States (1970); and the Helsinki Final Act (1975) (article 8).

35 The right generally is understood to have two dimensions: internal (democratic participation in the state) and external (the right to form a state). International law restricts the latter to a few limited circumstances. On the right to national self-determination in international law, generally, see Cassese (2005: 61–3); Crawford (2007: 415); Emerson (1971); Higgins (1994: ch. 7).

36 This norm is evidenced well by the Badinter commission's use of *uti possidetis juris* to understand the legitimacy of new states following the "dissolution" of the former Yugoslavia. On this and related qualifications to the right, see Weller (2005: 12–13); Emerson (1971: 464); Higgins (1994: 119–21); Chambers (2004).

37 Jackson (2003: 321–5). Again, the classic example of this compromise and the juridical nature for state borders is adherence to the principle of *uti possidetis juris* by emerging states in the decolonization processes in South America, Asia, and Africa (particularly, the fervent support for the principle by the Organization of African Unity and the use of the principle in the dissolution of Yugoslavia).

38 See Gurr (1993).

minorities to struggle for national self-determination, while also motivating states to seek solutions to the perceived problem.

Given the problem of fit, the struggles by national minorities for self-determination, and the resulting instability they cause, are perhaps not so surprising. While difficult to quantify, in 2008, approximately 174 struggles for national self-determination were identified.[39] Only some of these struggles included instances of violence, with a large number involving the use of "conventional" political means and others standing as examples where conflict-management practices are applied.[40] In those struggles that turn violent, the implications for peace and security are clear. From the 1950s, intrastate warfare has made up the vast majority of conflict and has risen significantly.[41] National self-determination struggles fuel many of these conflicts (with some 87 such conflicts emerging since the 1950s).[42] As noted earlier, while the point is still contested, a lack of congruence between the territorial boundaries of states and ethno-national groups, especially when groups are territorially concentrated or cut across multiple state borders, significantly increases the probability of conflict breaking out.[43]

It is not only through violent struggles that national minorities challenge political authority. Peaceful struggles can also work to delegitimize a political system. Through these struggles, national minorities put forth arguments for autonomy and stress the need for congruence between the boundaries of the nation and the state – something that resonates as a key tenet in modern political discourse. Consequently, their existence and actions present a paradox: they seek congruence between their nation and a state in a world where the value of the nation-state as an ideal is elevated in political discourse and theories of legitimacy, but is rarely, if ever, found. Thus, on a fundamental level, national minorities and their struggles for autonomy destabilize the compromise whereby national self-determination and sovereignty have been merged by showing that the nation-state equation does not work for all.

---

39 See Quinn (2008: 36–7).

40 Of these 174 struggles, some 28 can be placed in the first category, 100 in the second, and 46 in the third; see Quinn (2008: 36–7). These figures and three categories were adapted from his ten.

41 Hewitt (2008).

42 See Quinn (2008: 34).

43 See Montalvo and Reynal-Querol (2005); Gurr et al. (2008: 9); Toft (2003); Kaufmann (2011).

These struggles are mirrored by state action seeking to deal with national diversity and the resulting instability. Following Jennifer Jackson Preece and others, there are three broad ways that states have sought to solve the problem of national minorities.[44] First, states seek to eliminate national minorities through extermination or making borders match the "facts" by redrafting them or transferring populations. There are many pertinent examples of this approach, including the numerous genocides perpetrated in the twentieth century such as the Holocaust,[45] East Timor, and the Ibo in Nigeria; the mass population transfers involving Greece and Turkey following the Treaty of Lausanne in 1923 or Milosevic's ethnic-cleansing practices in the former Yugoslavia; and, while less common, border revisions in the case of Bangladesh or the split of Czechoslovakia. Second, states seek to facilitate or actively assimilate national minorities into a larger nation.[46] Opening up space for the "melting pot" culture in America and the attempted assimilation of Aboriginals in Canada through the residential school system are examples of the two broad ways states undertake these types of assimilation. Finally, states can accommodate national minorities by granting rights or through institutional design. Minority-rights provisions promoted by the League of Nations and the European Union, the establishment of a federal state in Canada (following the unpopularity of Lord Durham's proposed course of assimilating the Québécois), and the devolution of power in the United Kingdom reflect elements of this broad approach.

The "Solution" of Federalism

Throughout the twentieth century federal systems have gained prominence among policymakers and academics as a favourable mechanism to address the perceived problem of national diversity. Today, federalism is increasingly promoted as a useful compromise that can accommodate national minorities while maintaining the territorial integrity

44 See Jackson Preece (1998); McGarry and O'Leary (1993), from which the following three points are drawn.

45 The fact that it was referred to as the "final solution" is telling about how minorities are viewed as a problem to be solved.

46 See Jackson Preece (2008: 611) on the difference between facilitating assimilation (i.e., social pressure to assimilate) and proactive state policies designed to assimilate minorities.

of a state. At the same time, the practice can also be promoted and implemented to achieve assimilation. Accordingly, one can see discernible waves of federalism as a response to national diversity in the twentieth century, with federal systems being employed in the nation-building enterprises of the mid-twentieth century and becoming a popular option in the more accommodation-focused enterprises of the post-1990 period.[47]

When thinking about federal systems, I follow the practice of distinguishing between federations as a form of government and federalism as an ideology.[48] Federalism should be seen as a normative position directed at mobilizing political action, with the specific purpose of promoting a combination of shared and self-rule between two or more orders of government.[49] The ideology of federalism is best understood as a "second-tier" perspective, the presumptions inherent in the overarching ideology of nationalism having already been accepted. As Benedict Anderson and others have pointed out, the overarching character of nationalism places it in a class of ideologies separate from those like liberalism or socialism.[50] As subsequent analysis will show, federalism and federal theory tend to accept the value of congruence between the boundaries of "the nation," "the people," and "the state" that lies at the heart of national self-determination (and nationalism), as a means both to legitimize political authority and to suppress conflict.

The particular form of government federalism promotes is the federation.[51] While federations do differ, they share a set of key characteristics that distinguish them from other systems of government, including having at least two orders of government with a formal distribution of powers; a (written) constitution; a formal dispute-arbitration

47 See Watts (1994: 3–4, 10). On the general shift in international society from an assimilation-based to an accommodation-based approach to national minorities, see Jackson Preece (1998, 2008); Fink (2000).

48 See Watts (1994: 7–8; 1998; 2007: 225–8); King (1982); McGarry and O'Leary (2007: 180).

49 See King (1982: esp. at 1–3); Watts (1994: 8); Watts (1998: 120); Watts (2007: 226); McGarry and O'Leary (2007: 180). Daniel Elazar uses the term "federalism" more as a description for systems of government based on federal principles. For him, federalism is a "theoretical and operational concept"; see Elazar (1987: ch. 2, esp. at 38). A recent example following this more descriptive use of federalism is Hueglin and Fenna (2006: ch. 2).

50 See Anderson (1991: 5); Norman (2006: 6–9).

51 Along with other types of federal systems, like unions, consociations, confederations, leagues. I focus here on federations proper. For a review of these other systems, see Elazar (1987: 38–64); Watts (1998, 2008).

mechanism (i.e., a federal arbiter, usually a court of law); and intergovernmental cooperation mechanisms.[52] Accordingly, a federal system of government can be understood as a deliberate policy choice – as the implementation of a specific set of institutional mechanisms in a particular context in line with the principles of federalism.[53] At the same time, the breadth of choice is often limited in practice because federations tend to seek an acceptable compromise between sets of actors in a state seeking unitary forms of government and those seeking autonomy (while trying to build trust, or loyalty, towards the resulting system).[54] In addition, federations are sometimes "inherited," being the result of pre-existing structuring conditions (such as colonial decisions about the borders of political systems).[55]

The study and promotion of this form of government has led to a corpus of federal theory. Within this field my focus tends to be on those who study and promote federal systems as a means to manage national diversity.[56] While there are many that do promote the value of federalism, it is important to note that most scholars and policymakers do not see it as a panacea for all the world's ills: in general, those that point to the promise of federal systems also recognize their limits.[57] The work of Richard Simeon (among others) exemplifies the search for a balance between promoting federalism while also recognizing the many conditions and qualifications that limit comparative analysis and the application of general models.[58] Some of Simeon's later work provides a useful overview of the key factors to consider when thinking

52 Watts (1994: 8–9). Federations tend to differ in the extent they are centralist or decentralist, territorially or ethnically based and democratic or not.

53 See Hueglin and Fenna (2006: 28).

54 For a discussion of the constraints, the need for compromise, and the generation of trust in federal design, see Zahar (2013) and McGarry (2013).

55 See Simeon (2013: 287); Smiley (1987).

56 For examples of this type of work see Kymlicka (1998); McGarry and O'Leary (2007); O'Leary (2001); Gagnon (2007); Lijphart (2008). There are many divergent approaches and focuses within the field of federal theory, including those that focus on the various aspects of federations that intersect with economic, social policy, or democratic issues.

57 For recent examples of nuanced and informative discussions on the promise of federalism, see the contributions to Skogstad et al. (2013).

58 In Simeon's own words, in an essay reflecting on his "federalist life" he notes that when looking to "spread federalism ... students of federalism do have an array of possibilities, successes, and failures, which may, in the rights circumstances, be helpful" (2013: 289).

about a comparative analysis of federal systems or when promoting their value, including the context of the cases being studied (such as the historical legacies, social demography, nature of the political system, and its institutions); the starting point for negotiations over constitutional and institutional design (including who is participating in such negotiations); and the broader social norms and values in play.[59] At the same time, while it is clear that there is still a robust debate on the value of federal systems to manage ethno-national diversity and related conflict,[60] there are many within this debate who promote this form of government.

Among scholars who study federations there is a distinction between those who focus on the legal-institutional elements of federal systems and those who focus on their sociological basis.[61] Despite this split, when promoting federalism the enterprise of both camps is similar: to design institutional mechanisms that bring about congruence between the boundaries of the nation and the state. The underlying logic of the legal-institutionalist camp is to find methods of institutional design that either reflect or shape the socio-cultural basis of the association.[62] The policy prescriptions from the socio-cultural camp, by contrast, start with a desire to understand properly the link (or gap) between institutions

---

59 For a discussion of these conditions, qualifications, and limits to the promotion of federal systems, see Simeon (2011, 2009). Ronald Watts's reflections on the comparability of federal systems echo many of these points; see Watts (2008: 1–27). I return to discuss this topic and the limits of my own analysis in the conclusion.

60 As noted earlier, the debate roughly involves those who view "integrationist" approaches other than granting territorial autonomy as the most effective means to manage diversity and conflict, set against those who stress the value of accommodating groups through federal systems. The first group is represented by the "centripetalist" school, following the work of Horowitz (2000), Sisk (1996), and Reilly (2001). The second group is mainly associated with the "consociationalist" approach, following the work of Lijphart (2008) and McGarry and O'Leary (1993, 2007, 2009).

61 The classic examples for the legal-institutionalist and sociological perspectives are the work of K.C. Wheare and William Livingston, respectively; see Wheare (1963); Livingston (1952). For a review, from a scholar working within the sociological tradition, see Erk (2008: 3–6).

62 The promotion and defence of "asymmetrical" federal systems by John McGarry (and other liberal consociationalists), where there are some sub-state units that house national minorities, is indicative of the approach of reflecting underlying diversity; see McGarry (2007). At the same time, the approach of trying to integrate ethno-national diversity into a larger civic nation by designing sub-state units that cut across groups promoted by Horowitz (2007: 960–1) is also indicative of the view that institutions can shape the sociological basis of an association over time.

and society so as to better facilitate institutions reflecting their socio-cultural foundations.[63] Both perspectives thus point to the importance of congruence between the institutional design of a state and its national character, because they are both based on a presumption that the boundaries of federal institutions and social diversity must coincide over the long term for stability.[64] As Grace Skogstad et al. recently highlighted, a key unifying element of those arguing for the "global promise of federalism" is a broadly shared perspective that "the success of federal systems is closely related to their congruence with contextual (social, cultural, economic) factors," and so there is a focus on "getting federal institutions 'right' from the outset."[65] At the same time, there is recognition that federal institutions need to adapt over time to reflect shifting preferences, even though they can be remarkably rigid once put in place.[66] In any event, this recognition of the need for institutions to adapt over time also shows the underlying assumption that there is value in finding congruence between the design of federal institutions and the ethno-national character of a country.

This stress on "congruence" comes from the fact that federal theory (particularly its prescriptive bend) operates from within the confines of the ideology of federalism. As such, the broad perspective on how to deal with diversity has been to seek an alignment between the boundaries of the nation, the people, and the state (or between society and institutions, in federal theory parlance). This basic premise is seen as key to a functioning and legitimate federation because it is held up as the way to ensure stability and to counteract the centrifugal forces of the system.[67]

---

63 The argument from the sociological camp is that where federal societies do not have matching federal institutions, the situation ought to be rectified via institutional design. One of the best examples of this line of argument today is Will Kymlicka's multinational federalism; see Kymlicka (1995, 1998, 2001).

64 At the same time, I should point out that McGarry and O'Leary have argued that other key factors in the stability of federations include an overarching pan-state identity (a *Staatsvolk*), consociational arrangements within the central government, a commitment to democratic principles, consensual negotiations over institutional design, economic prosperity, and more than two sub-state units (2009: 12–20).

65 Skogstad et al. (2013: 7–10).

66 See Skogstad et al. (2013: 12–13). The ability of federal associations to be defined from the bottom up and reflect the salient political identities that may shift over time is also a key part of the more liberal stream of constitutional theory; see Wolff (2011: 167).

67 In addition to sources cited in the previous paragraph, see Erk (2008: 8–9); Almond and Verba (1963); Eckstein (1966); Eckstein and Gurr (1975).

Table 1.1. Three main approaches to managing national diversity via federalism

Approach to managing diversity	Federal and constitutional system as	Key aspects of federal institutions	Goal in dealing with national diversity	Key theorists
Trimming	Neutral framework based on an overlapping consensus	Symmetrical Territorial Centralized	Building a single pan-state (civic) nation	Rawls Trudeau
Trading	Background, neutral framework facilitating market-based politics	Symmetrical Territorial Decentralized	Facilitating a single pan-state (civic) nation	Hayek Dahl Horowitz
Segregating	Framework separating autonomous nations / political communities	Asymmetrical / symmetrical Ethnic / territorial Decentralized	Accommodating multiple nations within one state	Walzer Kymlicka

Within prescriptive federal theory, there are three key approaches towards the management of territorially concentrated national minorities (see table 1.1). Following the work of Richard Bellamy on liberal approaches to pluralism, I see these three approaches promoting federalism as a means to trim, trade, or segregate away national diversity.[68]

Trimming

The first approach, trimming diversity, aims to fix the constitution as a framework above politics. It is about demarcating the constitution from politics by establishing a set of principles that "provide the preconditions for politics."[69] Accordingly, the constitution is seen as a neutral framework that avoids any referent to a particular good life.[70] This is an objective clearly rooted in a Rawlsian attempt to "fix, once and for all," a basic structure based on an overlapping consensus.[71] It is an attempt to bypass the fact of pluralism by keeping the framework of politics neutral.[72]

68 Bellamy (1999, 2000); see also McGarry and O'Leary (2007); Gagnon (2007); Horowitz (2000, 2003).

69 Bellamy (2000: 200).

70 Ibid.

71 Rawls (1993: ch. 4, esp. at 161); Bellamy (1999: ch. 2).

72 Rawls (1993: 161, chs. 4, 7); Bellamy (2000: 201; 1999: 43–6).

Among federal theorists this approach leads to the promotion of federation as an overlapping consensus that avoids institutionalizing sub-state national identities. The federal approach promoted by Pierre Trudeau, the former prime minister of Canada who led a set of constitutional reforms in the early 1980s that included a bill of rights and domestic amending formula, epitomizes this perspective.[73] For him, a federal division of powers represents a lasting, rational consensus founded on reason, not ethno-national values or particularistic views.[74] This focus on neutrality and equality leads those following this approach to promote sub-state jurisdictions as merely territorial units (not ethno-national units) that are as equal in power and as symmetrical as possible.

With regard to national diversity, the trimming approach thus seeks to design federal systems as part of a nation-building enterprise.[75] A key part of this enterprise is promoting a strong central government, which reinforces a pan-state political identity. Accordingly, territorial autonomy for national minorities *as national minorities* is firmly rejected. Similarly, the trimming federal approach often promotes mechanisms that reinforce an overarching citizenship, such as a bill of rights that bases "the sovereignty of the ... people on a set of values common to all, and in particular on the notion of equality among all."[76]

In line with the stated goal of promoting federalism as the antidote to particularistic, archaic, and ethno-cultural values,[77] the objectives of the trimming approach are clearly to (1) build a single pan-state civic nation and (2) fix the core tenets of this civic national identity as the overlapping consensus in the constitutional federal structure. At its core, then, the approach maintains that the federation needs to reflect national values and a consensus among the members of one nation. Turning back to Trudeau, his vision of "un-hyphenated citizenship," of a singular pan-Canadian civic nation as the source of political legitimacy, is an example of how, despite the plurality of political communities in a federation, the nation and state are still seen to *necessarily*

73 Trudeau was also an active scholar before entering politics, studying at the London School of Economics, following the work of Elie Kadourie, and writing on federalism and nationalism in Canada.

74 Trudeau (1998: 97, 103, 117–18).

75 See, for example, Trudeau (1998: 120).

76 Trudeau (1998: 79).

77 McGarry and O'Leary (2007: 188).

coincide. In addition, Trudeau's political project of finalizing a constitutional amending formula for Canada and enshrining the Charter of Rights and Freedoms exemplify the desire to fix the basic structure of federation outside the realm of everyday politics. This desire is driven by a view that having "determined what justice requires, there can be no interesting argument for allowing it to vary from place to place" or to substantively change over time.[78]

Trading

The second approach, trading diversity, is about distributing power among a plurality of agents so that none can monopolize authority: it is about creating an effective bargaining environment and positions.[79] Central to facilitating this trading mentality is the creation of cross-cutting cleavages (multiple conflicting allegiances across many lines). These cross-cutting cleavages help ensure that no stable majority can be established in a federation (only shifting coalitions of groups depending on the issue).[80] The point of designing federal institutions in this way is to dilute diversity as the organizing principle of political conflict and thus to resolve disputes via mutually beneficial trade-offs.[81] The notion of a counterbalancing "polyarchy" at the heart of this approach is clearly drawn from the work of Robert Dahl and F.A. Hayek.[82] The core of the approach builds on Hayek's view that trading values through a free market is the best route to respecting pluralism.[83] In this view, the constitution ideally avoids regulating politics in line with a particular end. For those who subscribe to the trading perspective, constitutions should simply be a minimalist framework that facilitates a plurality of agents pursuing various purposes and bringing about a spontaneous system.[84]

In federal theory, this approach leads to the promotion of structural and distributive mechanisms that facilitate the trading and counterbalancing of difference. Drawing from elements of the wider school of

78 Levy (2007: 463).
79 Bellamy (2000: 202; 1999: ch. 1).
80 Bellamy (2000: 202–3).
81 Bellamy (2000: 202).
82 See Dahl (1956, 1989).
83 See Hayek (1973, 1960).
84 Hayek (1973: ch. 2, 55–9).

"centripetalism,"[85] the goal is to use federations as a means to disperse power through a decentralized system. This decentralization is seen to (1) facilitate correspondence between the heterogeneity of preferences and values of individuals and the policy agendas of the multiple sub-state governments;[86] and (2) provide a counterbalance to the concentration of power in the central government, thereby protecting the freedom of individuals from tyrannies of majorities or minorities.[87] The approach also promotes the design of symmetrical, and merely territorial, sub-state units to facilitate shifting allegiances and respect for plurality in the form of an overarching political identity.[88]

This emphasis on symmetry and territoriality for sub-state units is intended to strip national identity from the public and institutional realm. In so doing, the promoters of this approach are trying to use the federal system to build a civic nation[89] and create an environment that allows for the trading of difference to take place. The goal is to separate ethno-national identity from the political institutions and boundaries of the sub-state units, while elevating the importance of a pan-state civic identity. The logic of this nation-building enterprise is that it provides stability and allows plurality to be respected. The model and its promotion of structural and distributive mechanisms within a federal system thus work from the assumptions of national self-determination. The trading approach maintains that a single nation within a state is instrumentally and normatively preferable, as this is seen to promote stability and provide political legitimacy by creating and facilitating the environment to allow the trading of difference to take place at the political level.

Segregating

The third approach of segregating diversity is different in the way it recognizes and institutionalizes sub-state national identity. At the heart of this approach is adherence to the principle that groups should control

85 See Horowitz (2000); Reilly (2001).

86 Tiebout (1956: 419, 423–4).

87 Weinstock (2001: 76–8); Hueglin and Fenna (2006: 99–100); Levy (2007: 468–9).

88 McGarry and O'Leary (2007: 186); Levy (2007: 461). Some even promote the intentional creation of heterogeneous sub-state units to disperse national identities and facilitate cross-cutting cleavages; see Horowitz (2000: 601–28; 2007: 960–1); Wolff (2011: 169).

89 McGarry and O'Leary (2007: 187).

areas vital to their form of life, and so it promotes autonomy and power sharing for distinguishable sub-state groups.[90] The theoretical basis of the approach seeks to protect individual rights by protecting an individual's culture, which is what makes the protection of a group's values and identity via self-government instrumentally and normatively justifiable.[91] In this vein, the work of scholars like Michael Walzer underpins the approach, especially his linkage between the social construction of goods and identity and the justifiable protection of the autonomy of spheres within which this construction takes place,[92] as well as his argument that homogeneous political communities are a means to lessen conflict.[93] Also central is the idea that local government can be controlled better than a distant central authority, and that it is valid to demarcate local government along ethno-national lines.[94]

Within federal theory, the segregating approach is applied to achieve two complementary objectives: (1) protecting national minority identity; and (2) dispersing power as a counterbalance to central authority in order to protect freedom. Will Kymlicka's promotion of ethno-national sub-state units, or multinational federalism, is among the most prominent contemporary theories in this spirit.[95] Unlike the above approaches, this theory accepts that a measure of asymmetry among sub-state units is likely and acceptable, given that national minority identities may only line up nicely in certain regions (and thus some jurisdictions may be territorially based and some nationally based).[96] Decentralization is also a key part of this approach. It is promoted to ensure that nationally based sub-units have adequate powers to meaningfully exercise self-government,[97] while also protecting

90 Bellamy (2000: 204–5).

91 McGarry and O'Leary (2007: 189); see, e.g., Kymlicka (1995).

92 Walzer (1983: 7–10); Bellamy (1999: 68–70).

93 Bellamy (1999: 75).

94 Levy (2007: 462).

95 See Kymlicka (1998: ch. 10; 2001: ch. 5). For a review of this and other related works following the multinational federal model, see Schertzer and Woods (2011).

96 See Kymlicka (1998: 139). The defence of asymmetry follows the logic that since nationally based sub-state units can legitimately pursue particular purposes in line with their distinct culture, they need to have the policy levers to achieve these ends, which may exceed or differ from the policy levers other territorial jurisdictions need to manage themselves.

97 Kymlicka (1998: 139).

groups from the potential tyranny of the majority through a central authority.[98]

Multinational federalism is a structural response to the perceived "reality" of nationalism, taking minority nationalist claims for self-determination seriously and trying to accommodate them in a federal framework.[99] While the approach leads to a (welcome) attempt to accommodate national diversity, the commitment to take nationalism seriously betrays the approach's adherence to the doctrine of national self-determination. Clearly, the segregating approach drops the idea that each nation deserves and requires its own *state*, and in this way it properly rejects the overt assimilationist output of this equation being applied in the trimming and trading approaches.[100] At the same time, the equation that the nation and the state should be congruent is only slightly adjusted: in multinational federalism the view that legitimate political authority is based upon consent from "the nation" is only moved down a level to apply to sub-state jurisdictions. This adjustment assumes national minority groups are well established, politically organized, and already institutionalized to an extent.[101] Thus, the approach can tend to recognize and work from an "essentialist" understanding of national minority identity, selecting certain groups and particular views within those groups as the basis for institutional design.[102] Moreover, the accommodation of national minority self-government within this federal approach is generally only allowed to the extent that the powers and actions of self-government are consistent with liberal principles of individual freedom and equality.[103]

The above exemplifies the shared flaw with all three federal approaches: they are based upon a goal of "solving" the "problem" of national diversity by containing conflict through federal institutions that largely sit above political contestation. In a discussion of the shared nature of federal systems, Daniel Halberstam presented them as "constituting the framework within which daily politics takes place."[104] Each approach is based upon a justification of federal institutions and

98 Levy (2007: 466–7); Acton (1985).
99 Schertzer and Woods (2011: 204–6). See, e.g., Kymlicka (1998: 130–2, 134, 139).
100 McGarry and O'Leary (2007: 190–1).
101 Bellamy (2000: 208).
102 Wimmer (2008); Schertzer and Woods (2011).
103 See, for example, Kymlicka (1995, 1998, 2001).
104 Halberstam (2008: 143).

the distribution of power that reinforces the fixed and static nature of these institutions. The underlying theories are premised upon the view that politics legitimately happens *within* nations, and since the federal structure is the way groups are recognized as nations (or not), debate and conflict *over* the federal structure is removed from the political agenda. The trimming federal model seeks to suppress such political contestation by placing the federal structure above everyday politics as representing an overlapping consensus of the pan-state civic nation. The trading federal model seeks to resolve such conflict by removing the federal system from the field of political contestation. In the trading approach the federal system is part of the minimalist framework that is the expression of, and the key factor in establishing, a pan-state civic nation; so, political conflict takes place within this framework, not over it. The segregation model seeks to solve the problem of diversity by maintaining that legitimate politics takes place within nations, and the federal system is the framework that segregates these nations from each other (and so, the framework itself is not an object of politics). Of course, most scholars – despite pointing to the value of federal systems being part of a difficult to change constitutional order – also recognize the need for the institutions of government and the distribution of power and resources to respond to changing circumstances and preferences over time.[105] In this vein, the study of how federal systems do change over time, despite the sticky nature of federal institutions, is a core part of the field.[106] However, the underlying assumption of the main approaches within federal theory as a means to manage diversity work from a position of trying to get institutions "right" at the outset in terms of achieving congruence between the nation and the state, while ultimately elevating the federal system (as part of the constitutional order) above political contestation.[107]

Before elaborating further on why this shared basis is problematic, I want to contextualize my discussion by turning to Canada. By looking

105 For a discussion and overview, see Watts (2008: 157–70).

106 Jan Erk's (2008) study looking at the patterns of congruence between the institutions and society in five federations (Austria, Belgium, Canada, Germany, and Switzerland) is a case in point; see Arthur Benz and Jörge Broschek's (2013) edited volume on continuity and change in federations.

107 As Ronald Watts says: "In matters relating in any way to the relationship between federal and constituent unit governments, the ultimate supremacy of the federal constitutions over all governments has always been prescribed in federations" (Watts 2008: 158).

at how these three broad federal approaches are applied in Canada, I can better draw out the issues with an approach that seeks to trim, trade, or segregate away national diversity within a plurinational state, while also highlighting the value of an alternative understanding of, and approach towards, federalism in this country.

The Contested Federation

The status of Canada as a plurinational federation means it is inherently complex and contested. The result of this status is that there is no widely agreed upon description of the nature of the federal system. For some the federation grants the central government considerable power as the representative of a pan-state national community; for others, the system grants the provinces considerable power, while even giving Québec special powers to accommodate its nature as a minority nation. The distance between these competing understandings of the national composition of the country and the federal system drive ongoing political conflict, which manifests most explicitly as conflict over the federal division of powers, the constitutional amending formula, the impact of civil-liberties protections on provincial autonomy, and so on.

This conflict over the federal system manifests as, and is propelled by, competing perspectives of what the federation is and ought to be. Among these competing perspectives, three main federal models have emerged in Canada that represent competing positions about the actual and ideal institutional makeup of the federation driven by underlying views about the state's national character. Many scholars have contributed to, and employed, a taxonomy of federal models within Canada.[108] Of these, Rocher and Smith's work, which can be understood as a refinement of Edwin Black's taxonomy, stands apart for its in-depth treatment of the federal models as emanating from underlying perspectives on political identity and associated perspectives on the preferred institutional makeup of the state.[109] Reflecting on this taxonomy helps us understand not only the contested nature of the federation in Canada, but also how this contestation reflects the wider debates within federal theory on the approaches to manage diversity via federal systems.

108 Notably, see Black (1975); Mallory (1977); Swinton and Rogerson (1988); Cairns (1994); Noel (1994); Cooper (1994); Tully (1994); Rocher and Smith (2003); McRoberts (2003); Russell (2004).

109 See Rocher and Smith (2003) and Black (1975), respectively.

Rocher and Smith argue that actors and citizens in Canada subscribe to one of four "federal visions," which represent "diametrically opposed concepts, norms and values" with regard to the federation.[110] The differing institutional designs promoted by these federal visions – the set of "constitutional priorities" – are "based on different underlying definitions of political identity."[111] In other words, contrasting views of the sociological underpinnings of the polity drive related views about the ideal institutional structures of the federation. But, these are not just abstract concepts or theories: they inform political mobilization and activity by social actors in Canada (which serve to reinforce and shape the visions).[112] This reciprocal relationship, whereby the visions mobilize action based on a perceived reality, with the mobilization in turn helping to bring about that reality, points to one of the key attributes of these federal models: they are both purported descriptions of what the federation *is* and ideal models of what it *ought* to be.[113]

Drawing heavily from Rocher and Smith, but also from Black and the others cited above, I identify three key federal models in Canada: pan-Canadian, provincial-equality, and multinational (see table 1.2).[114]

Pan-Canadian

The pan-Canadian model has gone through a number of iterations since the nineteenth century, most recently being expressed by Prime Minister Trudeau from the 1970s.[115]

---

110 Rocher and Smith (2003: 22).

111 Rocher and Smith (2003: 22).

112 Rocher and Smith (2003: 37).

113 Black (1975: 2–3, 7).

114 Rocher and Smith's four visions have been collapsed into three as the pan-Canadian, provincial-equality, and multinational visions incorporate significant components of their fourth vision (rights-based constitutionalism); see Rocher and Smith (2003: 22, 38–40). For example, the core of the rights-based movement in Canada helps to solidify the pan-Canadian vision by projecting a shared citizenship for all Canadians; at the same time, the rights-based movement can act to protect and solidify minority national identity, thus supporting the multinational vision (i.e., when group rights are recognized through ethno-cultural identifiers). In addition, I find support for my three categories from Black, where he is actually identifying three *models* (central, compact, and dualist) and two additional *ways of undertaking* federation or processes of intergovernmental relations (administrative, coordinate); see Black (1975: ch. 1, 15–20, 225–6). The overlapping consensus between these two taxonomies of Canadian federal theory, then, is that there are three key models: pan-Canadian, provincial-equality, and multinational.

115 Rocher and Smith (2003: 34).

Table 1.2. Three Canadian federal models

Federal model	Approach to managing national diversity	Nature of federal system	Ideal federal structure	Key expressions of model
Pan-Canadian	*Trimming* diversity to create one bilingual, multicultural nation across Canada	Compact between members of one nation	– Symmetrical – Territorial – Centralized – Central institutions as national	– Substance of *Constitution Act, 1867* – Expansion of social programs in 20th century – Substance of *Constitution Act, 1982* – Defeat of Meech and Charlottetown Accords
Provincial equality	*Trading* diversity to facilitate a civic nation built on the equal diversity of provinces	Compact between equal *provinces*	– Symmetrical – Territorial – Decentralized – Central institutions representing provincial diversity	– Process of enacting *Constitution Act, 1867* – Provincial-rights movement in 19th century – Defeat of Meech and Charlottetown Accords – Fed.-Prov. Agreement on Internal Trade (1994) – Calgary Declaration (1999)
Multinational	*Segregating* diversity to accommodate multiple nations (Québécois, Aboriginals, and English Canada) within the state	Compact between already established *nations*	– Asymmetrical – Ethnic and territorial – Decentralized – Central institutions include special representation for minority nations	– *Royal Proclamation* (1763) and *Québec Act* (1774) – Process and substance of *Constitution Act, 1867* – "Québec Veto" over constitutional amendments – Aboriginal nationalism – Federal government recognition of Québec as distinct society and nation (1999 and 2006)

It clearly draws from the trimming approach in how it both views and deals with national diversity. At the heart of this model is a view of Canada as a bilingual, multicultural pan-state nation; accordingly, subscribers of this model seek to promote a single, comprehensive civic political identity for every citizen within the territory of the state.[116]

This understanding of the nation, in combination with a view that the federation is and ought to be an overlapping consensus between the members of a single community fixed above politics, informs the key policy prescriptions of the federal model. Placing the central government as the locus of pan-Canadian political identity, the model promotes a centralized federal system where national standards are the benchmark against which provincial autonomy to act is measured.[117] In addition, since the plurality of the single nation is seen as represented in central institutions, the provinces are understood as subordinate territorial/administrative units, symmetrical in their status.

To support their position, subscribers of this model point to the extensive powers granted to the central government in the Constitution Act, 1867 (particularly unlimited tax-and-spend powers and the reserve and disallowance powers). They also point to the process of patriating, and the substance of, the Constitution Act, 1982 and the defeat of the Meech Lake and Charlottetown Accords as demonstrating the continued relevance of the pan-Canadian model.[118]

Provincial Equality

The provincial-equality model similarly has roots in the nineteenth century, stressing that Canada is the result of a "compact" between four autonomous political entities in 1867.[119]

The theoretical foundation of the provincial-equality model shares a great deal with the trading approach in its view and approach to national identity. The subscribers of this model try to facilitate allegiances that cut across ethno-national lines, enabling mutually beneficial trade-offs between (and among) the provinces and central government. While the provincial-equality model stresses that the provinces represent the

116 Rocher and Smith (2003: 34); Webber (1994: 143); McRoberts (2001: 703–7).

117 Rocher and Smith (2003: 34–5).

118 Rocher and Smith (2003: 34–7).

119 Rocher and Smith (2003: 23); Russell (2004: 48–52); Romney (1999).

primary political community of belonging, subscribers see the sum of these communities as a singular Canadian nation – a nation that is the result of respecting the *equal diversity* of its constitutive elements.[120]

This understanding of Canada leads to a position that the federation is the background neutral framework that facilitates the desired market-based politics between jurisdictions. As the provincial-equality model presents the central government as the sum of its provincial parts, its supporters promote a decentralized federation; this stress on decentralization is based on equality, though, since the original compact is seen to be between equal partners.[121] Accordingly, not only are central institutions supposed to represent equally the regional diversity of the country, but each province is seen as a symmetrical territorial unit, none being any more distinct than the rest.

To stress the historical lineage of this model, its supporters highlight the political process of adopting the Constitution Act, 1867 (i.e., representing this as a compact between four equal partners), and the subsequent provincial-rights movement following confederation.[122] The promoters of the provincial-equality model also point to the more recent unanimity clauses in the constitutional amending formula, the Federal-Provincial Internal Trade Agreement (1994), the Social Union Framework (1999), and the Calgary Declaration (1999) as a basis for the model's continuing importance.[123]

Multinational

Originally stressing a bi-national character for Canada as the driving force for federation, the multinational model has moved beyond an exclusive anglo-franco dynamic to incorporate Aboriginals.[124]

The multinational model draws on the segregation approach to accommodate national diversity. It starts with a basic understanding of Canada as comprised of multiple sociological nations: the Québécois, Aboriginals, and English Canada.[125] Accordingly, the model holds that some mixture of autonomy and power sharing for the Québécois and

120 Rocher and Smith (2003: 24–6).
121 Rocher and Smith (2003: 23–6).
122 Russell (2004: ch. 4).
123 Rocher and Smith (2003: 25–7).
124 Rocher and Smith (2003: 28–33); McRoberts (2003: 89–91, 102–4).
125 See Resnick (1994); Schertzer and Woods (2011: 203).

various Aboriginals is justified. This is a federal model that is about protecting values and culture seen as intrinsic to the identity of Québécois and Aboriginal groups through forms of self-government.

Given the adoption of the multinational character of Canada as fact, the supporters of this model understand and try to reinforce a view of the federation as the framework that separates these nations into autonomous political communities. Thus, from its beginnings as a compact between founding nations,[126] the Canadian federation is seen as the means by which various nations within Canada are segregated from each other and enjoy the autonomy required to develop as nations. From this basis, those subscribing to the multinational model hold that sub-state jurisdictions can be understood as either ethno-national (Québec, Nunavut, and Aboriginal communities) or territorial units (the remaining provinces).[127] Moreover, as national minority identities in Canada only line up nicely in certain units (and thus the majority of provinces are territorially based), asymmetry between these jurisdictions is accepted and promoted.[128] Finally, the objective of protecting minority national identity from coercion by the majority leads to the promotion of both special representation for national minorities in the institutions of central government and decentralization of powers to the sub-state jurisdictions.

The promoters of this model point first and foremost to the political circumstances driving confederation to support its validity (e.g., the Great Coalition between anglophone and francophone leaders in the Province of Canada and the implementation of federalism to accommodate the francophone nation).[129] In addition, to support their understanding of the federation in Canada, they point to the practice of a Québec "veto" over the rounds of constitutional negotiation from "Fulton-Favreau" to "Victoria" in the 1960s and 1970s.[130] Multinationalists also draw attention to a number of more recent developments to argue that their model ought to be the governing paradigm for contemporary federal design in Canada; notably, they highlight the rise of Aboriginal nationalism and the Assembly of First Nations in the mid-twentieth century in response to assimilationist policies and the

126 On the competing "compact" theories see, e.g., Sabetti (1982: 17–23).
127 Kymlicka (1998: ch. 10; 2001: ch. 5).
128 Kymlicka (1998: 139); McRoberts (2001: 711).
129 On the relevant process of confederation, see Russell (2004: 18–33).
130 On the rounds of constitutional negotiation, see Russell (2004: ch. 6).

central government's move towards recognition of national diversity and asymmetry from the 1990s (e.g., the Meech Lake and Charlottetown Accords, the 2004 first ministers' meeting on the future of healthcare, and the recognition of Québec as a distinct society and then nation through motions in the federal parliament in 1999 and 2006).

There are clear points of contention between the federal models. And, I would argue, this is largely based upon different views of the national character of the country, with associated views on how the federation does and should account for this reality. At the same time, while the differences between the institutional designs expressed in these three federal models are evident (between centralist, decentralist, and asymmetrical approaches), a direct correlation between one's view of the sociological reality of the state and an institutional model is not necessarily as clear as I have implied. Nuance is lost and lines are presented as brighter than they are in reality when one creates a taxonomy of socio-political views and phenomena. In this case, there are elements of crossover between each federal model (e.g., a general acceptance of some form of pan-national community). There is even the possibility that actors with a view of the sociological underpinnings of the state as multinational would argue for a centralized, pan-Canadian institutional design (perhaps to either offset the centrifugal force of this reality or because accommodation is possible outside the federal system). Or, there may be those with a view of Canada as inherently uninational who would argue for asymmetrical decentralization (perhaps as a matter of practical politics to alleviate conflict with those mobilizing for autonomy). Despite this qualification, I argue that the principal driver for the three competing federal models in Canada is an underlying view of the ideal sociological nature of the state as a pan-national community, a compact among provinces, or a compact among nations. In addition, the space between these main perspectives, and the fact that different groups tend to adhere to different models,[131] undeniably leads to conflict in the political arena – something that has been reflected in the development of the federation.

In this regard, each model represents a legitimate perspective on the nature of the federation in line with my earlier discussion of legitimacy. The Canadian federation has developed in response to the conflict

131 In simplified form, the pan-Canadian vision generally finds its greatest support within Ontario and Maritime Canada, the provincial-equality view in the western provinces, and the multinational vision is favoured by Aboriginals and Québécois.

between the subscribers of the federal models in a way that reflects elements of each perspective. As a result of this political mobilization and the resulting incorporation of elements of each competing model, the state has been able to maintain the loyalty of groups with the competing perspectives. Over and above the points just noted, even a cursory glance at Canada's constitutional documents supports this view.

Canada has had at least six main constitutions since 1769 that have reflected and impacted the evolution of the federal system in the state (see tables 1.3 and 1.4). At first glance, it seems that each constitution implements an overarching vision for the political community and the federation. Each document could be seen as representing a perceived reality and ideal model for the state and the relationships between political identity, institutions, and authority. However, as tables 1.3 and 1.4 indicate, each document can also be interpreted as an imperfect agreement between key social actors who held competing perspectives on the nature of the political community and thus competing ideal constitutional and federal models.

So, while the socio-economic and political context may have influenced which social actors were able to position their federal model as the dominant one, the process and outcome of constitutional negotiation led to inevitable compromise and at least marginal inclusion of the competing perspectives. These constitutions thus stand as representations of the then-achievable agreement between the key social actors who held competing perspectives on the nature and ideal form of Canada. Accordingly, the constitutions of Canada reflect an increasing complexity in their presentation of the political community. This complexity is not just associated with the technological thrust of modernity. It reflects the fact that the constitutions represent the outcome of negotiations over the very nature of the federation between increasingly wider sets of social actors and movements that held increasingly solidified views on the link between authority and ethno-cultural diversity (spurred on by the doctrine of national self-determination). The solidification and perceived validity of these views necessitated a level of inclusion in the negotiations and final document for the association to remain legitimate (as not including them would risk the loyalty to the association among the subscribers of the federal visions).

An understanding of the constitutions of Canada as iterations in a process of integrating competing perspectives on the nature of the association allows us to see the dialectic that takes place between key social actors representing movements that subscribe to the various federal models and the federal structure of Canada. This understanding

Table 1.3. Key constitutions for Canada, 1763–1840[132]

Constitution	Key aspects	Relation to federation in Canada	Approach to managing national diversity
Royal Proclamation (1763)	Established territory of Québec under administration of a British governor and council; established a large section of land "reserved" for "Indians" that could only be ceded by treaty with the Crown	Sought to establish a singular, unified colonial territory for British settlers	Assimilation of Catholic francophone settlers by excluding them from political administration and by implementing Protestant schools and churches
		Established the key territorial and legal entity foregrounding the Government of Canada	Purported to treat Aboriginals as sovereign legal entities with rights to negotiate ceding of lands with Crown as equals
Québec Act (1774)	Expanded territory of Québec; maintained administration under a British governor and council; permitted free practice of Catholicism	Sought to maintain and solidify a unified colonial territory of anglophones and francophones under British rule	Accommodated Catholic francophones in Québec by allowing free practice of Catholicism, practice of French civil law, and by granting them access to public office
		Foundational example of accommodating francophone diversity	Significantly expanded territory of Québec into lands reserved for Aboriginals via treaties (legitimacy of treaties is contested)
Constitutional Act (1791)	Segmented territory of Québec into Upper Canada (Ontario) and Lower Canada (Québec); established elected legislative assemblies for both colonies	Provided a measure of autonomy for the anglophones and francophones (through separate territories and representative institutions)	Accommodated Catholic francophones by establishing separate territory and representative institutions from those of the anglophone United Empire Loyalists settling in Upper Canada
		Key early use of territorial autonomy to accommodate national diversity	Newly created territories (especially Upper Canada) expanded into lands reserved for Aboriginals through treaties (legitimacy of treaties is contested)

(*Continued*)

132 Information and analysis draws from listed constitutional documents, as well as Russell (2004).

Table 1.3. Key constitutions for Canada, 1763–1840 (Continued)

Constitution	Key aspects	Relation to federation in Canada	Approach to managing national diversity
Act of Union (1840)	Reunited Upper Canada and Lower Canada into single territory with one legislature; provided guaranteed equal representation in legislature for the subsequent provinces of Canada East and Canada West (the borders being the same as for Upper and Lower Canada)	Following Durham report, sought to reverse autonomy for francophones and maintain stability of territory through centralized representative government Key early use of centralized government to seek stability (following the rebellions of 1837); but also established power-sharing arrangements (via guaranteed equal representation for francophones and anglophones in legislature)	Retreated from accommodation through autonomy, seeking assimilation of francophones. Nevertheless, guarantee of equal representation in the legislature, maintenance of the provinces of Canada East and West, and implementation of responsible government facilitated the continued operation of the state as a quasi-federation Preceding and following the Act of Union, treaties continued to be signed with Aboriginals to cede land (e.g., the Niagara Treaty of 1838)

Table 1.4. Key constitutions for Canada, 1867–1982[133]

Constitution	Key aspects	Relation to federation in Canada	Approach to managing national diversity
Constitution Act (1867)	Established a federal state with power divided between two orders of government, having four provinces (Ontario, Québec, Nova Scotia, and New Brunswick) and a bicameral central parliament (that retained powers of reserve and disallowance) Authority to amend the constitution and arbitration of intergovernmental disputes remained with the imperial parliament	Established the foundational division of powers and responsibilities between the two orders of government, which is still in force The three main federal models find support in the process of establishing, and in the substance of, the act. For example, it (1) creates and provides significant powers to a central government; (2) forms this government out of an agreement among the three original provinces; and (3) represents a compact between francophones and anglophones (through the "Great Coalition" within the Province of Canada)	Reversed the course of assimilation set in the Act of Union by establishing a federal state where both anglophones and francophones had a measure of political autonomy. Minority-rights provisions were also included for francophone and anglophone minority-language communities and denominational schools Responsibility for Aboriginals (including the negotiation of treaties and the establishment of lands reserved for them) was granted to the central government
Constitution Act (1982)	Following federal-provincial negotiation (but without approval from Québec) enshrined a domestic amending formula with various permutations; a pan-state bill of rights; and Aboriginal treaty rights	Solidified pan-Canadian model through the *Charter of Rights and Freedoms* and exacerbated tensions with Québec (through the content and process of enshrining the act) The two other federal models are also expressed in the act; for example: the provincial-equality model through the bilateral and unanimity clauses in the amending formula; and the multinational model through the Aboriginal-rights provisions and sec. 1 and 33 of the Charter	Through the *Charter seeks* to build a pan-state identity, but also accommodates Québec's autonomy (sec. 1 and 33) Aboriginal treaty rights are affirmed, with the goal of negotiating land claims and treaties in good faith on a nation-to-nation basis (a symbolic reversal of the policy approach of assimilation adopted throughout the 20th century)

133 Information and analysis draws from listed constitutional documents, as well as Russell (2004).

provides an appreciation of the relationship between, on the one hand, things like the 1837 rebellions for representative government, opposition to the Act of Union and the political stalemate of the 1860s, and the rise of Aboriginal nationalism and Québécois nationalism in the mid-twentieth century, and, on the other hand, key constitutional and federal developments in response. In other words, by accounting for the dialectic processes of constitutional and federal politics we are able to see how the federal system has endured over time in the face of considerable political conflict and centrifugal forces (driven by things such as ethno-national diversity, geography, and geo-political factors).

This brief review of Canadian constitutional history also shows that there is no single triumphant perspective on the nature of the federation; rather, actors can and do draw on a number of persistent competing perspectives that have roots deep into the past. The substance of the Canadian constitutions, and the process by which they were struck, exemplify the competition and conflict between various actors over the nature of, and the ideal model for, the Canadian federation. The six constitutions of Canada thus also help show why each of the three federal models noted above can be seen as legitimate. The three federal models have received long-standing and continuing support from sets of actors. The political mobilization by these actors in support of the federal models demonstrates an acceptance of them as valid principles to organize political activity. Importantly, this mobilization has resulted in elements of each perspective being incorporated into the constitutional framework of the state over time, which sets the three federal models apart as valid descriptions of the nature of the federal system. And, this inclusion in the constitutional framework not only generates loyalty to the federal system itself (as representing the particular perspectives of different sets of actors), it also reaffirms the validity of each vision in the eyes of its subscribers. Accordingly, we can see a mutually constitutive process whereby the legitimacy of the visions can be increased with inclusion in the federal system in some form and, at the same time, the legitimacy of the federal system can be increased through this inclusion. In other words, including elements of each federal model in the constitutions of Canada has the potential to generate loyalty to the model itself (as valid) and to the wider system (as representative).

Conclusion

The above discussion of the way national minorities challenge political authority, how policymakers try to solve this problem through federalism, and the way this plays out in the Canadian case sets up a number of points for the remainder of the book.

The first relates to the nature of the issue. Understanding how national diversity (and particularly national minorities) challenges political legitimacy provides insight into the proposed responses. Appreciating how national minorities draw attention to the lack of congruence between the boundaries of the nation and the state can show that many responses seek to solve this problem. This perspective thus shows that some policy responses are about generating legitimacy for a state or government through social or institutional manipulation with the underlying goal of making the boundaries of the nation and the state one and the same.

Reflecting on this point also provides a sense of the importance legitimacy plays in politics. Instability and violence are often (rightly) the focus of policymakers and academics. Political instability, though, is generally a manifestation of a loss of legitimacy on the part of governments and states. In a large number of instances, this loss of legitimacy and violence are the result of ethno-national diversity and groups struggling for national self-determination (and not realizing their goal). The maintenance of peace and order is thus, in no small way, linked to the maintenance of political legitimacy. In diverse federations the link is particularly strong – as geographic, institutional, and demographic factors often combine to create centrifugal forces that threaten state unity. This is the context that informs my own study of Canada, and one of the key motivations for looking at the critical role the federal arbiter plays in managing conflict over the federation and in maintaining the legitimacy of the system both there and in other federations. In other words, the narrative in this chapter has been about setting up the point that stability and unity in a federation require the generation and maintenance of legitimacy for the political system.

Federalism is often promoted as a means (a compromise) to achieve such stability. At the same time, the three approaches described in this chapter all seek to generate the required legitimacy by implementing an institutional structure of government that is informed by the logic of national self-determination. Each approach is about finding (or building) congruence between the boundaries of the national community and political authority. This congruence is a way of containing political conflict within nations, using the federation as the means to either build or separate these national communities. Thus, even with the recognition that federal systems are contested by the members of the association and that to remain legitimate they have to (and do) adapt over time, the starting point for the main approaches to promoting federal systems is about finding an alignment between the boundaries of the nation and the state (or society and institutions).

Drawing out the links between the broad approaches to federal design and the main federal models in Canada helps to show the flaw in this underlying logic of designing federal systems. The similarities in the underlying perspectives and goals of the three federal models and the broader approaches to federal design show how both the models and approaches represent normative positions on the best way to deal with national diversity.[134] The three federal models (on their own) do not stand as comprehensive, accurate depictions of the Canadian federation. Rather, each is a partial perspective that merges a view of what the federation is and what it ought to be – with supporters going on to promote an institutional structure that reinforces and brings about their own ideal. In this regard, each federal model is both based upon a particular understanding of the sociological basis of the polity and an attempt to reflect and reinforce that understanding in the institutional designs of the federation. The continued contestation between the subscribers of these competing views challenges the premise that a federation can be a neutral framework that achieves congruence. Conflict over the very nature of what the federation is and ought to be has taken place since before the Canadian state was founded. This conflict, and the models that drive it, accordingly seem to be indeterminate. The view that implementing one approach will resolve this conflict simply fails to account for this fact.

The Canadian federation is thus properly understood as contested and dynamic. Conflict over the nature of the system between different groups has been the norm, and will continue to be so. The principal mediums through which this contestation over national identity and the federation takes place in the state are the models noted above. Importantly, this political conflict has had an effect on the federal system. We can see how the constitution has adapted over time, changing to reflect the various positions through an evolving institutional structure.

134 It should be noted that in some respects, given Canada's importance as a key case in federal theory, the particular models have also informed broader theory, particularly in the case of the Canada School of multinational federalists (led by Will Kymlicka); see Schertzer and Woods (2011: 204).

This dynamic is what informs my argument that federal theory needs to better account for the inherent conflict over national identity and the federation in plurinational federations like Canada. A defensible federal theory cannot only work from the premises of, and work towards the ideal of, one federal approach and model. Simply seeking to solve the problem of national diversity by suppressing conflict through rigid institutional structures that try to build one civic nation or separate nations fails to adequately account for (and manage) this dynamic of conflict. The inevitable result of such an approach is to push conflict over the federation and the way it recognizes national identity outside the political process and into the realm of violence.[135] The alternative approach, which I outline and argue is preferable in the next chapter, is to account for the inherent conflict that takes place in a plurinational federation and try to generate and maintain legitimacy for the system in the way it manages this conflict. This chapter has established the groundwork for this claim, and the argument that the federal arbiter plays an important role in managing the conflict that takes place within and over federation in Canada (and thus in the generation and maintenance of legitimacy).

135 Schertzer and Woods (2011: 214).

Chapter Two

The Role of the Federal Arbiter in a Diverse Federation

The central objective of this chapter is to show that conflict over the federation (particularly in a plurinational state) means the federal arbiter is important for the development and maintenance of legitimacy in the system. Central to this role, and its effect on legitimacy, is how the federal arbiter exercises its duties. As I discuss below, while there is a strong tradition of work considering the role of the Supreme Court of Canada in the development of the Canadian federation, the federal arbiter is relatively under-examined and under-theorized in the broader field of comparative federal and conflict management studies. To the extent the federal arbiter has been considered, there has been a tendency to promote a role that has the potential to delegitimize the conflict-management process and the federation more generally. Seeking to address this issue, I argue here that when studying and promoting federal systems, we need to start with an understanding of them as dynamic institutional arrangements that are shaped by ongoing negotiation. By starting from this point, we can appreciate the critical role the federal arbiter plays in managing conflict when negotiation breaks down, and that how it fulfils this role matters. As I argue here, how the Court manages this conflict can either negatively affect the legitimacy of the federal system or generate legitimacy. The SCC can potentially generate legitimacy by reinforcing the dynamic elements of the system, and thus seek to manage conflict by facilitating ongoing negotiation, where possible.

The chapter begins with a brief discussion on the nature of federal systems as contested normative frameworks, while making the point that conflict over these associations is only enhanced in plurinational states like Canada. Reflecting on the various forums where this type of conflict plays out and the mechanisms that are used to manage it, I look in depth at the vital role of the federal arbiter (which in Canada is the judiciary, and ultimately the Supreme Court of Canada). In doing this, I highlight why the judiciary is an important mechanism to manage conflict (viz., because its decisions affect the development of the federation and the legitimacy of the system). I then lay out how federal theory has generally presented the ideal role for the judiciary as federal arbiter, arguing that the three main roles for the Court (as umpire, branch of government, or guardian) are problematically linked to the broader approaches of trimming, trading, or segregating diversity. Finally, I present an alternative federal theory: one that accounts for the contested nature of a federation and promotes an ideal role for the federal arbiter that could help to generate and maintain legitimacy for the system.

Conflict over the Federation and the Forums of Management

The previous chapter has demonstrated that the Canadian federation is contested by groups subscribing to competing perspectives on the nature of the system and its ideal direction. This seemingly indeterminate conflict is driven by two related factors: the nature of the federation as a normative framework and the plurinational character of the state.

In the Introduction I argued that a federation is properly understood as a system governed by a set of norms (in both their regulating and regularizing aspect).[1] Federal systems are actually one of the most explicit examples of a normative framework. They are systems that arise out of contestation over the way identities are recognized, and power and resources accordingly distributed via the governing norms (what James Tully terms an "intersubjective normative framework)."[2] Federations are only one type of intersubjective normative system within the gambit of political associations (which are all governed by intersubjective normative systems); going back to the last chapter, a federation is distinguished from other systems of rule, though, in the way it explicitly constitutes multiple orders of government within a state and distributes power and resources accordingly.

1 On normative systems, see Tully (2004: 88); Butler (1997: 1–105).

2 See Tully (2004, 2001); on the link between recognition and distribution, see Tully (2000b: 469–71).

One of the central elements of intersubjective normative systems is that conflict is an inherent part of the association. The multiplicity of perspectives among those subject to the system on its true and ideal nature means that consensus on how to organize the association – even on its basic rules – is virtually impossible. As Tully argues, these systems and the struggles over them are "too complex, unpredictable and mutable to admit of definitive solutions."[3]

This inherent conflict over the federation in Canada is also driven by the fact it is a plurinational state. As discussed in the Introduction, the idea of "plurinationality" is best explained by noting the difference between the category of "multinational" (implying multiple sealed national groups within a state) and "plurinational" (where the very concept of nationality is contested and plural).[4] The idea of plurinationality is enhanced by linking it to the work of John Hutchinson, which shows how nations are best understood as "zones of conflict" where multiple movements and understandings compete over time to define the nature and direction of the group.[5] This link allows us to see that national identity itself is contested, and that it is through this contestation that the nation emerges and re-emerges.[6] In plurinational states, then, social and political actors compete over time to define and set the future agenda for their respective national projects, and also for the national character of the state as a whole.

The contested nature of national identity is observable in the case of Canada. For example, within Québec there are both Québécois nationalists and pan-state nationalists. Also, inside the Québécois nationalist project there are sets of actors competing over what it means to be Québécois (e.g., those espousing an "ethnic" or "civic" core for the group).[7] At the same time, there are English Canadians outside Québec who are both English Canadian nationalists and pan-state nationalists,

3 Tully (2001: 5).

4 See Keating (2001: 27; 2002: 361).

5 See Hutchinson (2005).

6 The point is to recognize that nations, as imagined communities, have a rather fluid nature and that contestation over the idea of the nation takes place among various sets of actors with competing visions. See Anderson (1991); Brubaker (1996, 2004); Hutchinson (2005).

7 These differences were readily observable during the hearings of the "Consultation Commission on Accommodation Practices Related to Cultural Differences" within Québec. The final report is available at https://www.mce.gouv.qc.ca/publications/publications.htm.

while there are also those who are sympathetic to Québécois and Aboriginal nationalism, displaying what might be thought of as a type of "multinational nationalism."[8] In other words, there is conflict within groups that identify as nations and between these groups over the way the state recognizes their identities or not.[9]

The underlying conflict between these groups is sometimes obscured by the success of one group promoting its understanding as the correct one in the political arena or at times of institutional and constitutional design. The varying nature of Canada's constitutions noted in the first chapter is a case in point. In this regard, the emergent view shared by many anglophone scholars and policymakers of Canada as multinational, where the Québécois and Aboriginals are accepted as nations within the wider polity paired with reduced levels of support of sovereignty in Québec, would seem to be a signal the country is moving beyond a period of conflicting nationalisms. The clarion call of this view is the parliamentary motion recognizing the Québécois nation within a united Canada in 2006.[10]

However, such a view is in danger of missing the sometimes episodic, yet indeterminate, nature of this conflict between the subscribers of competing understandings of the national community. Moreover, this view fails to account for the inherent complexity and ambiguity of national identity. For example, as Kenneth McRoberts has noted, the very concept of multinational as a descriptor for Canada has so many different meanings for scholars and policymakers (e.g., referring to multiple sociological, political, minority, or internal groups) that plurinational as a category is much better suited to account for this variation.[11] Such variation and conflicting views are even observable in the 2006 Québec nation motion, which "recognize[s] that the Québécois form a nation within a united Canada." While the ambiguity of the wording is designed to hide this fact, the motion is intended

8 For example, see Kymlicka (1998); for a discussion of this, see Schertzer and Woods (2011). Also see Woods (2012) for an overview and discussion of the different national projects in Canada.

9 See Schertzer and Woods (2011).

10 See, for example, how the Multicultural Policy Index (http://www.queensu.ca/mcp) frames the evolution of Canada's recognition of multinationalism as growing from a largely pan-Canadian view in the 1980s towards an acceptance of Québec's status as a nation, with the 2006 parliamentary motion cited as the culmination and evidence of an affirmation of this view in the late 2000s.

11 McRoberts (2001: 683–8).

to appease soft nationalists within Québec and multinationalists outside Québec through the recognition of a "sociological nation"; but also pan-Canadianists inside and outside Québec since the "nation" is not recognized as congruent with the borders of the provincial political community and as a group that resides within a strong Canadian polity.

The benefit of noting Canada's plurinational character, along with the federation's nature as a normative system, then, is that this conceptualization illuminates key elements of the intra-state conflict that takes place within and over the federation. First, the concept helps show how contestation between the subscribers of the federal models is driven, in no small way, by a struggle over the way identities are recognized by the federation (or not). Struggles within and over the federation are thus exacerbated by the plurinational character of the country as the usual conflict related to resource competition mixes with identity politics, while debates over the character of Canada as *uninational or multi*national play out as debates over the federation. The result is continual conflict between the orders of government, as well as between private actors and governments, over the distribution of resources and power via the federal system. Appreciating the dynamics of conflict over national identity and the federation in Canada recasts these struggles as more than simple competition over resources. This appreciation shows that these struggles are not struggles *for* recognition of a particular federal power or right; rather, they are struggles *over* the very way the recognition of national identity takes place and powers and responsibilities are accordingly distributed.[12]

Struggles of this general type (i.e., struggles over recognition) play out in various forums and are managed through a number of mechanisms. Identifying these forums and management mechanisms involves three related steps of analysis: (1) looking at the specific type of struggle that is taking place; (2) considering the mediums through which the struggle manifests itself; and (3) determining where the struggles are explicitly and implicitly managed.[13]

The type of struggle I focus on here is conflict over national identity and the federation. In particular, I examine struggles over the way a federation either recognizes or imposes particular conceptions of national identity in distributing power and resources. This type of struggle tends to focus on two related areas: the substantive provisions of a

12 See Tully (2004: 87–8); Schertzer (2008: 106–7).

13 Schertzer (2008: 107); Tully (2004: 88–90).

federation (i.e., the constitutional division of powers) and the political practices that underpin a federal structure.[14] Moreover, Stephen Tierney has identified four specific areas to which disaffected groups within a plurinational state direct their struggles: the recognition of nationality; representation in central decision making; control over constitutional amendments; and group autonomy.[15]

The mediums through which these struggles manifest are diverse. There are numerous ways in which actors go about struggling against a constitutional and federal system they see as an imposition (or act in defence of a system they see as recognizing their position). Such action is clearly observable in the legal and political realm, both in the everyday practice of political actors and at more extraordinary junctures (so-called mega-constitutional politics).[16] This conflict also takes place, though, in the cultural realm (e.g., through artistic activity supporting or criticizing the distribution of power via the federation), in the media, in the economic sector (e.g., with private actors pursuing economic activity and policies that reinforce or challenge the distribution of resources via the federation), and even outside politics as violence.

The forums where conflicts between actors over nationality and the federation are explicitly managed are more limited. I have identified five main forums: (1) central government institutions (i.e., Parliament, the executive, and the bureaucracy); (2) intergovernmental relations mechanisms (i.e., regular intergovernmental cooperation and coordination, official bilateral and multilateral meetings and committees, and more extra-ordinary federal-provincial conferences); (3) public discourse (i.e., through the media and public debates, as well as through public inquiries and commissions); (4) arbitration mechanisms (i.e., the judiciary, constitutional courts, and referenda); and (5) international forums (i.e., multilateral institutions and tribunals).

So, in states like Canada there is continual conflict within and over the federation, and this conflict happens in many places and is managed in many different ways. In general, these conflict dynamics draw our attention to the fact that politics does not just take place within the legal and political framework of a federation; it happens over that framework as well. The nature of this continuing conflict is what has led me (and others) to look at the critical role these forums of managing

14 See Tierney (2009: 93).
15 See Tierney (2009: 92; 2003).
16 On "mega-constitutional politics," see Russell (2004: 75–6).

conflict over the federal system play in the association's development (and for me, in maintaining its legitimacy).[17]

The Judiciary as Federal Arbiter

Among the mechanisms that manage conflict over national identity and the federation the federal arbiter occupies a special status. A key feature of all federations is that they have a constitution and assign a division of responsibilities between different orders of government. This basic characteristic leads to the necessary functions of interpreting and applying the supreme law of the land and adjudicating disputes that arise between the orders of government over the scope of their respective powers and responsibilities in line with this supreme law.[18]. The necessity of these functions are what make the federal arbiter so crucial: it is the institution that allows difficult conflicts over the distribution of powers and resources via the federation to be managed within the domestic political sphere. And so, in exercising its duties, the federal arbiter has a critical role in the development of the system and, ultimately, in *maintaining its legitimacy*.

Different perspectives on how this role should be fulfilled – notably whether it should be left to legal experts and technocrats or be a more inclusive, democratic process – have resulted in different approaches to establishing the institution.[19] In practice, there are two distinct approaches: using courts of law or relying on referenda.[20]

Within the courts-of-law approach there are two related ways the role of federal arbiter is institutionalized. The first model grants the highest appellate court in a country (the apex court) the status as ultimate federal arbiter. This "apex court" approach, which tends to be employed in common-law jurisdictions, is used in the majority of federations (fifteen

---

17 Within the Canadian context there are many examples of important work on the role played by these forums of management in the development of the system; notable is the foundational work of Richard Simeon on intergovernmental relations (Simeon 2006), Watts on central (intra-state) institutions (Smiley and Watts 1985) and Alan Cairns on the judiciary (Cairns 1971).

18 On this point, see Watts (2008: 157–8).

19 See Watts (2008: 158).

20 Set somewhere between these two approaches is the unique case of Ethiopia, where the federal upper chamber (the House of Federation, made up of representatives from the states) has the exclusive responsibility to interpret the constitution; see Watts (2008: 48, 159).

in total: the United States, Canada, Australia, India, Argentina, Brazil, Mexico, Venezuela, Malaysia, Nigeria, Pakistan, Comoros, Micronesia, Belau, and St Kitts and Nevis).[21] In general, in these federations, a private citizen, corporation, or government can challenge the constitutionality of an order of government's actions or legislation by requesting judicial review from a court of law staffed with justices who have a broad jurisdiction to hear all questions of law. Often these challenges start with lower-level courts, with decisions being appealable up to the apex court. In practice, whether issues work their way through the court system via appeals or are referenced directly to the supreme court, apex courts tend to hear and ultimately decide upon the constitutionality of an order of government's actions and legislation (particularly, when the conflict is between orders of government and is about which has responsibility for an area).

The other related model of using courts of law is to rely on a body that specializes in constitutional issues. This approach is used mainly in civil-law systems and is followed in eight federations (Germany, Austria, Russia, Bosnia and Herzegovina, the United Arab Emirates, Belgium, Spain, and South Africa).[22] The distinction between this approach and the apex court model is that in these eight federations the constitutional court sits apart from the system of courts responsible for non-constitutional matters. Accordingly, the constitutional court is the sole body dealing with issues of constitutional interpretation. In this model, the constitutional court is thus a specialized body that holds the exclusive jurisdiction to act as the supreme arbiter for constitutional challenges and judicial review, whereas other matters of law (e.g., criminal, civil) progress through a separate appellate court system.[23]

Both of these approaches can be grouped together given their legalistic approach of judicial review to enforce the constitutional division of responsibilities between orders of government in federations. Moreover, both models are implemented in virtually every federation in a way that seeks to protect the independence of the institution and to ensure it has a

21 List compiled from review of federations, as well as Watts (2008), Saunders (2006), and Hueglin and Fenna (2006: 277–8).

22 This list is compiled from a review of federations, as well as Watts (2008) and Saunders (2006).

23 Note that in South Africa, lower courts with ordinary jurisdiction can hear appeals on the constitutionality of government action, but appeals of these matters culminate at the Constitutional Court; see Saunders (2006: 368).

measure of representativeness.[24] While there are different approaches to protecting the independence of the apex or constitutional court (through some combination of constitutional provisions, political conventions, administrative structures, and public pressure), federations operate with the premise that the federal arbiter should be perceived as independent of any one order of government. In addition, whether the body is an apex or constitutional court, most federations have adopted some process to seek a measure of representation for sub-state units by giving them a role in the appointment of members to the federal arbiter, either directly or indirectly through consultation. The key distinguishing factor between these models, then, is quite minor: it comes down to the place of the ultimate federal arbiter within the institutional structure of the court system (one being at the apex of the courts of general jurisdiction, the other having a separate body to deal with constitutional issues).

The similarity of these two models of relying on courts of law comes into relief when considering the other key approach to federal arbitration: referenda. In line with the long-standing use of direct democratic measures in Switzerland, referenda are used to adjudicate whether a federal law is within the scope of power granted by the constitution. Nevertheless, the courts-of-law approach is still used for cantonal laws in Switzerland, which are subject to judicial review by the Federal Tribunal.[25]

The variation in approaches noted above strengthens the argument that conflict is inherent in federations, as is the need for arbitration. Some form of arbiter can be identified in every federation. I focus here on the judiciary (i.e., the apex court model) for two main reasons. First, it is the most prominent form of federal arbitration (especially since there is a propensity to understand federations from a legal lens and, in the absence of other suitable alternatives, the federal arbiter has tended to be the judiciary).[26] Analysis of the apex model is also generally applicable to the constitutional court model, since both are mechanisms to allow for the judicial review of government action with a view to providing fair and representative constitutional interpretation; adapt the constitutional and federal structure; and manage intergovernmental conflict.[27] Second, the apex model is the one used in Canada – the state

24 On this see Watts (2008: 159–60).

25 See Watts (2008: 159); Saunders (2006: 367).

26 Hueglin and Fenna (2006: 275).

27 On these three related objectives of the federal arbiter, see Burgess (2006: 159), citing Watts (1999: 100).

representing a foundational case within federal theory, while also providing a rich history of actors subscribing to differing federal models conflicting in court battles.[28]

Accordingly, a study of this approach in Canada can be used as the basis to reflect on the role of the federal arbiter in nearly all federations (save, perhaps, Switzerland with its unique referenda model and also Ethiopia, which relies on the upper house to conduct judicial review). As I discuss in the conclusion, there are limits to making generalizations based on any single case study: context and detail matter a great deal when thinking about how to apply political and legal analysis. Indeed, the above should not imply that there are no important differences in how the federal arbiter and court systems are structured in federations across the globe. For example, there is variation in the structure of courts (between nationalized systems, dual national/sub-state systems, and hybrids), the appointment procedures for the ultimate federal arbiter (nominations being the remit of heads of state, the sub-state units, or some measure in between), and the respect given to the independence of the body itself by political actors. Setting other qualifications aside, though, the institutional role and objective of the federal arbiter is similar enough across federations to allow for useful insights to be generated from a single case study conducted with a view to generating analysis applicable to other federations.

Returning to my point at the end of the last section, while understanding a federation's contested nature illuminates the important role the judiciary plays as federal arbiter, it also helps show the benefit of (and need for) negotiation between actors to manage their differences. Central government institutions, intergovernmental relations, and public discourse play a vital role in maintaining peace within, and legitimacy for, federations. At the same time, the inherently adversarial nature of conflict, especially that which combines identity politics and resource competition, means that negotiation and cooperation often break down. Moreover, structural and material inequalities mean that forums of negotiation can be irreparably unfair, with parties that feel wronged often seeking outside actors to help arbitrate disputes. In Canada, and in many other federations, parties (both private and

28 I have already discussed Canada's role as a key case in the field; just glancing at recent comparative federalism texts demonstrates the important role Canada plays in thinking about federations; see in particular Hueglin and Fenna (2006); Burgess (2006); Erk (2008); Baier (2006).

public) call upon the judiciary when negotiations break down or there is a perceived need for arbitration. And, it is when the courts are called upon that they are often acting as the last line of defence to keep the management of conflict over the federation within the domestic political sphere.

This position means the judiciary significantly affects the development of the federation over time. In Canada, conflicts over national identity and the federation have a tendency to manifest themselves as conflicts between the orders of government (and between private actors and an order of government) over the constitutional distribution of powers. These conflicts over which order of government has authority over a particular issue place the courts in the position of having to decide the validity of a government's action or legislation by engaging in a "process of classification to determine whether [it] comes within a federal or provincial class of powers."[29] In arbitrating such disputes and interpreting the constitution, the courts' federalism jurisprudence defines the very structure of the federal system. Federalism jurisprudence is one of the main ways that the constitutional and federal system develops over time.[30] The judiciary represents one of the central mechanisms through which the federation adapts in response to challenges and thus remains a dynamic system.

The judiciary's position as federal arbiter also means it has a vital role in maintaining the legitimacy of the association. It is called upon to mediate some of the most important and heated conflicts within and over the federation.[31] Over the past thirty years, the SCC has been a major player in many constitutional events, as well as dealing with hundreds of comparatively lower-level intergovernmental and private-actor conflicts over the federation. The Court's decisions in these cases – which represent selections between competing arguments put forth by parties about the actual and ideal nature of the federal system – have significant effects on the legitimacy of the conflict-management process and the association more generally.

29 Swinton (1990: 26).

30 Baier (2003: 111–12); Tremblay (1991: 164).

31 These situations represent some of the most intractable and acrimonious conflicts. Taking a party to court is a significant decision. It involves considerable financial implications and risk (including the consideration that it damages future relations with a party).

There are two general aspects of a court's decision that can affect the legitimacy of federation: the decision-making process and the outcome.

How the federation is depicted in rationalizing a decision can help to reinforce the system's nature in line with a party's particular perspective, or not. This aspect of the decision-making process can have implications for a party's loyalty to the federation, allowing them to see it as either recognizing their perspective or imposing a competing perspective, while ultimately also affecting their status within the system. In a related way, the decision can be seen either as biased against a party's perspective on the nature of the federation, or as recognizing their perspective and protecting this view. The implication here is that the decision-making process can affect the support of various parties for the conflict-management system.

With regard to the decision outcome, the process can be seen as either taking account of, or ignoring, perceived facts about the nature of the federation. The potential issue here is that ignoring a party's perspective on the nature of the system can raise questions about the validity of the conflict-management process. More important, the outcome that stems from a court's decision can either alienate a group from the federal system, or it can work to create linkages between a group's ideal picture of the federation and the evolving association. In the same vein, a decision outcome can have significant effects for the distribution of powers, responsibilities. and resources to groups within the federation. Consequently, a decision can affect a group's status and power within the federation and ultimately the connection they feel to the system (i.e., affecting their self-perceived, and actual, status as political insiders or outsiders).

Given the importance of the judiciary as federal arbiter in the majority of federations, how does federal theory account for this role and the activity of judicial review? As noted in the Introduction, there is a general lack of in-depth theorization on the judicial role in diverse federations within the broader comparative field and conflict-management theory.

That being said, there is a particularly strong lineage of work on federal judicial review in the Canadian context. This work tends to highlight the important role the SCC has played in the development of the federation.[32] Among scholars focusing on the SCC's federalism

32 Examples of this line of work include Hogg (2009, chs. 8 and 15; 2007); Russell (2004, 1987, 1983); Monahan (1987); Saywell (2002); Swinton (1990); Kelly and Murphy (2005); Verelli (2008); Wright (2014); and Cairns (1971, a foundational overview of the influence of the predecessor to the SCC, the Judicial Committee of the Privy Council, the court of last resort in Canada before 1949).

jurisprudence, there is a split between those who frame it as primarily a court of law and those who stress its more political nature.[33] In a related manner, there is an ongoing debate about the extent to which the Court's federal judicial review is balanced, or acts as a centralizing force that favours the federal government.[34] Much of this debate, with the associated arguments about the need for judicial restraint or activism and the democratic or anti-democratic nature of judicial review, mirrors work on the Supreme Court in the United States.[35] And, while this traditional focus on the SCC's federalism jurisprudence has largely given way to work on its civil rights decisions with the introduction of the Charter of Rights and Freedoms in 1982,[36] it remains an important body of work that can be drawn upon for reflecting on the role of the judiciary in diverse federations more broadly.

Within comparative federal and conflict management theory, though, comprehensive and *integrated accounts of the links* between the activity of judicial review, the role of the judiciary and the functioning of federal systems are less developed.[37] There are case studies of judicial review in a number of important federal systems, but this work tends to stop short of integrating this analysis into a broader consideration of the role of the federal arbiter in managing diversity and conflict.[38] A recent overview of the study of judicial review in federations does make important linkages between the often-disparate political and legal case studies of the activity (while arguing in favour of a role for federal arbiters as umpires of the system).[39] In other words, while there

33 Peter Hogg (2009) and Gerald Bair's (2006) work exemplify the former, while Weiler (1974), Monahan (1984), and Schertzer (2008) exemplify the latter perspective.

34 Within this debate Hogg (1979) and Baier (2003, 2006, 2012) argue the Court is generally a balanced federal arbiter, while Bzdera (1993), Leclair (2003), MacKay (2001), and Greschner (2000), among others, argue the SCC tends to favour the central government.

35 The debate about the role of the judiciary in America is voluminous; for an overview of the central positions that still holds up today, see Bobbitt (1982, 1991) and Swinton (1990: 34–55, 325–31).

36 For example, see Morton and Knopff (2000); Manfredi (2001); Mandel (1994); Kelly (2001).

37 Notable studies include McCrudden and O'Leary (2013); Hirschl (2013); Baier (2006); Hueglin and Fenna (2006: ch. 10); Radmilovic (2010, 2011); Tierney (2009); Schertzer (2008); and McHugh (2000).

38 I discuss a number of these case studies as they relate to India, Spain, and South Africa, in particular, in the Conclusion.

39 See Halberstam (2008).

are gaps, the courts are not ignored in the study of federations, with the literature establishing a corpus of theory on the role of the judiciary as the independent enforcer of the constitution.[40] And, where the functioning of the arbiter is assessed through the prism of this role, critiques are often made that the Court deviates from this ideal of independence.[41]

The general consensus on the need for federal arbiters to be independent likely stems from the way one's view of the constitutional and federal system drives one's view of the courts' role within that system. In other words, perspectives on the courts' role and theories of judicial review within a federation represent part of a wider understanding of what federal systems are and ought to be: legal, institutional regimes. For example, the very concept of judicial review presupposes the constitution as supreme law and the judiciary as the enforcer of that law.[42] From this perspective, judicial review as the action of invalidating legislation that is deemed to contravene the constitution seems logical. Federal judicial review is thus seen as legitimate in two situations: (1) where one order of government's legislation or action offends the established division of powers and responsibilities; and (2) where one order of government's legislation or action, while within its federal jurisdiction, violates some other constitutional provision (i.e., individual rights).[43] This formulation largely finds it roots in the line of argument in *Marbury v. Madison* in 1803,[44] which laid out a mandate for the Supreme Court of the United States to act as the umpire of the federation and the protector of a constitution understood as supreme law, which federal theorists have largely accepted.[45] For example, we see this understanding of federal systems and the judiciary's role in the work of influential constitutionalist A.V. Dicey and federal theorist K.C. Wheare.[46] And, it is the

40 For an overview, see Halberstam (2008). However, there are those who argue that the political nature of federations and the role of the Court as federal arbiter means judicial review on federal grounds is generally illegitimate, see Weiler (1974) and Monahan (1984).

41 The debate over apex courts as "centralizers" is a good example of this; see Bzdera (1993). The focus of such work tends to call for courts to be better umpires, rather than moving on a step and accounting for the nature of arbitration in the federal structure and revising federal theory accordingly. For a more contemporary example, see Vaubel (2009).

42 Hueglin and Fenna (2006: 276–7).

43 Hueglin and Fenna (2006: 276–9).

44 *Marbury v. Madison*, [1803] 5 U.S. 137.

45 See Hueglin and Fenna (2006: 287–9); Tierney (2009: 97–100).

46 See Dicey (1982) and Wheare (1963).

wide acceptance of this form of judicial review on federal grounds that contributes, at least in part, to the under-theorization on the role of the federal arbiter beyond the idea that the institution is needed and that it ideally should be an independent and neutral body.

Turning back to Canada, within the general consensus on the independence of the judiciary as federal arbiter there is a measure of variation. This variation comes from scholars adopting a particular understanding of the constitutional and federal system, which leads them down a path towards an associated notion of the courts' ideal role.[47] Here, I discuss three of the key ideal roles for the judiciary as federal arbiter, which are linked to the three approaches and models noted in the last chapter. These three roles are the judiciary as umpire, branch of government, or guardian of the federation (with links to the trimming, trading, and segregating approaches and the pan-Canadian, provincial-equality, and multinational federal models, respectively) (see table 2.1).[48] The conceptual links between the broader federal approaches and the federal arbiter roles are not quite as clear as they are presented in the following paragraphs. With such categorization and analysis nuance is often lost; for example, all three roles (of umpire, branch of government, and guardian) promote a measure of independence for the judiciary, while the umpire and guardian roles share an aim of ensuring the courts enforce the rules of the association. Nevertheless, each federal approach *at its core* has links to the basic characteristics of one of the three ideal roles for the judiciary. Thus, despite their variation, these three roles still work from a shared understanding of the basic structure of the federation as largely placed above political contestation. In line with this view, the judiciary's role is ultimately to uphold and enforce the federal system. Accordingly, these roles do not fully account for the inherently contested and political nature of the federation, nor for the integral way the federal arbiter helps to maintain the legitimacy of the system.

---

47 A good example of how this sequence of thought takes place – how a theorist's view of the federation leads to a particular view of the judiciary's role – can be seen in the work of Strayer (1988).

48 For a review of these three prominent views of the judiciary in Canada, see Greschner (2000); Swinton (1992). See also Wright (2014: 279–90). These ideal roles can also be seen in wider federal theory.

Table 2.1. Three roles for the judiciary as federal arbiter

Role	Related approach / Model	Key aspects of role	Court's objective as federal arbiter
Umpire	Trimming / Pan-Canadian	Neutral and independent arbiter	Implement the constitutional consensus and stay above the fray of politics
Branch of government	Trading / Provincial equality	Equal to other institutions (e.g., central and provincial parliaments) and providing checks and balances to their power	Facilitate market-based politics by upholding the minimalist framework that creates cross-cutting cleavages
Guardian	Segregating / Multinational	Superior to other institutions as the protector of the constitution	Protect the federal arrangement and uphold the means by which nations and political communities are segregated

The Judiciary as an Umpire

The judiciary as the umpire of the federation is a logical role for those promoting the trimming approach and pan-Canadian federal model.[49] From this view, the courts must act in a neutral fashion, adjudicating disputes fairly in accordance with pre-established rules. The judiciary presented as an umpire promotes a restrained approach to judicial review, as the institution occupies a truly important position in the development of the federation, but not the pre-eminent one.[50] It is a body that must, above all else, display appropriate balance and independence to stay above the fray of politics.[51]

The idea of keeping the courts above politics, simply enforcing the pre-established rules, draws attention to how this ideal role for the courts is linked to the trimming federal approach and pan-Canadian model. As Donna Greschner puts it: the umpire view of the courts assumes that the "'game' has 'rules' … and that the umpire's job is to apply them."[52] From this view, these rules – the constitutional and the

49 See, for example, Rawls (1993); Wheare (1963); Trudeau (1998).

50 See Russell (1969: 123); Lederman (1975: 615); Greschner (2000: 56–7, 61).

51 See Lederman (1975: 619); Greschner (2000: 57).

52 Greschner (2000: 65).

federal structure – are constitutive of the political game within which the orders of government find themselves.

So, we can see how the federal structure, as presented by the trimming approach and pan-Canadian model, dictates the courts' role as an umpire; in this approach and model the federal structure is (1) above politics; (2) a neutral framework; and (3) legitimate as it represents the overlapping consensus of a single nation. Accordingly, the arbiter of disputes over the federal structure, as an umpire, (1) must act to regulate politics, not be part of it; (2) must apply the neutral framework fairly and in a balanced way, so as to let the neutrality of the framework mediate disputes; and (3) must act in accordance with the rules, interpreting them, not changing them, so as to maintain their legitimacy as an overlapping consensus.

The Judiciary as a Branch of Government

The judiciary viewed primarily as a branch of government is presented as an equal institution to the legislative and executive branches of the orders of government.[53] This view thus promotes the Canadian federation as one where courts and parliament(s) are participants in a conversation about the compatibility of laws and actions within the supra-legal constitutional association.[54] Seeing the courts as a branch of government is a position that stresses the separation of powers and, to pick up on the above metaphorical language, treats them not as an "umpire" of the "game" of politics, but, in a way, as one of the "players."[55] Thus, the perceived need for an arbiter that upholds the supra-constitutional law manifests here in line with the perspective on the constitution as distributing power among the various branches of government to ensure checks and balances. Accordingly, no branch, the courts included, can be the sole actor in the development of the federation.

Stressing the need for the courts to act as an equal branch of government is linked to the trading federal approach and provincial-equality model. The trading federal model presents the federal structure (1) as dispersing power among multiple centres, within the central

53 See Greschner (2000: 55).

54 Greschner (2000: 49). Though Greschner labels this view of the courts as promoting "dialogue," I prefer to highlight that the Court is seen as an equal branch of government. On this role for the courts in Canada, see Hogg and Bushell (1997).

55 Greschner (2000: 70).

government and between orders of government; and (2) as resolving conflict by enabling political trading, but still acting as a minimalist fixed framework to regulate this activity. Accordingly, the judiciary, understood as a branch of government in line with this approach and model, (1) provides an additional locus of power in the federal system, checking the monopolization of power in either order of government; and (2) upholds the background framework of constitutional law; but, as power is distributed between multiple centres, does not itself monopolize power and is seen as only one of the many actors involved in the development and implementation of the federal structure.

The Judiciary as a Guardian

The notion of the judiciary as the guardian of federation promotes a more activist role for the courts than the umpire role (which stresses balance and a measure of deference) and the view of the courts as a branch of government (which stresses that the courts should not supplant the role of parliaments in establishing the federal structure, but rather work with them). In this view, the judiciary is understood as the protector of the constitutional and federal system (rather than just its enforcer);[56] this, in turn, means that intervention by the judiciary to uphold the supreme law against contravening legislation or action is a requirement. This perspective thus promotes a hierarchical relationship between the judiciary and parliaments[57] – the courts having the higher authority to interpret and protect the system that gives rise to the orders of government.[58]

The idea of the courts as the protector of the structure that gives rise to politics draws attention to its linkages with the segregation approach and multinational model. In this approach and model, the federal structure is viewed (1) as elevated above politics; (2) as fixing an agreement between groups for autonomy; and (3) as protecting identifiable groups, such as national minorities, by protecting their political autonomy from encroachment by the majority or central power. Accordingly, the judiciary as guardian of the federal structure (1) must act above politics and

56 Greschner (2000: 54).

57 Greschner (2000: 54).

58 This is not like the umpire, who applies clear rules of a game, but rather the commissioner of the league, who settles disputes and oversees the relationships between the clubs.

protect the federal agreement from political interference; (2) regulate politics in line with the predetermined agreement; and (3) act as the key enforcer and protector of the agreement that in turn protects the autonomy of those groups thought to be vulnerable to coercion or abuse at the hands of either majority or minority interests. We can see these principles in the work of those like Lijphart, for example, who says the courts need to be a "forceful protector of the constitution."[59] Along these lines, theorists promoting the need to protect sub-state autonomy will often present a court's role as upholding the compact between the orders of government to respect mutually exclusive jurisdictions; these scholars will often then evaluate the courts as a guardian of sub-state autonomy, generally portraying them as a failure in this regard and noting their tendency to centralize federations.[60] In addition, this line of thinking leads theorists promoting the segregation model to prescribe that identifiable minority groups (i.e., national minorities) be given special representation within the judiciary (i.e., a selection of judges on the apex court representing the minority), so as to ensure it acts accordingly in its role as a guardian of the federal structure.[61]

This brief review demonstrates the links between each ideal role for the judiciary and a federal approach and model, showing how each role is based on a particular understanding of the federation working towards an ideal association. The shared characteristic of these roles, then, is that each seeks to enforce a particular constitutional and federal system that ultimately stands beyond political contestation. The shared problem of these roles is thus the failure to take into account the fact that the federal structure itself is inherently contested. And, this shared flaw means that these ideal roles fail to account for the potential for the judiciary to *impose particular perspectives* on the nature of the federation and thus affect the legitimacy of the system. Promoting a role for the Court as neutral arbiter (be it as umpire, branch of government, or guardian) can allow the judiciary to impose particular federal models under the veil of neutrality, invites it to do this, or raises expectations of neutrality that simply cannot be met.[62] Each of these situations can

59 See Lijphart (2008: 85).

60 See Elazar (1987: 182–3, 214–17); Bzdera (1993); Tierney (2009).

61 See Kymlicka (1998: 114).

62 As I discuss below, the Court cannot meet the standard of neutrality because it is not independent of the struggles over which it presides. Courts are part of the federal system that is being challenged in such conflicts.

negatively affect the legitimacy of the federation, as they call into question the validity of the conflict-management process and the status of the federal system as free and fair.

This shared flaw with the main ideal roles for the judiciary as federal arbiter stems from not linking theories of judicial review to theories of federation. Drawing a bright line between the two leads to problems for both. It allows theories of federation to simply assume that the judiciary will act as a neutral arbiter and enforce a particular model, while also underestimating the importance of the courts in the development of the federation and in maintaining the legitimacy of the system. At the same time, a theory of judicial review promoting a role for the Court as either umpire, branch of government, or guardian can fail to appreciate that this role is linked to a particular and partial understanding of the federation, and thus the roles fail to account for, and adequately manage, the contested nature of the federation. In contrast, understanding the inherently contested nature of a federal system, and appreciating the role the federal arbiter plays in managing this conflict, allows us to see what should drive our ideal of the Court's role: the *management* of conflict within and over the federation with an explicit purpose of *generating legitimacy* for the system (while rejecting the imposition of any particular federal model as the law).

There are those who do link an understanding of the Canadian federation as contested to their reflections on the Court's role as federal arbiter. The general trend among those who have done this, though, is to still strive for neutrality. Katherine Swinton's earlier arguments exemplify this approach: while noting that there are competing models of the Canadian federation and that this has implications for the way courts select and impose particular perspectives on the federation, she argues for a balanced approach to judicial review where the courts act in an unbiased role as an umpire.[63] Similarly, Donna Greschner has noted that the Canadian federation is contested by actors holding multiple understandings of the nature of the arrangement, going on to suggest that the Court's role is to umpire the conflict that stems from

63 See Swinton (1990: 5, 21–55, 195–200). In subsequent work Swinton does seem to shift towards a model more in line with the one proposed below, which promotes a role for the Court as primarily the facilitator of conflict between orders of government; see Swinton (1992: 138), where she says the Court "has a role to play in managing conflict and change in the federalism system, but its role is secondary and, ideally, facilitative."

this diversity.[64] More broadly, Daniel Elazar has also pointed out that a federation can be understood as more than a final, fixed structure, arguing it is also a dynamic process;[65] nevertheless, he goes on to imply that the role of the courts in a federation is to uphold the "perpetual compact," and its activity should be evaluated against this role.[66]

At the same time, a number of scholars have put forward theories on the judicial role that move beyond the "independent arbiter" mould, even linking them with an understanding of federations as dynamic processes. For example, Patrick Monahan has argued that the influence federal theories can have on the political work of courts raises questions about the validity of the federal arbiter role.[67] Similarly, Paul Weiler has argued that the political nature of the courts' work managing conflict over the federation means the apex-court model of federal arbitration should be virtually abandoned.[68] Also, in Swinton's later work she seems to move towards the view that the contested nature of federation means the courts should operate as a facilitator of negotiation between political actors.[69] Similarly, work by James Kelly and Michael Murphy highlights the SCC's recent turn to embrace a facilitator role.[70] In addition, Vuk Radmilovic has made a strong case for understanding the SCC's work (in its federalism jurisprudence and more broadly) as focused on cultivating legitimacy for the institution itself.[71] Similarly, while focused more on the internal institutional dynamics of the Court, Emmett Macfarlane's recent study argues we can only understand the Court's activity through a "role-centric" analysis that considers the influence of the broader structures and institutional factors of the Canadian political system.[72] While I build on the work of these studies, ultimately this stream of analysis does not account for the importance and need for a federal arbiter (the issue with Monahan's and Weiler's arguments), nor does it provide comprehensive, integrated accounts of the contested nature of federal systems with an associated understanding of the actual and ideal role the judiciary plays as the arbiter of this

64 See Greschner (2000, esp. at 71–6).
65 Elazar (1987: 67–8).
66 See Elazar (1987: 157, 182–3, 214–17).
67 See Monahan (1984, 1987).
68 See Weiler (1974).
69 See Swinton (1992: 138).
70 Kelly and Murphy (2005).
71 Radmilovic (2010).
72 Macfarlane (2013).

contestation (the issue with the Swinton, Kelly and Murphy, Radmilovic, and Macfarlane pieces). In the next section, I begin to address these issues by sketching a federal theory that accounts for its contested nature and the important role the courts play in the system.

A Dynamic Federal Theory and the Judiciary as Facilitator and Fair Arbiter

What the above leaves us with is that there is a need for a theory that accounts for (1) the contested nature of the federation, and (2) the important role the courts play in managing this conflict and maintaining the legitimacy of the system. I argue these two needs can be addressed through a theory that sees federal systems as the process and outcome of negotiation, with the federal arbiter's ideal role being to reinforce this aspect of the constitutional order when it is called upon to mediate a dispute. In fulfilling its role in this way, the judiciary can thus facilitate ongoing negotiation between the conflicting parties as the means to manage disputes.

A theory promoting federal systems as the process and outcome of negotiation has a different theoretical basis than those discussed in the last chapter. It is an approach that seeks to *manage* conflict over the nature of a federation, not to trim, trade, or segregate away diversity and conflict from the political agenda. This perspective, which builds on the work of James Tully and others,[73] starts by recognizing that conflict within federations are often struggles *over* the very nature of the system and that institutional mechanisms can be designed to manage and harness this conflict beneficially.

The fundamental difference between seeking to manage conflict over seeking to eliminate it can be achieved by promoting federal systems as orders of non-domination in line with broader republican principles.[74] In this vein, the goal of a federation should be to respect and protect the free agency of actors to define, control, and actively participate in the intersubjective normative systems to which they are subject.[75] Doing so ensures that the federation remains legitimate, as the association can

73 See Tully (1995, 2000b, 2001, 2004). It also builds on the work of Ludwig Wittgenstein, which informs much of the relevant aspects of Tully's work; see Wittgenstein (1967).

74 In addition to Tully (1995), see also Petite (1997) and Bellamy (2007).

75 Tully (2004: 91–5).

generate and maintain loyalty to the way it recognizes and manages conflict over the way identities are accounted for (or not) in the distribution of power and resources.

In promoting this more dynamic model of federal systems, I am also seeking to build on the work of Carl Friedrich.[76] For Friedrich, a federation "should not be seen only as a static pattern or design ... [It] is also and perhaps primarily the process of federalizing a political community."[77] The central point for my own work here is that we need to consider how a federation can adapt over time to reflect the ways different communities understand the association to maintain legitimacy. As Friedrich points out, the different levels of community and government within a federation "constantly interact, as the human beings operating them argue, fight, cooperate, and compromise with one another."[78] The implication of this view is that "any federally organized community must therefore provide itself with instrumentalities for the recurrent revisions of its pattern or design."[79] In promoting a model of dynamic federation, then, a key consideration is how to develop institutions that fulfil this purpose – particularly for those institutions with the explicit mandate of managing conflict over the federation, like the federal arbiter.

Tully and others have provided a set of principles and conventions that can inform the design of institutional mechanisms to account for conflict over the federation.[80] The key goal of these principles is to generate

---

76 See, in particular, Friedrich (1968: 3–10, 30–40, 173–85).

77 Friedrich (1968: 7). While similar, it should be noted that Friedrich's focus and my own differ slightly. Friedrich is emphasizing the "process of federalizing," which looks in particular at how a "federal order may be operating in the direction of both integration and differentiation; federalizing being either the process by which a number of separate political units ... enter into and develop arrangements for working out solutions together ... or the reverse process" (177). My own focus is not as much on the unifying or decentralizing processes within federations, but more on how conflicts between groups over the nature of the federal system are managed and the institutional structure responds over time. In this way, my own work is informed by the contemporary scholarship on identity, diversity, and nationalism to a greater extent (though it should be said that Friedrich does briefly investigate the relationship between federalism and nationalism; see 1968: 30–40).

78 Friedrich (1968: 3).

79 Friedrich (1968: 7; see also 177).

80 I recognize that the following "principles" are drawn from practices and conventions in particular historical contexts. In this regard, their applicability as universal principles to guide federal institutional design to manage diversity and conflict is limited. I discuss some of the limitations of their applicability in the Conclusion.

legitimacy for associations like federations in the way they manage conflict between actors over the normative system. In this regard, the principles provide a basis to develop a broad federal theory – and an associated role for the courts – that seeks to recognize and reinforce the dynamic nature of diverse federations.

The first principle is *quod omnes tangit ab omnibus approbetur* (what touches all, must be approved by all).[81] This principle promotes the active participation of key actors in establishing the process by which normative arrangements are negotiated, approved, and contested over time – as well as being incorporated in the act of negotiation, approval, and contestation of the normative arrangement.[82] *Quod omnes tangit*, then, shares a similar logic to that of Jürgen Habermas's principle D: "Only those norms can claim to be valid that meet (or could meet) with the approval of all affected in their capacity as participants in a practical discourse."[83]

The second key principle is *audi alteram partem* (listen to the other side).[84] The core of this principle is that the actors negotiating, approving, and contesting a normative system listen to other actors' reasons and justifications for their positions vis-à-vis the normative system (including those actors speaking in defence of the current norms); moreover, the principle places an active responsibility on actors to respond in kind in an act of dialogue (including those actors speaking in defence of the current norms).[85] *Audi alteram partem* is particularly important to institutionalize, as it facilitates the actualization of *quod omnes tangit*; necessitating the duty to listen to the other side and to reply pushes those in a dominant position to engage in a process where actors actively participate in the negotiation, approval, and contestation of a governing normative system.

---

81 Tully (2004: 92). This principle immediately raises a key issue: in what ways and to what extent can *everyone* subject to a norm be incorporated into the active process of approval? On this see Luhmann (1996: 884–7). For my purposes it suffices to say that the actors contesting the federation include all the citizens of a state, either through their representatives in the democratic system of government or as individual actors, if they so choose (through mechanisms like the courts).

82 In addition to Tully (2004), on the establishment of governing norms in line with the *quod omnes tangit* principle (as part of the reconception of liberalism and democracy as mutually constitutive) see Habermas (2001, esp. at 776–8).

83 Tully (2004: 92); Habermas (1995: 66).

84 Tully (2004: 94–5).

85 Tully (2004: 99).

These principles clearly need to be brought down from the realm of abstraction to effectively guide institutional design. Tully's earlier work on constitutionalism helps ground these principles by outlining three related conventions that can usefully guide the design of a federal model that accounts for conflict over the system and garners legitimacy in the way it does this.[86] The first such convention is that institutions must *recognize* actors' self-selected identities. This recognition seeks to ensure that the way actors see themselves as participants in the activity of negotiating, approving, and contesting norms is as free from domination by others as possible. The second convention is that institutions must account for the *heterogeneity and indeterminacy of identity*. Accounting for this aspect of identity seeks to account for the fact that prior to, through, and after the negotiation, approval, and contestation of normative systems, the identities of participating actors remain, but also can change in complex ways.[87] The third convention is that the institutions based on the negotiation, approval, and contestation of normative systems must receive the *active consent* of those subject to their authority. Active consent seeks to ensure that the ongoing struggles over the normative system are accounted for – that, given the indeterminate contestation over a federation itself noted in the last chapter, the federal system is not removed from the political agenda.

This last line indicates the fundamental purpose behind a model promoting a federation as the process and outcome of negotiation: to enable the management of the inherent struggles over the norms that govern political associations in a way that garners loyalty to the association (and thus legitimacy). And, this purpose should, in turn, illuminate some of the key differences between the promotion of federal systems as a process of negotiation and the trimming, trading, and segregating approaches.

First and foremost, there is a fundamental difference in the way the constitutional and federal systems are understood and promoted. As the previous chapter explains, the three main approaches and federal

86 See Tully (1995), from which the subsequent three conventions are drawn.

87 The work of the more liberal bend of the consociationalist school of conflict management to avoid "essentializing" ethno-national identities during institutional design can help explain this point; see Wolff (2011: 167). My goal here is to ensure that institutional design does not lock *particular* identities into place, while allowing institutions to adapt over time in response to the inherent shifts and conflicts that take place within groups over their nature and direction.

models all work from an understanding of the constitution and federation as something that is fixed above contestation and as giving rise to politics. Thus, a "modern constitutionalism" is shared by each of the three perspectives.[88] I have laid out above a contrasting basis for a federal model, one that understands constitutions are, and can be, based on political conventions and processes.[89] The point here is that constitutions are not immune from the conflict that takes place over them, nor should they be; there is a dialectic that does, and ought to, take place between the actors subject to an association and the association itself (as my discussion of the evolution of the Canadian constitutional and federal systems demonstrated in the last chapter). Accordingly, a constitution should be promoted as the tool to manage conflict over its nature, while also being the representation of agreements stemming from such conflict. The very basis of a federation – the legal and institutional structure upon which identities are recognized and power and resources are distributed – can be seen as the *process* and *outcome* of imperfect agreements between actors holding competing perspectives, not a fixed framework that sits above this contestation in an attempt to trim, trade, or segregate away the offending diversity.

The above principles, conventions, emphasis on conflict management, and turn away from modern constitutionalism inform a federal model that stands in contrast to the pan-Canadian, provincial-equality, and multinational models.

The core objective of this federal model is to manage the conflict among key social actors holding competing perspectives on the nature and direction of the federation (i.e., between the subscribers of the pan-Canadian, provincial-equality, and multinational models). This approach rejects the claim that a *particular* model can solve conflict within and over the Canadian federation. The idea is not to promote an ideal balance of power. The goal is not centralization or decentralization. Similarly, the model does not seek to distribute power symmetrically or asymmetrically. Rather, the balance of powers in the federation

88 On modern constitutionalism – with its key tenets that a constitution exists as a tangible fact and gives rise to the state and government – see Tully (1995); McIlwain (1947). Thomas Paine's work exemplifies the foundations of modern constitutionalism.

89 On the links between this view of the constitution and a more "ancient constitutionalism," which highlights the way conventions dictate political action and set the norms of an association, see Tully (1995). On ancient constitutionalism see McIlwain (1947). The key tenets of this approach are exemplified by Edmund Burke's work.

is understood as dynamic, as validly shifting in response to debates over the ideal way power and resources should be distributed in the association based on the political, social, and economic context. The key, then, is to promote the mechanisms through which this negotiation takes place (i.e., ad hoc and structured intergovernmental relations, citizen-government forums, as well as an effective and fair arbitration mechanism).

The objective of centralized or asymmetrical federal systems, along with the other oft-focused-on ways of manipulating the federal structure, like the nature of central institutions or the relationship between the orders of government, should not be the primary concern of a federal model. Instead, the focus should be to implement a set of institutional processes that incorporate the key conventions noted above – to facilitate key social actors reaching agreements that take into account the conflicting and various views over the nature of the federation. For Canada, there is thus no ideal federal model; rather, the federation should be promoted as a process through which the actors subscribing to the pan-Canadian, provincial-equality, and multinational visions work to reach agreement.

Now, with negotiation there is conflict, and conflict is rarely fully settled. The indeterminate nature of conflict is one of the key reasons why a fixed federal model is problematic: it fails to implement a real consensus, because no real consensus is possible. Federations, then, should be understood and promoted as indeterminate. The competing visions of the federation in Canada have endured in some form or another for nearly two centuries, and they are not likely to go away any time soon. Consequently, a core component of any federal model for Canada should be to ensure the federal structure remains open to continual contestation through arbitration and amendment.

To say this is a core component of a federation may imply support for never-ending discussion and debate (i.e., celebration of debate for its own sake). That is not my intention. The macro-political nature of constitutions – the idea that they need to be removed from everyday partisan politics if they are to be effective at all – is important.[90] So, the more mundane processes of contesting and adapting the federal structure should be facilitated and accessible (i.e., intergovernmental-relations mechanisms and arbitration), while the more extra-ordinary measures

90 See Loughlin (2003: 44); but also, on the problematic positivist logic that can stem from this point, see Loughlin (2003: 44–52).

like constitutional amendment should be just that, extra-ordinary, but still possible. Amending the constitution should not be easy, but the process and formula to do so should also not make it impossible. The principal means by which a federation adapts over time – intergovernmental relations, arbitration, and amendment – should be designed to ensure the federation is not a "straitjacket."[91]

As with the other approaches and models, how national identity is understood drives aspects of this federal model.[92] The previous chapter argued that the three Canadian federal models work from, and seek to reinforce, particular perspectives on the national composition of the state. They see Canada as either uninational or multinational, and seek congruence between this understanding of the state's sociological nature and its political institutions. The trimming and trading approaches are underpinned by a constructivist understanding of national identity that seeks to build a pan-state community by overcoming sub-state national diversity (which is understood as elite-driven and discursive).[93] The multinational model is underpinned by a more primordialist-inspired understanding of Canada's sociological nature and tries to accommodate this fact through rigid institutional structures.[94]

Working from a more nuanced understanding of national identity can help avoid the limitations of these approaches. As discussed in the introduction, I stake out a middle ground between the constructivist and primordialist perspectives. Following the ethno-symbolic approach, the nation can be understood as an imagined and discursive community, but one that does exist and is defined by a combination of shared myths, symbols, and cultural markers.[95] In other words, there are competing narratives about the nature of the nation, but these are structured by and work from the same set of resources.[96] This view of national identity allows us to see that it cannot simply be ignored: it drives political mobilization both due to its emotive force and also because it is a central aspect of politics and the way authority is legitimized. At the same time, an ethno-symbolist position avoids taking the

91 See Tully (2000a: 21–31).

92 On the link between one's view of nationality and how it affects one's approach to conflict-management strategies, see Woods, Schertzer, and Kaufmann (2011).

93 On the constructivist approach to nationality and its effect on conflict-management approaches, see Wolff (2011: 171–5).

94 Schertzer and Woods (2011: 203–6); Wolff (2011: 171–5).

95 See Hutchinson (2005); Smith (2009).

96 See Zimmer (2003); Kaufmann (2009, 2008).

claims of some nationalists too seriously, as they are likely only representing a particular narrative within the wider national community.

This discussion shows the problem with the constructivist and primordialist underpinnings of the three federal models. Denying that the Québécois or Aboriginal groups are nations, or selecting aspects of these identities and trying to invalidate pan-state identity, are equally problematic positions to start from when designing institutions to manage national diversity. In other words, failing to account for the plurinational character of the state by promoting only one of these positions is problematic. Implementing a model based on one perspective risks delegitimizing the federation for those who do not subscribe to the underlying view of the national composition of the state.

What a federal model seeking to manage national diversity in Canada should promote, then, are processes and institutional mechanisms that allow actors from the various national groups to negotiate how the federation ought to recognize their group in the distribution of resources and power via the federation. Focusing on the conflict and negotiation that takes place between the various established political units in Canada (i.e., between provinces, the central government, and to an extent Aboriginal band councils), the key is to promote a model that seeks to take national identities seriously while not reifying and institutionalizing certain identities to the detriment of others. Accordingly, the goal should be to accept, but not promote, ethno-national-based political units within the federation. Similarly, the asymmetry that often accompanies the recognition of ethno-national units should be accepted, but not promoted. In other words, the federation should open up the space for the system to accommodate difference based on nationality (i.e., it does not need to openly reject asymmetry for Québec or Nunavut based on a status as political units overwhelmingly representing national groups). At the same time, the federation needs to actively promote institutions and mechanisms that represent the pan-state community to reinforce this important element of state unity. These institutions, however, must be designed in a way that represents the plurality of views on the national character of the state (i.e., through so-called intra-state federal mechanisms, like representation in the executive for members of the different groups).[97] Essentially, in trying to manage national diversity through the federation, a governing

97 On intra-state federal measures, see Smiley and Watts (1985); Kymlicka (1998: 114–20); Baier and Bakvis (2007: 89).

principle should be to avoid dogmatic support to either distributive or structural mechanisms in line with constructivist or primordialist perspectives; the key is to rely on many different mechanisms and allow the federation to develop through processes of negotiation.[98]

The benefit of such an approach to federal design is that it can walk the line between recognizing the importance of national identity without reifying it as the only way to legitimize authority. It is an approach that can recognize and account for the emotive power of nationality and its ability to mobilize political action, while, at the same time, seeking to manage national diversity from outside a paradigm that sees political legitimacy as emanating from some ideal congruence between the nation and the state. This approach thus avoids the problem of some post-modernist work that downplays the importance of nationality in modern politics, reducing it to only one of the multiplicity of identities that humans hold.[99] Similarly, it does not legitimize the federal system as the embodiment of some overlapping consensus on how to recognize national identity through a federation. Instead, it seeks to recognize and accommodate those that see Canada as both uninational and multinational through processes and institutions that grant these perspectives validity, while treating the actors holding these views with equality in status. The means by which the legitimacy of the system is generated is thus shifted to how the federation recognizes the various competing perspectives on the nature of the state's national composition and the federation, and to how the system manages the conflict between the actors subscribing to these views.

One of the key differences between this approach and the main federal models is the starting point: this approach begins with a comprehensive and accurate account of the nature of national identity and the federation, rather than a partial picture. It avoids the problem of collapsing the categories of what is and what ought to be at the heart of each of the three models discussed in the last chapter. Appreciating the contested nature of nationality and the federation illuminates the fact that each federal model represents a partial (and proper) description

98 On the need to avoid working from within either constructivist or primordialist perspectives and the attendant promotion of only distributive or structural conflict-management mechanisms (as well as the related turn towards "complex power sharing"), see Wolff (2011, 2009).

99 As is the case with Tully (1995).

of the nature of the Canadian federation. At its base, then, this model recognizes what Canada is, and ought to be: a dynamic federation.

Recognizing and promoting federal systems as dynamic processes draws our attention back to the role of the federal arbiter. As noted above, starting with an appreciation of the inherently conflicted nature of nationality and the federation points to the importance of political and institutional mechanisms that facilitate negotiation, but also points to the vital role the judiciary plays in the development of the system and in maintaining its legitimacy when negotiations stall or break down. The lack of consideration for this role noted above, and the problems with those ideals that start from and reinforce partial perspectives on the nature of the federal system can be avoided within a model that understands and promotes the federation as a process and outcome of negotiation between the subscribers of legitimate perspectives.[100]

First, the understanding of the federation as a dynamic entity not only allows for an appreciation of the courts' role in a federal system, but also allows a better understanding of the judiciary itself. Seeing federations as normative systems helps show how the judiciary is part of these systems, given its function of managing conflict over the association. In other words, the judiciary does not, and cannot, sit above conflict as a neutral umpire, an independent branch of government, or a guardian of the system, because it is part of the system. The fact that the courts reduce "inherently political questions to matters of legal judgement" does obscure this point.[101] But, in conflicts over the federation, the courts are part of the field of struggle.[102] As Ran Hirschl argues, "Constitutional courts and their jurisprudence are integral elements of a larger political setting and cannot be understood as isolated from it."[103]

Appreciating the political nature of the judicial role shows that when courts deal with struggles directly challenging the legitimacy of the constitutional and federal systems, they are also facing challenges to their own legitimacy. Striving for neutrality in this situation is thus a false hope. In such conflicts, there is simply no neutral ground to which

100 A complementary formulation of courts as facilitators of negotiation can be found in Wright (2010, 2014, esp. at 284–9).

101 Hueglin and Fenna (2006: 312).

102 Tully (2004); Schertzer (2008).

103 Hirschl (2008: 97). On this, and Hirschl's wider argument about the "judicialization" of politics and his concept of "juristocracy," see also Hirschl (2004).

the courts can retreat.[104] The process of decision making can be influenced by base presumptions, understandings, and perspectives on the nature of the federation held by judges themselves.[105] What is needed, then, is not to hope for neutrality and independence, or to mandate that courts protect a particular perspective; rather, what is needed is a judiciary that accounts for its potential to impose particular understandings of the federation and to ask courts to actively recognize the various perspectives on the nature and ideal direction for the system.

To sum up, the need to promote an ideal role for the courts that differs from the umpire, branch of government, or guardian roles stems from (1) the contested nature of nationality and a federation; (2) the realization that the courts play a key role in the development and maintenance of legitimacy in the system; and (3) the fact that in federalism conflicts the courts generally cannot operate in a meaningfully independent and neutral fashion. It is these three factors, combined with the principles underpinning the promotion of a federation as the process and outcome of negotiation between the subscribers of legitimate perspectives on the nature of the system, which also illuminate the path towards a more defensible institutional model for the federal arbiter.

The driving ideal of this role and associated theory of judicial review is that courts in diverse federations should seek to reinforce the flexible and dynamic nature of the federal system. The above understanding of federations as inherently contested associations points to the importance of negotiation and political compromise as vital elements of an effective and legitimate system. When negotiation breaks down and political actors turn to the courts to help arbitrate their dispute, this underlying nature of the federal system should not be abandoned; it should be embraced. That is, in this more explicitly political form of judicial review, the courts should be guided by a view of the constitution as built upon competing viewpoints on its very nature. Rather than adopting more traditional forms of legal reasoning that seek to objectively interpret and apply the legal rules of the association, federal judicial review requires the Court to embrace the political nature of its role. There are two avenues a court can take to reinforce the dynamic nature of a federal system when they are called upon to mediate a dispute: (1) explicitly pushing the conflicting parties back into political negotiations to reach an

104 Schertzer (2008: 120); Bellamy (2000: 201).

105 See Swinton (1990: 26–31, esp. at 29). See also my discussion of this in the next chapter.

outcome; or (2) rejecting a zero-sum approach by reaching an outcome that validates and accounts for the competing perspectives of the parties. The intended effect that links these two role-perceptions is to *facilitate the continued use of political mechanisms and negotiation to manage conflict over the federation* to the greatest extent possible. While I elaborate on these two related elements of a broad facilitator role for a federal arbiter in a diverse federation over the remainder of the book, a brief discussion of their central tenets here is important.

On the first aspect, the more *explicit facilitator role*, the ideal is that the judiciary manages conflict within and over the federation by directing parties to negotiate through political processes. This approach means that when the courts are called upon to help manage a conflict over the distribution of powers and resources, they should – to the extent possible – direct the conflicting parties and governments to work to find solutions through the established constitutional and institutional mechanisms that enable negotiation, while also being deferential to outcomes worked out through these mechanisms. In practice this means promoting the use of a host of intergovernmental-relations mechanisms (such as bilateral and multilateral forums or intergovernmental agreements) to encourage mutually agreeable outcomes to conflicts over the division of powers and responsibilities. It also means recognizing and reinforcing that there is significant crossover between each order of government's areas of responsibility – even if they are presented as "exclusive" to a particular order in the constitution; accordingly, the courts should be deferential to, and promote, forums for joint priority setting, management, and decision making where policies or programs have a national-level impact (or where regional-level policies and programs impact national-level priorities). The focus on facilitating negotiation also means that courts should allow and encourage the delegation of authority between governments, despite the tendency of constitutions to grant responsibilities to one order or the other. Finally, this approach also means that the courts, in making their decisions, should reinforce and protect the status of central institutions as forums for the representation of, and negotiation between, national-level and regional-level actors and interests. Thus, in exercising their duty as federal arbiter, the courts should both defer to decisions taken by the orders of government through forums of negotiation over the nature of the federation, and also push the use of these mechanisms as avenues to manage ongoing conflict. As I discuss in chapter 4, the SCC provided a key example of pushing conflicting parties to negotiate in the *Secession Reference*, where a framework of constitutional principles was laid out that could inform any future negotiations relating to the separation of a province from the federation.

This core aspect of the ideal facilitator role entails embracing the inherent conflict that takes place in diverse federations over their national and institutional character, rather than suppressing it by enforcing a partial, fixed idea of the system. Starting from this perspective also means that the guiding principle for the judiciary's decision-making process should be to ensure that it reinforces the legitimacy of the various perspectives on the nature of the federation (rather than imposing one perspective and working to delegitimize competing ones). Similarly, federalism jurisprudence should also explicitly seek to establish and protect access to (and the free and fair functioning of) the political and institutional mechanisms that serve as forums for the negotiation of conflict over the federal system. These institutions should be validated as avenues to allow for discussion and cooperation between the subscribers of different perspectives on the federal and national character of the state. And, the principal way courts can go about such validation is to push conflicting parties to use these mechanisms to manage their conflict, while also being deferential to the outcomes of these negotiations. The implication of such deference is that a court should not impose its own interpretation of the federal system in the place of negotiated settlements on how the federation is to be operationalized between the orders of government.

At the core of this call for courts to be more explicit facilitators are the principles and broader approach of a dynamic federalism. Recognizing the legitimacy of the conflicting perspectives on the nature of the federation and the institutional mechanisms that allow for negotiation and cooperation helps ensure that those subject to the federal structure participate in its development. To the extent that courts are part of the federal system, they can act as a forum of recognition by accounting for the status of the different parties subject to the association – listening to their perspectives and responding in kind through jurisprudence. This facilitator role is better integrated into a broader understanding of federations as dynamic systems than a more independence-inspired ideal. The facilitator role-perception calls on the institution to act as a key mechanism that can reinforce the more dynamic aspects of a federation. Building on what I said above, institutionalizing elements of *audi alteram partem* in the role of federal arbiter helps establish the principle of *quod omnes tangit*: necessitating the duty for the courts to listen to all sides and pushing them to reply sets up a process where the conflicting parties actively participate in the approval and contestation of the federal system.

Of course, negotiation and cooperation between the subscribers of different (conflicting) perspectives on the nature of a federal system (often represented by different orders of government) are not always possible, especially in conflicts that get as far as the legal realm. Court disputes are inherently adversarial, often resulting in acrimonious relations in high-stakes situations. Any account of the judiciary's ideal role as a federal arbiter needs to keep this reality in mind. When further negotiation and cooperation is not a viable option, or the fact situations of a particular case warrant it, the courts may have to make binding decisions. In such situations, an understanding of a federation as a dynamic system calls for decisions that reject the imposition of one particular, partial perspective on the nature of the association. Instead, in line with the underlying principles of a more dynamic federal model (recognition, participation, and listening to all sides in a conflict), courts should seek to account for the validity of the various perspectives on the nature of a federation. Through this recognition, the courts can, even in binding decision, reinforce both (1) the underlying nature of the federation as the process and outcome of previous negotiation and (2) the validity of the competing perspectives on the nature of the federation, which can inform future negotiation. In this regard, a broad facilitator role for the federal arbiter does not mean the courts cannot reach binding decisions, it just calls on them to do so fairly and in an inclusive manner.

The core of this second aspect of the facilitator role – which focuses on *fair arbitration* – is how a court approaches the decision-making process and enforces a binding outcome to a dispute. With regard to the decision-making process, ideally federal arbiters should work from an inclusive understanding when interpreting the division of powers and federal structure. This inclusivity involves incorporating elements of the main, established perspectives on the nature of the system in the decision-making rationale. Such an approach entails working from a comprehensive view of the constitutional law and institutional structure of the state. From this wider view, the Court is able to account for the various streams of law and convention that support the competing perspectives on the nature of the system. In other words, decisions should be built upon an interpretation of the constitution that recognizes the inherent flexibility and contested nature of the division of powers and responsibilities. In this regard, the competing perspectives on the nature of the federation should be drawn upon to inform the interpretation of the constitution and related conventions. In the process, they are reinforced and rooted in the constitutional law and convention.

At the same time, the actual disposition of an appeal is arguably the critical way courts exercise influence as federal arbiters. Decision outcomes have practical political and material effects: they help establish the very nature of the federal system through constitutional interpretation that sets precedent, which influences future judicial decisions. The outcomes of cases also shape our understanding of the federation, which can affect the standing of parties in future negotiations and political conflicts. Accordingly, within a dynamic federal theory, the courts should rule in a way that, ideally, (1) avoids imposing a particular party's perspective on another party; (2) reaffirms the legitimacy of a losing party's perspective; and (3) mitigates any loss for a party to the extent possible, while also seeking to highlight that continued disagreement is reasonable. In other words, where possible, federal arbiters should reject a zero-sum outcome, given the inherently political nature of decision making in federalism cases and the likelihood of continued contestation.

This ideal role for the judiciary, that of a broad facilitator of negotiation that pushes conflicting parties to use political processes to manage disputes and reinforces the flexible nature of the federal system through its decisions, is inherently linked to an understanding of the federation as a dynamic process of negotiation. This outline of a theory of judicial review is also meant to serve as the first step in accounting for the Court's role within a broader theory of how federations can be used to manage diversity. It is a theory that is based upon a view that the courts play a critical role in the development and maintenance of legitimacy for the federation in a plurinational state.

There are a number of potential benefits to this approach to federal judicial review and conflict management. First, this position does not create an ideal of neutrality and independence for the courts that simply cannot be achieved (thus removing the negative repercussions of falling short of this ideal). Instead, this approach invites the courts to seek ways of encouraging parties to manage their own conflicts, and calls on the courts, when acting as arbiter, to recognize their own partial perspectives and seek to have decisions that recognize the various other positions on the nature of the federation. Such an approach would result in decisions that are not held over the heads of parties in any future negotiations; instead, these decisions could work to grant status and legitimacy to the main federal models and their subscribers, leading to freer and fairer negotiations in the future. Ultimately, a federalism jurisprudence seen in this light should be one that properly accounts for the legal and institutional landscape (rather than focusing on particular aspects of the constitutional law that reinforce partial perspectives on the nature of the federation). Similarly, recognizing and incorporating the plurality of perspectives on the federal system should lead to more optimal outcomes in federalism jurisprudence (by representing the plurality of perspectives on the law). Accordingly, the role of facilitator and fair arbiter should lead to decisions that generate legitimacy for both the conflict-management process and the resulting system.

PART TWO

The SCC's Federalism Jurisprudence, 1980 to 2010

Chapter Three

Investigating the SCC's Federalism Jurisprudence

The second section of the book answers a number of empirical questions stemming from the first section, notably: how has the judiciary in Canada managed conflict over national identity and the federation? In addressing this question, the remainder of the book explains and reflects on the findings of a comprehensive review of the Supreme Court of Canada's (SCC) federalism jurisprudence over a thirty-year period. This analysis focuses on the extent to which the Court's decisions draw from and reinforce the key federal models previously discussed and the self-selected role the Court takes in arbitrating disputes.

From this review I have identified two streams of federalism jurisprudence: decisions that recognize and account for conflict over national identity and the federation, and those that do not. Reflecting on these two streams illuminates the problem with the latter, notably the potential negative effect such decisions can have on the legitimacy of the federation. At the same time, this review shows the possible benefits of a federal arbiter recognizing and accounting for the contested nature of nationality and federal systems (i.e., the potential for this to generate legitimacy for the system).

This chapter acts as the introduction to the second, more empirical, section of the book. It explains how I conduct my review and defends some of the key premises informing my analysis. Accordingly, I explain below why and how I analyse the SCC and its federalism jurisprudence, and, importantly, how I determine that a decision adheres to and imposes one particular federal model or recognizes the federation as the process and outcome of negotiation between the subscribers of competing models.

The chapter begins by discussing the key issues related to the scope of the study. It explains why I focus on the SCC from 1980 onward, as well as justifying my case-selection criteria. I then provide and explain the framework that informs my analysis of SCC decisions, while also discussing some of the finer points of Canadian constitutional law to contextualize subsequent analysis.

The Scope of the Study

When one plans a study of the way federal arbiters manage conflict within and over a federation a number of questions immediately arise with regard to the scope. For my own study, the central questions are: why focus on the SCC, why start in 1980, and what cases should be considered? In this section I answer the first two questions together, then turn to discuss the case-selection criteria.

The reason I focus on the SCC from 1980 forward is because it has played an important role as the ultimate federal arbiter in Canada – a position that was crucial in mediating the heated conflicts over the nature of the federation that took place in the early 1980s and which have dictated the tone of federal politics ever since. In other words, the SCC matters. It has played a vital role in the development of the federation and in maintaining legitimacy for the association in the face of serious challenges to its unity and survival. How it makes decisions also matters: imposing particular federal models or recognizing the legitimacy of multiple models can affect the development and legitimacy of the system, particularly at moments of heated political conflict.

As indicated in the last chapter, the central role of Canada's apex court in the development of the federation is an oft-made point.[1] The SCC was established in 1875, but only became the state's apex court, at the top of its judicial system, in 1949.[2] Prior to 1949, the Judicial Committee of the Privy Council (JCPC) acted as the final court of appeal for Canada. As a result, many of the early decisions shaping federation were handed down from the JCPC in the United Kingdom, not

1 For an overview, see Mahler (1987: ch. 2); Baier (2003: 111–12); Russell (2004: 40–6, chs. 7–8).

2 For a historical overview of the SCC from 1875 to 2000, see Lamer (2000). On the Canadian court system, see Morton (2002: ch. 3); Fitzgerald and Wright (2000: 95–103); Iacobucci (2002).

from the SCC.[3] In the period following confederation (from 1867 to the 1930s) the JCPC was an integral element in the rise of the "provincial rights" movement.[4] There is a general consensus that the JCPC consistently sided with those promoting a decentralized view of federation in battles over the system, interpreting the constitution in a way that expanded provincial jurisdiction while limiting central powers.[5]

In the post–Second World War period, and with the rise of the welfare state, there was a notable shift towards centralization in the federation, with an increasingly important central government and the need for the orders of government to cooperate to deliver social services.[6] This trend is demonstrated well when one looks at the increase in central spending going to the provinces: in 1949 cash transfers to the provinces made up 5.9 per cent of central government expenditures; by 1971 this rose to 23 per cent.[7] At the outset of this period we can see the JCPC halting the tide of decentralizing decisions, a signal that was ultimately taken up by the SCC when it replaced the JCPC as the state's court of last resort.[8]

From the 1960s and into the 1970s, intergovernmental relations were hostile in Canada, being marked by a number of failed attempts to negotiate a domestic constitutional amending formula and by the rise of Québécois nationalism.[9] At the outset of this period the SCC was of lesser importance in the development of the federation (the mechanisms of executive federalism instead taking centre stage);[10] however,

---

3 For an overview of the JCPC, see Cairns (1971); Vaughan (1986); Saywell (2002).

4 Russell (2004: ch. 4).

5 Baier (2003: 117–20); see also Mahler (1987: 35–43). The result is that the initial reading of the Constitution Act, 1867, which provides the impression the system is significantly centralized, is not how the federation developed in practice; see Wheare (1963: 20); J. Smith (2003: 52–6). For an alternative take, arguing that other decentralizing forces were at play (not just the JCPC), see Cairns (1971).

6 Particularly since the increasingly important issue areas of the time (healthcare, social services, and education) are provincial matters of competence, while the central government has the resources and ability to establish national-level programs. On this era of "cooperative federalism," see Smiley (1980); Cameron and Simeon (2002).

7 Monahan (1987: 145); Dowd and Sayeed (1985) (cited in Monahan 1987).

8 A key signal is *Edwards v. Attorney General for Canada*, [1930] A.C. 124, which also marked the emergence of the progressive interpretive approach discussed below; on this see Mahler (1987: 43–4); Baier (2003: 119–20).

9 On this period of executive federalism, see Smiley (1980); Cameron and Simeon (2002); Russell (2004: chs. 6–7).

10 Monahan (1987: 149–50); see also Smiley (1970, 1980).

by the latter part of the 1970s the Court was increasingly being called upon to mediate disputes over the division of powers.[11]

With tensions increasing into the 1980s, a lineage of conflicts between the orders of government related to the "patriation" of the constitution and the nature of the federation emerged, with the SCC playing a central role.[12] A key moment in this line of conflict was the *Senate Reference* in 1980.[13] The SCC's decision to reject Prime Minister Trudeau's plan to take unilateral action on areas thought to be within central control (Senate reform, the SCC's composition, and a federal charter of rights) led to the subsequent patriation round of negotiations. The first round of these negotiations in September 1980 failed, with the prime minister declaring in October 1980 he would "go over the heads" of the provinces by unilaterally patriating a constitutional package from the UK. The legality of the intended unilateral action by the central government was quickly challenged in the courts by the provinces of Québec, Newfoundland, and Manitoba. The resulting *Patriation Reference*[14] in 1981 broke the impasse in negotiations by legally allowing unilateral action by the central government, while also advising that constitutional convention mandates substantial provincial consent for the kind of constitutional amendments Trudeau sought. The result was an agreement producing the Constitution Act, 1982, which included an amendment formula and charter of rights, with all provinces, except Québec, signing on to the document.

The process and substance of the Constitution Act, 1982 have informed constitutional politics ever since. Québec took to the courts to argue that a constitutional agreement without its assent was illegitimate; in the *Quebec Veto Reference*[15] in 1982 the SCC disagreed, saying the constitution was in force and that Québec had no veto over constitutional negotiations. In 1987 a new central government received unanimous consent from the executive branches of the provinces on a package of constitutional amendments designed to entice Québec

11 The number of cases receiving federal judicial review between 1950 and 1959 was 30; between 1960 and 1969, 36; and between 1970 and 1979, 54; see Monahan (1987: 150–1). Some of these cases, notably *Reference re Anti-Inflation Act*, [1976] 2 S.C.R. 373, were important and heated disputes over the very nature of the federation.

12 See Russell (2004: ch. 7, 107).

13 *Reference re Authority of Parliament in Relation to the Upper House*, [1980] 1 S.C.R. 54.

14 *Reference re Resolution to Amend the Constitution*, [1981] 1 S.C.R. 753.

15 *Reference re Objection by Quebec to a Resolution to Amend the Constitution*, [1982] 2 S.C.R. 793.

back into the constitutional family (the Meech Lake Accord); however, in the face of concerns over the elite-driven process, perceived over-accommodation of Québec, and failure to account for Aboriginal interests, the accord failed to be ratified by the legislative assemblies of Manitoba and Newfoundland. In an attempt to address these concerns, a new round of negotiations was struck (the Canada Round), with the resulting package of amendments (the Charlottetown Accord) ultimately going forward to a country-wide referendum in 1992 (the package was rejected, both inside and outside Québec, with some 55 per cent of Canadians opposed).

The subsequent period was one of even higher tensions, with nationalist Québec politicians pushing for secession. The culmination was a 1995 province-wide referendum on secession in Québec, with the federalist option winning with a mere 50.6 per cent of the vote. As part of the central government's well-known plan to combat the sovereignty movement, the legality of unilateral secession by a province was referred to the SCC. The court responded in the *Secession Reference*[16] that, technically, unilateral secession is illegal, but constitutional principles dictate that a clear vote on a clear question places a duty on all orders of government to negotiate secession. Both the central government and Québec declared victory and conflict continued with the central government's enactment of the *Clarity Act* in 2000, which seeks to define a "clear question" and a "clear majority."[17]

Following the battles around the *Clarity Act* there has been a noticeable easing of tension in federal and constitutional politics, with a turn towards more asymmetrical and coordinated relations (as evidenced by the Accord on Health Care Renewal [2003], Parliament's recognition of the Québécois nation [2006], and attempts to address a fiscal imbalance through a renewed equalization formula [2007], among other things). This is the era some are calling "collaborative federalism."[18] However, to say that conflict has ceased is erroneous. Conflicts still regularly take place in the intergovernmental arena and before the courts, some of the most notable issues being inter-provincial labour mobility, financial regulation, and the composition of the Senate. Between 2000

16 *Reference re Secession of Quebec*, [1998] 2 S.C.R. 217.

17 S.C., 2000, c. 26.

18 Cameron and Simeon (2002). On the link between this new era of intergovernmental relations and the role of the SCC, see Baier (2012).

and 2010, the SCC rendered decisions in thirty conflicts over the division of powers.[19]

This review shows that Canada's apex court has played a central role in mediating disputes over the nature of the federal system. From the mid-twentieth century this duty has fallen to the SCC. While the Court hears all types of law cases,[20] and the importance of civil rights cases has taken over a considerable part of its docket from the mid-1980s, its role as the state's ultimate federal arbiter remains one of its most important functions.

This is why I focus on *the SCC, in particular*: it occupies a special place in the system. It is *the* final arbiter of federal disputes within the domestic sphere. Because it is the apex court, virtually all major disputes related to the federation that come before the judiciary are settled by the SCC. Moreover, given the high-stakes nature of even comparatively mundane disputes over the distribution of resources and power via the federation, the SCC is often called upon to mediate such conflict. In settling these disputes the Court sets the tone for the entire judiciary and for intergovernmental relations. Lower-court decisions are clearly taken into account, but when a conflict over the federation needs arbitration (because negotiations break down or an actor feels third-party help is needed), it is the apex court that is called upon.

The SCC thus represents an ideal focus for my study, which provides a picture of how the federal arbiter in Canada either imposes a particular model of the federation or recognizes the system as the process and outcome of negotiation between the subscribers of legitimate models.[21] The cases that reach the SCC, given the high resource investment and public scrutiny involved, tend to push actors to clearly and forcefully elaborate their positions. The nature of these conflicts force the Court to select between these competing perspectives on what the federation is and ought to be, with the outcomes shaping the federal system. So,

19 In addition, the Court has rendered decisions in two of the three areas just mentioned; see *Reference re Securities Act*, [2011] 3 S.C.R. 837 and *Reference re Senate Reform*, [2014]. Nevertheless, both areas remain points of contention and negotiation between the central and provincial governments.

20 As Canada's supreme appeal and constitutional court the SCC hears both private law (tort, contract, business, property, and family law) and public law (constitutional, criminal, administrative, tax, and labour law) cases; see Iacobucci (2002: 34).

21 Focusing on the SCC also serves a pragmatic purpose. Studying just SCC cases from 1980 to 2010 involves a consideration of 697 constitutional cases, 159 of which fall under the rubric of federalism jurisprudence. Including lower-court cases or expanding the period would make the project unfeasible.

by reviewing the SCC's federalism jurisprudence I am able to reflect on the role the federal arbiter plays in managing national diversity through the federation, and on the way its actions can potentially affect the legitimacy of the system.

The above review should also indicate why I begin in 1980. From the process and substance of the Constitution Act, 1982 a series of conflicts over the nature of the federation follow where the SCC played a particularly crucial role. These conflicts are all linked, and are examples of clashes between competing conceptions of what the Canadian federation is and ought to be.[22] From the wellspring of the 1980s, then, debates about the very nature of the federation become more explicit and hotly contested; the result is well formulated and elaborated positions, which have much to offer a study of the ways that nationality and the federation are contested, how this competition is managed in the federal system, and the role the federal arbiter plays in this process. Starting analysis in 1980 does mean I am investigating a heightened moment of conflict over the federation where the Court was particularly important. This starting point, though, should not imply that in other times the Court is unimportant. The state's federal arbiter has always played a key role in the development of the federation. Conflicts over the nature of the system have been the norm since confederation. Moreover, although the period of analysis covers recent years, where the extent of intergovernmental conflict seems to have eased, cases still regularly come before the Court.[23]

---

22 See Choudhry and Gaudreault-DesBiens (2007: 166–7). Justice Iacobucci, a key actor in the events, sees them as a causal string (see ibid., 186). These were not new conflicts, but in the run-up to patriation issues were "brought to the surface," and so "antagonisms that, in the past, had been left unstated" became part of constitutional politics (see ibid., 172–3).

23 Gerald Baier has argued that in the current period of collaborative federalism the Court's role as federal arbiter is becoming comparatively less important; though he does note that the Court is still called upon to "umpire" disputes over the federal division of powers (Baier 2012). My own perspective is that the Court's turn towards pushing parties to find negotiated outcomes to their disputes, when it is called upon, not only reflects a collaborative turn in Canadian intergovernmental relations, but is likely also a factor in this era of intergovernmental relations. Even when the SCC is not called upon to mediate a dispute, the actors' perceptions of what the Court would say if they took their case to the institution shapes intergovernmental relations. And, the stream of jurisprudence I discuss in chapter 6 that recognizes the competing perspectives of the various groups on the nature of the federation has the potential to push actors to find negotiated outcomes to their conflicts before seeking arbitration in the first place.

Despite asserting its independence and taking a central place in the political system, interestingly, the SCC has strong administrative and structural links to the central government. The Court is a creature of central government statute.[24] The institution's funding also comes from the central government.[25] Moreover, the central government appoints the nine justices of the Court for a term of good behaviour until the age of seventy-five. At the same time, the SCC often promotes judicial independence as a central principle of the Canadian constitution.[26] There are also conventions and rules that dictate justices represent regional diversity, that three justices be appointed from Québec, and that the Court operate as a bilingual institution. In a recent high-profile decision rejecting the appointment of a justice from the Federal Court of Appeal (Marc Nadon) as a representative from Québec, the Court expanded upon these two features of independence and regional representation. In this decision the SCC reasoned it has constitutional protection as an institution of government, stating that "the Supreme Court's evolution in the structure of the Constitution" and the amending rules in the Constitution Act, 1982 mean that unanimous consent by the central and provincial governments is required to alter "the composition of the Court" (including representation for Québec, while other levels of provincial consent would be required for changes to other essential features of the institution).[27] And so, on the one hand, the SCC appears to have many of the hallmarks of an independent arbitration body: it exercises its authority and plays a central role within the constitutional and political system;[28] it has considerable discretion to set its agenda;[29] and, it can strike out on new avenues of law (relatively) free from precedent.[30] On the other hand, it has significant links to the central government, and is often charged as a

24 See *Supreme Court Act*, R.S.C., 1985, c. S-26.

25 For a review of the Court's funding mechanisms, see Bilodeau (2010: 427).

26 See, in particular, *Reference re Remuneration of Judges of the Provincial Court of Prince Edward Island*, [1997] 3 S.C.R. 3 [*Judges Salary Reference*].

27 *Reference re Supreme Court Act, ss. 5 and 6*, [2014].

28 For example, the Court is not shy about overturning lower-court rulings; see Hogg (2009: 252, 264).

29 While the Court tends to allow appeals involving federal disputes, it does set its agenda (rejecting four of every five leaves to appeal); see Morton (2002: 97).

30 The Court is not bound by precedent (even that set by its own or JCPC rulings), though it does not often overturn its own precedent; see Hogg (2009: 252, 264).

nationalizing and centralizing force.[31] At the same time, the SCC operates as a bilingual institution and represents regional diversity on the bench, including special accommodations for Québec.[32] Accordingly, the Court can be perceived as (1) an independent body, (2) as a tool to impose a nationalist and centralizing agenda, or (3) as protecting and representing diversity and minority rights.

This historical, structural, and administrative context informs my analysis of the SCC, but this is not a study of the SCC *per se*; rather, it is a study of the way the SCC *as federal arbiter* manages conflict over nationality and federation.[33] What should be taken away from the above is that the institution of the Court is important in the development of the federation and has a number of institutional characteristics that can affect its perceived ability to fulfil this role successfully.

The idea of the SCC *as an institution* is important for my study. The subsequent chapters focus on the way the institution of the SCC either works to impose particular federal models or recognizes the system as the process and outcome of negotiation (while reflecting on the potential effect these approaches have on the legitimacy of the system).

At the same time, the Court is made up of individual justices. Accordingly, when looking at the way the SCC understands and reinforces ideas of what federation is and ought to be, I am taking into account how individual justices' ideas about the federation influence their decisions. Therefore, the shifting conceptions of what the federation is among SCC decisions noted in the next three chapters are no doubt related to the fact that the composition of the Court is continually in flux. Over the period of analysis (from 1980 to 2010) there have been four chief justices,[34] and

31 See Bzdera (1993). There are those who argue against this position, notably Hogg (1979) and Baier (2003, 2006).

32 In the recent decision on Marc Nadon, the SCC said that appointing three justices from Québec was part of "the historical compromise" and helps ensure the institution represents "Quebec's legal traditions and social values," while also working to "enhance the confidence of Quebec in the Court"; see *Reference re Supreme Court Act, ss. 5 and 6*, [2014] SCC 21. For more on the guarantee of justices from Québec as an accommodation, see Lamer (2000: 12). At the same time, an Aboriginal justice has never been appointed to the Court.

33 In this way, my own analysis – while complementary to and building upon some of his insights – stands apart from Emmett Macfarlane's (2013) recent study.

34 The chief justices being the Rt. Hon. Bora Laskin (1973–84), Rt. Hon. Brian Dickson (1984–1990), Rt. Hon. Antonio Lamer (1990–2000), and Rt. Hon. Beverley McLachlin (2000–).

an additional twenty-seven puisne (i.e., "ordinary") judges. Much can be gained from looking at individual justices and their role in decision making on the Court.[35] Clearly, the tone set by chief justices, and the individual characteristics and perspectives that come with new justices, affect the dynamics of decision making.[36] Indeed, many argue that an individual judge's understanding of the federation can be discerned from the corpus of their judgments.[37]

Such individual-level analysis, however, is not my objective here.[38] While interesting and perhaps shedding light on *why* the Court shifts its conception of the federation over time, this approach can obscure an understanding of the important role the Court fulfils as an institution. Ultimately, the SCC's power does not come from individual justices, but rather from the normative force it wields as the apex court of the state's judicial system. What the Court says in (and the outcome of) its decisions clearly matters in terms of the development and maintenance of legitimacy for the constitutional, political, and federal system; but, the name on the judgments matters far less than the fact that they come from the SCC.[39] While key actors in the federation may appreciate the different opinions (and regional ties) that inform an individual justice's decision record or tendencies, these actors (and the general public) are likely to consider the overall impact of the Court as an institution on the federation, rather than the impact of a particular justice or chief justice.

This view of the SCC as an institution is something that the Court itself seems to be embracing. The SCC has sought consensus among justices in delivering judgments in recent years.[40] We see this consensus

35 See, in the Canadian context, McCormick (2000, 2004, 2008); Ostberg et al. (2004); Songer et al. (2012).

36 See the revealing interview with Justice Binnie by Makin (2011). Macfarlane (2013) examines these intersections in the decision-making of the SCC in-depth.

37 See, for example, Sharpe (2000); Swinton (1990, 1991); Choudhry and Gaudreault-DesBiens (2007).

38 On the attitudinal model of analysis in the context of the SCC, see Ostberg and Wetstein (2007); Songer and Johnson (2007). For an overview (and critique) of this approach, see Macfarlane (2013: 21–6).

39 On the legitimacy of the Court in relation to its judgments, see Hausegger and Riddell (2004).

40 On unanimous judgments and the consensus approach, see Songer and Siripurapu (2009); Macfarlane (2010, 2013: 101–32). For a look at disagreement on the Court see McCormick (2004). Tellingly, in an interview Justice Binnie identifies this aspect of the Court's approach during his tenure (1998–2011): "You have an institutional

manifesting, for example, through an increasing tendency in federalism jurisprudence to deliver unanimous judgments, rather than having individual justices author dissenting or concurring opinions. Before the *Secession Reference* (from 1980 to 1999) some 48 per cent of the Court's federal decisions were completely unanimous; following the reference (from 1998 to 2010) this rose to 80 per cent.[41] This turn towards consensus is also observable in the more general shift over the last two decades towards a standardized format for decisions (which depersonalizes the judgments and presents them as emanating from an institution).[42]

The third issue related to the scope of the study is the case-selection criteria. As indicated previously, my focus is on the SCC's federalism jurisprudence. Federalism jurisprudence concerns constitutional law where the core of the case is a challenge to an order of government's jurisdiction to legislate or act under the constitutional division of powers.[43] It is an area of law separate from other aspects of constitutional law, most notably civil rights cases involving the Charter of Rights and Freedoms. Federalism jurisprudence is about *what order* of government has jurisdiction to legislate according to the constitutional division of powers (not *if* government has authority to act at all, which

---

responsibility to try to generate as much clarity and solidarity in the law as you can … The whole point of the Supreme Court is you are not dealing with individual judges penning their own thoughts. You are expressing the ideas of nine judges synthesized into one judgment"; and, speaking about the *Secession Reference*, he says: "The objective from the outset was to have a decision 'from the court' … We wanted an anonymous judgment which carries the authority of the whole court and avoids personalizing some particular judge's perspective. I think it was just understood that this was too important for people to be flying off at angles from the main thrust of the judgment." He goes on to note the concerted effort during his tenure within the institution of the SCC to ensure justices operated as a whole, rather than forming "cabals"; see Makin (2011).

41 Interestingly, while 13% of the Court's unanimous federal decisions are delivered as "The Court" (a practice that tends to be used in federal references), even where an individual justice is identified as the author of a unanimous decision the judgment always begins with the text "The Judgment of the Court was delivered by …" By "completely unanimous" I mean there was no dissenting or separate concurring opinion.

42 McCormick (2009).

43 The division of powers and responsibilities between the orders of government is laid out (generally) in ss. 91–95 of the Constitution Act, 1867. Other sections, such as the judicature sections (96–101) and s. 35 of the Constitution Act, 1982 dealing with Aboriginal rights, also play an important role in federalism jurisprudence.

is the question in Charter jurisprudence).[44] The associated legal principle is that when a government enacts legislation outside its jurisdiction it is invalid, hence the dichotomy of rulings in federal cases between *intra vires* (valid, being within the legal power of a government) and *ultra vires* (invalid, being beyond the legal power of a government).[45] Of course, in many areas of constitutional law, and particularly Charter jurisprudence, issues do arise about the way identities are recognized and power is distributed.[46] The difference, though, and the reason I focus on federalism jurisprudence, is that these cases deal *explicitly* with the recognition of identities and the distribution of power and resources *via the federation.*

In cases where the issue is which order of government has jurisdiction, there are three main ways impugned legislation is attacked: on (1) the validity of the law (the question here is if the law falls within or outside an order of government's jurisdiction); (2) the application of the law (the question here is if the law, while validly enacted within a government's jurisdiction, has aspects that apply to another order's area of competence); and (3) the operability of the law (the question here is if a validly enacted law is inoperative because it conflicts with another order of government's validly enacted law). In essence, then, the central issue in a federal case is if legislation is within an order of government's power or if it infringes on another government's jurisdiction.[47] These challenges have associated legal doctrines developed over time to deal with them, which are discussed below. The point to make here is that these attacks beg questions about the scope of an order of government's jurisdiction, about when a law's application infringes this jurisdiction, and about when one order of government's law trumps the other. Consequently, answering these questions pushes the SCC into a process of selecting between competing perspectives on the very nature of the federation.

44 This is a distinction the Court often makes itself; see *Reference re Assisted Human Reproduction Act*, [2010] 3 S.C.R. 457 (at 44): "Whether a federal law falls within Parliament's criminal-law power under s. 91(27) of the *Constitution Act, 1867*, is a question of *which level* of government has jurisdiction to enact this law. This question relates to the powers of one level of government *vis-à-vis* the other, and it is resolved by determining the law's pith and substance. The degree to which the Act may impact on individual liberties is not relevant to this inquiry" (emphasis original).

45 Hogg (2009: 366).

46 See Kelly (2001); Clarke (2006).

47 In the instances where there is a conflict between validly enacted laws the doctrine of paramountcy comes into play; see Hogg (2009: 392, ch. 16).

In these cases the dynamics of conflict between key actors arguing for competing perspectives on the nature of the federation can take a number of forms. The most clear-cut dynamic is between the orders of government (i.e., conflicting provincial and central governments). Conflict takes place between the orders of government in 20 per cent of the decisions discussed in chapters 5 and 6. In a number of cases private actors (citizens, civil society, or corporations) challenge an order of government's legislative jurisdiction. In these cases, three dynamics can take place: (1) a private actor conflicting with an order of government (20 per cent of cases reviewed); (2) a private actor being supported in its case by an intervening order of government, turning the conflict into one between orders of government (29 per cent of cases); or (3) a private actor conflicting with an order of government that is being supported by another order of government (28 per cent of cases).[48] Finally, the dynamic of conflict can take place between two private actors (which happens only 3 per cent of the time in the decisions reviewed in this study). Regardless of the dynamic of conflict, though, these cases involve actors putting forth competing perspectives on the nature of the federation, with the Court interpreting the system in a way that either imposes a particular perspective or recognizes the legitimacy of multiple models.

Employing the criterion of identifying all decisions where the conflict is *explicitly* over the recognition of identity and the distribution of resources and power *via the federation*, I identify 159 SCC decisions delivered between 1980 and 2010. These cases are drawn from a review of all constitutional-law decisions delivered by the Court over this period (some 697 decisions),[49] selecting for further analysis those cases where one of the key questions is which order of government has the constitutional jurisdiction to legislate or act in relation to a matter.[50] The case review was conducted using the SCC's official, comprehensive online database of decisions.[51]

48 When a constitutional question is raised challenging an order of government's jurisdiction, all attorneys general are invited to intervene in the case.

49 Including (4) motions and court orders.

50 This includes cases where the principal issue is the division of powers and also those cases where some form of division-of-powers issue is raised.

51 The database provides public access to all SCC decisions; see http://scc-csc.lexum.com/scc-csc/en/nav.do. It includes the official text for all decisions from 1994 onward and is considered reliable for the period of study; see http://www.scc-csc.gc.ca/contact/faq/qa-qr-eng.aspx#f26.

In line with the study objectives, 28 decisions have been excluded from the initial pool of 159. These 28 decisions have been excluded for one of two reasons. First, a number of judgments simply do not contain sufficient text to analyse (typically a few sentences). These are so-called "stump decisions," where the Court meets to provide a judgment as a matter of formality. The decisions typically take the form of an oral judgment (with no written reasons), often citing a related decision as the basis for the outcome (making expanded reasons moot).[52]

The second reason decisions have been excluded is because the division-of-powers issue raised in the initial case filing is not considered at all by the SCC in its final decision. This "mislabelling" happens when the case is officially classified as relating to federalism jurisprudence because one of the parties, often a private entity, has contested the constitutionality of a particular federal or provincial law on both federal and civil rights grounds. In these cases, the SCC can opt to first consider whether a law violates civil rights under the Charter of Rights and Freedoms. In the decisions excluded from analysis, the SCC struck down the challenged law based on a civil rights violation. Accordingly, in line with legal principles of restraint, the Court does not consider the challenge on federal grounds. The result is that in these cases there was no text or decision for me to consider on the federal issue, and so the case was excluded.

After these 28 exclusions, there are 131 SCC decisions that play an important role in the development of the federation *and* represent a useful population to research the extent to which the Court either imposes a particular federal model or recognizes the legitimacy of multiple models and the federal system as the process and outcome of negotiation.

Given my objective, it is quite clear why I do not consider cases dealing exclusively with criminal, administrative, tax, or other areas of constitutional law; however, my case-selection criteria gets more complicated in relation to Charter cases and Aboriginal rights jurisprudence. As mentioned above, Charter cases often involve conflicts associated with identity recognition and the distribution of power and resources; however, in these cases this is (generally) not *explicitly* linked

52 *Robar v. The Queen*, [1982] 2 S.C.R. 532 and *Goldwax v. Montreal*, [1984] 2 S.C.R. 525 are classic examples of these stump decisions. However, the issue at hand in some of these stump decisions is indirectly considered in my analysis; the latter case was tied to *Westendorp v. the Queen*, [1983] 1 S.C.R. 43, which is included in my review.

to the distribution of resources and power *via the federation*. The lack of an *explicit* conflict over the distribution of resources and power via the federation across the breadth of Charter cases is why I exclude them from my analysis.[53] Of course, some cases involve both Charter issues and explicit division-of-powers issues. In cases where the division-of-powers issue is considered by the Court, it is included in the 131 decisions analysed in subsequent chapters.

With regard to cases involving Aboriginal issues, the approach is similar. I analyse those decisions where the key issue is which order of government has jurisdiction to legislate. Accordingly, two types of cases are included in the above-noted 131 decisions: (1) those where the question is which order of government (central or provincial) has the jurisdiction to legislate with regard to Aboriginal issues; and (2) those where a claim is made by an Aboriginal group that the constitution (via s. 35) grants them the right to *actively regulate themselves as an order of government* (i.e., a claim for self-government).[54] While the former is quite common, the second type is rather rare (I have identified only two such cases in the period of study).[55]

In line with the focus of study I exclude the two other streams of Aboriginal jurisprudence (i.e., classic Aboriginal rights cases and Aboriginal title cases).[56] The former includes cases where the central issue is if Aboriginal rights under section 35 of the Constitution Act, 1982 protect an individual or group from government regulation or action.[57] The latter includes cases where the issue is a proprietary claim to an area of land (including the standards to allow such a claim and what

53 This is not to say that some cases do not deal with this element of conflict. However, to select for analysis only those Charter cases where there was a clash between individual rights conceptions and perspectives on the ideal federal model would open up the study to case-selection bias. There are also practical constraints here: including Charter jurisprudence would significantly increase the number of cases reviewed. Exploring this jurisprudence does mark a future research direction.

54 S. 35 of the Constitution Act, 1982 states that "the existing aboriginal and treaty rights of the aboriginal peoples of Canada are hereby recognized and affirmed."

55 *R. v. Pamajewon*, [1996] 2 S.C.R. 821 and *Delgamuukw v. British Columbia*, [1997] 3 S.C.R. 1010. The latter only cursorily dealt with the issue. While self-government claims have been discussed in other Aboriginal rights cases (namely, *Mitchell v. M.N.R.*, [2001] 1 S.C.R. 911), they have only *explicitly* been dealt with in these two cases.

56 For an overview of the voluminous literature on Aboriginal jurisprudence, see Hogg (2009: ch. 28).

57 On Aboriginal rights, see Hogg (2009: 634–48).

rights, like mineral, hunting, or fishing rights, accompany the claim).[58] These decisions are not considered for the same reason Charter cases are excluded: they deal with the question of *whether* government can regulate an activity at all, not *which* order of government can regulate an activity. In other words, while these streams of jurisprudence involve conflicts over identity and the distribution of resources and power, they do not deal as directly with the distribution of the resources and power via the federation as more classic federalism jurisprudence.

One central issue remains relating to the case-selection criteria, as the set of 131 decisions includes both federal references and division-of-powers cases, which raises questions about the inclusion of both types of cases and their comparability.

References are advisory opinions (almost always on matters of constitutional law) given by the SCC in response to questions posed by the central or provincial governments.[59] It is often pointed out that, because they are technically opinions, references have no effect other than representing the views of the justices.[60] However, it should be remembered that references play a key role in determining whether proposed or recently enacted legislation is within the constitutional jurisdiction of an order of government.[61] Division-of-powers cases, by contrast, deal with *actual* conflicts of law or fact where the constitutional jurisdiction of a government's legislation is challenged. This is "traditional" federal judicial review with all its attendant enforcement mechanisms and doctrines (which makes up the brunt of federalism jurisprudence).[62]

There are three related issues with comparing federal references and division-of-powers cases. First is the position that sees references as overtly political, while division-of-powers jurisprudence is seen as a proper function of judicial review applying constitutional law to actual conflicts. This perspective is understandable given the lineage of heated political conflicts that have led to references where the Court employs

58 On Aboriginal title, see Hogg (2009: 643–7).

59 Provincial governments cannot directly refer questions to the SCC. They have an appeal to the SCC as a right following a reference to a provincial court of appeal; they thus have a de facto right to submit references to the SCC where they so choose; see Hogg (2009: 258–9).

60 Hogg (2009: 257–63); Strayer (1988: ch. 9).

61 Hogg (2009: 263).

62 For an overview, see Hogg (2009: 365–697).

unwritten principles and conventions.[63] Nevertheless, this position is flawed. In references, the Court is undertaking the same function it does in other areas of judicial review: the constitution is being interpreted and applied to a situation. Admittedly, this interpretation can take the form of elaborating fundamental principles and conventions of the constitution; however, conventions are properly understood as the underlying assumptions and architecture of the constitution.[64] The result is that the legal framework worked out in the ("political") references is often applied in the ("legal") division-of-powers cases.[65] At the same time, the legal doctrine and precedents stemming from division-of-powers cases are often applied in references. Thus, while references tend to take account of the constitution as a broad normative framework and division-of-powers decisions tend to be more explicitly linked to precedent and the text of the constitution, the two are linked in that the constitution can only be interpreted and applied with recourse to both streams. The unwritten principles and conventions often identified in references provide the substantive provisions of the constitution with meaning, and vice versa.[66]

The second issue is the extraordinary element of most references. The context and issues raised by some references thrust the Court into overtly political battles and require it to make decisions about the very nature of the constitutional and federal system.[67] Can these references be compared to cases where mundane and technical issues arise, for instance over the jurisdiction to regulate the telecommunications or financial sector?

As argued in previous chapters, it is incorrect to segment "struggles over recognition" (as explicit struggles for modes of recognition based

---

63 See, for example, *Patriation Reference*, *Quebec Veto Reference*, *Judges Salary Reference*, *Secession Reference*, and also *Re Manitoba Language Rights*, [1985] 1 S.C.R. [*Manitoba Language Rights*]. On the recourse to unwritten principles in the Court's work, see Hogg (2007: 90–3).

64 See *Secession Reference* [1998] at 32.

65 See Leclair (2002: 396–7, 412–13, 439); Russell (1983: 228); Hogg (2009: 418–23).

66 See *Judges Salary Reference* [1997] at 95; *Secession Reference* [1998] at 52; Leclair (2002: 394); Russell (1983: 217). In the *Secession Reference* [1998] the Court noted (at 52) that the four unwritten principles identified "assist in the interpretation of the [constitutional] text," and specifically that they inform the "delineation of [the] spheres of jurisdiction" (i.e., division-of-powers jurisprudence).

67 See Choudhry (2008b: 214–15, 219–20, 228); Choudhry and Howse (2000); Tierney (2003: 170).

on identity) from "struggles over distribution" (as explicit struggles over economic, social, and political power).[68] Separating these struggles is incorrect because "challenges to a prevailing norm of intersubjective recognition to which citizens are subject also challenges in some way the prevailing relations of political, economic, and social power that the norm of recognition legitimates, and *vice versa*."[69] If references are where the norms related to identity recognition are more directly challenged and division-of-powers cases are where conflicts arise as to the economic, social, and political distribution of power, the two must be seen as intimately linked. Also, not all references are particularly extraordinary (there are those dealing with taxation issues, firearms regulation, and the regulation of human reproduction).[70] Similarly, many division-of-powers cases deal with hotly contested issues where the disposition of rights and powers has far-reaching effects on the nature of the federation.[71]

Third, as references are by their nature hypothetical cases, valid questions arise about the different context and its effect on the decision approaches and outcome.[72] Nevertheless, the hypothetical nature of the case does not mean a conflict over the federation is not taking place (the core issue in each federal reference discussed is the nature of the federal system). It also needs to be realized that in no reference

68 Tully (2000b).

69 Tully (2000b: 471).

70 See *Re: Exported Natural Gas Tax*, [1982] 1 S.C.R. 1004; *Reference re Firearms Act (Can.)*, [2000] 1 S.C.R. 783; *Reference re Assisted Human Reproduction Act*, [2010] 3 S.C.R. 457. The point is that not every reference is about the validity of the constitution or the ability of a province to secede.

71 See *Multiple Access Ltd. v. McCutcheon*, [1982] 2 S.C.R. 161; *R. v. Crown Zellerbach Canada Ltd.*, [1988] 1 S.C.R. 401; *Bell Canada v. Quebec (Commission de la santé et de la sécurité du travail)*, [1988] 1 S.C.R. 749; *General Motors of Canada Ltd. v. City National Leasing*, [1989] 1 S.C.R. 641; *Friends of the Oldman River Society v. Canada (Minister of Transport)*, [1992] 1 S.C.R. 3; *Ontario Hydro v. Ontario (Labour Relations Board)*, [1993] 3 S.C.R. 327; *R. v. Hydro-Québec*, [1997] 3 S.C.R. 213; *Kitkatla Band v. British Columbia (Minister of Small Business, Tourism and Culture)*, [2002] 2 S.C.R. 146; *Canadian Western Bank v. Alberta*, [2007] 2 S.C.R. 3.

72 There "does appear to be some link between reference cases and [a higher percentage of] rulings of *ultra vires*" when compared to division-of-powers cases; however, this is likely because governments refer particularly contentious legislation and also the very process of the reference may tip off courts that there are questions as to the constitutionality of the legislation, rather than some systemic difference in approach; see Monahan (1987: 154–5).

has the opinion of the SCC ever been ignored – the normative force of the "opinions" in references clearly result in a binding decision on parties.[73] In any event, the difference between an *opinion* of the Court and a *decision* is questionable: the law, as a normative system, is only binding to the extent it is followed. Finally, the procedures of the two streams are nearly indistinguishable, with both seeking to determine the jurisdiction to legislate based on an understanding of what the constitution mandates – something the SCC itself noted in the *Secession Reference.*[74]

The Analytical Framework

The above provides a picture of the overall scope of the study. This section covers the finer points of the research design and introduces the analytical framework used to review SCC decisions.

The general design of the study is rather simple. The broad methodology is textual analysis. The scope is all federal decisions delivered by the SCC in the period 1980–2010 (131 cases).[75] The objective is to determine the extent to which these decisions demonstrate the Court is adhering to, and reinforcing, particular federal models in its federalism jurisprudence (or alternatively, if it understands and reinforces the system as the process and outcome of negotiation between the subscribers of legitimate models). To facilitate this objective I developed and employed an analytical framework to review and assess the SCC decisions.

Analysing the text of SCC decisions is one of the only viable means to determine what the Court thinks about the nature of the federation. Other seemingly applicable methods such as survey or elite-level interviews have considerable constraints: SCC justices and their legal clerks generally do not discuss the particulars of judgments and the rationales

73 See Hogg (2009: 260–1). It should also be noted that the Court struck down legislation and issued a binding decision in *Manitoba Language Rights*.

74 See Hogg (2009: 261); *Secession Reference* [1998] at 25.

75 My analysis excludes dissenting opinions within these decisions because they are generally of lesser importance and for reasons of efficiency. Also, in line with my focus on the Court qua institution, I tend to treat the SCC as a corporate entity. However, the first time a decision is substantively discussed I do identify via a footnote how the decision is reached (i.e., if it is a unanimous or majority judgment) and the primary author of the unanimous, majority, and concurring opinions, where appropriate.

behind them.[76] Moreover, what the Court says in a decision, and how it says it, is important. Text is the only way the SCC can fulfil its role as federal arbiter and exert its power.[77]

Despite the recent push to standardize judgments, it is correct to say that SCC decisions have always followed a general structure, having a factual background, discussing lower-court actions, conducting analysis that gives reasons for a decision, and ending with an explanation of the outcome.[78] At the same time, they have changed over the years, notably becoming longer and departing from the practice of *seriatim* judgments in a move towards consensus-orientated decisions that represent an institutional product.[79] Importantly, though, decisions have almost always included an analytical component, where constitutional interpretation explicitly takes place and is applied to the legal or factual issue at hand. This is the section I tend to focus on in my review.

In federalism jurisprudence, this analytical component has traditionally followed a two-step process.[80] The first step is to characterize the challenged law's pith and substance, or the true and dominant matter of the law, including a consideration of its purpose and effect.[81] The second step is to identify the appropriate "head of power" to which the law should be assigned (which involves an explicit or implicit consideration of the scope of the various areas of legislative competence assigned to the orders of government and the nature of the federal system).[82] These two stages are recognized as inherently linked. Defining the matter of

---

76 See Macfarlane (2013: 7–8) on the difficulty of collecting information on the SCC via interviews. His study is remarkable not only because he managed to secure 28 not-for-attribution interviews, but also because, as he notes, internal SCC directives prohibiting such interviews in the future as breaches of stringent confidentiality agreements mean further studies using this research method are unlikely.

77 McCormick (2009: 36–7).

78 McCormick (2009: 45). The "standardization" in the last twenty years comes from adherence to a particular format for decisions with the use of the above-noted generic subheadings.

79 McCormick (2009: 37, 38, 42, 51, 58); see also L'Heureux-Dubé (1990). A *seriatim* decision takes the form of each justice writing a full reason for the decision as if it is the only judgment.

80 For a discussion of how the Court undertakes judicial review, see Laskin (1955: 114); Lederman (1975); Finkelstein (1986: 242); Hogg (2009: 370–91).

81 See Hogg (2009: 370–91). This process has involved the development of a number of legal doctrines, discussed below, to assist the Court in the process of characterization.

82 A voluminous set of doctrines relating to each order of government's areas of legislative jurisdiction has developed to assist the Court in this stage of analysis; for an overview see Hogg (2009: chs. 17–33).

a law is done in relation to the areas of jurisdiction, and the areas of jurisdiction are given meaning through the classification of permissible and impermissible activities within them.[83]

Reflecting on these two steps in the decision-making process of federal judicial review draws attention to the way understandings of the nature of the federal system can influence the decision, as well as how these decisions reinforce particular perspectives as legal fact. Choosing the essential matter of a law is generally determinative of its validity (if the law is classified one way, it is a valid exercise within an order of government's jurisdiction; classified another way, it is not).[84] The process of characterization thus comes down to a choice that is made knowing full well the result determines the validity of the statute and shapes the federal structure. And, in making this choice, the Court draws from a perspective on the nature of the national community and the ideal federal system, particularly where the relevant statute or precedent is unhelpful in determining a law's pith and substance.[85] At the same time, determining the scope of an order of government's jurisdiction is a more overt act of taking an understanding of the federation and giving it form through legal reasoning.

By combining these two steps and rendering a decision, the Court provides a legal rule that either sanctions or disallows a law as falling within or outside a government's jurisdiction. The decision-making process thus *actualizes* a particular perspective of the federation by defining the scope of these powers and the nature of the system.

To investigate how SCC decisions draw from and reinforce particular understandings of the federation (and so impose or recognize a federal model) I analyse three related components of the 131 above-noted judgments. First is how the federation is depicted, including the use of legal forms of argument to reinforce the validity of this depiction. Second is the outcome of the case. Third is the self-selected role adopted by the Court in the decision.

There are two potential methods by which the next three chapters could discuss the empirical analysis stemming from a review of the SCC's federalism jurisprudence. One method is a series of in-depth case reviews of important decisions, followed by a summary of the data pertaining to the 131 judgments. Another method is to demonstrate how

83 Laskin (1955); Hogg (2009: 370).

84 Hogg (2009: 385).

85 See Hogg (2009: 385–7); Lederman (1981: 241); Simeon (1984: 131).

key aspects of all 131 decisions exemplify the central characteristics of the ideal-type imposing or recognizing decision approaches. The first selective "case review" approach is an onerous and impractical method of presenting analysis given the breadth of decisions investigated in this study. Taking this approach would also open up the analysis to criticisms of selection bias, as the presentation of in-depth analysis would hinge on a handful of decisions that I have deemed important to highlight. Most importantly, though, the case-selection approach does little to advance the overall objective of the book, which is to investigate the extent to which the SCC in the breadth of its federalism jurisprudence between 1980 and 2010 either imposes particular federal models or recognizes competing ones. Accordingly, I use the second method.

Chapters 4 through 6 are structured to present my analysis of the SCC's federalism jurisprudence in a way that reflects the key elements of imposing and recognizing decisions. Each chapter provides examples of how the Court, over the breadth of its work, depicts the federation, uses constitutional law to support its depiction, reaches an outcome, and self-selects its role as federal arbiter. Structuring the empirical chapters around these themes is well suited to meet the book's overall objective for three related reasons. First, this approach does not require the reader to have an in-depth knowledge of particular cases or Canadian constitutional law to assess the argument. Instead of asking the reader to follow the legal reasoning on which a particular judgment purportedly turns, the focus is on how key elements of many decisions demonstrate that an apex court can (and does) undertake imposing or recognizing federalism jurisprudence. Second, my focus is not only on the outcomes of decisions (generally expressed in the *ratio decidendi*), but also on how the Court understands and depicts the federation and its own role in the system (typically found by looking deeper into both the *ratio decidendi* and the *obiter dicta*). Presenting a partial picture of this information by reviewing a few cases is insufficient, while presenting it for each case is impractical. Accordingly, the three subsequent chapters provide examples of how the Court reaches, presents, and employs an understanding of the federation in the two categories of imposing and recognizing decisions across the breadth of its federalism jurisprudence. Finally, chapters 4 through 6 demonstrate how federal arbiters can actually go about fulfilling their role in line with the ideal approach of recognizing competing conceptions of the federal and national system. They provide a sustained case for the potential problems and benefits of how the Court actually operates (and implicitly how it should act) by looking at how the SCC depicts the federation, uses legal argument to support these depictions, reaches outcomes, and self-selects its role across the breadth of its work.

Structuring my analysis in line with the key elements of an imposing and recognizing decision has at least two limitations. One is that it still necessitates providing enough information to allow the reader to assess both the political and legal aspects of my analysis. To provide sufficient information, I have taken three steps. The first is an in-depth review of one case, the *Secession Reference*.[86] An entire chapter is dedicated to this case because of its significance to my argument (it is the marquee example of a recognizing decision). But, I also dedicate considerable space to the case because it provides a detailed example of how I have conducted my case review. The analytical approach that underpins the discussion of the *Secession Reference* in chapter 4 was mirrored for all 131 cases analysed in this study. The second step is to provide a summary of key details for each of the remaining 130 decisions at the outset of chapters 5 and 6. This detail includes the key case identifiers, the issue at hand and related area of jurisprudence, as well as how I have classified the decisions. Finally, as a third step, throughout the text I have provided extensive footnotes that outline essential case information and reference the applicable key elements of the decision.

The second possible limitation of how I have structured my empirical analysis is that, despite the attempt to avoid issues with case-selection bias, my approach raises potential questions for how the decisions have been categorized as either imposing or recognizing. To help address this possible issue I have developed an analytical framework (see tables 3.1 to 3.4) that provides the indicators and benchmarks for assessing how a decision adheres to and reinforces a federal model. I employed this framework to analyse the depiction, outcome, and self-selected role for the Court in each of the 131 decisions. Reviewing this framework – and the indicators of adherence to a federal model for each aspect of a decision – helps to explain my subsequent analysis and provides transparency on how cases were classified as imposing or recognizing.

Depiction of the Federation

The way the SCC depicts the federation matters. It illuminates how the Court understands the system, which drives the outcome of a case.

---

86 *Reference re Secession of Quebec*, [1998] 2 S.C.R. 217.

Table 3.1. Indicators for depicting the federation in line with a federal model

Aspects of Federal Model	Federal models			
	Pan-Canadian	Provincial-equality	Multinational	Dynamic
National character	Uninational	Uninational	Multinational	Plurinational
Nature of constitution	Overlapping consensus	Background neutral framework	Separates and protects national communities	Contested normative system
Nature of federation	Compromise given diversity	Compact between equal provinces	Compact between founding *nations*	Process and outcome of negotiation
Purpose of federation	Trim diversity and conflict	Trade away diversity and conflict	Segregate diversity to suppress conflict	Manage diversity and conflict
Balance of powers	Centralized	Decentralized	Decentralized	No ideal (fluid in response to conflict)
Distribution of powers	Symmetrical	Symmetrical	Asymmetrical	No ideal (fluid in response to conflict)
Nature of provinces	Territorial	Territorial	National *and* territorial	National *and/or* territorial
Nature of central institutions	National	Equally representing provinces	Guaranteeing special representation for minority nations	Representing actors to facilitate dialogue and cooperation
Relationship between orders	Centre superior to provinces	Provinces equal among selves and with centre	Québec, Nunavut, and Aboriginals have special status	Equality in status to allow fair negotiation (system of non-domination)

How the federation is presented by the Court in a decision also has broader effects, influencing the public's understanding of the association, the perceived legitimacy of the various federal models, and the status of the subscribers of those models.

Unpacking the depiction of the federation in a decision involves looking at a number of aspects that play into the Court's understanding of the system and its ideal form. These aspects include the perceived nature of the constitution, purpose of federation, ideal balance and distribution of power, relationship between the orders of government, the national character of the state, and so on. Building on the last two chapters, I have identified how each of the federal models depict the federation in relation to these aspects (see table 3.1). In reviewing the SCC's decisions I looked for correspondence between these ideals and the Court's depiction of the federation to indicate adherence to particular federal models.

Use of Legal Argument

An important element of the Court's decision-making process is how it goes about interpreting the constitution and formulating legal arguments. As Phillip Bobbitt points out, the presence of a constitution means that it has to be construed in some way and there are a number of *accepted* ways this is done in legal analysis.[87] For this study, it is particularly important to consider how these methods of constitutional interpretation are employed to buttress the depiction of the federation. It is through accepted forms of legal argument that the imposition (or recognition) of a federal model is validated *as law* – how mere theories are given creditability and anchored in the constitutional law.

To investigate this aspect of the SCC's federalism jurisprudence, I apply a framework that looks at how the key methods of constitutional analysis are applied in the 131 decisions (focusing on the extent to which they are employed to reinforce an imposing or recognizing depiction of the federation) (see table 3.2).

Some additional explanation of this framework and the use of legal argument is required to contextualize subsequent analysis. This framework builds on Bobbitt's taxonomy of accepted ways of interpreting the constitution and formulating legal arguments about its nature.[88] The "constitutional modalities" listed above are the method through which legal propositions about the constitution are given a meaning as true – the formulation of a legal argument in their image is what generates legitimacy for the argument and for the constitution.[89] While Bobbitt's work focuses on the use of these approaches in the United States,

87 Bobbitt (1991: 5, ch. 3; 1982); see also Barber and Fleming (2007, esp. chs. 1, 4). For an overview of the more Canadian-specific methods of interpretation see Hogg (2007, 2009: ch. 15).

88 See Bobbitt (1982, 1991).

89 Bobbitt (1991: 9, 11–12).

Table 3.2. Methods of constitutional interpretation

Interpretative Approach	Manifestation	Reinforces depiction
Historical	yes/no	yes/no
Textual	yes/no	yes/no
Doctrinal	yes/no	yes/no
Structural	yes/no	yes/no
Prudential	yes/no	yes/no
Ethical	yes/no	yes/no
Progressive	yes/no	yes/no

the underlying point that there are a set of accepted forms of legal argument that inform constitutional interpretation is a broadly applicable insight. As Robin Elliot argues, and subsequent analysis demonstrates, the breadth of approaches discussed by Bobbitt (with the exception of the ethical modality) are regularly employed by the SCC in its federalism jurisprudence.[90]

The first modality, the historical approach, stresses that the constitution should be interpreted and applied in line with the original intent of the framers.[91] Second is the textual method, which involves looking to the meaning of the words of the document as they would be understood by the "man on the street."[92] Third is the doctrinal approach, which applies the rules and principles developed from precedent to understand and interpret the constitution.[93] Fourth is the structural mode of analysis, which infers constitutional rules from the institutional relationship established by the constitution.[94] Fifth is the prudential approach, which seeks to make wise rules that balance the costs and

90 See Elliot (2001: 71–4).

91 Bobbitt (1982: ch. 2; 1991: 12). This mode of analysis is thus also referred to as "original intent" or "originalism."

92 Bobbitt (1982: ch. 3; 1991: 12).

93 Bobbitt (1982: ch. 4; 1991: 13).

94 Bobbitt (1982: ch. 6; 1991: 12–13). To explain further, a structural constitutional argument would go as follows: (1) an uncontroversial statement is made about the constitutional system and institutional structure it sets up; (2) a relationship is inferred from this structure; (3) a factual assertion is made; and (4) a conclusion is drawn that provides the constitutional rule. So, as an example: (1) Canada distributes legislative power between the central and the provincial governments; (2) this means that the two orders of government are equal in status; and so (3) the ability of the central government to unilaterally alter the federal system in a way that would affect provincial powers is (4) invalid, because the two orders are equal.

benefits of the rule.[95] Sixth is the ethical modality, which seeks to derive rules from the cultural ethos of the polity reflected in the constitution.[96] The final modality, the progressive approach, is specific to the Canadian case. Often touted as the dominant approach in Canada, it stresses flexibility in interpreting the text of the constitution in line with the changing social, economic, technological, and regulatory context.[97] It recognizes the constitution is not frozen and should adapt over time (and is thus also known as the "living tree doctrine").[98] This alternative moniker illuminates the fact that the progressive modality actually walks the line between an approach to constitutional interpretation and a legal doctrine relying on precedent to establish a constitutional principle.

Reflecting on the use of these modalities in federalism jurisprudence shows that each can be employed to impose (or recognize) a particular federal model. Of course, the first three modalities do provide a measure of structure the interpreter has to contend with (i.e., the historical record, the text of the constitution, or the case law). Nevertheless, when using these approaches, the Court has sufficient room to interpret the constitution in a way that reinforces a particular view of its nature and that of the federal system. Regardless of the modality used, their flexibility allows for different aspects of the source of interpretation to be highlighted to support a particular view of the federation. This flexibility is even more evident in the final four modes of interpretation. For example, there is significant leeway to determine what the structure of federation is, what is prudent and wise, what the ethical ethos of the constitution is, and what sociopolitical changes the document should reflect. In other words, what is important is not the use of particular modalities, but *how* they are used by the Court to reinforce particular depictions of the federation.

---

95 Bobbitt (1982: ch. 5; 1991: 13).

96 Bobbitt (1982: ch. 7; 1991: 13, 20). This rather abstract approach is rarely used by the SCC. Bobbitt argues that the ethos of the American constitution is limited government, which is discernible through the consequence that rights in the American system are defined as those choices beyond the power of the government to compel; see Bobbitt (1991: 20–1).

97 Hogg (2007: 87).

98 See Hogg (2007: 86). This view of the constitution was laid out in *Edwards v. Attorney General for Canada*, [1930]. The view is set against the formalism at the heart of other modalities like the historical and textual approaches; see Hogg (2007: 87).

A more in-depth explanation of the prominent modality of doctrinal reasoning serves a few functions. First, it demonstrates how a modality can be used to either impose or recognize a federal model. Second, it addresses an important critique to my approach (that doctrine structures SCC decisions, not theories of federation). And, finally, it provides necessary context for later analysis of SCC decisions (in relation to some of the finer points of Canadian federalism jurisprudence). Accordingly, a review of the key "division-of-powers doctrines" employed by the SCC in its federalism jurisprudence is warranted.

The first doctrine – the pith and substance doctrine – is a key part of the process of characterizing a law discussed above. This doctrine establishes that a law is characterized in relation to a head of power by its central and dominant matter, even though it may have other aspects that relate to other areas of jurisdiction.[99] The doctrine thus allows a law passed by one order of government to have an "incidental effect" on another order of government's jurisdiction.[100] It is the concept of incidental effect that demonstrates how the doctrine can be employed to impose a particular federal model: a generous interpretation of what is "incidental" to a law can justify a centralized federation in line with the pan-Canadian model, while a narrow interpretation of incidental effect can protect provincial autonomy in line with the provincial-equality model. At the same time, a nuanced test, which recognizes each order of government has core areas of jurisdiction, but that these are not static, watertight compartments, can reinforce that the division of powers is dynamic and able to respond to conflicts over the system.

Also important to the process of classifying legislation is the double-aspect doctrine. This doctrine explicitly recognizes that a law may have more than one *dominant* matter, falling within central government jurisdiction in one respect and within provincial jurisdiction in another respect (and so, both orders of government can validly pass laws relating to the issue).[101] It is clear how this doctrine can be employed to reinforce a view of the federation and balance of powers as dynamic – as the process and outcome of negotiation that remains flexible in response to conflicts. However, the doctrine can also be employed to impose the pan-Canadian model, as the increasing tendency to note that almost any issue has a double aspect means the

99 See Hogg (2009: 371–4).
100 See Hogg (2009: 373).
101 See Hogg (2009: 375–7).

doctrine of central paramountcy can allow for the federation to be considerably centralized.

This principle of federal paramountcy represents a general understanding of how the division of powers is to be operationalized. The doctrine holds that where central and provincial laws are validly enacted, but inconsistent and conflicting, the central government's law prevails.[102] The way this doctrine can be used to impose a particular federal model comes down to the test of what constitutes a conflict: a broad test (saying that parallel laws or minor inconsistencies between them constitutes a conflict) allows and promotes a centralized system, whereas a narrow test (saying that conflict exists only where there is significant operational conflict between laws) protects provincial autonomy in line with the provincial-equality view. At the same time, the test for paramountcy can be employed to recognize both the ultimate superiority of central government legislation (in line with the pan-Canadian model) and the need to protect provincial autonomy (in line with the provincial-equality view), while also recognizing the respective positions by only "reading down" the aspects of provincial laws that explicitly conflict with central laws (rather than striking down the conflicting law).[103]

Another key doctrine dealing with the general understanding of how to operationalize the division of powers is the interjurisdictional immunity doctrine. This doctrine holds that each order of government's jurisdiction has a "basic, minimum and unassailable" core that is immune from the application of another government's legislation.[104] Again, the key to understanding how this doctrine can impose a federal model is the test employed by the Court to determine the scope of an order of government's immunity: a broad scope for central immunity in an area can lead to a centralized system, or a broad scope for immunity in a provincial area can reinforce a decentralized one. At the same time, restricting the applicability of this doctrine and reinforcing a narrow test of immunity can work to recognize the dynamic and inherently

102 See Hogg (2009: ch. 16).

103 This general direction on paramountcy is evidenced in the Court's thinking on the doctrine, which is summarized in *Canadian Western Bank v. Alberta*, [2007]. On the reading-down principle, see Hogg (2009: 390–1).

104 See *Bell Canada v. Quebec*, [1988] at 839; *Canadian Western Bank v. Alberta* at 33; Hogg (2009: 392–404). It should be noted that the Court in *Canadian Western Bank v. Alberta* voiced its concern with this doctrine and indicated it has fallen out of favour.

contested nature of the federal system, as well as its ability to adapt as a process of negotiation.

Finally, there are numerous principles and doctrines that inform the Court's interpretation of the various heads of power in ss. 91 and 92 of the Constitution Act, 1867. For example, there is the precedent and doctrine around the scope and nature of the central government's residual power to make laws for peace, order, and good government, or the provinces' power over property and civil rights, to name only two.[105] These doctrines related to the heads of power, even more so than the doctrines noted above, can be employed to impose particular federal models. Selecting aspects of the case law and emphasizing certain precedents can help to reinforce the scope of a head of power in line with a particular federal model. In fact, the question needs to be asked: what informs the initial development of doctrine around heads of power if not theories of what the federation is and ought to be?

This question draws attention to the final point I want to make about doctrine and the use of legal argument before moving on: while doctrine is properly understood as a structuring factor in a decision, its influence should not be overstated. As Gerald Baier points out, the force of previous decisions and the principles contained in doctrine do shape the SCC's federalism jurisprudence.[106] However, what underlies the development and application of doctrine is preconceived understandings of the nature of the federation. The development of doctrine over time is simply the statement of legal principles that stem from, and operationalize, views of what the federation is and ought to be. This is a point that is borne out through the next three chapters, which clearly show how federal models inform the Court's understanding of the federation and drive decision outcomes that provide precedent and doctrine, which in turn lead to the application of this doctrine in future cases.

Outcomes

While the way the federation is depicted is an important element of how SCC decisions draw from and reinforce particular understandings of the federation, equally important is a consideration of the outcome of the case. The decision outcome has practical political and material

105 For an overview, see Hogg (2009: chs. 17–33).
106 See Baier (2006).

effects, while working to align the constitutional and federal system with the way it is depicted in the decision and establishing precedent that influences future decisions. The outcome is thus a central element of a decision either imposing a particular model or recognizing the legitimacy of multiple models and the system as the process and outcome of negotiation (and accordingly has implications for the legitimacy of the conflict-management process and the federation).

Looking at how an outcome plays into the judgment either imposing or recognizing federal models involves investigating two aspects of the decision (see table 3.3). The first is the actual disposition of the appeal (i.e., who wins, and how they win). The second aspect is the broader effect of the outcome for the federal system. The ideal-type of an imposing decision involves a zero-sum outcome (where one jurisdiction wins outright and the other loses), with the effect being to align the federal system with a particular model (i.e., reinforcing through the decision that the federation *is* as a model says it *should be*). The opposite ideal-type is a decision that rejects the zero-sum approach to disposing of the appeal (seeking positives for all jurisdictions, or at least mitigating the loss for a party) while rendering a ruling that reinforces the legitimacy of multiple models and the system as the process and outcome of negotiation.

Self-selected Role

The way the federation is depicted and the decision outcome combine with the Court's self-selected role to form a broader conflict-management approach in any given case where it is acting as the federal arbiter. At the same time, how the SCC perceives its role within the federation plays an important part in both its decision-making approach and the outcome in a case. The SCC's perception of its function in the federation is part of how it understands the constitutional and federal system and also informs how it goes about disposing of the case. Therefore, the role the Court adopts (and projects for itself) as federal arbiter has important implications for the legitimacy of the conflict-management process and the broader federal system.

Accounting for the Court's self-selected role involves identifying the links between its perceived position in the federation and the various federal models (see table 3.4). As noted earlier, there are links between the federal models and the ideal role the Court should play as federal arbiter (i.e., between the pan-Canadian, provincial-equality,

Table 3.3. Decision outcomes indicating adherence to a federal model

	Federal models			
	Pan-Canadian	Provincial-equality	Multinational	Dynamic
Winner	Positive central government	Positive all provinces	Positive particular jurisdictions (Québec, Aboriginals)	Positive all (or mitigates loss)
Effect	Reinforces pan-Canadian model	Reinforces provincial-equality model	Reinforces multinational model	Reinforces dynamic model

and multinational models and the umpire, branch of government, and guardian roles, respectively). When assessing if a decision imposes a particular federal model, I look at how the Court adopts and promotes an ideal role for the judiciary in line with what a particular federal model expounds it should be; and also the extent to which this role is used to justify an outcome that reinforces the legitimacy of a particular model. At the same time, I also investigate the extent to which the Court operates with an understanding of the federation as the process and outcome of negotiation and accordingly adopts and promotes its role as the facilitator of this negotiation and a fair arbiter when it breaks down.

Even when each case is coded according to the indicators outlined in this framework, there are challenges and limits to the analysis that need to be recognized. A measure of subjectivity is inevitable in qualitative textual analysis such as this that seeks to make links between a set of phrases and broader ideas and concepts. The complexity of cases compounds this issue by making it difficult in certain situations to pinpoint the exact nature of the decision as imposing or recognizing. For example, in a number of decisions elements of the legal reasoning can indicate support for multiple federal models within a broader decision that seems to reinforce a particular model or reach an outcome where only one side wins. In other instances, an otherwise lengthy decision can include only limited reflections on either a law's pith and substance or the scope of a federal power, and so it does not provide a sufficient amount of text to determine with certainty the underlying federal visions at play. For these reasons, reasonable disagreements can be expected about how some decisions are coded.

At the same time, the research design of the study takes these limitations into account. The analytical framework, grounded in the theory

Table 3.4. Self-selected roles for the judiciary

	Self-selected role			
	Umpire	Branch of government	Guardian	Facilitator / Fair arbiter
Indication	yes/no	yes/no	yes/no	yes/no

and context of Canadian federalism, is explicitly designed to show how decisions may indicate support for different views of the national and federal community across a range of potential topics. In addition to this and the other above-noted elements – such as the use of the *Secession Reference* as an in-depth demonstration of the review method and extensive footnotes throughout – I have structured the classification of decisions as impositions or recognitions to address these issues. Notably, decisions are placed on a scale that accounts for the variation in the extent to which they either adhere to the ideal-type of an imposing or recognizing decision. The scale is based upon how the key parts of the decision (the depiction of the federation, the use of legal argument, the outcome, and the self-selected role for the Court) combine to either reinforce the legitimacy of one federal model or recognize the legitimacy of multiple models. As I explain further in chapters 5 and 6, the classification also takes into account the method used to depict the federation and reach an outcome. For example, imposing decisions can depict the federation by relying exclusively on one model, by primarily using that model (along with other models), or by delegitimizing competing models. Similarly, the outcome of an imposing decision can provide an absolute victory for one order of government or it can reach a result that has varying levels of ambivalence to the different orders and stakeholders. Similarly, a recognizing decision can directly reinforce the dynamic nature of the constitution, balance multiple models off one another in depicting the federation, or take a more minimalist and ambiguous approach to depicting the federation that avoids reinforcing any particular model. In such cases the outcome can reject a zero-sum outcome in a number of ways: directly granting all sides a victory, mitigating the loss for one side, or even leaving elements of the conflict unresolved and thus pushing parties back to the negotiation table. It is the combination of these different methods of decision making along with an appreciation of the complexity of the particular case and of the ways that judicial doctrine and other contextual factors influence decisions that informs the overall ranking of a decision on the scale from highly imposing to highly recognizing. Predictably, as the analysis shows in chapters 5 and 6, the majority of the decisions fall somewhere in the middle of these two poles on the lower ends of the imposing and recognizing spectrum.

Situating the Study

This study focuses on the SCC and the way it either works to impose particular federal models through its decisions or recognizes the system as the process and outcome of negotiation (while reflecting on the potential effect these approaches have on the legitimacy of the system).

This focus differs from the two most prominent approaches often adopted to study the judicial role: legal positivists and attitudinalists.[107] Legal positivists contend that constitutions and precedent act as independent variables structuring judicial decision making.[108] Accordingly, given the inherent separation between law and politics, justices can reach relatively objective decisions applying legal rules, with analysis of this activity focusing on the extent to which courts reach this benchmark and how the law itself influences the outcomes.[109] Attitudinalists, in line with wider developments in the study of political behaviour, contest the role of the law as a structuring agent, arguing that legal rules and doctrine are only used to rationalize decisions made in line with the personal values and beliefs of the justices.[110] Central to this perspective is studying how justices' ideological views shape their decision-making patterns (along with other personal characteristics such as gender, religion, age, region of birth, and ethnicity).

Sitting somewhere between these two perspectives is neo-institutionalist scholarship that stresses the importance of institutional structures, values, and ideas in shaping judicial decision making.[111] This work ranges from those who argue it is the key institutional structures of a polity that impact judicial decision making (e.g., the nature of the

107 See Macfarlane (2013: 17–31), from which the analysis in the next two paragraphs draws.

108 See, for example, Hart (1961).

109 A classic example is Epstein and Kobylka (1992), who argue (at 7) "the law and legal arguments … most clearly influence the content and direction of legal change."

110 See Segal and Spaeth (1993, 2002: 53); Macfarlane (2013: 21).

111 As I discuss in chapter 4, the focus on how institutional structures influence decisions can also be contrasted with more strategic accounts of judicial decision making that argue judges are mainly concerned with legitimacy cultivation.

federation established by the constitution)[112] to those who apply a more sociological institutionalist lens to argue that underlying, competing normative positions on the nature of the polity influence judicial decision making.[113] As Emmett Macfarlane's recent overview and application of this broader perspective shows, there is also a middle ground here that focuses on a justice's role perception cultivated by institutional structures and wider social norms that shape decision-making.[114]

The underlying perspective of this study – that the Court's adherence to particular federal models influences its decisions – has a pedigree in Canadian scholarship.[115] Given the nature of constitutional interpretation in general, and federal judicial review as mainly a political activity, the element of discretion the courts are afforded to interpret and apply the constitution allows preconceived understandings of the federation to influence decisions.[116] As Justice Binnie has said: "Nobody arrives at the Supreme Court of Canada without baggage. We have all had experiences. We all have views as to how society operates."[117] Chief Justice Laskin has also admitted as much: "Do we lean? Of course we do, in the direction in which the commands of the constitution take us *according to our individual understandings*."[118] The relevant element of analysis thus becomes *what those understandings are*, the extent *particular understandings of the federation and the constitution* play into the approach and outcome of federalism jurisprudence, and their *effect on the development and legitimacy of the system.*

In analysing these elements of federalism jurisprudence, this book differs from previous related studies in three respects.

---

112 See Baier (2006).

113 See Monahan (1984); Schertzer (2008).

114 Macfarlane (2013).

115 For example, Monahan explores how federalism jurisprudence is influenced by judges' adherence to normative theories of federalism (rather than legal arguments or principles); see Monahan (1984: 48–9, 70, 71, 84–7, 89–90, 92; 1987); see also Weiler (1974); Lederman (1983); Saywell (2002: xvii).

116 See Monahan (1984: 64–5, 68–9); Weiler (1974); Lederman (1964). Even Peter Hogg notes the discretionary aspect of constitutional interpretation, specifically with regard to federalism jurisprudence; see Hogg (2009: 138, 140). However, the work of Hogg (and his followers such as Baier) can be contrasted to these scholars' work, as they generally see the Court as conducting legal reasoning separated from political decision making; see Baier (2006).

117 Makin (2011).

118 Cited in Saywell (2002: xvii) (emphasis added).

First, I disagree with the general conclusions of some that since the Court is undertaking a political practice in its federal judicial review, its role as federal arbiter should be abandoned altogether.[119] My viewpoint builds on Stephen Tierney's distinction between substantive and process-orientated prescriptions for constitutions in plurinational states.[120] When thinking about prescriptions for existing federal arbiters in diverse federations, the more pragmatic and logical starting point is "process-orientated" changes to adapt already existing institutional structures (like the role of the courts in the system), rather than wholesale, substantive changes to the macro-constitutional system. In other words, from a pragmatic standpoint, it is logical to keep federalism jurisprudence (which has developed in a legal environment) in the hands of the SCC and linked to the other streams of constitutional law.[121] More importantly, though, abandoning the idea of a federal arbiter and leaving the resolution of conflict completely to the political process fails to account for the reality that certain actors have material and political power advantages. The federal arbiter can play an important role in keeping the federation a free and fair system (or rather, it should do so). In a related way, the judiciary can also be a useful mechanism to achieve a balance: protecting the constitutional and federal system from partisan political manipulation while remaining open and dynamic enough to respond to conflicts over the system.

Second, I take issue with studies that focus only on the outcomes of court decisions. I argue the *approach* adopted by the SCC in its federalism jurisprudence (i.e., the way decisions are rationalized, how the constitution is interpreted, and the very act of recognizing, or not, the other models) is important, both in terms of its influence on decision outcomes and the affect the approach can have on the legitimacy of the federal system.

119 See Weiler (1974); Monahan (1984). I similarly reject the view that federalism jurisprudence is wholly "legal" in the traditional understanding; accordingly, striving for a neutral-umpire approach, as noted in the previous chapter, is not sufficient.

120 The former focusing on structural changes to the constitutional and federal system via amendment, the latter looking at more incremental changes like the way constitutions are interpreted by actors in the system. See Tierney (2009: 93).

121 See Hogg (2009: 270). This approach recognizes that issues in all areas of constitutional law often intertwine. Having one body deal with them allows for a coherent and up-to-date perspective from the federal arbiter.

Finally, I provide a study that is up-to-date, takes into consideration all federalism jurisprudence over a period of time (not just a few cases),[122] and, finally, takes the step past description towards theory generation.[123]

Nevertheless, this study is only worthwhile if federal judicial review has an effect on the federal system. The opposite case – that federalism jurisprudence has no discernible impact on the choices made by government – has been made by Patrick Monahan with something he calls the maxim of federalism: it is always possible to do indirectly what cannot be done directly.[124] His argument rests on a distinction between internal and external perspectives on federal judicial review. The internal perspective is that of participants in the process itself, for whom "consistency or rationality of constitutional decision-making are necessarily and inherently important"; while the external perspective is that outside the judicial enterprise rulings matter only if "they have significant impacts on other political institutions or on citizens."[125] In other words, federal judicial review does not really matter because outsiders only care about the final policy outcome (and ultimately governments can work around negative decisions).

I disagree with this position on three fronts. First, on the internal/external perspective, who is really external to the process of judicial review when it deals with constitutional law? By its very definition, constitutional law encompasses the interests of the entire state; accordingly, the approach and outcome of federal judicial review matters for everyone, and particularly for those who see the entire system as set against their particular view. Second, it is not just the outcomes that matter to parties, but also the process itself and the way the system seeks to deal with conflict over the nature of the federation. A process that generates loyalty to the way it manages conflict, rather than

122 This approach addresses selection-bias issues. While Saywell (2002) does look at a large selection of federalism jurisprudence from confederation through to the *Secession Reference*, his study lacks a clear and consistent application of a framework of federal theory to inform his analysis (which is thus slightly ambiguous in its conclusions). Baier (2006), while covering a number of important cases does not conduct a comprehensive review of the Court's work.

123 These last two points set my work apart from a study by Nadia Verelli (2008), where the Court's adherence to the key federal models is investigated in four references.

124 Monahan (1987: iv, 8–11, 161–2, 224, 239).

125 Monahan (1987: 8–9).

derogating the position of participants, is vital to a legitimate federal system. Finally, the fact that actors actually continue their negotiations in other forums after a decision is an important observation; but it supports the claim that federalism jurisprudence acts as a step in the process and outcome of federation (which does not mean it is unimportant and does not influence outcomes).[126]

Conclusion

This chapter provides the necessary context for subsequent analysis while explaining and justifying some of the key choices of my study. It explains why I focus on the SCC's federalism jurisprudence from the 1980s forward, namely, because the Court plays a particularly important role in the development and maintenance of legitimacy for the system (a function that became especially important in the face of heated conflicts from the 1980s). It also lays out my analytical framework and research method to determine if the Court is imposing a particular federal model in a decision or if it is recognizing the system as the process and outcome of negotiation between the subscribers of legitimate models. Over the next three chapters, I apply this framework and method to argue that a significant proportion of the Court's work as federal arbiter has the potential to erode the legitimacy of the federation by imposing particular federal models. At the same time, there is a stream of the SCC's federalism jurisprudence that shows how it can act to reinforce the dynamic nature of the federal system and thus facilitate negotiation between the subscribers of legitimate federal models, and, in so doing, manage conflict in a way that can generate legitimacy for the federation.

126 For an interesting study of the strategic use of SCC judicial review and its role in intergovernmental relations, see Riddell and Morton (2004).

Chapter Four

The Exemplar of the *Secession Reference*

This chapter discusses one decision, in-depth: the *Secession Reference.*[1] It presents this important decision as an exemplar in two senses. First, the reference represents the decision that most closely adheres to the ideal-type of a decision that recognizes and reinforces the federation as the process and outcome of negotiation between the subscribers of legitimate federal models (rather than imposing one federal model). The chapter thus provides a benchmark that informs analysis in the next two chapters, which look at those decisions that fail to live up to the approach followed in the reference, and those that substantially follow the lead of the *Secession Reference.* Second, through a detailed discussion of the reference, the chapter demonstrates how the remaining 130 decisions are analysed in the two subsequent chapters by showing how I employ the analytical framework introduced in chapter 3.

The chapter begins by discussing the context surrounding the case, highlighting the seriousness of the situation and the fact that the reference dealt with issues that directly challenge the legitimacy of the federal system. I then discuss the way the federation is depicted in the reference, noting the inclusive nature of the Court's understanding of the association. The third section examines the use of legal argument to reinforce the legitimacy of this inclusive depiction. The fourth section discusses the outcomes of the case, particularly the Court's rejection of a zero-sum approach and the attempt to ensure each side can find a positive aspect in the opinion. The next section discusses the SCC's self-selected role within the federation and how this draws from and

1 *Reference re Secession of Quebec*, [1998] 2 S.C.R. 217. The reference was a unanimous opinion (authored by "The Court").

reinforces the broader conflict-management approach in the decision. I then reflect on the possible reasons why the Court recognized the legitimacy of multiple federal models, promoted the system as the process and outcome of negotiation, and adopted a role as the facilitator of this negotiation. I argue the Court took this approach because it was the best way to reinforce the legitimacy of the federal system in the face of a severe legitimacy crisis and a direct challenge to the survival of the system with the potential unilateral secession of Québec.

Context

As discussed in the previous chapter, the *Secession Reference* represents the culmination of a tumultuous decade marked by considerable nationalist mobilization in Québec, heated intergovernmental conflict, and continuous constitutional negotiation.

Following the patriation of the Constitution Act, 1982 without the signature of Québec was the *Quebec Veto Reference*,[2] where the SCC told Québec the document was in force regardless of a perceived veto and special status for the province. A number of attempts followed that tried to bring the province into the constitutional fold, notably the Meech Lake Accord (which included a controversial clause recognizing Québec's distinct status) and the Charlottetown Accord (which included the "Canada Clause" recognizing Québec's distinct status along with Aboriginal rights to self-government and the equality of the provinces). Both of these attempts to amend the Constitution ultimately failed, the latter rejected by a pan-state referendum. Ironically, this process, which started as an attempt to accommodate Québec, actually exacerbated Québec–Canada relations and fuelled separatist sentiment. The result was a 1995 provincial referendum initiated by the Québec government seeking a mandate to secede.

With the federalist option winning the referendum by the slimmest of margins (securing only 50.6 per cent of the vote), the central government mobilized to combat separatist forces. A two-pronged strategy was implemented (so-called Plan A and Plan B).[3] Plan A was to actively

2 *Reference re Objection by Quebec to a Resolution to Amend the Constitution,* [1982] 2 S.C.R. 793.

3 On Plan A and B, and the link to the *Secession Reference,* see Drache and Monahan (1999); Gibson (1999); Greschner (1999). On these approaches and their branding, see the 1997 speech by then minister of intergovernmental affairs for Canada Stéphane Dion, "Beyond Plan A and Plan B" in Dion (1999).

promote a united Canada and stress the benefit to Quebeckers of staying in the federation. Among other things, this took the form of appeasing "soft-nationalists" by recognizing Québec's distinct status through a motion in the House of Commons, committing to recognize a Québec veto over constitutional amendment proposals, and sponsoring pro-Canada activities in the province.[4]

Plan B was to take a harder line that accentuated the costs associated with separation and made it difficult to achieve. The *Secession Reference* was a central component of Plan B.[5] The reference, initiated by the central government, asked the Court three related questions: (1) Can Québec legally, under Canadian constitutional law, unilaterally secede from Canada? (2) Under international law and the concept of self-determination does Québec have the right to unilaterally secede from Canada? (3) In the event of a conflict between domestic and international law, which would take precedence?

The validity of the entire court process was explicitly challenged by Québec. The province argued the move was an attempt to interfere in its domestic politics and constrain its democratic rights, while maintaining the SCC was biased against its position.[6] Québec even refused to participate in the reference, and so the SCC had to appoint an *amicus curiae* (friend of the Court) to defend the position in favour of unilateral secession.[7] In addition, thirteen parties intervened in the decision, including the provinces of Manitoba and Saskatchewan, the governments of the Yukon and Northwest Territories, various Aboriginal groups (e.g., the Grand Council of the Crees and the Chiefs of Ontario) as well as other advocacy associations. The general thrust of the interventions was against the right of Québec to unilaterally secede. Nevertheless, the dynamic of conflict in the case was between the central government and the Québec government, represented through the *amicus curiae*.[8]

4 On the latter point, and the ill-fated $100 million Sponsorship Program that was plagued by issues of corruption and accountability, see Hubbard and Paquet (2007).

5 As was the central government's response to the decision, the *Clarity Act* passed in 2000.

6 See Schneiderman (1999: 4–5).

7 There is a general consensus that the *amicus curiae*, a self-proclaimed separatist, represented Québec's position faithfully and forcefully (including challenging the validity of the reference itself); see Schneiderman (1999: 6–7).

8 The SCC indicated as much by reserving its questions mainly for the central government and the *amicus curiae* in the oral hearing; see Schneiderman (1999: 7).

The reference was marked by a high level of public engagement. The hearing and decision received significant media coverage and in the first few hours of the decision's posting online, it was accessed over 20,000 times.[9] The justices took note of this aspect of the process, and provided an opinion aimed not only at the participants of the case, but also at the general public.[10] The text of the opinion is quite long (over 21,000 words) and comprises three key sections. The first deals with the Court's role and its ability to hear the case (paragraphs 3–31). The second focuses on the identification and definition of four unwritten principles that underpin the constitution and are applicable to the issues in the case (these being federalism, democracy, constitutionalism and the rule of law, and minority rights) (paragraphs 32–82). The third section applies these principles to the issue, which gives rise to the key opinions of the case (paragraphs 83–147). Despite the extraordinary nature of the issue in the case (and the recourse to unwritten principles), the reference has a general structure similar to that of other federal decisions: it interprets the constitution and applies that interpretation to a question of law or fact to render its opinion.

The court's opinion rejected the *legal* right of Québec to unilaterally secede, under either Canadian or international law. However, Québec was given solace in the ruling. If a clear majority of Quebeckers voted for secession in a referendum with a clear question, a duty to negotiate in good faith would be placed upon both orders of government. Following the decision, both the central government and Québec claimed victory, the former stressing the legal aspect of the ruling and the need for clarity in any future referendums, the latter stressing the duty to negotiate following a referendum.[11]

---

9 Gaudreault-DesBiens (1999: 793).

10 See McHugh (2000, esp. at 446, 459); Des Rosiers (2000: 182). See also Tully (2000a: 3), where the decision is presented as "an exercise in public reason[ing]." As Justice Binnie says of the intense public interest and reception of the decision by the public: "My feeling then and now is that, although the judges are aware of this environment outside the courtroom, the focus is very concentrated on the issue and sense of responsibility to get it right regardless of how it is to be perceived. Personally, I was very pleasantly surprised that it was so well received by all sides … It seemed to me it was a hugely important function for the court to perform – to say that it's not our decision; it's the decision of the people of Canada"; Makin (2011).

11 For an interesting example of this see the 25 August 1999 open letter from Canada's then minister of intergovernmental affairs, Stéphane Dion, to Lucien Bouchard, then premier of Québec, on why the central government won the case; available in Dion (1999).

Because of this Solomonic approach (seen by many as a deft political move) and the issues raised by the reference, it is often heralded as the most important decision the Court has ever made.[12] What was at stake in the case was nothing less than the dissolution of the federation initiated by Québec. The case thus resonates with broader international issues: the unity of a state being challenged by a national minority group claiming a right to unilaterally secede, while the central government fights this endeavour. The reference thus forced the Court to grapple with issues that directly challenge the legitimacy of the constitutional and federal system (including the role of the courts within the system).[13] This extraordinary element no doubt led the Court to shift its conception of the federation and the constitution.[14] Many have noted an important part of this turn, focusing on the rejection of positivism in the opinion and the Court's recourse to unwritten constitutional principles to deal with the extraordinary legitimacy crisis.[15]

While I discuss these elements below, my focus goes beyond the direct political implications or the novel legal reasoning of the decision. My analysis instead focuses on uncovering the federal and judicial theory that underpin the decision's approach and outcome, while reflecting on the potential implications this can have for the legitimacy of the federal system. In this regard, I turn away from the explicitly legal positivist accounts of the decision, as well as those that frame it as only an exercise in strategic decision making.[16] My analysis here seeks to highlight how the Court can fulfil its role as federal arbiter in a way that recognizes and reinforces the federation as the process and outcome of negotiation between the subscribers of legitimate federal models, while acting as the facilitator of this negotiation.

---

12 On the Court mimicking King Solomon's judgment in the "Mothers' Case" (though having a rather negative interpretation of this), see Mandel (1999).

13 See Tierney (2003: 170–3).

14 See Tully (2000a: 3–7); Schertzer (2008: 119).

15 See Leclair (1999); Walters (1999: 384); Choudhry and Howse (2000: 150); Choudhry and Gaudreault-DesBiens (2007: 191–2); Choudhry (2008b: 215–28).

16 The latter position is exemplified by Radmilovic (2010). However, as I discuss later in this chapter, my argument and analysis do not contest the broader point of Radmilovic or others who focus on the strategic nature of judicial decision making. Rather, I seek to complement and help refine this view of judicial behaviour and better integrate it with more institutionalist accounts of the judicial role in diverse federations.

Depiction of the Federation

The first step in my analysis is to look at how the Court depicts the federation in the *Secession Reference*. How federation is depicted is important. It signals the Court's understanding of the system that drives the outcome, while also playing an important role in legitimizing (or delegitimizing) the various federal models.

As previously discussed, the federation is depicted in relation to a number of characteristics, such as the balance and distribution of power, the nature of the constitutional and federal system, the relationship between the orders of government, the nature of central institutions, and the national composition of the state. These different characteristics represent "points of conflict" for the subscribers of the various federal models. Each model presents a different perspective on the actual and ideal nature of the federation through these points. Accordingly, how the Court depicts the federation in relation to these criteria is indicative of the extent to which it either imposes a particular federal model or recognizes the legitimacy of multiple models and the system as the process and outcome of negotiation.

In the *Secession Reference*, we see the Court depict the federation in a way that recognizes the legitimacy of multiple models and the system as the process and outcome of negotiation in two related ways. First, it provides a *balanced depiction* of the federation. Second, it *explicitly* highlights that the federation is a dynamic process of negotiation.

With regard to the first approach, the Court's depiction of the federation is balanced to the extent it highlights how aspects of each of the three main federal models find support in the institutional and political structures of the federation.[17]

For example, the pan-Canadian model finds support in the Court's presentation of the nature of the federation and the role of the central government: "Canada as a whole is ... a democratic community in which citizens construct and achieve goals on a national scale through a federal government."[18] This point is accentuated by the Court's depiction of the constitution as an overlapping consensus that "was an act of nation-building."[19] In line with this view, Canada operates on the

17 Schertzer (2008: 114–15).

18 *Secession Reference* [1998] at 66.

19 *Secession Reference* at 43.

premise of "constitutional supremacy"[20] and "the *basic structure of our Constitution* ... contemplates the existence of certain political institutions, including freely elected legislative bodies at the federal and provincial level."[21] The combination of statements here places the federation and the constitution above politics – as a consensus that takes place among one nation, which gives rise to the different orders of government, an understanding of the constitutional and federal system that closely aligns with the trimming approach and pan-Canadian model.

At the same time, the Court's depiction of the federal and constitutional system recognizes the legitimacy of the provincial-equality model. While reflecting on the principle of federalism, the SCC consistently discusses the provinces as a block and as one of two orders of government, implying equality among them and with the central government.[22] Also, the idea of the federation as a compact among equal provinces is a strong undercurrent of the decision. The Court argues that without a federal system "neither the agreement of the delegates from Canada East nor that of the delegates from the maritime colonies could have been obtained."[23] The point of the federation, in this view, is thus not to "weld the Provinces into one, nor to subordinate Provincial Governments to a central authority, but to establish a central government in which these Provinces should be represented, entrusted with exclusive authority only in affairs in which they had a common interest. Subject to this each Province was to retain its independence and autonomy and to be directly under the Crown as its head."[24] It is clear here that the Court elaborates upon an understanding of the federal and constitutional system that recognizes that the provinces have considerable autonomy as equal jurisdictions to pursue their own and collective self-interests (and thus draws from and reinforces that view that the federation is about facilitating the trading of interests).

There is also considerable support for an understanding of the federation and constitution in line with the multinational model. The

---

20 *Secession Reference* at 72.

21 *Secession Reference* at 62 (emphasis added).

22 See *Secession Reference* at 55–60; for example, at 56 the Court says: "In a federal system of government such as ours, political power is shared by two orders of government: the federal government on the one hand, and the provinces on the other. Each is assigned respective spheres of jurisdiction by the *Constitution Act, 1867*."

23 *Secession Reference* at 37.

24 *Secession Reference* at 58, citing *Re the Initiative and Referendum Act*, [1919] A.C. 935 [P.C.] at 942.

Court clearly states that the federation "facilitates the pursuit of collective goals by *cultural and linguistic minorities* which form the majority within a particular province. This is the case in Québec, where the majority of the population is French-speaking, and which possesses a *distinct culture*."[25] Despite the above comments on the nature of the federation as a compact among equal provinces, the SCC also says that "the social and demographic reality of Québec explains the existence of the province of Québec as a political unit and indeed, was one of the essential reasons for establishing a federal structure for the Canadian union in 1867."[26] The federal system, in this view, is "a legal response to the underlying political and cultural realities that existed at Confederation and continue to exist today."[27] The adoption of "constitutional supremacy" cited above,[28] when combined with comments saying the constitution is a tool to protect national minorities,[29] thus also sustains a view of the federal and constitutional system as a framework segregating various nations in line with the multinational model.

These seemingly irreconcilable positions are not the product of faulty logic or incoherent reasoning; rather, when the decision is read carefully it is clear that support for one model is qualified in turn by important aspects from a competing model. For example, when weight is given to the idea of Canada as a mere quasi-federation (in line with a centralist pan-Canadian view) it is qualified by noting the importance of provincial autonomy and the federation as a compact among provinces; this view is then further qualified by highlighting that provincial autonomy is used to protect distinct cultural groups, their existence being the driving force behind confederation.[30] The balancing of perspectives is indicative of the respect the SCC affords to the complexity of the issues at hand and its task of interpreting the constitution in the face of competing perspectives on it and the federation.[31] The apparent support for each model is thus easier to grasp: it is about rejecting a singular perspective and seeking to embrace the complexity of the way the constitution and the federation are understood by key actors.[32]

25 *Secession Reference* at 59 (emphasis added).

26 *Secession Reference* at 59.

27 *Secession Reference* at 43.

28 *Secession Reference* at 72.

29 *Secession Reference* at 79–82.

30 See *Secession Reference* at 55–60.

31 *Secession Reference* at 1; Gaudreault-DesBiens (1999: 794–5); Des Rosiers (2000: 182–3).

32 See Gaudreault-DesBiens (1999: 794–5).

The Court's recognition of the complexity of the issues and of the federal and constitutional system plays into the second way it depicts the federation as the process and outcome of negotiation.

We see the Court presenting such a view of the federation in the identification, definition, and discussion of the relationship between the four unwritten principles at the heart of the decision (federalism, democracy, constitutionalism and the rule of law, and minority rights).[33] The Court clearly provides the purpose of the four unwritten principles: they are a vital part of the "global system of rules and principles which govern the exercise of constitutional authority" in Canada; they act as the architecture of the constitution, addressing gaps and abeyances in the text, and thereby providing the basic normative system as the "fundamental and organizing principles of the Constitution."[34] The principles are seen to emerge from political conflict over the federation and constitution, which produce patterns of adherence[35] – conflict that has pushed the governing institutions (like the federal system) to adapt to changing social and political values.[36] In other words, we can see the Court accepting that the normative system of the federation is brought about through the custom and process of actors who hold competing understandings of Canada reaching agreements (and continuing to disagree). Accordingly, the principles carry a normative force: they *may* give rise to substantive legal obligations and bind the actions of individuals, governments, and courts.[37] They are also necessarily enforced in the legal, political, and social forums[38] – something that helps to show how the constitution and the federation is conceived in this case as an intersubjective normative process.[39]

The Court's view of the federation as the process and outcome of negotiation rests largely on the link it provides between democracy and

33 Much has been written about the use of unwritten principles in the *Secession Reference*, both favourable and critical. For an overview see Hogg (2009: 418–23); Leclair (2002); McLachlin (2006). My focus here attempts to go beyond narrower legal debate to engage with wider issues of constitutional and federal theory, as have a few notable pieces such as Tully (2000a); Choudhry and Howse (2000); Choudhry (2008b); Tierney (2003, 2009).

34 *Secession Reference* at 32, 49–52.

35 *Secession Reference* at 48.

36 *Secession Reference* at 33.

37 *Secession Reference* at 54, 71–2; Walters (1999: 385)

38 See *Secession Reference* at 54, 98–103; Walters (1999: 389–90)

39 *Secession Reference* at 52, 58, 68, 88, 150; (Tully 2000a).

federation, with the federation facilitating democracy and vice versa.[40] In presenting democracy as a continual process of discussion, compromise, and negotiation among actors holding competing perspectives, it also presents the federation in the same light.[41] The federal system in this view is not static – it is not a straitjacket – but, rather, is a process and outcome of contestation, and it is legitimate to the extent that it remains a democratic system of continual deliberation.[42] It is in the relationship between democracy and the federation, then, that the Court can coherently see the federal system as incorporating the competing federal models (viewed as contingent perspectives, with the federation representing the process and outcome of contestation between the subscribers of these contingent perspectives).[43]

To say these models are contingent does not mean they lack legitimacy. It is just that the interaction between the federation, democracy, and constitutionalism gives rise to the view of them as contingent, while showing that the federation is the process and outcome of mediating the tension between these contingent views.[44] This point, taken in conjunction with the Court's presentation of the genealogy and purpose of the principles, is further evidenced by the Court's opinion that the principles are interdependent and so no one can trump the others.[45] This is an important aspect of the decision, because each principle is privileged by different constituencies in this case (and within the federal models). Accordingly, to ensure that the constitution and federation remain legitimate, no particular principle can be privileged.[46]

---

40 *Secession Reference* at 58–9, 65, 66, 74–6; Schertzer (2008: 115).

41 See *Secession Reference* at 68.

42 See *Secession Reference* at 68, 150; Tully (2000a: 21–31); Schertzer (2008: 115–16). For a discussion of the link between federalism and democracy in the more general sense, see Hueglin (2013).

43 On the Court seeing the competing federal models, or narratives, as contingent, see Gaudreault-DesBiens (1999: 836); *Secession Reference* at 66.

44 *Secession Reference* at 75–8, and particularly at 66, where the Court says that "the relationship between democracy and federalism means, for example, that in Canada there may be different and equally legitimate majorities in different provinces and territories and at the federal level. No one majority is more or less 'legitimate' than the others as an expression of democratic opinion." It goes on to say (at 68) that "at both the federal and provincial level, by its very nature, the need to build majorities necessitates compromise, negotiation, and deliberation. No one has a monopoly on truth."

45 *Secession Reference* at 49.

46 On the reference as a battle between democracy (as Québec's interest) vs. constitutionalism (as Canada's interest), see Tierney (2003: 178); McRoberts (1999).

This view of the federation, and the reconciliation of competing perspectives, is also closely linked to the Court's understanding of the national character of Canada. In the reference, it is clear that the Court recognizes the plurinational character of the state. Just as the competing perspectives are all legitimate, so too is their basis in differing self-selected identities.[47] In other words, each conception put forth by the competing federal models (i.e., Canada as uninational or multinational) is legitimate, and in this way Canada is plurinational. As the SCC states: "[I]n Canada there may be different and equally legitimate majorities in different provinces and territories and at the federal level ... [T]he function of federalism is to enable citizens to participate concurrently in different collectivities and to pursue goals at both a provincial and a federal level."[48] So, a picture of the state as comprising various sets of key political actors is painted, with each holding their own contingent perspectives on nationality and the federation.[49]

Given the seemingly strong support in the decision for a depiction of Canada as a *multinational* (rather than plurinational) state,[50] and the implications such a view would have for my reading of the *Secession Reference*, it is prudent to briefly address this interpretation of the decision. Interpreting the decision as supporting a multinational depiction of Canada rests on the Court's presentation of Québec as a distinct culture[51] and the possibility that the Québécois even form a people.[52] What matters, though, is not the presence of this support for the multinational model, but *how it is placed relative to competing conceptions of nationality* in line with the other federal models. Since Canada is plurinational, and the understanding of Canada as multinational is one of the key perspectives on nationality, the recognition of this view in the reference is understandable.

The point, then, is that the Court does not only afford the multinational understanding of Canada validity. It recognizes the plurinational character of Canada in the relationship it sees between the competing conceptions of nationality. As shown above, the Court balances each perspective and model off one another and shows how each is

47 *Secession Reference* at 66, 68, 75–8.

48 *Secession Reference* at 66.

49 See *Secession Reference* at 92, 98, 100, 101, 110, 153; Joffe (1999); Walters (1999: 379).

50 For examples of analysis along these lines, see Walters (1999: 381); Turp (1999); Joffe (1999); Tierney (2003).

51 *Secession Reference* at 59.

52 *Secession Reference* at 125.

represented in the federal and constitutional system. Thus, despite the support for the multinational model, acceptance of plurinationality helps to explain the Court's avoidance of the controversial term "dualism" and reluctance to declare the Québécois "a people" under international law.[53] In other words, the Court does recognize a multinational Canada, but it identifies this *as one of the many views on nationality* that exist in Canada. The result is that the *Secession Reference* forces both the Québécois and the rest of Canada to question the validity of their particular national narratives as natural, universal, and true.[54]

Thinking about the overall depiction of the federation in the reference shows us how the Court draws from and reinforces elements of each of the three main federal models. This balanced depiction is coherent because the Court also explicitly presents the federation as the process and outcome of negotiation between the subscribers of these legitimate federal models. The *Secession Reference* thus rejects an imposing depiction of the federation, instead putting forth an understanding of the system as a dynamic and free association of non-domination.

Use of Legal Argument

This section looks at how accepted forms of legal argument are used in the reference to reinforce the validity of how the federation is depicted in the decision.[55] As explained in chapter 3, one of the central ways the Court legitimizes its depiction of the federal system is to employ

53 See Ryan (2000) on the absence of the term.

54 Gaudreault-DesBiens (1999: 837–8).

55 As noted above, the Court's approach to constitutional interpretation in the *Secession Reference* has been the focus of significant analysis, with most arguing the reliance on unwritten principles is a departure from a more positivist approach towards a more progressive approach; see Choudhry and Howse (2000: 154–7); Choudhry (2008b: 216–18); Tierney (2003: 182); Leclair (1999, 2003: 449); Walters (1999: 384); Gaudreault-DesBiens (1999: 825). Not everyone welcomes this turn; see Hogg (1999: 2–3; 2007: 73–4, 90–3). Despite the correct assessment that the decision was a remarkable example of anti-positivism (in particular, the understanding of the constitution and federation as a contested normative system), there were aspects of positivism that should not be overlooked. For example, the Court relied on a positivist approach to buttress the primary legal opinion that secession (via unilateral amendment to the constitution) by a province is illegal; it also employed a decidedly positivist approach in interpreting and applying international law in the decision, with international statutes having pride of place; see *Secession Reference* at 84, 109–39; Walters (1999: 376).

the various constitutional modalities to present its perspective as the law. In this way, when it imposes a particular model or recognizes the legitimacy of multiple models, the Court says that this understanding simply reflects the nature of the federation as dictated by the framers' intent or the text of the constitution or legal doctrine, and so on.

In the *Secession Reference* each of the seven modalities of constitutional interpretation discussed in chapter 3 (historical, textual, doctrinal, structural, prudential, ethical, and progressive) is employed to support the depiction of the federation. Among these modes of interpretation, the structural, doctrinal, and textual approaches are used most prominently. Moreover, the Court even explicitly says it uses the doctrinal, textual, and historical approaches to interpret the (unwritten aspects of the) constitution in the decision.[56] However, it is not so much the use of particular approaches (or their frequency) that is important for my purpose. As previously argued (and demonstrated below), any modality of interpretation can be shifted to support a particular depiction of the federation. What is really important, then, is *how* these modalities are employed to reinforce the nature of the federation. Looking at this aspect of the decision helps us better understand the way imposing or recognizing depictions (and the related decision outcomes) are validated, and thus how decisions can affect the legitimacy of the federation.

In the *Secession Reference*, legal argument is used to reinforce the federal depiction in two related ways. First, constitutional modalities are employed to reinforce the legitimacy of each of the three federal models. Second, accepted forms of legal argument are used to reinforce the legitimacy of the system as the process and outcome of negotiation between the subscribers of these legitimate federal models.

With regard to the first approach, we see the Court explicitly reinforcing the pan-Canadian model, for example, by saying the federation is a centralized system representing a pan-state nation *because* "the vision of those who brought about Confederation was to create a unified country, not a loose alliance of autonomous provinces."[57] In addition to this historical support for the pan-Canadian model, we also see the Court say that the text of the constitution reinforces the validity of this model: "[O]n paper, the federal government retained sweeping powers which threatened to undermine the autonomy of the provinces."[58]

56 *Secession Reference* at 32; see also (Tully 2000a: 11–12).
57 *Secession Reference* at 96.
58 *Secession Reference* at 55.

At the same time, we see the Court qualifying this support for the pan-Canadian model by saying, in the same paragraph, that the constitutional structure of Canada as a federation protects provincial autonomy and has led to the central government's sweeping powers (like the ability to disallow provincial legislation) falling into disuse.[59] This support for the provincial-equality model through the structural modality is also employed to present the federation as a decentralized system.[60] And, citing relevant precedent to support its view, the Court says it is a system that came about through a compact between equal provinces.[61]

Yet, we also see the Court resorting to the intentions of the drafters to paint the federation as something more than an association between equal territorial units. Following a lengthy citation of one of the key framers (George-Étienne Cartier), the Court summarizes his intentions as supporting the view that "the federal-provincial division of powers was a legal recognition of the diversity that existed among the initial members of Confederation, and manifested a concern to accommodate that diversity within a single nation by granting significant powers to provincial governments."[62] This clear support for the multinational

59 See *Secession Reference* at 55: "Our political and constitutional practice has adhered to an underlying principle of federalism, and has interpreted the written provisions of the Constitution in this light. For example, although the federal power of disallowance was included in the *Constitution Act, 1867*, the underlying principle of federalism triumphed early. Many constitutional scholars contend that the federal power of disallowance has been abandoned."

60 See *Secession Reference* at 58: "The principle of federalism recognizes the diversity of the component parts of Confederation, and the autonomy of provincial governments to develop their societies within their respective spheres of jurisdiction. The federal structure of our country also facilitates democratic participation by distributing power to the government thought to be most suited to achieving the particular societal objective having regard to this diversity."

61 See *Secession Reference* at 58: "The scheme of the *Constitution Act, 1867*, it was said in *Re the Initiative and Referendum Act*, [1919] A.C. 935 (P.C.), at p. 942, was not to weld the Provinces into one, nor to subordinate Provincial Governments to a central authority, but to establish a central government in which these Provinces should be represented, entrusted with exclusive authority only in affairs in which they had a common interest. Subject to this each Province was to retain its independence and autonomy and to be directly under the Crown as its head." The Court goes on to cite two additional cases in this paragraph to support this view.

62 *Secession Reference* at 43. The Court also (at 82) resorts to the historical approach (in conjunction with the doctrinal modality) to say that it was the intent of the framers of the Constitution Act, 1982 to protect the rights of Aboriginal peoples with section 35 (a view that reinforces the purpose of the federation in line with the multinational model).

model's understanding of the federation as a compact between founding nations is further buttressed by the Court highlighting that the very structure of the federation supports a view of Québec as a nationally based province.[63] Moreover, the multinational model's support for asymmetry between provinces is reinforced by saying that the structure of the federation allows provinces "to develop their societies" and that doctrine supports the view that "differences between provinces 'are a rational part of the political reality in the federal process.'"[64]

This reasoning demonstrates one of the ways the Court can coherently balance the competing federal models in its depiction of the federal system. Through the various interpretive approaches, the Court finds support for each model in the constitutional law. And, this activity of anchoring each federal model in the constitutional law illuminates something about the models and the interpretative approaches themselves. With regard to the federal models, it shows that the Court can see the validity of each perspective. By using the various modes of analysis the Court highlights how each federal model finds expression in Canada's constitution. With regard to the forms of legal analysis, the use of the various forms in this reference shows how a modality can be shifted to support any model. In the decision the historical approach was used to present the framers' intent as creating a centralized, unified federation *and* one that devolves considerable autonomy to minority nations to protect their diversity. We also see how the structure of the federation supports both an understanding of the federation as a compact between equal, territorial provinces *and* a compact between founding nations where provinces can represent national groups and exercise their authority in an asymmetrical manner. The other side of this ability to use forms of legal argument to validate the different federal models is that we need to closely scrutinize decisions where the Court imposes a particular federal model by saying the constitutional law (interpreted through a particular modality) dictates a particular understanding of the federation and an associated outcome.

---

63 See *Secession Reference* at 59: "The principle of federalism facilitates the pursuit of collective goals by cultural and linguistic minorities which form the majority within a particular province. This is the case in Québec, where the majority of the population is French-speaking, and which possesses a distinct culture. This is not merely the result of chance. The social and demographic reality of Québec explains the existence of the province of Québec as a political unit and indeed, was one of the essential reasons for establishing a federal structure for the Canadian union in 1867."

64 *Secession Reference* at 58.

With regard to the second way legal argument is used to explicitly reinforce the dynamic depiction of the federation, we see this happening with the Court highlighting that the "federal principle, inherent in the structure of [Canada's] constitutional arrangements" translates into the view that "federalism is a political and legal response to underlying social and political realities."[65] In other words, the very structure of the federation reinforces a view of the system as the outcome of negotiation and conflict about how "social and political realities" are represented. Even more explicitly, the Court links the structure of the constitutional order as a democracy and a federation to relevant doctrine to say that the system "necessitates compromise, negotiation, and deliberation."[66] The Court goes on to anchor this view of the federation in the text of the constitution: "The *Constitution Act, 1982* gives expression to this principle, by conferring a right to initiate constitutional change on each participant in Confederation."[67]

This last line also indicates how the Court employs modalities to reinforce and justify a decision outcome. The Court's ruling that there is a duty to negotiate with a party that initiates a constitutional amendment proposal, which as I discuss in a moment reinforces the dynamic model, is reached in part by noting this is mandated by the text of the constitution.[68] At the same time, the finding of a duty to negotiate is clearly justified by the Court through prudential reasoning:

> For both theoretical *and practical reasons* ... we hold that Quebec could not purport to invoke a right of self-determination such as to dictate the terms of a proposed secession to the other parties: that would not be a negotiation at all. As well, it would be naive to expect that the substantive goal of secession could readily be distinguished from the practical details of secession. The devil would be in the details ... No negotiations could be

65 *Secession Reference* at 56–7.

66 *Secession Reference* at 68.

67 *Secession Reference* at 69. The Court is referring here to s. 46(1) of the Constitution Act, 1982, which allows both the central and provincial governments to initiate negotiations over a constitutional amendment.

68 See *Secession Reference* at 69: "The *Constitution Act, 1982* gives expression to this principle, by conferring a right to initiate constitutional change on each participant in Confederation. In our view, the existence of this right imposes a corresponding duty on the participants in Confederation to engage in constitutional discussions in order to acknowledge and address democratic expressions of a desire for change in other provinces."

> effective if their ultimate outcome, secession, is cast as an absolute legal entitlement based upon an obligation to give effect to that act of secession in the Constitution. Such a foregone conclusion would actually undermine the obligation to negotiate and render it hollow.[69]

The decision outcome is clearly reached through a consideration of what is wise policy.[70]

We can thus also see how the various constitutional modalities are employed to reinforce the dynamic federal model. These examples show how the Court can move past the confines of the three federal models and towards a more inclusive understanding of the association. In other words, the accepted forms of constitutional interpretation are used in the *Secession Reference* to reinforce an understanding of the federation as the process and outcome of negotiation *as constitutional law.*

Outcome

I turn now to focus on the outcome of the case, which is an important aspect of the decision recognizing and reinforcing the legitimacy of the federation as the process and outcome of negotiation between the subscribers of legitimate federal models. The outcome of any federal case is important because it has practical, material, and political effects. The Court's judgment influences the distribution of power and resources, a party's standing in the federation, and the development of the association more generally. Of course, the depiction of the federation and the outcome are linked: how the constitutional and federal system is understood drives the way the Court goes about disposing of the appeal. Moreover, it is the combination of the two components of a decision that allow us to understand the overall extent to which it imposes a particular federal model, or not.

As explained previously, I analyse two elements of a decision outcome: who wins the case and how they win; and its effect on the

69 *Secession Reference* at 91 (emphasis added).

70 At the same time, there is a need to divorce this aspect of reaching the decision (its prudential element) from a view that sees the *entire* judgment as an act of prudential reasoning. While prudential considerations clearly inform the Court's overall approach (a line of analysis that is clearly identifiable in the literature; see Schertzer 2008: 118–19; Choudhry and Howse 2000: 164–8; Hogg 2007: 96–100; Rocher and Verrelli 2003: 211; Tierney 2003: 174–5, 196), this should not obscure the fact that the Court makes its decision (in the main) through other forms of constitutional interpretation.

federation more generally and the extent it reinforces any particular federal model. In the *Secession Reference,* these two elements display remarkable adherence to the ideal-type of a decision that seeks to generate legitimacy for the conflict-management process and the federation more generally by reinforcing it as the process and outcome of negotiation between the subscribers of legitimate perspectives.

As the above implies, the *Secession Reference* is a complex case that deals with many issues. Accordingly, there are a number of outcomes that stem from the decision. I have already indicated what the main ones are, but it is worth summarizing the four key outcomes again for clarity.[71] First is the opinion that it is technically illegal for Québec to unilaterally secede.[72] Second is the constitutional duty placed on both orders of government to negotiate, in good faith, with a government that wants to amend the constitution (i.e., secede).[73] Third is the declaration that any referenda initiating negotiations related to secession needs to have a clear question, with a clear result.[74] Fourth is the opinion that international law does not sanction Québec's unilateral secession.[75] When speaking about the reference, it is thus proper to talk of its outcome as the sum of these four points. Focusing on only one of them fails to comprehend the approach the Court took to arbitrating the dispute.

Looking at these four points in tandem allows us to see that the Court handed each jurisdiction a positive outcome, while mitigating negative outcomes. For example, deciding it is illegal for a province to unilaterally secede (under either Canadian or international law) is clearly a positive outcome for the central government, as is the ruling that only a clear reference question with a clear majority can trigger secession negotiations. These outcomes meet the objectives of the central government going into the case: to erect roadblocks for the secessionist movement.[76] At the same time, the ruling that there is a constitutional duty to negotiate *in good faith* with a province seeking to secede also hands Québec

71 In addition to these four outcomes there is also the ruling that the Court has jurisdiction to hear the case and that the questions are justiciable, which is discussed in the next section.

72 See *Secession Reference* at 104, 106–7, 149.

73 See *Secession Reference* at 84, 88, 90–2, 96, 150.

74 See *Secession Reference* at 87, 100, 148.

75 See *Secession Reference* at 111, 130, 137, 154.

76 On how the central government employed the roadblock of the clarity mandate via the Clarity Act, see Rocher and Verrelli (2003).

a significantly positive outcome. This aspect of the opinion lends the secessionist movement legitimacy, pushing the other parties in the federation to recognize the validity of Québec's position in the face of a positive vote to secede (rather than simply being intransigent). The legitimacy the Court affords Québec's position in this regard also helps to mitigate the negative outcome for it in the form of the illegality of unilateral secession and the clarity mandate (i.e., while Québec cannot unilaterally secede, if its people declare they want to leave the federation, the other members of the system have to work to make that a reality in good faith). Moreover, the Court mitigates the negative aspects of the ruling for Québec by saying that, while *not granting legality* to the process, ultimately, the determinative element of any secession is if it is effective on a practical and political level.[77] In addition, Aboriginal groups are handed a positive in the ruling for a duty to negotiate, with the Court clearly saying that their interests need to be represented and accounted for in any negotiations that affect their lands and rights.[78] Similarly, all other provinces also receive a positive element in the decision with the ruling that one of them alone could not legally alter or destroy the federal system and with the implication that any negotiations over secession would have all provinces represented at the table.[79]

---

77 See *Secession Reference* at 106: "Although under the Constitution there is no right to pursue secession unilaterally, that is secession without principled negotiation, this does not rule out the possibility of an unconstitutional declaration of secession leading to a *de facto* secession. The ultimate success of such a secession would be dependent on effective control of a territory and recognition by the international community."

78 See *Secession Reference* at 139: "[A] clear democratic expression of support for secession would lead under the Constitution to negotiations in which aboriginal interests would be taken into account." On this aspect of the decision, see Joffe (1999); Tierney (2003: 181–2, 188–9).

79 The Court seems to take for granted that the provinces would participate in the negotiations, though it does remain somewhat ambiguous on the point; see *Secession Reference* at 88: "The clear repudiation by the people of Quebec of the existing constitutional system would confer legitimacy on demands for secession, and place an obligation *on the other provinces* and the federal government to acknowledge and respect that expression of democratic will *by entering into negotiations*." See also at 90: "One of those propositions is that there would be a *legal obligation on the other provinces* and federal government to accede to the secession of a province, *subject only to negotiation of the logistical details of secession*" and (at 92) "Negotiations would be necessary to address the interests of the federal government, of Quebec *and the other provinces*, and other participants, as well as the rights of all Canadians both within and outside Quebec" (emphasis added).

These outcomes also clearly have broader effects that reinforce the legitimacy of each of the main federal models. The ruling that under international law a sub-state unit cannot secede (and that Québec is not technically "a people" under international law) reinforces the superiority of the central government and a view of the provinces as subordinate territorial units in line with the pan-Canadian model. At the same time, giving all provinces a seat at the table in any negotiations over secession reinforces their status as equals in line with the provincial-equality model. Finally, ruling that there is a duty to negotiate with Québec, and the inclusion of Aboriginal interests in the process, reinforces a view of the federation as comprising and protecting national minorities.

What we see in the sum of the reference's outcomes, then, is a concerted effort by the Court to balance positives and negatives off one another for each jurisdiction and for the supporters of the various federal models. In other words, the Court rejects a zero-sum approach to managing the dispute. Each jurisdiction can point to a positive outcome, while the negative outcomes are also generally mitigated in some way. At the same time, the sum of the outcomes indicates how the federal system has developed, and will continue to develop, in a way that reflects elements of each federal model. The decision thus generates legitimacy for each model, while highlighting that there is a place for its subscribers in the federation by showing that the system has developed, and will continue to develop, in line with their perspective.

Now, equally important is how the outcomes also explicitly reinforce the legitimacy of the federation as the process and outcome of negotiation. I focus here on the elements of the decision related to the duty to negotiate, discussing the other elements in the next section (as they tell us a great deal about the Court's adopted role in the reference). The opinion that there is a duty upon all parties to negotiate in good faith if Québec expresses a clear desire to secede reinforces three key elements of the dynamic federal model.

First, it reinforces that the federation is – and its legitimacy rests upon – a process of negotiation. In other words, it reinforces that the constitution is not, and cannot be, a "straitjacket."[80] The decision solidifies the idea that the principles underpinning the constitution mandate that the federal system be a process that responds to conflicts over the system

80 *Secession Reference* at 150.

through dialogue and negotiation between those in conflict.[81] The perceived necessity of negotiation rests on the recognition that there are a number of key social actors that hold competing perspectives on what Canada is and ought to be.[82] Highlighting this contested nature of the federation forces both the Québécois and the rest of Canada to question the validity of their particular national narratives as natural, universal, and true.[83]

Second, the outcome reinforces an equality of status between the subscribers of the various federal models. Mandating that the duty to negotiate falls upon all within the federation (that each jurisdiction and their interests must be involved in the process of negotiation and that the position of Québec with regard to its place in the association and its right to leave it is valid) reinforces both the self-perceived status of each group and the validity of its perspective. Moreover, holding that negotiations must be conducted in good faith – that they must be free and fair – buttresses the point that no one perspective can trump the others (i.e., that each model and perspective is legitimate).

Finally, by highlighting that negotiations will be difficult and disagreement is a reasonable part of the process,[84] the Court reinforces the federal system as a continual process. This aspect of the outcome strengthens the view that the federation cannot solve conflict, but rather must work to manage it over time. It helps to establish that conflict over the system and the process of dealing with it is indeterminate.

Role of the Court

The Court's self-selected role in the *Secession Reference* is an integral part of the decision recognizing and reinforcing the federation as the process and outcome of negotiation between the subscribers of legitimate

81 See *Secession Reference* at 88: "The federalism principle, in conjunction with the democratic principle, dictates that the clear repudiation of the existing constitutional order and the clear expression of the desire to pursue secession by the population of a province would give rise to a reciprocal obligation on all parties to Confederation to negotiate constitutional changes to respond to that desire."

82 See *Secession Reference* at 66, and the analysis of this component of the decision above.

83 Gaudreault-DesBiens (1999: 837–8).

84 See *Secession Reference* at 96–7, for example: "No one can predict the course that such negotiations might take. The possibility that they might not lead to an agreement amongst the parties must be recognized."

federal models. As argued earlier, there is a link between a court's understanding of the constitutional and federal system and the role it adopts. Accordingly, there are links between the umpire, branch of government, and guardian roles and the pan-Canadian, provincial-equality, and multinational models, respectively. In the *Secession Reference*, we see the Court generally eschew these roles and adopt one of an explicit facilitator and also fair arbiter. In this way, the Court both draws from and reinforces an understanding of the federation as the process and outcome of negotiation through its adopted role of a broad facilitator of this negotiation.[85] The adopted role of facilitator is particularly evident in two areas of the reference: the determination of the referred questions as justiciable and the rulings related to clarity and a duty to negotiate.

With regard to the determination of the referred questions as justiciable, the Court explicitly links its ruling to its self-perceived "proper role" as facilitator.[86] The SCC was clear that its proper role is only to identify and consider the legal aspects of the global system of rules and principles that comprise the constitution.[87] Accordingly, the Court established itself as a facilitator of the democratic process by clarifying the legal framework within which democratic will manifests.[88] This role is quite different from the other roles the Court could have adopted as federal arbiter: it did not seek to uphold and implement the framework as a neutral umpire; nor did it act as an equal branch of government and simply dictate the rules of the game to the other branches; nor did it only seek to protect the framework from adaptation by the political

85 The facilitator role of the SCC in the *Secession Reference* has been noted by others, see Des Rosiers (2000: 173, 182); Choudhry and Howse (2000: 157–64).

86 See *Secession Reference* at 24–31 and particularly at 27, where the Court says: "As to the 'proper role' of the Court, it is important to underline, contrary to the submission of the *amicus curiae*, that the questions posed in this Reference do not ask the Court to usurp any democratic decision that the people of Quebec may be called upon to make. The questions posed by the Governor in Council, as we interpret them, are strictly limited to aspects of the legal framework in which that democratic decision is to be taken."

87 The Court says (at 27 and 32) that the constitution "includes the global system of rules and principles which govern the exercise of constitutional authority," going on to say (at 100) that "the role of the Court in this Reference is limited to the identification of the relevant aspects of the Constitution in their broadest sense. We have interpreted the questions as relating to the constitutional framework within which political decisions may ultimately be made."

88 See *Secession Reference* at 27, 100.

actors. Instead, the Court, in line with its view of the constitution as a normative framework, sought to facilitate discussion and negotiation over the framework itself (while also managing the conflict).[89]

The adopted role of facilitator is also apparent in the way the Court approached the issue of defining clarity. Notably, the SCC didn't dictate what clarity meant (i.e., that a referendum question on secession had to say "x" and that "x" number of people were required to support that question).[90] It was careful to not impose its own will on the process: "[I]t will be for the political actors to determine what constitutes a clear majority on a clear question."[91] In this way, the need for clarity is presented as an outgrowth of democracy (the lack of ambiguity allowing a clear expression of democratic will) and as something that supports democracy by instigating a reciprocal duty among all parties within Canada to negotiate constitutional change.[92] This approach places the SCC as the facilitator of a legitimate and free process of contestation over the federation and the constitution, rather than as an imposer of a particular perspective.[93] The ambiguity and deference that allows the political actors to define what "clarity" entails has unquestionably resulted in debate and political contestation;[94] but, arguably, the SCC imposing a particular definition of clarity, or leaving the entire issue of what instigates the duty to negotiate untouched, would have caused greater controversy.[95]

The function of facilitator, and the way it draws from and reinforces a view of the federation as the process and outcome of negotiation, is even more evident in the Court's identification of a reciprocal duty to negotiate in the event of a positive referendum on secession. The

89 It is from this view of the constitution, and its role within it, that the Court laid out a three-tier approach to justiciability: the first is (written) law enforced by the courts; the second is (unwritten) legal principle, which *is* enforced in the political and social realm and *may* also be enforced in the legal realm; and the third is constitutional convention, which is *only* enforced in the political and social realms; see *Secession Reference* at 54, 98, 102; Walters (1999: 389).

90 See *Secession Reference* at 87–8.

91 *Secession Reference* at 153, 100.

92 See *Secession Reference* at 87–8, 153.

93 Des Rosiers (2000: 173, 182).

94 See Rocher and Verrelli (2003).

95 Surely more contention would have resulted by allowing Québec to claim the decision was illegitimate if too harsh a level of clarity was defined by the Court, or by allowing the federal government to reject the decision as illegitimate if the issue was not broached or too lenient a standard was identified as instigating the duty to negotiate secession.

constitutional obligation on the members of the federation to enter into good faith negotiations over secession emanates from all four of the unwritten principles.[96] The Court clearly says that its role is limited to identifying the duty to negotiate in good faith stemming from these principles.[97] The conduct of parties in negotiations, the ability to reconcile their positions to reach an outcome, and any sanctions for perceived breaches of conduct in negotiations are matters for the political actors.[98] At the same time, the Court does not eschew its important role as a fair arbiter within the federation if negotiations were to break down. It still maintains the constitutional framework gives rise to *legal* obligations, with *legal* repercussions enforceable through the judiciary, if necessary.[99] The facilitator role similarly runs through the SCC's treatment of the parties to the negotiation: the Court is sufficiently vague on who is constitutionally guaranteed a spot at the table[100] and shows restraint when prescribing what amending formula would apply to implement a change to the constitution stemming from secession negotiations.[101]

---

96 See *Secession Reference* at 90: "The conduct of the parties in such negotiations would be governed by the same constitutional principles which give rise to the duty to negotiate: federalism, democracy, constitutionalism and the rule of law, and the protection of minorities."

97 In addition to the above, see *Secession Reference* at 100: "We have interpreted the questions as relating to the constitutional framework within which political decisions may ultimately be made. Within that framework, the workings of the political process are complex and can only be resolved by means of political judgments and evaluations."

98 See *Secession Reference* at 100: "The Court has no supervisory role over the political aspects of constitutional negotiations," and at 101, where it says "[T]o the extent that the questions are political in nature, it is not the role of the judiciary to interpose its own views on the different negotiating positions of the parties, even were it invited to do so. Rather, it is the obligation of the elected representatives to give concrete form to the discharge of their constitutional obligations which only they and their electors can ultimately assess ... Having established the legal framework, it would be for the democratically elected leadership of the various participants to resolve their differences."

99 See *Secession Reference* at 102: "The non-justiciability of political issues that lack a legal component does not deprive the surrounding constitutional framework of its binding status, nor does this mean that constitutional obligations could be breached without incurring serious legal repercussions. Where there are legal rights there are remedies"; see also at 105.

100 See *Secession Reference* at 88, 92–3, 103, 139, 151–2; Choudhry (2008b: 217).

101 By not explicitly elaborating a required amending formula the SCC avoids imposing the related particular federal model, while also avoiding issues associated with trying to legitimize that model in a case that is all about the divergence and competition between various understandings of the federation. On the vagueness, see *Secession Reference* at 84; Choudhry (2008b: 227); Gaudreault-DesBiens (1999: 825); Hogg (1999).

The discussion above indicates more than just the Court's self-selected role in the reference (important as this is in its own right). Establishing the links between the Court's adopted role, its understanding of the constitutional and federal system, and the way it disposes of the appeal shows how the SCC draws from and reinforces a view of the federation as the process of negotiation, with it being a key facilitator of this negotiation. In other words, the adopted facilitator role is indicative of how the Court is following a broader approach to manage conflict (not seeking to resolve it) in the decision. The Court's clear goal in the reference is to push the management of the conflict back into the political realm (while facilitating the conditions for free and fair negotiations). It does not impose a particular vision of the federation or a final solution to the problem; rather, it sees the process of contestation in the political sphere as indeterminate (and ultimately remains open to the possibility that it will have to step in again as a fair arbiter). It is this broad approach that reinforces the idea of the federation as a contested normative framework, particularly because the Court did not simply assert this was its role: it explicitly linked this "proper role" to the very nature and structure of the constitutional and federal system.[102]

I turn now to briefly reflect on this broader conflict-management approach (and understanding of the federal system) in terms of both the possible reason the Court adopted it in the case and its potential implications.

An Approach Focusing on Legitimacy and Conflict Management

The above discussion provides a comprehensive picture of the *Secession Reference* as an exemplar of a decision that recognizes and accounts for the contestation over nationality and the federation in Canada. It depicts the federation in an inclusive manner, with the Court employing accepted forms of legal analysis that demonstrate how the federation reflects aspects of each federal model and as the process and outcome of negotiation. Building on this understanding of the federation, the decision reaches an outcome that rejects a zero-sum approach, while reinforcing the legitimacy of the inclusive depiction. And, running through the overall approach in the decision is the Court's self-selected role as the facilitator of negotiation between conflicting parties,

102 See *Secession Reference* at 98–101.

rather than the imposer of a particular solution. In this way, the reference both draws from, and reinforces, the federation as the process and outcome of negotiation between the subscribers of legitimate models. As a whole, then, the decision provides a benchmark for how the Court can potentially generate legitimacy for the conflict-management process and the system more generally in the way it manages conflict over the federation.

As I have already indicated (and will demonstrate in subsequent chapters), the approach adopted in the *Secession Reference* represents a significant shift in its approach to federal arbitration.[103] It stands in contrast to the proportion of the SCC's federal decisions that impose a federal model (i.e., those decisions that draw from and reinforce a single model in the depiction of the federation and the outcome). The shift in the character of this reference is most evident in the fact that some 64 per cent of the Court's decisions prior to the reference impose a particular federal model, while only 25 per cent of those following it do so. The *Secession Reference* thus marks a noticeable change in the Court's general approach to federalism jurisprudence. Moreover, even among those cases that follow the general approach of the *Secession Reference*, as discussed in chapter 6, this reference stands apart given the extent to which it adheres to the ideal-type.

This disjuncture raises two important questions: Why did the Court adopt such a significantly different approach in this particular case? and, can it then usefully be compared to other cases? On the first question, as mentioned above, the likeliest answer is that the Court was forced to find a way to save the federation in the face of a direct challenge to the legitimacy of the constitutional and federal system. While all federalism jurisprudence involves conflict over the nature of the federation (i.e., over the way identities are recognized and power and resources are distributed), the uniqueness of the *Secession Reference* is the direct and serious nature of the conflict. The case was about a party to the federation challenging the survival of the system. Moreover, the Court battle took place shortly after a near referendum victory for the separatist option. The *Secession Reference*, then, was one of the rare occasions where the entire legal and political system was in flux and in danger of dissolution. In the face of this crisis, the Court was required – as the apex body of the legal system and the ultimate federal arbiter – to

103 For a similar argument about the nature of the reference, see Tully (2000a).

find an innovative way to rescue the legitimacy of the entire political and legal system.[104]

In such situations, it is important to recognize that the "tendency of judges may be to struggle to save the system from collapse."[105] In a case like this, the judges are forced to deal with a direct challenge to the legitimacy of the constitutional order and to their own place within the system. In other words, conflicts like the one in the *Secession Reference* highlight how courts are themselves part of the field of struggle.[106] Accordingly, the SCC fought in the reference to "find a way to ensure that legal continuity, stability and above all legitimacy would be maintained."[107] In this way, the reference is best understood as an explicit attempt to generate and maintain legitimacy for the constitutional and federal system, as well as for its federal arbiter and the way in which it fulfils its role.

This reading of the case complements the largely accepted view that the *Secession Reference* was a classic example of strategic decision making. Vuk Radmilovic argues the decision abides by the four key characteristics of a strategic act focused on reinforcing the legitimacy of the Court within the political system. First, the key outcomes, notably the duty to negotiate, aligned with public opinion inside and outside Québec. Second, the decision avoided pronouncing on controversial matters, such as the meaning of clarity, and so avoided an overt clash with the political actors. Third, the Court adopted a restrained approach. Fourth, the judicial doctrine developed in the decision, notably the need to negotiate, was largely informed by and upheld the political status quo.[108] The sum total of the approach – informed by a view that justices are rational actors – is that the *Secession Reference* allowed the Court to cultivate its own institutional legitimacy and to "strengthen its position as an unbiased arbiter of Quebec-Canada relations."[109] I largely agree with the broader point that the Court in this case, and more generally, is

---

104 This is an argument made by many (though the focus tends to be on the political astuteness of the decision); see Schertzer (2008: 117–19, from which the next two paragraphs are drawn); Choudhry and Howse (2000: 164–8); Hogg (2007: 96–100); Rocher and Verrelli (2003: 211); Tierney (2003: 170–5, 196); Walters (1999).

105 Walters (1999: 371); Hart (1961: 114).

106 Tully (2004: 86).

107 Schertzer (2008: 119).

108 Radmilovic (2010: 857–9).

109 Radmilovic (2010: 865).

informed by a desire to cultivate legitimacy.[110] At the same time, there are elements of this account of the *Secession Reference* and the broader focus on judicial decision making as a strategic enterprise that I take issue with.

Justices are not *only* strategic actors making rational choices designed to increase their position in the political system; the institutional context also structures their decision making. As I noted at the end of chapter 3, judges are influenced by broad normative values and positions on the nature of the constitutional and political association. Accordingly, while elements of the *Secession Reference* certainly support Radmilovic's account – the outcomes did align with popular opinion and it was purposefully ambiguous on points of contention – other aspects show how broader normative values and positions on the nature of the federation influenced the decision. The Court did not simply act as a restrained, neutral umpire; it also sought to actively identify and reinforce the dynamic elements of the federal system and the validity of the competing positions, with the explicit objective of facilitating negotiation to help manage ongoing conflict. In this regard, it also did not maintain the status quo of an irreconcilable impasse; it adopted a rather novel conflict-management approach that helped to reconceive the constitutional and federal association as a process of contestation and negotiation. The decision thus stands as an example of how the Court is focused not only on its own role in the system, but also on the wider political association and how the different conceptions of the federation both influence the Court and need to be accounted for by the justices.

The innovation in this decision, then, comes in *how* the Court sought to maintain and generate legitimacy for itself and the wider polity. Rather than imposing a particular perspective (informed by a trimming, trading, or segregating logic), the Court turned to recognize, account for and manage the conflict that takes place over the federation. Seeing itself as part of the system of government as its federal arbiter, the Court used what it had at hand to save the system: the law. The goal for any government in such a situation is to maintain order and legitimacy. The Court recognized in the case it could not achieve this goal by imposing a particular perspective on those in the association as a "neutral umpire." It saw the benefits of recognizing the legitimacy

110 For a discussion of the more general activity of the SCC and strategic decision making, see Manfredi (2002).

of the various federal models and the federation as the process and outcome of negotiation.

The potential benefits of this more inclusive approach to federalism jurisprudence are exemplified in the *Secession Reference* itself, namely, its ability to generate legitimacy for the conflict-management process and the federation more generally. The inclusive way the federation is depicted in the reference (rather than imposing one party's perspective) demonstrates to the parties that the federal arbiter takes their perspectives into account (thereby addressing any questions of bias). This inclusivity creates "buy-in" to the conflict-management process and the federal system, reinforcing the sense that both reflect each party's perspective of what the federation is and ought to be. Similarly, rejecting a zero-sum outcome in the reference allows the subscribers of the federal models to find positive aspects in the decision (and to see that elements of the outcome reaffirm the legitimacy of their perspective and standing in the association). In other words, the approach to disposing of the issue in the *Secession Reference* generates legitimacy for the federation because it does not align the system with any one perspective; rather, it shows the subscribers of each federal model that the association will develop in a way that reflects aspects of their perspective. Finally, the facilitator role adopted by the Court in the reference helps to ensure the conflict-management process is seen as unbiased, free, and fair, while also legitimizing the institutional and political mechanisms of the federation by pushing parties to use these processes to manage conflict.

On the second question, the comparability of the *Secession Reference*, the unique context and nature of the decision does need to be recognized as a potential limit on its basis as a test case for my theory. This was a reference case – a function that is not widely adopted by judiciaries in other federations. And, the tendency to rely on the reference procedure in politically charged contexts, combined with the hypothetical and technically non-binding nature of such opinions, means this is an overtly political form of judicial review. I have already made a case for comparing references to more traditional division-of-powers jurisprudence; but the unprecedented and high-stakes nature of the reference does raises questions about the applicability of the approach adopted by the Court in other contexts. Indeed, as I just argued, it may be that the nature of the case, which required the SCC to contemplate the dissolution of the federation, is what pushed the Court to reinforce the dynamic nature of the system and legitimize the association and its place within it. In this regard, the existential threat of secession may have acted as a catalyst for this relatively novel approach, with the Court picking up on some earlier streams of federalism jurisprudence and further developing the approach in its subsequent work. It is for this reason that I do not see the unique political context of this case as a problem: the *Secession Reference* is not the only example of the Court adopting a more facilitative role; rather, it stands as an early marker of a broader shift towards this approach.

Over the next two chapters I elaborate on this shift, along with the potential benefits of the approach taken in the *Secession Reference* and the problems with decisions that impose a federal model. Confining my analysis to the *Secession Reference* – important as the case is – would only tell part of the story. To leave things here would be to accept what may just be a temporary (or even rhetorical) turn by the Court in a rather extraordinary case without examining the broader jurisprudence.[111] By looking beyond this case (but, still keeping it in view) we are able to gain a more comprehensive account of the Court's work as federal arbiter and better evaluate the extent to which the SCC can fulfil its role in a way that generates legitimacy for the federation.

111 Something others have done; see (Tully 2000a) in particular.

Chapter Five

The SCC's Imposing Federalism Jurisprudence

In this chapter I turn from the *Secession Reference* to look at the SCC's problematic decisions that impose a particular federal model. The chapter analyses how these decisions reinforce specific views of what the federation is and ought to be over others. Such decisions are problematic because they fail to recognize the inherent conflict that takes place over nationality and the federation in Canada. The goal of this chapter, in the overall context of the book, then, is to demonstrate how the SCC can negatively affect the legitimacy of the federation and thus why federal theory needs to better account for how arbiters can fulfil this role.

The specific argument of this chapter is that a substantial proportion of the SCC's federalism jurisprudence imposes a particular federal model: in sixty-one division-of-powers cases (55%) and thirteen federal references (65%), the Court reinforces the legitimacy of one federal model over the others. As already argued, the federal arbiter should recognize the legitimacy of multiple models and the federation as the process and outcome of negotiation *in every decision*. The ideal is a federalism jurisprudence with no imposing decisions. Accordingly, this tendency to impose particular models needs to be addressed if the federal arbiter and the federation itself are to remain legitimate (particularly since the Court tends to impose the pan-Canadian model, while displaying virtually no support for the multinational model, something that does not sit well with the reality of Canada as a plurinational state).[1]

1 As explained earlier, a plurinational state is one where there is conflict over the national character of the state (as either *uni*national or *multi*national). This is distinguishable from a "multinational state," where it is generally accepted that there are multiple national groups within one state housed in defined territorial zones.

The ideal-type of a decision that imposes a particular federal model has three key characteristics. First is how the federation is depicted. A decision that imposes a federal model presents the federation in a way that corresponds with, and legitimizes, only one federal model (while also potentially delegitimizing other models). Furthermore, this particular perspective of what the federation is and ought to be is presented as a fact through the use of accepted forms of legal argument and modes of constitutional interpretation. The second characteristic is that the outcome of the case follows and reinforces the depiction of the federation. Accordingly, in imposing decisions, the outcome favours a specific jurisdiction, and does so in a way that aligns the federal system with the ideal of the imposed federal model. The third characteristic is that the Court's adopted role reinforces the legitimacy of the federal depiction and further justifies the outcome.

When all these factors combine, a decision substantially adheres to the ideal-type of an imposition. For example, a decision that imposes the pan-Canadian model would depict the federation as centralized, with a central government that is superior to the provinces, a situation that is presented as a legal fact supported by the text of the constitution, which the Court as umpire is bound to enforce. Building on this depiction, the central government could, for example, unilaterally amend funding agreements it has reached with the provinces (as was the case in the *Canada Assistance Plan* reference).[2] In other words, a decision imposes a federal model when the depiction and outcome, supported by the way the constitution is interpreted and the courts' role, all work *to reinforce the same model*. The *Ontario Hydro* case[3] also exemplifies this well; in this decision, the federation is presented as centralized with a superior central government through its broad power to declare something for the advantage of Canada and

2 *Reference Re Canada Assistance Plan (B.C.)*, [1991] 2 S.C.R. 525. The issue in this case is whether the central government can unilaterally amend funding agreements with the provinces. It was a unanimous decision (authored by Sopinka J).

3 *Ontario Hydro v. Ontario (Labour Relations Board)*, [1993] 3 S.C.R. 327. The issue in this case is whether provincial or central labour-relations legislation applies to workers at provincially owned atomic energy generation stations. The core of the issues is the scope of the central government's power to declare something for the "general advantage of Canada" under s. 92(10)(c) of the constitution, which allows it to assume legislative jurisdiction for the matter. It was a majority decision (authored by La Forest J, with Lamer CJ concurring).

to thus assume complete jurisdiction for the matter.[4] This view of the federation is supported with recourse to the text of the constitution and related doctrine, which give rise to legal rules the Court says it must enforce as an umpire.[5] And, by enforcing these rules the central government is granted exclusive jurisdiction to regulate labour relations at provincially owned atomic energy facilities (despite labour relations generally falling within provincial jurisdiction). Not all decisions so clearly draw from, and reinforce, a particular model in the decision approach and outcome. As my analysis shows, there are varying degrees of adherence to the ideal-type. However, the basic characteristics of an imposing decision are evident in each of the seventy-four cases discussed below.

This basic architecture of an imposing decision informs the structure of the chapter. The first section discusses how the federation is depicted in line with one model, looking at the extent this takes place in all the seventy-four cases and going on to exemplify how this is

4 See *Ontario Hydro*, [1993] at 370–2: "The power conferred on Parliament to declare that works wholly situate within the province are for the general advantage of Canada or for the advantage of two or more of the provinces, is obviously a far-reaching power. Parliament is the sole judge of the advisability of making this declaration ... [I]t vests in Parliament exclusive legislative authority over the local work which it removes from the provincial to the federal field of jurisdiction. There is no authority supporting the view that the declaratory power should be narrowly construed. Quite the contrary ... the courts, including this Court, have never shown any disposition to so limit its operation, and a wide variety of works – railways, bridges, telephone facilities, grain elevators, feed mills, atomic energy and munition factories – have been held to have been validly declared to be for the general advantage of Canada ... The declaratory power is not the only draconian power vested in the federal authorities. The powers of disallowance and reservation accorded the federal government by ss. 55–57 and 90 of the *Constitution Act, 1867* give it unrestricted authority to veto any provincial legislation ... The declaratory and veto powers were frequently used in tandem in the early years following union to accomplish the original constitutional mandate by establishing the authority of the central government and its policies, and in particular to ensure the construction of the intercontinental railway. Later, the declaratory power was effectively used as a tool to regulate the national grain market in the pursuit of the constitutional vision of integrating the western region of Canada into the country."

5 In *Ontario Hydro* the Court counters the argument that it ought to narrowly construe the declaratory power of the central government to protect the federal principle by saying (at 371) that such an "argument evinces a misunderstanding of the respective roles of law and politics in the specifically Canadian form of federalism established by the Constitution" and (at 372) that the rules of the constitution are to be enforced by the courts, while "protection against abuse of these draconian powers is left to the inchoate but very real and effective political forces that undergird federalism."

done in specific decisions. I do the same in subsequent sections, looking at the way the Court reinforces the legitimacy of particular models through legal argument, the outcomes of decisions, and the Court's adopted role. Following this structure (rather than reviewing cases in their entirety) best accomplishes my goal of demonstrating how the Court imposes particular federal models in these seventy-four decisions. It allows for in-depth analysis of the way these cases exemplify the various characteristics of an ideal-type imposition. This structure also facilitates clear comparison with those decisions that tend to adhere to the opposite ideal-type of recognizing the legitimacy of multiple models.

I conclude the chapter by reflecting on my analysis, discussing some key points related to the wider arguments of the book. I start by comparing the division-of-powers decisions and references, arguing that despite some differences they are essentially similar in their imposition of specific federal models over others. This shared tendency highlights the difference between these seventy-four decisions and the *Secession Reference*, demonstrating the latter's focus on legitimacy generation and approach to conflict management. I then elaborate on why these imposing decisions are problematic, focusing on the way they hinder the ability of the federation to generate and maintain loyalty in the plurinational state of Canada. I highlight four specific trends in these seventy-four decisions that negatively affect the legitimacy of the Court as the federal arbiter and the federation more generally: (1) the tendency to impose the pan-Canadian model more than others; (2) the lack of support afforded the multinational model; (3) the creation of stark winners and losers in the outcomes of the cases; and (4) the propensity of the Court to adopt a role for itself that reinforces the legitimacy of particular federal models.

Context

The analysis in this chapter stems from a comprehensive review of every decision dealing with federalism issues delivered by the SCC between 1980 and 2010. As discussed in the third chapter, this period has been marked by intergovernmental conflict and nationalist mobilization, with the result being considerable litigation in the Courts. The clear initiator of this heightened era of conflict (and particularly the recourse to the Courts to arbitrate the conflict) was the process of establishing a domestic constitutional amending formula (and enshrined bill of rights) in the early 1980s. From this process stemmed a trilogy of references to the SCC (the *Senate,*[6] *Patriation,*[7] and *Quebec Veto*[8] references) that decisively set the tone of constitutional politics and intergovernmental relations in the following decades. Even outside the realm of this "mega-constitutional politics," a climate of hostility informed the more traditional conflicts over the nature of the federation taking place between governments and between private actors and governments. While this has been discussed in previous chapters, what has not been explained are the specific issues brought before the SCC over this period.

As tables 5.1 and 5.2 indicate, the issues that arise in these imposing cases span a range of matters. Within the division-of-powers cases there are many that deal with the scope of the central government's criminal-law power (20), with the extent of the central government's power over its works and undertakings (8),[9] with the role and scope of the judiciary's power in the federation (6), and matters such as trade (4), maritime law (4), taxation (4), and Aboriginals (3). Similarly, in addition to the two high-profile references related to constitutional amendment, there are those that deal with the role and scope of the judiciary's power in the federation (4), natural resources (3), as well as those that mirror division-of-powers cases where the jurisdiction of a government to pass economic or social legislation is challenged (4 cases). This range of issues is not surprising given the inherent conflict that is expected in any federation – and particularly in a plurinational federation like Canada, where conflict over the distribution of power and resources mixes with nationalist mobilization and identity politics.

---

6 *Re: Authority of Parliament in Relation to the Upper House*, [1980] 1 S.C.R. 54. The opinion in this reference was unanimous (authored by "The Court").

7 *Re: Resolution to Amend the Constitution*, [1981] 1 S.C.R. 753. The opinion in this reference was split between two majorities (one on the legal issue and one on the convention issue).

8 *Re: Objection by Quebec to a Resolution to Amend the Constitution*, [1982] 2 S.C.R. 793. The opinion in this reference was unanimous (authored by "The Court").

9 The centre's "works and undertakings" are those matters that fall under exclusive central control as a result of s. 92(10) of the Constitution Act, 1867. This generally includes enterprises such as inter-provincial transportation (like railways, steamships, and aviation) and telecommunications, as well as matters declared by the central government to be for the general advantage of Canada, like atomic energy.

Table 5.1. Issues in imposing federal references, 1980–2010

Reference	Primary (and related) area of jurisdiction	Issue
Senate [1980]	Constitutional amendment	Central law changing composition of Senate
Residential Tenancies Act [1981]	Courts (s. 96)	Provincially established tribunal
BC Family Relations Act [1982]	Courts (s. 96)	Provincially established tribunal
Exported Natural Gas Tax [1982]	Natural resources (s. 125)	Central tax on export of natural gas
Quebec Veto [1982]	Constitutional amendment	If Québec has veto over constitutional amendment proposals
McEvoy [1983]	Courts (s. 96)	Centrally established tribunal
Upper Churchill [1984]	Natural resources (extra-territorial effect)	Newfoundland expropriating power station partly owned by Québec
Strait of Georgia [1984]	Natural resources	Ownership of Strait of Georgia seabed
Goods and Services Tax [1992]	Tax (property and civil rights)	Central value-added tax (if infringes provincial jurisdiction)
Canada Assistance Plan [1991]	Central spending power	Centre unilaterally altering funding agreement with provinces
Quebec Sales Tax [1994]	Tax	If provincial tax direct and within province
NS Residential Tenancies Act [1996]	Courts (s. 96)	Provincially established tribunal
Firearms [2000]	Criminal law (property and civil rights)	Central regulation of firearms (if infringes provincial jurisdiction)

The seventy-four imposing decisions are classified as such by applying the framework introduced in the third chapter (which facilitates analysis of the extent to which decisions draw from and reinforce the pan-Canadian, provincial-equality, multinational, or dynamic federal models in their approach and outcome). As previously discussed in chapter 3, I have identified these imposing decisions by reviewing all of the Court's constitutional law work reported between 1980 and 2010 (almost 700 decisions), selecting 159 cases where a key issue is raised with regard to the jurisdiction of an order of government to act. From these 159 decisions, 28 have been excluded from my analysis because they do not provide sufficient information on the relevant federalism

Table 5.2. Issues in imposing division-of-powers cases, 1980–2010

Case	Primary (and related) area of jurisdiction	Issue
Labatt Breweries v. Canada [1980]	Trade (criminal law, POGG)	Central law regulating production and labelling of beer
Four B Manufacturing [1980]	Aboriginals (s. 91.24, labour)	If provincial labour regulations apply to Aboriginal business
Ritcey v. The Queen [1980]	Admin. of justice (courts)	Provincial law relating to administration of courts
Fowler v. The Queen [1980]	Fisheries (environment)	Central fisheries legislation
Northwest Falling Contractors [1980]	Fisheries (environment)	Central fisheries legislation
The Queen v. Sutherland [1980]	Aboriginals (s. 91.24)	Provincial law regulating Aboriginal hunting
Boggs v. R. [1980]	Criminal law	Central criminal sanction for provincial offence
Crevier v. QC [1981]	Courts (s. 96)	Provincially established tribunal
AB v. Putnam [1981]	Criminal law (admin. of justice)	Jurisdiction to investigate and sanction central police
Massey-Ferguson v. SK. [1981]	Tax	If provincial tax direct
Moore v. Johnson [1982]	Fisheries (property and civil rights)	Regulation of seal hunt
NB v. Simpsons-Sears [1982]	Tax	If provincial tax direct and within the province
Municipality of Peel v. Mackenzie [1982]	Criminal law (municipalities)	Centrally imposed fee on municipalities via Young Offenders Act
Canada v. Law Society of BC [1982]	Courts (property and civil rights)	Centre shielding law from provincial court review; application of central law to regulate provincial law society
Capital Regional District [1982]	Courts (s. 96)	Provincially established tribunal related to pollution control
Westendorp v. The Queen [1983]	Criminal law (municipalities)	Municipal legislation relating to prostitution
Canada Labour Relations Board [1983]	Federal undertaking (labour, courts)	Central regulation of labour, centre shielding law from provincial court review
Zavarovalna Skupnost [1983]	Maritime law	Central law regulating marine insurance
Northern Telecom [1983]	Federal undertaking (labour, courts)	Central regulation of labour
Bisaillon v. Keable [1983]	Criminal law (admin. of justice)	Provincial commission mandate (if infringes on criminal law)

(*Continued*)

Table 5.2. Issues in imposing division-of-powers cases, 1980–2010 (Continued)

Case	Primary (and related) area of jurisdiction	Issue
Canadian National Transportation [1983]	Criminal law (admin. of justice)	Centre's prosecutorial power (re: anti-competition law)
R. v. Wetmore [1983]	Criminal law (admin of justice)	Centre's prosecutorial power (re: food and drug law)
QC v. Grondin [1983]	Courts (s. 96)	Provincially established tribunal relating to landlord-lessee affairs
Skoke-Graham v. The Queen [1985]	Criminal law	Criminal code provision (re: disturbing religious service)
R. v. Big M Drug Mart [1985]	Criminal law	Criminal code provision (re: Sunday shopping)
Scowby v. Glendinning [1986]	Criminal Law (s. 96)	Provincial commission mandate (if infringes on criminal law)
R. v. Crown Zellerbach [1988]	POGG (environment)	Central law regulating dumping at sea
Clark v. Canadian National Railway [1988]	Federal undertaking (property and civil rights)	Central law regulating civil actions related to railways
Devine v. QC [1988]	Criminal law (trade)	Provincial law regulating language use for commerce
Sobeys v. NS [1989]	Courts (s. 96)	Provincially established tribunal related to labour relations
City National Leasing [1989]	Trade (property and civil rights)	Centre's anti-competition law
Quebec Ready Mix [1989]	Trade (property and civil rights)	Centre's anti-competition law
Irwin Toy v. QC [1989]	Federal undertaking (criminal law)	Provincial law regulating advertising to children
YMHA v. Brown [1989]	Labour (employment insurance)	Application of central labour laws to centrally funded enterprise
MacKeigan v. Hickman [1989]	Criminal law (courts)	Provincial commission mandate (if infringes on criminal law)
Bank of Montreal v. Hall [1990]	Banking (property and civil rights, paramountcy)	Jurisdiction to regulate seizure of property in security of a bank loan
Knox Contracting v. Canada [1990]	Criminal law (tax, admin. of justice)	Provision of centre's income tax act (if valid as criminal law)
National Battlefields Commission [1990]	Federal undertaking	Provincial transport regulations (if apply to federal undertaking)
Central Western Railway [1990]	Federal undertaking (labour)	Jurisdiction over labour relations for particular railway line
Whitbread v. Walley [1990]	Maritime law (property and civil rights)	Central law regulating civil action relating to maritime matters
Monk v. Island Fertilizers [1991]	Maritime law	Central law regulating civil action relating to maritime matters

Table 5.2. Issues in imposing division-of-powers cases, 1980–2010 (Continued)

Case	Primary (and related) area of jurisdiction	Issue
R. v. Swain [1991]	Criminal law (health)	Criminal code provision (re: detention of mentally ill)
Ontario Hydro [1993]	Federal undertaking (POGG)	Jurisdiction to regulate labour at provincial atomic power stations
R. v. Morgentaler [1993]	Criminal law (health)	Provincial abortion laws (if infringe on criminal law)
Hunt v. T&N [1993]	Courts	Province prohibiting removal of corporate documents from province
Allard Contractors v. Coquitlam [1993]	Tax (licensing)	Provincial levy charging variable fees
BC v. Canada [1994]	Transportation	If centre must continue rail service on Vancouver Island
RJR-MacDonald v. Canada [1995]	Criminal law (POGG)	Central law regulating advertising of tobacco products
Husky Oil v. Canada [1995]	Bankruptcy (paramountcy)	Provincial law relating to bankruptcy
R. v. Hydro-Québec [1997]	Criminal law (municipalities)	Central law regulating toxic substances
Delgamuukw v. BC [1997]	Aboriginals (self-govt., s. 91.24)	Aboriginal right to self-government. If provinces can extinguish Aboriginal rights
Westcoast Energy v. Canada [1998]	Federal undertaking	If particular natural gas operation is a federal undertaking
Consortium Developments [1998]	Criminal law (municipalities)	Provincial commission mandate (if infringes on criminal law)
Ordon Estate v. Grail [1998]	Maritime law (property and civil rights)	Central law regulating civil action relating to maritime matters
M & D Farm [1999]	Paramountcy	Jurisdiction relating to seizure of property
Unifund Assurance [2003]	Extraterritorial effect	Extraterritorial effect of provincial law
R. v. Malmo-Levine [2003]	Criminal law	Criminalization of marihuana possession (if valid as criminal law)
R. v. Demers [2004]	Criminal law	Criminal code provision (re: detention of person unfit to stand trial)
BC v. Imperial Tobacco [2005]	Extraterritorial effect	Extraterritorial effect of provincial law
Kirkbi AG v. Ritvik Holdings [2005]	Trade	Central law regulating unregistered trademarks
Dunne v. QC [2007]	Tax	If provincial tax direct and within the province

issue to determine if they impose a particular model or recognize multiple models.[10] This leaves 131 decisions, 74 of which (57%) are classified as impositions. Of these 74 imposing decisions, 61 are division-of-powers cases, and 13 are references.

As discussed in chapter 3, while division-of-powers cases and references can be considered two separate streams of federalism jurisprudence, they share the fundamental similarity of dealing with conflicts over the nature of the federal system. These decisions share the characteristic of imposing a specific view of what the federation is, in cases where the SCC is asked to settle a conflict over the very nature of the federation. This conflict over the nature of the federation is particularly evident in most references, where the disagreement tends to be between the orders of government over key aspects of the federal system (i.e., the process of constitutional amendment).[11] Similarly, in many division-of-powers cases the nature of the conflict is between orders of government, either directly or because one order of government has intervened to support a private actor challenging an opposing order of government.[12] These seventy-four decisions taken together are thus judgments where a particular view of what the federation is and ought to be is imposed by the Court in conflicts between social and political actors holding competing perspectives on the very nature of the association. Moreover, the range of issues outlined in tables 5.1 and 5.2 shows the breadth of critical areas where these imposing decisions have played a role in shaping the development of the federation. The outcomes of these cases, dealing with a wide range of matters, both individually and cumulatively, align the nature of the federation with specific federal models.[13]

---

10 As discussed in chapter 3, the lack of information in these 28 decisions stems from (1) the reasons for the decision being too brief to determine the rationale behind the Court's decision, so-called stump decisions of about one paragraph, often delivered orally; or (2) the division-of-powers issues not being considered at all by the Court given that the appeal is disposed of on another point of law (generally civil rights issues).

11 In 16 of the 21 references discussed in the book (76%), the conflict dynamic is between the orders of government.

12 While only 9% of division-of-powers cases (10 of 110) involve direct government-to-government conflict, an additional 35% (38 of 110) involve an order of government intervening in support of a private actor to turn the conflict into one between the orders of government.

13 As explained below, a single decision can significantly affect the federal system (e.g., *R v. Crown Zellerbach Canada Ltd.*, [1988] 1 SCR 401, which centralizes the federation by legitimizing the central government's ability to take exclusive jurisdiction

In the sections that follow, I discuss how the Court's division-of-powers and reference work to impose particular models. Within each section I discuss the shared characteristic between the division-of-powers and reference decisions that leads them to impose a federal model, going on to discuss how the two streams of decisions do this separately. I reflect on some of the key similarities and differences between these two streams in the concluding section of this chapter and in subsequent chapters.

Imposing Depictions

The Court's depiction of the federation rests on how it perceives the association in relation to a number of "points of conflict." The key points of conflict are the balance of powers (as centralized or decentralized), the distribution of powers (as symmetrical or asymmetrical), and the nature of the provinces (as equal territorial units or as housing national minorities), among others.[14] It is from a particular understanding of the federation vis-à-vis these points of conflict that the Court goes on to depict the federal system. And, the way the federation is presented by the Court – the way it explains what the federation *is* – is a central component to a decision imposing a specific model. This is because the Court's understanding of what the federation is drives the outcome of a case, and through the decision the Court can either align the federation with a particular model or reinforce the system as the process and outcome of negotiation between the holders of legitimate competing models.

It is important to note at the outset that in these seventy-four decisions the federation is depicted in a way that primarily reinforces the legitimacy of either the pan-Canadian model (44 decisions) or the provincial-equality model (29 decisions) (see table 5.3).[15] However, while

---

over matters of "national concern" like environmental protection); at the same time, the cumulative effect of imposing decisions can be noteworthy (i.e., the centralizing effect of the line of decisions that reinforce a broad scope to the central order's criminal-law power).

14 As outlined in chapter 3, the focal points of conflict over what the federation is generally include: the way the constitution is represented; the nature of the federation; the purpose of the federation; the distribution of powers; the balance of powers; the nature of the provinces; the nature of central institutions; the relationship between the orders of government; and the national composition of the country.

15 The federal system is depicted primarily in line with the multinational model in one decision: *Attorney General of Quebec v. Grondin*, [1983] 2 S.C.R. 364. The decision was unanimous (authored by Chouinard J).

Table 5.3. Summary of imposing SCC decisions, 1980–2010

Rank	Case	Depiction				Outcome		Court's role
		Model imposed	Secondary support	Approach	Primary modality	Winner	Model reinforced	
High	Senate [1980]	Provincial		One	Text, Historical	Provinces	Provincial	Branch (Facilitator)
	Canada v. Law Society of BC [1982]	Provincial		One	Doctrine	Provinces	Provincial	Branch
	Quebec Veto [1982]	Pan-Can		One	Doctrine, Prudent	Centre	Pan-Can	Umpire
	Canadian National Transportation [1983]	Pan-Can	Provincial	Primary	Text	Centre	Pan-Can	Umpire
	R. v. Wetmore [1983]	Pan-Can		Minimal	Doctrine	Centre	Pan-Can	—
	Scowby v. Glendinning [1986]	Pan-Can	Provincial	Primary	Text	Centre	Pan-Can	Umpire
	R. v. Crown Zellerbach [1988]	Pan-Can	Provincial	Primary	Doctrine	Centre	Pan-Can	—
	Bank of Montreal v. Hall [1990]	Pan-Can	Provincial	Primary	Prudent, Doctrine	Centre	Pan-Can	(Branch)
	Whitbread v. Walley [1990]	Pan-Can		One	Doctrine	Centre	Pan-Can	—
	Canada Assistance Plan [1991]	Pan-Can		One	Text	Centre	Pan-Can	Umpire
	Hunt v. T&N [1993]	Pan-Can		One	Doctrine, Structure	Centre	Pan-Can	Branch
	Ontario Hydro [1993]	Pan-Can	Provincial	Primary	Text, Doctrine	Centre	Pan-Can	Umpire
	RJR-MacDonald v. Canada [1995]	Pan-Can		One	Doctrine, Prudent	Centre	Pan-Can	(Branch)
	Husky Oil v. Canada [1995]	Pan-Can	Provincial	Primary	Doctrine	Centre	Pan-Can	(Branch)
	NS Residential Tenancies Act [1996]	Provincial		One	Doctrine, Progress	Provinces	Provincial	Branch
	Ordon Estate v. Grail [1998]	Pan-Can		One	Doctrine, Prudent	Centre	Pan-Can	Branch
	Firearms [2000]	Pan-Can	Provincial	Primary	Doctrine	Centre	Pan-Can	Umpire
	Unifund Assurance [2003]	Provincial		One	Doctrine, Structure, Prudent	Provinces	Provincial	Umpire, Branch

Medium	Four B Manufacturing [1980]	Provincial		One	Doctrine	Provinces	Provincial	—
	Ritcey v. The Queen [1980]	Provincial		One	Text, Doctrine	Provinces	Provincial	—
	Boggs v. R. [1980]	Provincial	Pan-Can	Primary	Doctrine, Text	Provinces	Provincial	—
	Residential Tenancies Act [1981]	Pan-Can		One	Doctrine, History	Centre	Pan-Can	Umpire
	Municipality of Peel v. Mackenzie [1982]	Provincial	Pan-Can	Primary	Doctrine	Provinces	Provincial	Branch
	Westendorp v. The Queen [1983]	Pan-Can		One	Text	Centre	Pan-Can	—
	Devine v. QC [1988]	Provincial		One	Doctrine, History, Text	Provinces	Provincial	—
	Sobeys v. NS [1989]	Provincial	Pan-Can	Primary	Doctrine	Provinces (Centre)	Provincial	Branch
	Irwin Toy v. QC [1989]	Provincial		One	Doctrine	Provinces	Provincial	—
	MacKeigan v. Hickman [1989]	Provincial		One	Text, Doctrine	Provinces	Provincial	Branch
	Knox Contracting v. Canada [1990]	Pan-Can	Provincial	Primary	Doctrine, Text	Centre	Pan-Can	—
	Monk v. Island Fertilizers [1991]	Pan-Can		One	Doctrine, Progress	Centre	Pan-Can	—
	Goods and Services Tax [1992]	Pan-Can	Provincial	Primary	Doctrine	Centre	Pan-Can	—
	R. v. Morgentaler [1993]	Pan-Can	Provincial	Primary	Doctrine, Text	Centre	Pan-Can	Umpire
	BC v. Canada [1994]	Pan-Can		Minimal	Text	Centre	Pan-Can	—
	R. v. Hydro-Québec [1997]	Pan-Can	Provincial, Dynamic	Primary	Doctrine, Prudent	Centre	Pan-Can	(Branch)
	M & D Farm [1999]	Pan-Can		Minimal	Doctrine	Centre	Pan-Can	Umpire
	R. v. Malmo-Levine [2003]	Pan-Can		One	Doctrine	Centre	Pan-Can	Umpire
	BC v. Imperial Tobacco [2005]	Provincial		One	Doctrine	Provinces	Provincial	—
	Kirkbi AG v. Ritvik Holdings [2005]	Pan-Can	Provincial	Primary	Doctrine	Centre	Pan-Can	—
Low	Labatt Breweries v. Canada [1980]	Provincial	Pan-Can	Primary	Doctrine	Provinces	Provincial	—
	Fowler v. The Queen [1980]	Provincial	Pan-Can	Primary	Doctrine	Provinces	Provincial	—
	Northwest Falling Contractors [1980]	Pan-Can, Provincial		Balance	Doctrine	Centre	Pan-Can	—

(*Continued*)

Table 5.3. Summary of imposing SCC decisions, 1980–2010 (Continued)

Rank	Case	Depiction				Outcome		Court's role
		Model imposed	Secondary support	Approach	Primary modality	Winner	Model reinforced	
Low	The Queen v. Sutherland [1980]	Pan-Can	Provincial, Multinat.	Primary	Doctrine, Text	Centre	Pan-Can	—
	Crevier v. QC [1981]	Pan-Can		Minimal	Doctrine	Centre	Pan-Can	Umpire
	AB v. Putnam [1981]	Pan-Can	Provincial, Dynamic	Minimal	Doctrine	Centre	Pan-Can	—
	Massey-Ferguson v. SK [1981]	Provincial		Minimal	Doctrine	Provinces	Provincial	—
	BC Family Relations Act [1982]	Pan-Can	Provincial	Balance	Doctrine, Progress	Centre (Provinces)	Pan-Can	Umpire
	Moore v. Johnson [1982]	Pan-Can	Provincial, Multinat.	Primary	Text	Centre	Pan-Can	—
	NB v. Simpsons-Sears [1982]	Provincial		Minimal	Doctrine	Provinces	Provincial	—
	Exported Natural Gas Tax [1982]	Pan-Can	Provincial	Primary	Text	Centre (Provinces)	Pan-Can	Umpire (Facilitator)
	Capital Regional District [1982]	Provincial		One	Doctrine, Text	Provinces	Provincial	Branch
	Canada Labour Relations Board [1983]	Provincial	Pan-Can	Primary	Doctrine	Provinces	Provincial	Branch
	Zavarovalna Skupnost [1983]	Pan-Can	Provincial	Primary	Doctrine	Centre	Pan-Can	—
	McEvoy [1983]	Provincial		One	Doctrine	Provinces	Provincial	Branch
	Northern Telecom [1983]	Pan-Can	Provincial	Primary	Doctrine	Centre	Pan-Can	Umpire (Branch)
	Bisaillon v. Keable [1983]	Pan-Can	Provincial	Primary	Doctrine	Centre	Pan-Can	—
	QC v. Grondin [1983]	Multinat.	Provincial, Dynamic	Primary	Doctrine	Multinat.	Multinat.	Facilitator
	Upper Churchill [1984]	Provincial		Minimal	Doctrine	Provinces	Provincial	Umpire
	Strait of Georgia [1984]	Provincial		One	Doctrine, Text	Provinces	Provincial	—

Low	Skoke-Graham v. The Queen [1985]	Pan-Can		Minimal	Doctrine	Centre	Pan-Can	—
	R. v. Big M Drug Mart [1985]	Pan-Can	Provincial, Dynamic	Primary	Doctrine	Centre	Pan-Can	Facilitator
	Clark v. Canadian National Railway [1988]	Provincial	Pan-Can, Dynamic	Primary	Doctrine	Provinces	Provincial	Branch
	YMHA v. Brown [1989]	Provincial	Pan-Can	Primary	Doctrine, Text	Provinces	Provincial	Facilitator
	City National Leasing [1989]	Pan-Can	Provincial, Dynamic	Primary	Doctrine	Centre	Pan-Can	Facilitator
	Quebec Ready Mix [1989]	Pan-Can	Provincial, Dynamic	Primary	Doctrine	Centre	Pan-Can	Facilitator
	National Battlefields Commission [1990]	Pan-Can, Provincial		Balance	Doctrine	Centre	Pan-Can	—
	Central Western Railway [1990]	Provincial	Pan-Can	Primary	Doctrine	Provinces	Provincial	—
	R. v. Swain [1991]	Pan-Can	Provincial	Primary	Doctrine	Centre	Pan-Can	—
	Allard Contractors v. Coquitlam [1993]	Provincial		Minimal	Doctrine	Provinces	Provincial	—
	Quebec Sales Tax [1994]	Provincial		Minimal	Doctrine	Provinces (Centre, Multinat.)	Provincial	—
	Delgamuukw v. BC [1997]	Pan-Can	Provincial	Primary	Doctrine	(Centre) (Provinces)	Pan-Can (Provincial)	Facilitator
	Westcoast Energy v. Canada [1998]	Pan-Can, Provincial		Minimal	Doctrine	Centre	Pan-Can	—
	Consortium Developments [1998]	Provincial		One	Doctrine	Provinces	Provincial	—
	R. v. Demers [2004]	Pan-Can	Dynamic	Primary	Doctrine	Centre	Pan-Can	Facilitator
	Dunne v. Quebec [2007]	Provincial		Minimal	Doctrine, Text	Provinces	Provincial	—

the tendency to present the federation in line with one specific model (the pan-Canadian model) is significant, what is more important is *how these decisions depict the federation* by drawing from, and reinforcing, a particular perspective of what the federation is and ought to be (regardless of which model is adhered to).

In the sixty-one imposing division-of-powers decisions, the primary way the Court tends to depict the federation is in relation to the balance of powers and the relationship between the orders of government. In virtually all of these decisions the federation is depicted in line with either the pan-Canadian or provincial-equality model by either presenting the federation as granting broad powers to the central government, with the added ability to infringe on the legislative jurisdiction of the provinces; or saying the federation grants the provinces broad powers and an autonomous legislative jurisdiction that is to be free of infringement from the centre.[16] *Scowby v. Glendinning*[17] is indicative of the former, with the central government's criminal-law power presented in the "widest sense of the term" and as having a "destructive force" on those provincial laws that encroach on the centre's broad and superior jurisdiction (even if the provincial law is passed in relation to its own power over civil rights).[18] Similarly, in *Kirkbi AG v. Ritvik Holdings*,[19] despite the recognition of a measure of provincial autonomy in areas like the regulation of local trade,[20] the federation is ultimately presented as centralized via a broad and superior trade and commerce power that allows the central government to infringe on the provinces' jurisdiction over property and civil rights.[21] Whereas in *MacKeigan v.*

16 In *Quebec v. Grondin* the federation is depicted in line with the multinational model with the distribution of powers being presented as asymmetrical (at 382–3) and the constitution as protecting this historical compromise (at 377).

17 *Scowby v. Glendinning*, [1986] 2 S.C.R. 226. The issue in this case is whether a provincial human rights board can investigate the conduct of central police officers relating to the arrest and detention of individuals. It was a majority decision (authored by Estey J).

18 *Scowby v. Glendinning* at 238; see also at 233–8, 240–1.

19 *Kirkbi AG v. Ritvik Holdings Inc.*, [2005] 3 S.C.R. 302. The issue in this case is the validity of a central law regulating unregistered trademarks (i.e., if the law is within the central order's trade and commerce power). It was a unanimous judgment (authored by LeBel J).

20 See *Kirkbi AG v. Ritvik Holdings*, [2005] at 15–16, 23.

21 In *Kirkbi AG v. Ritvik Holdings* the Court clearly establishes a broad scope to the central order's trade and commerce power (at 17–19), arguing this centralization of power is necessary to ensure consistency in the law across the country (at 28–9, 32–3) and saying that the central government can validly infringe on the jurisdiction of the provinces when acting under its trade and commerce power (at 20–1, 23–7, 32–3).

Hickman[22] the provinces are seen to have a broad scope of power over the administration of justice, including autonomy over aspects relating to *criminal* justice, despite section 91(27) of the constitution granting the central government jurisdiction over criminal law and procedure.[23] And in *YMHA v. Brown*[24] the Court reinforces a broad and autonomous scope to the provinces' jurisdiction over labour relations, while questioning the scope of the central government's power to bring matters under its regulatory authority by simply using its power to distribute funds.[25]

In a number of cases (27), the view of the federation as centralized or decentralized is augmented by depicting the federal system in line with other key aspects of the pan-Canadian or provincial-equality models. For example, in *Sobeys v. Nova Scotia*,[26] the federation is presented as a

---

22 *MacKeigan v. Hickman*, [1989] 2 S.C.R. 796. The division-of-powers issue in this case is whether a provincial commission mandate is ultra vires because it relates to matters of criminal law and procedure (an area of exclusive central jurisdiction under s. 91(27) of the Constitution Act, 1867). It was a majority judgment (authored by McLachlin J, with La Forest J and Lamer CJ concurring).

23 See *MacKeigan v. Hickman* at 834, where the Court notes that the provinces' power over "the 'administration of justice' should be interpreted broadly as including criminal justice … [and] given a fair, large and liberal construction" (see also at 809–10). In addition, the Court (at 834–5) implies that the central government and provinces have autonomy over their respective spheres relating to criminal law, procedure, and justice (with the first two being areas of central jurisdiction and the latter a legitimate area of provincial competence).

24 *YMHA Jewish Community Centre of Winnipeg Inc. v. Brown*, [1989] 1 S.C.R. 1532. The issue is whether provincial labour-relations standards apply to work undertaken as part of a centrally funded job creation program. It was a unanimous judgment (authored by L'Heureux-Dubé J).

25 See *YMHA v. Brown*, [1989] at 1540, where the Court explicitly follows the "fundamental principle that legislative competence over labour relations is provincial" and thus works from "the assumption that there is provincial competence over labour relations in the present case." The Court goes on (at 1548) to note that the "scope and extent of [the federal spending power] has been subject to some speculation," implying a shaky basis for the central government's ability to distribute resources to areas that may fall outside its jurisdiction, while further narrowing this power by saying (at 1550) "it [is] difficult to believe that simply by providing federal money to promote employment in a region or sector, the federal government can obtain jurisdiction over the workers employed by virtue of the grant."

26 *Sobeys Stores Ltd. v. Yeomans and Labour Standards Tribunal (N.S.)*, [1989] 1 S.C.R. 238. The issue in this case is whether a provincially established tribunal dealing with labour relations infringes on the authority of superior courts protected by s. 96 of the constitution. The judgment was unanimous (authored by Wilson J, with Beetz, La Forest, and L'Heureux-Dubé JJ concurring).

compact between provinces,[27] which results in a symmetrical distribution of powers between equal territorial units[28] (a view that reinforces the provincial-equality model to the detriment of key aspects of the multinational depiction of the federation). Similarly, in *Unifund Assurance*[29] the Court presents the system as one where the provinces are equal in status, with broad and symmetrical powers and autonomy to act free of influence from outside jurisdictions.[30] By contrast, in *Hunt v. T&N*[31] a depiction of the federation as centralized[32] is reinforced by presenting

27 See *Sobeys v. Nova Scotia*, [1989] at 263–4, where the Court refers to the process of union in 1867 as the "original bargain" or the "Confederation bargain."

28 See *Sobeys v. Nova Scotia* at 264–6, where the Court says the validity of a provincially established tribunal must be determined by investigating the conditions in *all four of the original confederation provinces* (treating them as equals at the time of union and as having the same jurisdiction to establish tribunals after union). In addition, at 265–6 the SCC laments the asymmetry in powers that results from a misapplication of this aspect of the test to determine the validity of provincially established tribunals. The key point is that the Court rejects the view that asymmetrical judicial arrangements in pre-confederation jurisdictions like Québec (i.e., the special inferior courts in Québec in 1867) allow *only* Québec to establish similar tribunals in the contemporary period, and this reinforces the view that all the provinces were, and are, equal in status with symmetrical powers. Compare this depiction with that of *Quebec v. Grondin*, [1983].

29 *Unifund Assurance Co. v. Insurance Corp. of British Columbia*, [2003] 2 S.C.R. 63. The core issue in this case is the validity of a province's law that affects an insurance company in another province. It was a majority decision (authored by Binnie J).

30 See *Unifund Assurance*, [2003] at 50–1: "[I]t is well established that a province has no legislative competence to legislate extraterritorially ... [T]his territorial restriction is fundamental to our system of federalism in which each province is obliged to respect the sovereignty of the other provinces within their respective legislative spheres, and expects the same respect in return. It flows from the opening words of s. 92 of the *Constitution Act, 1867*, which limit the territorial reach of provincial legislation: 'In each Province the Legislature may exclusively make Laws in relation to' the enumerated heads of power" (emphasis original). This depiction of equality with broad and autonomous powers is made elsewhere in the decision (at 23–4, 56, 73–5) and further buttressed by equating provincial boundaries with those of sovereign states that have a monopoly on domestic law (at 28, 30, 60–2, 68–71, 73–5). A similar depiction can be seen in *British Columbia v. Imperial Tobacco Canada Ltd.*, [2005] 2 S.C.R. 473 (*BC v. Imperial Tobacco*).

31 *Hunt v. T&N plc*, [1993] 4 S.C.R. 289. The issue in this case is whether a provincial statute prohibiting the removal of documents from a business in that province, by order of a court in another province, is valid. The decision was unanimous (authored by La Forest J).

32 See *Hunt v. T&N* at 322–3, where the Court notes the broad scope of powers afforded the central government, contrasted against a narrow interpretation of provincial powers (at 319–20).

Canada as a pan-state (legal and economic) community, where "thick" intra-state boundaries are inefficient and unjust,[33] and where the courts act as a unifying national institution.[34] Or in *Whitbread v. Walley*[35] the Court depicts the federation in line with the pan-Canadian model, saying the central government *necessarily* holds broad and superior powers to enact a national body of maritime law to deal with pan-state issues, and these powers allow it to infringe upon provincial areas of responsibility (i.e., the regulation of torts under the provinces' jurisdiction over civil rights).[36]

33 At the outset of *Hunt v. T&N* (at 295–6) the Court states: "Legal systems and rules are a reflection and expression of the fundamental values of a society, so to respect diversity of societies [*sic*] it is important to respect differences in legal systems. But if this is to work in our era where numerous transactions and interactions spill over the borders defining legal communities in our decentralized world legal order, there must also be a workable method of coordinating this diversity. Otherwise, the anarchic system's worst attributes emerge ... Developing such coordination in the face of diversity is ... one of the major objectives of the division of powers among federal and provincial governments in a federation." Following this foregrounding, the Court goes on (at 321–2) to equate strong provincial autonomy with an "outmoded conception of the world that emphasized sovereignty and independence, often at the cost of unfairness," while also (at 322) depicting the federal system as having "the obvious intention ... to create a single country" with "common citizenship," "interprovincial mobility of citizens," and a "common market."

34 See *Hunt v. T&N* at 312, where the SCC (citing a previous case) says that (provincial) superior courts "are not mere *local* courts for the administration of the local laws" (p. 19), but "are the Queen's Courts, bound to take cognizance of and execute all laws, whether enacted by the Dominion Parliament or the Local Legislatures" (p. 20) (emphasis added); a view the Court goes on to apply to itself, where it says (at 318) that the SCC "can thus play a 'unifying jurisdiction' over the provincial courts ... This is consistent with the mandate given it under the *Supreme Court Act* which establishes it as 'a General Court of Appeal for Canada.'"

35 *Whitbread v. Walley*, [1990] 3 S.C.R. 1273. The issue in this case is the applicability of central maritime law in relation to civil actions that stem from incidents on provincial waters. The decision was unanimous (authored by La Forest J).

36 *Whitbread v. Walley* at 1294–5: "[T]he very nature of the activities of navigation and shipping, at least as they are practised in this country, makes a uniform maritime law which encompasses navigable inland waterways a practical necessity ... The Fathers of Confederation thought it necessary to assign the broad and general power over navigation and shipping to the central rather than the provincial governments, and ... the courts quickly accepted that this power extended to the regulation of navigation on inland waterways." Similar depictions of the central order's power over maritime matters as necessarily broad and superior to provincial jurisdiction (through a uniform body of national maritime law) are made throughout the decision, see at 1286, 1288–9, 1292–3, 1298–9.

Even in the 12 cases among these imposing decisions where the Court undertakes a relatively minimal depiction of the federation, it is still evident that the way the federation is understood and presented reinforces a specific federal model. These depictions tend to take the form of the Court working from presumptions about the nature of the federal system and simply stating contested points as legal fact. *R. v. Wetmore*[37] exemplifies this approach, where a broad scope to the central government's criminal law and trade power was simply assumed,[38] as was the superiority of the centre to determine how criminal prosecutions take place in the country.[39] *M & D Farm*[40] and *Allard Contractors v. Coquitlam*[41] are also indicative of this same pattern of presuming contested aspects of the federal system as settled and going on to rationalize a decision based in large part on the presumption.

---

37 *R. v. Wetmore*, [1983] 2 S.C.R. 284. The issue in this case is the ability of the central government to prosecute offences under its food and drug legislation. The prosecution of criminal offences is traditionally the purview of provincial attorneys general (as mandated by the central government's Criminal Code and, the provinces argue, as part of their power over the administration of justice). It was a majority judgment (authored by Laskin CJ, with Beetz and Lamer JJ concurring).

38 See *R. v. Wetmore* at 288–9, where the Court, in brief reasons, simply states that the challenged legislation has three purposes (protecting physical health and safety, protecting the moral health of the public, and regulating marketing and controlled drugs), the first two "properly assigned to the criminal law" and the last falling under its trade and commerce power.

39 See *R. v. Wetmore* at 287, where the Court flatly states that criminal prosecutions by the provinces have always "depended and continues to depend on federal enactment" passed under the central government's broad criminal-law power (implying both that the provinces' power over the administration of justice does not encompass this jurisdiction and that the provinces exercise the power only at the behest of the central government).

40 *M & D Farm Ltd. v. Manitoba Agricultural Credit Corp.*, [1999] 2 S.C.R. 961. The issue in this case is a conflict between a provincial and central law relating to the seizure of farms. The unanimous decision (authored by Binnie J) in favour of the central government was premised on the principle that central laws are paramount (at 17, 40) in conjunction with broad scope afforded central competence (thereby limiting the available scope for conflicting provincial legislation) (at 25–6).

41 *Allard Contractors Ltd. v. Coquitlam (District)*, [1993] 4 S.C.R. 371. The issue in this case is if municipal by-laws authorizing variable fees are valid (since they impose what is, in effect, an indirect tax contrary to the constitution's only granting provinces and municipalities the ability to enact direct taxes). The Court, via a unanimous judgment (authored by Iacobucci J), legitimizes the power to impose indirect fees on the premise that they are within the provinces' broad jurisdiction to raise revenue in relation to their licensing and permit power (at 398–9, 402).

The basic pattern of depicting the federation as either centralized with a superior central government, or decentralized with provinces being equal in status to the central order, is also evident in federal references. For example, in *Upper Churchill*[42] the provinces are presented as equal, autonomous units that are protected from outside influence at the hands of another jurisdiction in their areas of competence.[43] In *Goods and Services Tax*[44] the SCC highlights that the central government can legitimately infringe on areas of provincial jurisdiction through its broad taxing power (thus presenting the central government as superior to the provinces and also the federation as considerably centralized).[45] There is a measure of legitimacy afforded the provincial-equality model in this reference; however, it simply takes the form of an assurance that the provinces do enjoy autonomy in some areas and that the test to determine if the central government can infringe this autonomy "is clearly a strict one."[46] A similar depiction of the federation as

42 *Reference re Upper Churchill Water Rights Reversion Act*, [1984] 1 S.C.R. 297. The issue in this case is the effect of one province expropriating a power station partly owned by another province. The opinion was unanimous (authored by McIntyre J).

43 See *Upper Churchill*, [1984] at 321, 326, 332, and particularly 328, where the Court says that "the territorial limitation on provincial legislative competence is contained in the *Constitution Act, 1867*. The opening words of s. 92 are: 'In each Province ....' Subsection (13) of s. 92 gives the Provinces exclusive legislative authority over 'Property and Civil Rights in the Province,' and subs. (16), similarly, is confined to matters of a purely local or private nature in the Province" (original emphasis). In addition, the Court highlights the extensive powers of the provinces, noting (at 324–5) that in accordance with the provinces' power over property and civil rights, they may subject even federal incorporated companies to "all laws of general application in the province ... Provincial legislation may license and regulate the activities of federal companies within the field of provincial competence and may impose sanctions for the enforcement of its regulations" so long as this regulation does not destroy the essential status or capacities of the company.

44 *Reference re Goods and Services Tax*, [1992] 2 S.C.R. 445. The issue is if a central value-added tax is valid (or if it infringes on provincial jurisdiction). The opinion was unanimous (authored by Lamer CJ, with La Forest and L'Heureux-Dubé JJ concurring).

45 *Goods and Services Tax* at 470–1, 483–5, and particularly 468, where the Court says: "[T]he GST Act has no purpose other than to raise revenue for the federal government ... The GST Act has significant effects upon matters within provincial jurisdiction, but it is impossible to say that the purpose of the Act is to produce these effects. The purpose of the Act is to raise revenue for the federal government, and the effects produced by the scheme on matters within provincial jurisdiction are incidental to this purpose."

46 *Goods and Services Tax* at 469; see also at 478, 481–2, and 494, where the SCC notes the constitution limits the ability of the central government to tax the lands, property, resources, and consolidated revenue funds of the provinces.

permitting the central government to infringe on the autonomy of the provinces via its broadly defined powers is also evident in *Firearms*.[47]

Just as with the above division-of-powers decisions, there are those federal references that augment the basic depiction of the federation as centralized or decentralized by highlighting how the system aligns with other aspects of a specific federal model. For example, in *Residential Tenancies Act*[48] the Court presents the federal system *as a compromise* that protects *national unity* through a judiciary that acts as a *national institution*, while also affording the central government a *superior position* to establish and appoint the justices of s. 96 superior courts.[49] Such adherence to a particular model in the depiction of the federation can also take the form of delegitimizing competing models, as was generally the case in *Quebec Veto*. Here the Court said that the federal system does not include a convention recognizing a requirement for unanimous provincial consent to amend the constitution[50] (denying a core element of the provincial-equality view), while also saying there is no

47 *Reference re Firearms Act (Can.)*, [2000] 1 S.C.R. 783. The issue in this case is whether central legislation requiring firearms be licensed infringes on provincial jurisdiction over property and civil rights. In the unanimous opinion (issued by "The Court"), the SCC (at 26, 29, 31, and particularly 28) states: "[C]riminal law, as this Court has stated in numerous cases, constitutes a broad area of federal jurisdiction ... [and it] ... often overlaps with provincial jurisdiction over property and civil rights." Additionally, in line with the pan-Canadian model, the Court (at 2–3) implies that the constitutional and federal system is neutral and fixed above the political controversy at hand.

48 *Re: Residential Tenancies Act, 1979*, [1981] 1 S.C.R. 714. The issue in this case is whether a provincially established tribunal infringes on the jurisdiction of superior courts protected by s. 96 of the constitution. The opinion was unanimous (authored by Dickson J).

49 See *Residential Tenancies Act* at 728: "[S]ection 92(14) and ss. 96 to 100 represent one of the important compromises of the Fathers of Confederation. It is plain that what was sought to be achieved through this compromise ... [was] a strong constitutional base for national unity, through a unitary judicial system ... Section 96 has thus come to be regarded as limiting provincial competence to make appointments to a tribunal exercising s. 96 judicial powers and therefore as implicitly limiting provincial competence to endow a provincial tribunal with such powers."

50 See *Quebec Veto*, [1982] at 807–8: "... one essential requirement for establishing a conventional rule of unanimity was missing. This requirement was acceptance by all the actors in the precedents. Accordingly, there existed no such convention." The Court went even further here to say explicitly (at 812) that "the opinion expressed in the *First Reference* that there existed no conventional rule of unanimity should be re-affirmed."

special veto for Québec in such situations[51] (denying a core element of the multinational view).

These examples demonstrate how the Court can, and does, depict the federation in line with one particular federal model in its federalism jurisprudence. In a significant percentage of its federalism jurisprudence, the Court understands and presents the federation in line with particular federal models. The imposing approach to understanding the federation happens in each of the seventy-four decisions reviewed in this chapter (even in those few instances where a measure of validity is afforded competing models). In other words, in both its division-of-powers and reference work the Court draws from federal theories to understand what the federation is, while reinforcing these theories as fact by describing the federation in line with them in its reasons-for-decision.

Framing the Depiction through Legal Argument

The depiction of the federation is only one part of an imposing decision. The way a particular depiction is reinforced and validated by employing legal argument is also a key part of understanding how a decision imposes a specific federal model. In all seventy-four of these decisions the Court presents what is ultimately a contested aspect of the federal system as a legal fact by using accepted forms of legal argument and constitutional interpretation.[52]

As table 5.3 indicates, in these imposing decisions the Court primarily employs the doctrinal modality to reinforce the depiction of the federation in line with a particular model (either by citing supportive case law or adapting and applying the host of "division-of-powers doctrines"

51 See *Quebec Veto* at 814–15: "[N]either in his factum nor in oral argument did counsel for the appellant quote a single statement made by any representative of the federal authorities recognizing either explicitly or by necessary implication that Quebec had a conventional power of veto over certain types of constitutional amendments … Furthermore, a convention such as the one now asserted by Quebec would have to be recognized by other provinces. We have not been referred to and we are not aware of any statement by the actors in any of the other provinces acknowledging such a convention."

52 As explained in chapter 3, the generally accepted forms of legal argument and methods of constitutional interpretation are the doctrinal, textual, historical, prudential, structural, ethical, and progressive modalities.

discussed in chapter 3).[53] At the same time, the textual modality plays an important role as both a primary and secondary way of reinforcing the various depictions of the federation (as do the prudential and structural forms of reasoning).[54] As already discussed, however, the frequency of the various modes of constitutional interpretation is not what really matters to a decision imposing a model, as the Court can employ a range of modalities and adapt them to reinforce a particular depiction of the federation.[55] To better understand how the Court imposes a federal model in these decisions the focus must be squarely on *how the Court employs* these modes of legal argument to reinforce a specific depiction of the federation.

There are numerous examples in the sixty-one division-of-powers cases of how the Court employs doctrine to reinforce the legitimacy of a particular depiction of the federation. For example, *Fowler v. The Queen*[56] is indicative of the way the Court can emphasize selective

53 This modality is employed in all 74 cases, and is the primary way the constitution is interpreted and the depiction given support in 66 of the 74 cases. The doctrinal modality is employed to support both the pan-Canadian model (in 37 cases), the provincial-equality model (in 28 cases), and the multinational model (in one case) by selecting case law that supports the particular model imposed, or by highlighting aspects of the applicable "division-of-powers doctrines" (i.e., the paramountcy doctrine, the interjurisdictional immunity doctrine, the pith and substance and incidental effect doctrine, etc.) to reinforce key elements of the particular model imposed.

54 Textual analysis is employed as the primary modality to support a depiction in 20 decisions, and as a secondary mode of interpretation in an additional 22 cases. Prudential analysis is employed in support of a depiction as a primary form of legal argument in 7 decisions and as a secondary form of argument in 11 decisions. Structural analysis is employed as a primary form of argument in only 2 cases, but as a secondary form of argument it is used in 16 cases to support a specific depiction of the federation.

55 As argued previously, the various modes of legal argument can be shifted to support any model – both those more "constraining modalities" (the textual, historical, and doctrinal modes) and those more "flexible modalities" (the structural, progressive, prudential, and ethical modes). In this way, correspondence between specific modalities and specific depictions offers limited analytical value. Simply pointing out that doctrine is employed in support of the pan-Canadian model in 37 decisions and in support of the provincial-equality model in 28 decisions does not add much to our understanding of how the Court imposes particular models and the problematic element of this (because this modality, and all the others, can easily be used to reinforce other models). What is important to point out, then, is *how* the modalities are used to reinforce specific models.

56 *Fowler v. The Queen*, [1980] 2 S.C.R. 213. The issue in this case is whether the central government's fisheries act (which prohibits the putting of debris into water frequented by fish) is within its legislative competence (or if it infringes provincial jurisdiction over property and civil rights). The judgment was unanimous (authored by Martland J).

aspects of the case law to support a view of the central government's power over fisheries as relatively narrow in scope, when compared to the broad provincial power over property and civil rights[57] (thereby legitimizing a depiction of the federation in line with the provincial-equality model). By contrast, in *R. v. Crown Zellerbach*[58] the Court pulls from the case law a set of principles that legitimize a view of the federation where the central government can usurp legislative jurisdiction for a matter from the provinces under the "national concern" branch of its reserve power[59] (legitimizing a view of the federation as centralized with a superior central government). Similarly, in

57 See *Fowler v. The Queen* at 221–3, where the Court highlights the following from the applicable case law on the scope of the central fisheries power: "[T]he legislation in regard to 'Inland and Sea Fisheries' contemplated by the *British North America Act* was not in reference to 'property and civil rights' – that is to say, not as to the ownership of the beds of the rivers, or of the fisheries, or the rights of individuals therein, but to subjects affecting the fisheries generally ... To all general laws passed by the Dominion of Canada regulating 'sea coast and inland fisheries' all must submit, but such laws must not conflict or compete with the legislative power of the local legislatures over property and civil rights ... Their Lordships are of opinion that the 91st section of the *British North America Act* did not convey to the Dominion of Canada any proprietary rights in relation to fisheries ... There is everywhere a power of regulation in the Dominion Parliament, but this must be exercised so as not to deprive the Crown in right of the Province or private persons of proprietary rights where they possess them ... Federal power in relation to fisheries does not reach the protection of provincial or private property rights in fisheries through actions for damages or ancillary relief for injury to those rights."

58 *R. v. Crown Zellerbach Canada Ltd.*, [1988] 1 SCR 401. The issue in this case is whether a central law prohibiting the dumping of substances at sea (in waters that are within the boundaries of the province of BC) is valid (the key issue being if the law falls under the national-concern branch of the central order's reserve power to pass laws for the peace, order, and good government of Canada). It was a majority judgment (authored by Le Dain J).

59 *R. v. Crown Zellerbach* (at 423–4) reinforces the legal principle that the central government can legitimately legislate on an issue that has become a national concern (i.e., an issue that has moved beyond the scope of a merely local or provincial issue) under its reserve power. Drawing from the applicable case law, the Court (at 432–4) ascribes a broad scope to what constitutes an issue of national concern, arguing that such issues do not need to be national emergencies (at 427–8, 431–2) and encompass a wide range of issues, such as aeronautics (at 425). Ultimately, the Court establishes that the federal system includes a legal principle that allows the central government to usurp provincial jurisdiction in relation to a matter that was previously considered local and is now determined (by the Court) to be of national concern.

Ordon Estate v. Grail[60] the Court employs what it perceives to be an established legal principle to support a depiction of the federation as centralized with a superior central government. Employing the "inter-jurisdictional immunity doctrine," the Court says that "each head of federal legislative power under the *Constitution Act, 1867*, possesses a basic, minimum, and unassailable content, which the provinces are not permitted to regulate indirectly through valid laws of general application," and accordingly, the central government's broadly construed jurisdiction over maritime matters creates "a body of law, uniform across the country, within which there is no room for the application of provincial statutes."[61]

These three examples demonstrate the range of ways doctrine is used to support a particular depiction of the federation in these imposing decisions: from citing case law to legitimize a broad or narrow scope to a government's powers; to developing a perspective on the scope of a government's powers into a legal principle; to the application of an established legal principle that reinforces a specific depiction.

In the division-of-powers decisions where modalities other than doctrinal reasoning are employed, the approach is broadly similar: the Court uses an accepted form of legal argument to reinforce the legitimacy of a depiction of the federation. So, for example, in *Canadian National Transportation*[62] the Court presents the text of the constitution as the supreme law of the country (fixed above influence from political practice),[63] one

60 *Ordon Estate v. Grail*, [1998] 3 S.C.R. 437. The issue in this case is whether the central government's maritime law applies to regulate a set of private tort actions stemming from claims of negligence in boating accidents (or if provincial law regulating tort actions through its jurisdiction over property and civil rights applies). The decision was unanimous (authored by Iacobucci and Major JJ).

61 *Ordon Estate v. Grail* at 486, 497; also see at 489–91 and 496–9.

62 *A.G. (Can.) v. Can. Nat. Transportation, Ltd.*, [1983] 2 S.C.R. 206. The issue in this case is whether the central government can prosecute an offence under its anti-competition law (or if criminal offences must be prosecuted by provincial attorneys general, given past political practice and the provinces' jurisdiction over the administration of justice). The case is essentially about the scope of the central government's criminal-law power in relation to the provinces' power over the administration of justice. The decision was unanimous (authored by Laskin CJ, with Dickson, Beetz, and Lamer JJ concurring).

63 See *Canadian National Transportation*, [1983] at 235: "[T]he issue must be decided on the basis of the language of ss. 91 and 92 [of the Constitution] and the principles of federal exclusiveness and paramountcy embodied therein. It would be one thing to assert that

that mandates a centralized federation[64] with a superior central government.[65] In *RJR-MacDonald v. Canada*[66] the Court clearly uses prudential reasoning to buttress the legitimacy of its depiction of the central government's broad criminal-law power.[67] This broad criminal-law power is rationalized as allowing the criminal prosecution of tobacco advertisers, which is presented as an innovative solution to a public evil that is necessary given the difficulties of banning tobacco advertising wholesale.[68]

---

practical considerations would best be served by recognizing provincial prosecutorial authority in the general run of criminal law offences, but this is a matter to be considered by the legislature that has constitutional authority to enact the relevant provisions. It cannot of itself determine where that constitutional authority lies."

64 See *Canadian National Transportation* at 223: "Language and logic inform constitutional interpretation, and they are applicable in considering the alleged reach of s. 92(14) and the allegedly correlative limitation of criminal procedure in s. 91(27). I find it difficult, indeed impossible, to read s. 92(14) as not only embracing prosecutorial authority respecting the enforcement of federal criminal law but diminishing the *ex facie* impact of s. 91(27) which includes procedure in criminal matters. As a matter of language, there is nothing in s. 92(14) which embraces prosecutorial authority in respect of federal criminal matters. Section 92(14) grants jurisdiction over the administration of justice, including procedure in civil matters and including also the constitution, maintenance and organization of civil and criminal provincial courts. The section thus narrows the scope of the criminal-law power under s. 91, but only with respect to what is embraced within 'the Constitution, Maintenance, and Organization of Provincial Courts … of Criminal Jurisdiction.' By no stretch of language can these words be construed to include jurisdiction over the conduct of criminal prosecutions. Moreover, as a matter of conjunctive assessment of the two constitutional provisions, the express inclusion of procedure in civil matters in provincial Courts points to an express provincial exclusion of procedure in criminal matters specified in s. 91(27)"; see also at 216–17, 220–1, 240–1.

65 Note that in the previously cited paragraph from *Canadian National Transportation*, [1983] (at 235) the Court presents the constitution as mandating a superior role for the central government in the federation ("the language of ss. 91 and 92 and *the principles of federal exclusiveness and paramountcy embodied therein*"); see also at 212, 219, 221.

66 *RJR-MacDonald Inc. v. Canada (Attorney General)* [1995] 3 S.C.R. 199. The issue in this case is a central law regulating tobacco advertising. It was a majority judgment (authored by Iacobucci J, with McLachlin J concurring).

67 On the decision presenting the central order's criminal-law power as broad, see *RJR-MacDonald v. Canada*, [1995] at 240–2.

68 See *RJR-MacDonald v. Canada* at 252–3: "Parliament has been innovative in seeking to find alternatives to a prohibition on the sale or use of tobacco. In light of the practical difficulties entailed in prohibiting the sale or consumption of tobacco, and the resulting need for innovative legislative solutions, Parliament's decision to criminalize tobacco advertisement and promotion is, in my view, a valid exercise of the criminal-law power." See, also at 241–5 and 247–9, where the Court explicitly justifies the use of the criminal law because it says (at 247) that "a prohibition upon the sale or

This form of prudential argument is generally used in conjunction with other modalities to further legitimize a depiction of the federation (as was the case in *RJR-MacDonald v. Canada*).

This practice of layering legal arguments to rationalize a particular depiction is evident in most of the seventy-four imposing decisions, as *Bank of Montreal v. Hall*[69] exemplifies. In this decision the Court broadens the definition of what constitutes a conflict of laws under the paramountcy doctrine[70] (thereby reinforcing the notion that the rules of the federation promote a centralized system with a superior central government). This general depiction in line with the pan-Canadian model is further buttressed by the Court noting the policy reasons that support a centralized power over banking, given "the pressing need to provide, on a nationwide basis, for a uniform securities mechanism."[71] In *Senate*, the provincial-equality model is reinforced by highlighting that the text of the constitution mandates that Parliament include a body that represents the interests of the province,[72] while also noting that the fathers

consumption of tobacco is not a practical policy option at this time." Generally, this type of prudential reasoning is employed to justify a centralization of authority; however, there are also decisions that employ prudential reasoning to reinforce the legitimacy of other models. For example, in *Unifund Assurance*, [2003] (at 28, 68–71) the Court emphasizes the importance of provincial boundaries and autonomy as ensuring order and justice in the federal system.

69 *Bank of Montreal v. Hall*, [1990] 1 S.C.R. 121. The key issue in this case is whether a central law that lays out the procedure and conditions for a bank to seize property as security of a loan is subject to provincial laws that regulate the procedures for the seizure of property put up as security for a loan. The decision was unanimous (authored by La Forest J).

70 As explained in chapter 3, the paramountcy doctrine holds that when there is a conflict between a valid central and provincial law the former is seen as superior and applicable. In *Bank of Montreal v. Hall*, [1990] (at 152–4) the Court broadens the definition of conflict under the paramountcy doctrine by adding the notion that a mere frustration of the legislative intent of the central government engages the doctrine. This is a considerably broader test than that established in *Multiple Access Ltd. v. McCutcheon*, [1982] 2 S.C.R. 161 (discussed in the next chapter), which states that an operational conflict is needed for the paramountcy doctrine to be applicable.

71 *Bank of Montreal v. Hall*, [1990] at 146; also see at 134–5, 137–40.

72 See *Senate* [1980], at 71, 73–5, and particularly 68, where the Court says that "the place of the Senate in the exercise of federal legislative powers is determined by ss. 17 and 91 of the [Constitution] Act [1867] ... The power to enact federal legislation was given to the Queen by and with the advice and consent of the Senate and the House of Commons. Thus, the body which had been created as a means of protecting sectional and provincial interests was made a participant in this legislative process." On the use of the textual modality in this reference, see Monahan (1987: 175–9, esp. 178).

of confederation intended this to be the role of the Senate and that they viewed the federation as a compact among equal provinces.[73]

The use of doctrinal and other forms of legal argument to reinforce particular depictions of the federation is also evident in the Court's thirteen imposing references. For example, in *Exported Natural Gas Tax*[74] the Court presents the text of the constitution as establishing a centralized federation with a generally superior central order,[75] a view that is further justified by the relevant doctrine that allows the central government to infringe upon provincial jurisdiction.[76]

These examples demonstrate how various forms of legal argument and modes of constitutional interpretation (on their own and in combination) are used to reinforce the legitimacy of particular views of

73 See *Senate* at 77 and particularly 66–7, where the Court cites debates among the fathers of confederation to note their intention that "in order to protect local interests and to prevent sectional jealousies, it was found requisite that the three great divisions into which British North America is separated, should be represented in the Upper House on the principle of equality" and that "the very essence of our compact is that the union shall be federal and not legislative," statements immediately followed with the view that "a primary purpose of the creation of the Senate, as a part of the federal legislative process, was, therefore, to afford protection to the various sectional interests in Canada in relation to the enactment of federal legislation." On the use of the historical modality and the (lack of) historical accuracy in this decision, see Monahan (1987: 179–6).

74 *Re: Exported Natural Gas Tax*, [1982] 1 S.C.R. 1004. The issue in this reference is the validity of a proposed central tax on the export of natural gas. It was a majority opinion (authored by Martland, Ritchie, Dickson, Beetz, Estey, and Chouinard JJ).

75 See *Exported Natural Gas Tax*; while the majority find s. 125 of the construction protects provinces from the taxation of their property by the central order, importantly this protection is presented as an *exception* (at 1067); the general superiority of the central order through its taxation power and other heads of power is reaffirmed. And so, in a decision structured by reviewing relevant constitutional and legislative text the Court argues (at 1053–4) that "the federal government has the undoubted power in the exercise of its regulatory authority under s. 91(2), 'The Regulation of Trade and Commerce,' to affect directly and seriously the provincial proprietary interest notwithstanding that that effect might come through regulatory taxation and notwithstanding the presence of s. 125" – a position taken further still by the dissenting opinion (at 1031), and which also indicated that the central order's residual power to legislate for the peace, order, and good government of Canada contained in s. 91 of the constitution may apply in this instance (at 1041–2).

76 See *Exported Natural Gas Tax* at 1068: "While s. 125 restricts the federal taxing power, it does not limit the exercise of the other heads of power found in s. 91. Provincial Crown lands are not immune from the operation of Dominion laws made in exercise of competent authority affecting the use of such property. This proposition flows from the doctrine that laws 'in relation to' a federal head of power may 'affect' provincial jurisdiction or property."

the federation. They show what happens in each of these seventy-four decisions: the presentation of a particular and contested perspective of what the federation is as a legal fact.

Imposing Outcomes

The extent to which a decision imposes a federal model rests not only on how the federation is understood, presented, and legitimized via legal argument, but also on the outcome of the case.

As argued previously, imposing decisions reinforce the legitimacy of a particular federal model by bringing the federal system in line with the way that model says the federation ought to be. In such decisions, the jurisdiction that wins, and the way it wins, reinforces only one model (i.e., the outcome reinforces the view that the federation *is* as a model says it *should be*).

There is a close link between the way the federation is depicted and the outcome: the depiction of the federation establishes the nature of the association that drives the decision, and the outcome of the decision in turn reinforces the legitimacy of a particular depiction of the federation as legal fact. It is thus the correspondence between a specific depiction of the federation in line with a federal model and an outcome that reinforces the legitimacy of that model that is the hallmark of an imposing decision. Each of these attributes is evident in almost all of these seventy-four cases: in virtually each decision the outcome reinforces only one model (through the jurisdiction that wins and the way it wins); and in each decision there is a correspondence between the way the federation is depicted in line with a model and the way the outcome reinforces the legitimacy of that federal model.[77]

We can see these two attributes when looking at the thirty-seven division-of-powers decisions that depict the federation in line with the pan-Canadian model. In these decisions the central government is the primary winner and the outcomes actually work to better align the federal system with the ideal model in each instance. This outcome is exemplified in *Ontario Hydro*, where the Court (following a depiction of the federation as centralized with a superior central government) finds that central-government laws apply to regulate labour relations

77 The exceptions being *Re: B.C. Family Relations Act*, [1982] 1 S.C.R. 62 and *Reference re Quebec Sales Tax*, [1994] 2 S.C.R. 715, with the outcomes in both cases being positive to multiple jurisdictions (however, still tending to reinforce the legitimacy of one model).

at provincially owned atomic power stations. This outcome works to centralize the federation and solidify the superiority of the central government because it reinforces the ability of the central government to usurp legislative jurisdiction from the provinces via a broad interpretation of its declaratory power[78] and what constitutes a matter of national concern.[79] Similarly, in *R v. Hydro-Quebec*[80] the Court's decision to allow the centre to legislate with regard to the environment (i.e., to classify material as toxic and regulate its use) follows a broad depiction of the central order's criminal-law power[81] (which, in turn, works to reinforce the nature of the federation as centralized).

In the seven federal references that impose the pan-Canadian model the central government is also the primary winner and the outcomes

---

78 The declaratory power stems from s. 92(10)(c) of the constitution, which is seen to allow the central government to unilaterally bring a local work (which would otherwise be within the legislative remit of the provinces) within its exclusive jurisdiction by declaring that it is "for the general advantage of Canada." This power has been used over 470 times, though generally prior to 1970. On the power and its use see Hogg (2009: 132, 577–80). In *Ontario Hydro*, [1993] (at 362–3) the Court granted a broad scope to this power: "[W]hen such a declaration is made, any work subject to the declaration falls … within the legislative jurisdiction of Parliament … [and thus] provincial jurisdiction over the work is ousted." Summing up the basis of its decision on this point the Court (at 367) affirms that "the legislative jurisdiction conferred over a declared work refers to the work as a going concern or functioning unit, which involves control over its operation and management … Labour relations are integral and vital parts of the operation of a work … [accordingly,] legislation governing labour relations on such works is legislation in relation to that work and falls outside provincial legislative competence."

79 *Ontario Hydro* (at 379) adds to the expanding definition of what constitutes a national concern and so falls within the exclusive legislative jurisdiction of the central order via its reserve power (in a similar manner to that taken in *R v. Crown Zellerbach*, discussed above). While the outcome in this decision is based on the central government's declaratory power and jurisdiction over matters of a national concern, similarities in the way the outcome reinforces a broad and superior scope to the central government's power over federal works (including labour relations) can be seen in *Northern Telecom v. Communication Workers*, [1983] 1 S.C.R. 733 (*Northern Telecom*).

80 *R. v. Hydro-Québec*, [1997] 3 S.C.R. 213. The issue in this case is whether environmental protection legislation (clarifying what constitutes a toxic substance) is within the central government's jurisdiction (particularly under its criminal-law power). It was a majority decision (authored by La Forest J).

81 See *R. v. Hydro-Québec* at 118–19, where the central order's criminal-law power is presented as "plenary in nature" and is explicitly interpreted in its "widest sense"; following this interpretation the Court (at 123–4, 127, 146, 152) goes on to hold environmental pollution to be a public evil that allows for regulation through the broad criminal-law power.

also align the federal system with the ideal model. For example, in *Firearms* the "long-gun" registry is found to be a legitimate exercise of the central government's criminal-law power despite provincial objections[82] – a ruling that centralizes the federation and reinforces the superiority of the central government by legitimizing its ability to affect provincial jurisdiction over the regulation of property and civil rights.[83] In *Canada Assistance Plan*, the Court holds the central government can unilaterally alter funding agreements previously reached with the provinces,[84] which reinforces the pan-Canadian model adhered to in the depiction and approach by clearly establishing the central government as superior and the federation as centralized.[85]

The same pattern of an outcome following, and reinforcing, a particular depiction of the federation is evident in the six federal references that impose the provincial-equality model. For example, in *Strait*

---

82 See *Firearms*, [2000] at 31, 39, 40, and particularly 24: "[T]he effects of the law suggest that its essence is the promotion of public safety through the reduction of the misuse of firearms, and negate the proposition that Parliament was in fact attempting to achieve a different goal such as the total regulation of firearms production, trade, and ownership"; after applying a test that builds on relevant doctrine the Court (at 35) goes on to state that the "gun control law possesses all three criteria required for a criminal law."

83 See *Firearms* at 26, 28, 29, 50, and particularly 4: "[T]he gun control law comes within Parliament's jurisdiction over criminal law. The law in 'pith and substance' is directed to enhancing public safety by controlling access to firearms through prohibitions and penalties. This brings it under the federal criminal-law power. While the law has regulatory aspects, they are secondary to its primary criminal law purpose. The intrusion of the law into the provincial jurisdiction over property and civil rights is not so excessive as to upset the balance of federalism."

84 See *Canada Assistance Plan*, [1991] at 548, where the Court rules that the central order has "the power of repealing or amending [any Act, such as that giving rise to the agreement between the provinces and the central order] and of revoking, restricting or modifying any power" that stems from such acts – a ruling that is reinforced (at 557–8) by the Court holding that provincial expectations that the agreement would not be altered do not give rise to substantive legal rights.

85 See *Canada Assistance Plan*, [1991] at 548–9, 563–4, and at 560, where the Court says: "[A] restraint on the Executive in the introduction of legislation is a fetter on the sovereignty of Parliament itself"; and also at 567, where the Court goes on to argue "it was said that, in order to protect the autonomy of the provinces, the court should supervise the federal government's exercise of its spending power. But supervision of the spending power is not a separate head of judicial review. If a statute is neither *ultra vires* nor contrary to the *Canadian Charter of Rights and Freedoms*, the courts have no jurisdiction to supervise the exercise of legislative power." As Baier (2006: 147) also argues, the outcome of this reference clearly affirms "the superiority of the federal government in setting governmental priorities through its spending power."

of Georgia[86] the territory claimed by both the central and provincial governments was determined to be the property of the colony of British Columbia prior to joining Canada (and so, it was seen to be the territory of the province of British Columbia today);[87] this ruling reinforces the provincial-equality model adhered to in the depiction as it reinforces the very nature of the federal system as a compact between equal, already established, autonomous communities that retain this autonomy into and throughout the association.[88] We see a similar link between approach and outcome in *McEvoy*,[89] where the prohibition against establishing tribunals that infringe on s. 96 superior court functions is extended to the central government;[90] and, in this negative outcome for the central government we see the provincial-equality model reinforced, as both orders of government are presented as equal in their subordination to the independence of the judiciary.[91]

---

86 *Reference re: Ownership of the Bed of the Strait of Georgia and Related Areas*, [1984] 1 S.C.R. 388. The issue in this case is whether the central or provincial government owns the seabed (and the resources contained therein) of the Strait of Georgia. It was a majority opinion (authored by Dickson J).

87 See *Strait of Georgia*, [1984] at 410, 418, 421, 425.

88 See *Strait of Georgia* at 401: "[If] British Columbia can demonstrate [that the territory belonged to the colony prior to joining the federation] … it would *necessarily follow* that the lands in question were within British Columbia when it entered Confederation and consequently British Columbia has retained proprietorship" (emphasis added). It is the implication that the colony necessarily retains its status and autonomy even after it joins the federation (a system that thus is the result of the pooling of this sovereignty with other autonomous jurisdictions) that works to reinforce the nature of the federation as a compact in line with the provincial-equality model.

89 *McEvoy v. Attorney General for New Brunswick et al.*, [1983] 1 S.C.R. 704. The issue in this reference is if the central government can establish a tribunal that infringes on the jurisdiction of superior courts protected by s. 96 of the constitution. The unanimous opinion was issued by "The Court."

90 See *McEvoy* at 719–722: "[T]he judicature sections of the *Constitution Act, 1867* guarantee the independence of the Superior Courts; they apply to Parliament as well as to the Provincial Legislatures."

91 See *McEvoy* at 719–22, and particularly 720: "The traditional independence of English Superior Court judges has been raised to the level of a fundamental principle of our federal system by the *Constitution Act, 1867* … Under the Canadian constitution the Superior Courts are independent of both levels of government. The provinces constitute, maintain and organize the Superior Courts; the federal authority appoints the judges. The judicature sections of the *Constitution Act, 1867* guarantee the independence of the Superior Courts; they apply to Parliament as well as to the Provincial Legislatures" – a point which makes clear that the two orders are equals under the constitution, something the Court reiterates (at 722): the two orders are equal as there are elements of the constitution that "are beyond conjoint provincial and federal action."

These two attributes, all provinces being the primary winners of the case and the outcome aligning the federation with what the provincial-equality model says it is and ought to be, are also evident in the twenty-three division-of-powers decisions that impose the provincial-equality model. For example, in *Irwin Toy*[92] a provincial law prohibiting advertising to children was found valid, despite the fact it affects television broadcasting (an area of exclusive central jurisdiction). This outcome reinforces a broad scope for provincial powers as well as a measure of equality with the central order (by allowing provinces to affect central jurisdiction and the rejection of a broad application of central paramountcy in the case).[93] In *Devine v. Quebec*[94] the outcome also follows and reinforces a depiction of the provinces as having broad and symmetrical powers (while simultaneously delegitimizing the view that Québec can wield asymmetrical powers as a jurisdiction housing a national minority).[95] The Court's decision reinforces the provincial-equality view by finding that it is within the ability of all provinces (not just Québec) to validly regulate language use in relation to commerce, with the basis for this result being their shared authority over the regulation of commerce within the provinces.[96]

---

92 *Irwin Toy Ltd. v. Quebec (Attorney General)*, [1989] 1 S.C.R. 927. The issue in the case is whether provincial legislation prohibiting advertising to children is ultra vires because it infringes on federal jurisdiction over television broadcasters. It was a majority judgment (authored by Dickson, Lamer, and Wilson JJ).

93 See *Irwin Toy* at 950–1 and 957–8, where the Court works from a depiction of the order that allows provinces to legitimately pass legislation that affects areas of central jurisdiction, while (at 963–4) additionally applying the paramountcy doctrine in a way that protects provincial autonomy (i.e., employing the more stringent test that requires an operational conflict between laws for provincial legislation to be displaced by central legislation).

94 *Devine v. Quebec (Attorney General)*, [1988] 2 S.C.R. 790. The division-of-power issue in this case is whether Québec legislation that mandates the use of French for business is invalid because it infringes on the central government's power over the criminal law and trade and commerce. The case also involves Charter issues, which were determinative in the appeal. The unanimous judgment was issued by "The Court."

95 On this depiction and its link to the outcome see *Devine v. Quebec* at 807–9, where the Court rejects the view that a plenary authority over "language" is given to either level of government, instead deciding that provincial legislation regulating language must do so in relation to a head of power that all provinces share through s. 92 of the constitution (i.e., the power must be one exercised within the symmetrical jurisdiction afforded provinces as a level of government).

96 As just stated, it is the focus on the shared jurisdiction of all provinces in this area that reinforces the view of them as equal in status. This understanding of the nature of the provinces simultaneously delegitimizes the view that Québec holds an asymmetrical power to regulate language in the province.

Finally, despite *Devine v. Quebec* challenging the legitimacy of the multinational model, in *Quebec v. Grondin*[97] (the only case that imposes the multinational model), the outcome clearly follows and reinforces the view that the federation allows Québec to wield asymmetrical powers as a result of its distinct historical and cultural situation. The outcome of *Quebec v. Grondin* reinforces this view of the federal system by allowing Québec a unique and distinct power to establish an inferior court/tribunal that handles landlord-lessee affairs based on the fact that inferior courts within Québec dealt with such matters prior to confederation.[98] In other words, Québec (alone) is allowed to establish such a tribunal, based on the unique legal and historical circumstances of the jurisdiction – a ruling that legitimizes an asymmetrical arrangement based on the pre-confederation situation in Québec (i.e., recognizing a unique and enduring quality of Québec both as a colony prior to confederation and province after the union).[99]

What these examples demonstrate is that regardless of which model is imposed, the outcome and depiction in these seventy-four decisions work in tandem to reinforce the legitimacy of one particular federal model. They exemplify how a partial understanding of what the federation is and ought to be informs the outcomes of a case, and how in turn these outcomes reinforce the legitimacy of that partial view. They show how these decisions actually align the federation with what a model says it should be – how they merge the normative with the factual.

An Imposing Role

The SCC's adopted role within the federation can be an integral part of a decision imposing a particular model. As noted earlier, the ideal role for the judiciary as the federal arbiter is linked to a particular

97 The issue in this case is whether a tribunal dealing with landlord–lessee relations established by Québec violates superior court jurisdiction protected under s. 96 of the constitution (and the role of the central government in appointing and establishing such courts).

98 See *Quebec v. Grondin*, [1983] at 377 and 382–3, where the Court says that because inferior courts in Lower Canada (Québec) exercised this power prior to confederation, the province can establish a tribunal with such powers in the contemporary period.

99 Contrast the way this case reinforces the multinational view of the federation and distribution of powers (in the application of the *Residential Tenancies Act* test) with the way the provincial-equality model is reinforced to the detriment of the multinational model in *Sobeys v. Nova Scotia*, [1989], discussed above.

understanding of what the federation is and ought to be.[100] Generally, there are three ideal roles for the judiciary that stem from an understanding of the constitution and the federation as a fixed set of rules that are to be enforced and protected (the umpire, branch of government, and guardian roles).[101] Moreover, there are links between these three ideal roles and the three key federal models: the Court as an umpire draws from and reinforces elements of the pan-Canadian model; the branch of government model draws from and reinforces elements of the provincial-equality model; and the guardian role draws from and reinforces elements of the multinational model. What we see in a number of SCC decisions is the Court adopting and promoting one of these three roles in a way that works from, and also reinforces, particular understandings of the actual and ideal federal system.

As table 5.3 indicates, in the seventy-four imposing decisions I was able to determine the Court's self-selected role in 38 cases.[102] In these 38 decisions the Court adopts a role for the judiciary as an umpire in 16 cases and as a branch of government in 18 cases, while also displaying a measure of support for the judiciary as a facilitator of negotiation to manage conflict over the federal system in 9 cases.[103] Interestingly, there is also a high degree of correspondence between the identified role of umpire and the imposition of a pan-Canadian model (13 of 14 cases).

In any event, it is not the frequency of particular roles (or even the correspondence between particular roles and particular models) that

---

100 As argued in chapter 2, despite the lack of coherence within federal theory with regard to theories of the federation and theories of judicial review (i.e., the role of the Court within the system), there is an inherent link between these two things as the Court's role within the federation stems from how the actual and ideal constitutional and federal system are understood.

101 These three roles can be contrasted with the facilitator role, which starts from an understanding of the federation as a contested normative system and seeks to mange conflict over it by fostering negotiation.

102 The lack of information in a number of cases stems from the SCC tending to avoid theoretical discussions on points such as the role of the judiciary in the federation (unless the issue is raised by a party).

103 It is important to note that the Court can and does display support for multiple roles within a single decision. In all 9 of the decisions where the facilitator role is adopted there is a measure of legitimacy afforded multiple models in the depiction of the federation; because of this, and the support for the facilitator role, these cases tended to fall on the lower end of the scale of imposing decisions.

is of primary concern; what really matters is how the SCC employs a particular role to reinforce the legitimacy of a particular federal model, which happens in two key ways.

The first is when the Court actively employs its adopted role to reinforce a specific depiction of the federation in line with a federal model. A number of division-of-powers decisions exemplify this approach. In *Canada v. Law Society of BC*[104] a depiction of the federation as decentralized, with provinces being equal among each other and with the central government,[105] is buttressed by presenting the judiciary as a branch of government independent from both the central government and the provinces and as the arbiter between these two equal orders of government.[106] In contrast, *Hunt v. T&N* presents the judiciary as a branch of government that is essentially unitary in nature, acting as a national institution (with provincial superior courts being more than "mere local courts" and the SCC as having a "unifying jurisdiction" as an apex court).[107] This adopted role for the judiciary as a branch of government thus helps to reinforce the legitimacy of the depiction in the decision, which presents the federation as centralized and stresses the pan-state nature of the political community.[108] At the same time, in *Scowby v. Glendinning* the Court says that the constitutional law mandates a centralized federation with a superior central government, and that the Court's role is to enforce this law as an umpire, not to comment

104 *A.G. Can. v. Law Society of B.C.*, [1982] 2 S.C.R. 307. The issue in this case is whether central anti-competition legislation is applicable to provincial law societies. The decision was unanimous (authored by Estey J).

105 See *Canada v. Law Society of BC*. at 318, 334–6, 347, 349.

106 See *Canada v. Law Society of BC*. at 327, where the SCC notes the equality of both orders of government in relation to an independent judiciary: the provincial superior courts have always "occupied a position of prime importance in the constitutional pattern of this country ... They cross the dividing line, as it were, in the federal-provincial scheme of division of jurisdiction, being organized by the provinces under s. 92(14) of the *Constitution Act* and are presided over by judges appointed and paid by the federal government (sections 96 and 100 of the *Constitution Act*)," and that these provincially organized superior courts "are surely bound to execute all laws in force in the Dominion, whether they are enacted by the Parliament of the Dominion or by the Local Legislatures"; see also at 326–8 and 330.

107 See *Hunt v. T&N*, [1993] on the courts as unitary in nature (at 314), on the courts as more than mere local institutions (at 311–12), and on the SCC as a unifying apex court (at 318–19).

108 See the discussion of this depiction above.

on its wisdom[109] (thereby reinforcing a depiction of the federation in line with the pan-Canadian model as simply reflecting the rules of the constitution).

The SCC also employs an adopted role for the judiciary to reinforce the way it depicts the federation in its imposing references. For example, in *McEvoy* the SCC presents the judiciary as an independent branch of government, saying this role has been "raised to the level of a fundamental principle of our federal system" – a role that reinforces the provincial-equality model imposed in this reference because it means the courts are "independent of both levels of government" (reinforcing an equality between the two orders).[110]

The second way the Court's self-selected role can work to impose a federal model is by employing the adopted role to justify an outcome that reinforces the legitimacy of a particular model. The archetypal example occurs when the Court says that its role as umpire of the federation mandates it to enforce the rules of the constitution, regardless of their effect. This approach is exemplified in the division-of-powers case *Northern Telecom*.[111] Here, the finding that the central government can carve out the regulation of labour relations from provincial jurisdiction when it is related to federal undertakings is reinforced *as a legal rule* through the Court's self-selected role. The Court says its proper role is to enforce the constitutional division of powers that allows such action, and to police conflict that may arise as a result of those rules, not to act as a branch of government to adapt those rules or to facilitate negotiation over the rules.[112] Similar examples of the Court using the umpire

109 See *Scowby v. Glendinning*, [1986] at 238: "The terms of s. 91(27) of the Constitution must be read as assigning to Parliament exclusive jurisdiction over criminal law in the widest sense of the term. Provincial legislation which in pith and substance falls inside the perimeter of that term broadly defined is *ultra vires*. Parliament's legislative jurisdiction properly founded on s. 91(27) may have a destructive force on encroaching legislation from provincial legislatures, *but such is the nature of the allocation procedure in ss. 91 and 92 of the Constitution. Here we are not concerned with the result in law of the exercise by Parliament of one of its exclusive heads of jurisdiction*" (emphasis added).

110 *McEvoy*, [1983] at 720; see also at 719–21 generally.

111 The issue in this case is whether labour relations associated with a federal undertaking fall under central or provincial competence. The majority decision was authored by Estey J, with Dickson J concurring.

112 See *Northern Telecom*, [1983] at 742: "It is inherent in a federal system such as that established under the *Constitution Act*, that the courts will be the authority in the community to control the limits of the respective sovereignties of the two plenary

role to further justify an outcome that favours the pan-Canadian model can clearly be seen in *R. v. Malmo-Levine*[113] and *R. v. Morgentaler.*[114]

Despite these cases, in a number of decisions the Court embraces the branch of government role to allow it to consider the policy rationale of a particular law or action; importantly, in these decisions the Court often goes on to employ these policy considerations to help justify a law as legitimately within the scope of a government's jurisdiction. For example, in *RJR-MacDonald v. Canada* the Court justifies the outcome (which reinforces a broad scope to the central government's criminal-law power and allows it to regulate tobacco advertising) by implying its role permits it to consider this action as a practical necessity and an innovative policy solution.[115] Similarly, in *Bank of Montreal v. Hall* the Court justifies the outcome that reinforces a broad scope to the central government's power over banking by noting "the pressing need to provide, on a nationwide basis, for a [*sic*] uniform security mechanisms" (implying such policy concerns are within its proper role to consider).[116]

This approach of employing a particular role to rationalize and justify an outcome that reinforces a specific model is also evident in the SCC's federal references. In *Canada Assistance Plan* the Court explicitly rejects a role of guarding the federal principle or acting as an equal branch of government. Instead, it opts to explicitly enforce the rules of the constitution as an umpire, regardless of the effect on the balance of the federation or intergovernmental relations (even if, as in this reference, these rules are interpreted to legitimize the central government infringing on what is generally thought to be provincial jurisdiction).[117]

---

governments, as well as to police agencies within each of these spheres to ensure their operations remain within their statutory boundaries. Both duties of course fall upon the courts when acting within their own proper jurisdiction." See also at 745 and particularly 768–9, where the Court rejects the view that its role is to facilitate continued negotiation over the constitutional rules.

113 See *R. v. Malmo-Levine; R. v. Caine*, [2003] 3 S.C.R. 571.

114 See *R. v. Morgentaler*, [1993] 3 S.C.R. 463.

115 See *RJR-MacDonald v. Canada*, [1995] at 39.

116 *Bank of Montreal v. Hall*, [1990] at 146.

117 See *Canada Assistance Plan*, [1991] at 558–9 and particularly 567, where the Court responds to the argument "that the 'overriding principle of federalism' requires that Parliament be unable to interfere in areas of provincial jurisdiction. It was said that, in order to protect the autonomy of the provinces, the Court should supervise the federal government's exercise of its spending power. But supervision of the spending power is not a separate head of judicial review. If a statute is neither *ultra vires* nor contrary to the *Canadian Charter of Rights and Freedoms*, the courts have no

In both streams we can see examples of the SCC adopting and promoting an ideal role for the judiciary in line with what a particular federal model expounds it should be, while also employing this role in a way that reinforces key aspects of a federal model's depiction of the federation. In addition, there are a number of examples that demonstrate how the Court employs a selected role to justify an outcome that favours a jurisdiction and reinforces a federal model.

The Problem with This Imposing Jurisprudence

The above review establishes the difference between these seventy-four imposing decisions and the exemplar of the *Secession Reference*. Imposing decisions overwhelmingly depict the federation in line with only one model, while the *Secession Reference* recognizes the legitimacy of multiple models and the federal system as the process and outcome of negotiation between the subscribers of these models. Legal argument and constitutional interpretation are employed in the imposing cases to frame one perspective on what the federation is in the legitimacy of the law. This approach is generally rejected in the *Secession Reference*, where legal argument and methods of constitutional interpretation are used to lend legitimacy to multiple federal models. Similarly, the outcomes of these seventy-four imposing decisions diverge significantly from the *Secession Reference*; the former create stark winners and losers and reinforce specific federal models to the detriment of others; the latter rejects a zero-sum approach and seeks an outcome that benefits all parties to the conflict, while also working to reinforce the legitimacy of multiple federal models. Finally, the Court's adopted role in the *Secession Reference* facilitates negotiation and dialogue to manage the conflict between the actors subscribing to legitimate federal models. The tendency of the SCC in the imposing cases is to adopt a role in line with what a particular federal model mandates it should be, while also employing this role in a way that reinforces key aspects of a specific federal model's depiction of the federation and to justify outcomes that reinforce that model.

As the above analysis demonstrates, there is little difference between the SCC's imposing division-of-power decisions and its references. In

---

jurisdiction to supervise the exercise of legislative power." Gerald Baier (2006: 149) has also noted this aspect of the decision: "The court claimed that it could not supervise the exercise of the federal spending power even if the stability of intergovernmental compromise was at stake."

both streams the models imposed, and the way they are imposed, are substantially similar. For example, the pan-Canadian model is imposed a majority of the time in both streams (61% in division-of-powers decisions and 55% in references). Similarly, there is virtually no support for the multinational model across both streams. Moreover, the pattern of an imposing decision is generally followed, with all seventy-four decisions depicting the federation in line with a particular model and reaching outcomes that draw from and reinforce this depiction.

At the same time, and as already discussed in the methods chapter, there are some general differences between the two streams of federalism jurisprudence that should be noted. As the thirteen imposing federal references demonstrate, these cases tend to place the orders of government in direct opposition,[118] while a majority of the sixty-one imposing division-of-powers decisions (50) *begin* as conflicts between private actors and a government. Moreover, as discussed above, references are technically advisory opinions, whereas division-of-powers cases lead to an actual disposition of rights. However, these differences are offset by the fact that in a large number of the division-of-powers cases (25) governments intervene on behalf of the private actor to turn the conflict into one between orders of government,[119] as well as the reality that references are almost always followed as binding decisions.[120]

We can also see in these imposing decisions a slight difference in the apparent willingness of the Court to find a law unconstitutional (with rulings of ultra vires in approximately 45 per cent of imposing references, compared to about 34 per cent of imposing division-of-powers decisions). This discrepancy seems to support the view, already discussed, that the different context of the references leads to slightly different outcomes; however, this small difference is understandable, since the nature of a reference is to deal with especially contentious legislation.[121]

Ultimately, my concern is not only with which order of government wins a case, or the rate at which the Court overturns laws. I argue that

118 In 10 of the 13 imposing references the dynamic of conflict was between governments.

119 The result of these interventions is that in a majority of imposing decisions, some 58%, the orders of government are in direct conflict. Moreover, the orders of government are cooperating in these cases a mere 16% of the time (contrast this with the higher percentage of cooperation evident in those cases where the Court recognizes the legitimacy of multiple models, discussed in the next chapter).

120 See Hogg (2009: 260–1).

121 See the discussion on this point in chapter 3.

how these decisions are reached, and the extent to which they reinforce specific understandings of the federation to the detriment of others, deserves equal attention. And, on this front, the slight differences between these two streams of federalism jurisprudence are offset by their shared tendency to follow the pattern of an imposing decision. All of the seventy-four decisions discussed in this chapter, to some degree, depict the federation in line with one model; legitimize that depiction as a fact through accepted forms of legal argument; reach an outcome that draws from and reinforces the depiction of the federation in line with a particular federal model; while also adopting a role for the judiciary that reinforces the depiction and further justifies the outcome.

It is the shared nature of these decisions that supports the core argument of the chapter. The above analysis shows that the SCC can impose a particular federal model in its decisions, which it does in a significant proportion (57%) of its federalism jurisprudence between 1980 and 2010.

As argued earlier in the book, the problematic aspect of the SCC's imposing jurisprudence is that these decisions fail to account for the inherent conflict over nationality and the federation in Canada. Canada is a plurinational state. Accordingly, various groups hold conflicting views about the national character of the country (i.e., seeing Canada as uninational or multinational). Canada is also a federation. The nature of federal systems as normative frameworks leads to inherent disagreement about the ideal distribution of resources and power. Canada's dual nature as a *plurinational federation* thus leads to views on the national character of the state mixing with associated beliefs of how resources and power ought to be distributed via the federation. The result is a significant amount of conflict within and over the federal system. For the federation to remain legitimate in the eyes of those who are subject to the association, the way conflict is handled must generate a sense of loyalty to the system. This is why the Court's role as arbiter of conflict within and over the federal system is so important and also why its decisions that fail to recognize and account for the base sources of this conflict are potentially problematic.

When the SCC fails to recognize and account for the drivers of conflict over nationality and the federation in Canada, and rather picks a particular federal model to inform its decisions, those decisions have the potential to delegitimize its role as federal arbiter and the federation more generally. Such decisions may be seen by members within the association as imposing, because they can reinforce a particular perspective of what the federation is that they do not subscribe to. In these decisions, the "losing" parties have to absorb a negative outcome while also being told the way they understand the federation, at a base level, is an illegitimate perspective. This combination means that the Court can be seen as a biased and unfair institution, falling well short of the popular ideal of neutrality. Moreover, the outcomes in imposing decisions align the distribution of powers and resources closer to the ideal of the imposed federal model. This alienates those imposed upon, because the federation no longer lines up with what they believe it is and should be (while also leading them to perceive the federation as "stacking the deck" against them in future conflicts). The potential effect of all this is that loyalty to the federation and the way it manages conflict can suffer. Those groups that are imposed upon see the process of conflict management as unfair because their perspective on the nature of the federation is delegitimized in the process, and they are further alienated from the federal system that results from an imposed decision as it reflects a distribution of powers and resources that weakens the basis of their perspective into the future.

We can better understand the potential effects of these seventy-four decisions by looking at four specific trends. The first is the tendency of the Court in these decisions to impose the pan-Canadian model to a greater extent than the other models and to favour the central government in the outcomes.[122] The figures support this point: in forty-four of the seventy-four decisions (59%) the Court imposes the pan-Canadian model and reaches an outcome generally favourable to the central government. Also, the Court tends to find central laws valid at a considerably higher rate compared to provincial laws: 70 per cent of the time central laws are challenged they are upheld, compared to 55 per cent where the impugned legislation is provincial.

---

122 The debate over the SCC as a centralizing force in the federation is a perennial topic of Canadian political studies. There are those who argue the Court is biased in favour of the central government (Bzdera 1993; Leclair 2003; MacKay 2001; Greschner 2000) and those who see it as a generally "balanced" federal arbiter (Hogg 1979; Baier 2003, 2006). My own analysis recognizes the centralizing tendency in the Court's imposing decisions, but also notes that this is not always the case (particularly in the Court's decisions that afford a measure of legitimacy to multiple models, as I will argue in the next chapter). More importantly, focusing only on the outcomes of the SCC's decisions (and the extent to which they favour the central or provincial governments) misses significant aspects of the Court's work as federal arbiter. Equally important is the way these decisions are reached.

Looking at the raw figures of court decisions, though, does not always tell the whole story. One decision can fundamentally alter the federal system, while another string of decisions can deal with technical or relatively minor issues. However, considering the context surrounding these imposing decisions and the extent to which they actually affect the federation only strengthens the assertion that the SCC, at times, acts as a strongly centralizing force in Canada.

Compare, for example, some of the key outcomes of the federal references above. The net effect of the decisions in favour of the central government is to legitimize a constitution passed without the consent of Québec; allow the central government to unilaterally amend funding levels of key social programs established by agreements with the provinces; uphold the central government's ability to raise taxes by any mode or system regardless of the effect on provincial jurisdiction; and allow the central government to regulate and establish a registration system for "long-guns" under its criminal-law power regardless of the effect on the provinces' jurisdiction.[123] The decisions in the provinces' favour prohibit the central government from abolishing or fundamentally altering the Senate; grant ownership of the seabed between Vancouver Island and the west coast of British Columbia to that province; prohibit one province from expropriating the property of another province (as they are all barred from affecting extraterritorial rights); and allow provinces to establish tribunals that deal with landlord-tenant disputes.[124]

This same pattern is evident in the imposing division-of-powers decisions: the Court tends to expand the central government's scope of power in important areas and with far-reaching implications. The expansion of power is exemplified through the corpus of decisions that broaden the scope of the central order's criminal law power.[125] Similarly,

---

123 See, respectively, *Quebec Veto*, [1982], *Canada Assistance Plan*, [1991], *Goods and Service Tax*, [1992], and *Firearms*, [2000].

124 See, respectively, *Senate*, [1980], *Strait of Georgia*, [1984], *Upper Churchill*, [1984], and *Reference re Amendments to the Residential Tenancies Act (N.S.)*, [1996] 1 S.C.R. 186.

125 See, in particular, *Canadian National Transportation*, [1983] and *R. v. Hydro-Québec*, [1997]; see also *Attorney General of Alberta et al. v. Putnam et al.*, [1981] 2 S.C.R. 267; *Westendorp v. the Queen*, [1983] 1 S.C.R. 43; *Bisaillon v. Keable*, [1983] 2 S.C.R. 60; *R. v. Wetmore*, [1983]; *Skoke-Graham v. The Queen*, [1985] 1 S.C.R. 106; *R. v. Big M Drug Mart Ltd.*, [1985] 1 S.C.R. 295; *Scowby v. Glendinning*, [1986]; *Knox Contracting Ltd. v. Canada*, [1990] 2 S.C.R. 338; *R. v. Swain*, [1991] 1 S.C.R. 933; *R. v. Morgentaler*, [1993] 3 S.C.R. 463; *RJR-MacDonald v. Canada*, [1995]; *R. v. Malmo-Levine*, [2003]; and *R. v. Demers*, [2004] 2 S.C.R. 489.

there are the lines of decision that revitalize the central government's trade and commerce power;[126] establish a broad and exclusive jurisdiction for the central government over maritime matters;[127] and expand its power over banking and bankruptcy (while reinforcing the paramountcy of central-government laws when they conflict with provincial laws).[128] There are also the decisions that broadly define the core of a federal undertaking that is immune from provincial legislation[129] and reinforce the ability of the central government to usurp provincial jurisdiction over any work or undertaking through its declaratory power.[130] Finally, there are the cases that generously interpret the central order's ability to take legislative control over matters of "national concern,"[131] including the use of this and other broadly defined powers to regulate the environment.[132] The corollary of the expansion of central power has been, in most cases, to narrow areas of provincial jurisdiction or to allow the central government to affect matters within provincial competence.

At the same time, there are division-of-powers decisions that impose the provincial-equality model and favour the provinces. The few areas where provincial jurisdiction has been expanded include the ability to establish administrative tribunals[133] and the ability to levy variable and indirect fees.[134] There are also the select cases that effectively narrow

126 See *Canadian National Transportation*, [1983]; *General Motors of Canada Ltd. v. City National Leasing*, [1989] 1 S.C.R. 641; *Québec Ready Mix Inc. v. Rocois Construction Inc.*, [1989] 1 S.C.R. 695; and *Kirkbi AG v. Ritvik Holdings*, [2005].

127 See *Zavarovalna Skupnost, (Insurance Community Triglav Ltd.) v. Terrasses Jewellers Inc.*, [1983] 1 S.C.R. 283; *Whitbread v. Walley*, [1990]; *Monk Corp. v. Island Fertilizers Ltd.*, [1991] 1 S.C.R. 779; and *Ordon Estate v. Grail*, [1998].

128 See *Bank of Montreal v. Hall*, [1990]; *Husky Oil Operations Ltd. v. Minister of National Revenue*, [1995] 3 S.C.R. 453; and *M & D Farm*, [1999].

129 See *Northern Telecom*, [1983]; *National Battlefields Commission*, [1990]; *Ontario Hydro*, [1993]; and *Westcoast Energy Inc. v. Canada (National Energy Board)*, [1998] 1 S.C.R. 322.

130 See *Ontario Hydro*, [1993].

131 See *R. v. Crown Zellerbach*, [1988]; and *Ontario Hydro*, [1993].

132 See *Northwest Falling Contractors Ltd. v. The Queen*, [1980] 2 S.C.R. 292; *R. v. Crown Zellerbach*, [1988]; and *R. v. Hydro-Québec*, [1997].

133 See *Capital Regional District v. Concerned Citizens of British Columbia et al.*, [1982] 2 S.C.R. 842; and *Sobeys v. Nova Scotia*, [1989].

134 Either through an expansive reading of the provinces' power to exclusively enact direct taxes within their borders or a liberal interpretation of their power to raise levies in relation to a licensing scheme; see *Massey-Ferguson Industries Ltd. et al. v. Government of Saskatchewan et al.*, [1981] 2 S.C.R. 413; *Minister of Finance of New Brunswick et al. v. Simpsons-Sears Ltd.*, [1982] 1 S.C.R. 144; *Allard Contractors v. Coquitlam*, [1993]; and *Dunne v. Quebec (Deputy Minister of Revenue)*, [2007] 1 S.C.R. 853.

the central government's criminal-law power (i.e., in relation to the administration of justice within the province and the provinces' powers over property and civil rights).[135] The tendency, though, is for decisions to maintain (not expand) provincial powers, for example, in relation to property and civil rights[136] or labour relations.[137] This tendency is also exemplified by the decisions that allow provincial laws of general application to apply to federal undertakings and persons (but only to the extent provincial laws do not affect the core of federal jurisdiction over these matters).[138]

In these seventy-four decisions we can see the Court centralizing power in key areas. The relative importance of the decisions that favour the central government, in their effect on the overall federal system, is markedly different than those that favour the provinces. When the central government wins, the decision tends to fundamentally reinforce a generally centralized system with a superior central government. When the provinces win, the decisions tend to reinforce the legitimacy of select areas of provincial competence and to arbitrate rather technical issues (like the validity of a local levy). The impression of the Court's imposing decisions over the last three decades is thus one of an expanding central power in relation to stagnant, and even declining, provincial jurisdiction. As John Leclair has argued, this trend in the SCC's work is clear: the central government's powers have been liberally interpreted, while the provinces' powers have generally been held at bay or reduced.[139]

This centralist tendency, in and of itself, is problematic. Consistently siding with the central government delegitimizes the Court as arbiter of the federation for the subscribers of the provincial-equality

135 With regard to the administration of justice, see *MacKeigan v. Hickman*, [1989] and *Consortium Developments (Clearwater) Ltd. v. Sarnia (City)*, [1998] 3 S.C.R. 3; with regard to property and civil rights, see *Labatt Breweries of Canada Ltd. v. Attorney General of Canada*, [1980] 1 S.C.R. 914. However, these cases need to be placed in the context of a line of federalism jurisprudence that has significantly expanded the centre's criminal-law power over the past thirty years.

136 See *Fowler v. The Queen*, [1980]; and *Clark v. Canadian National Railway Co.*, [1988] 2 S.C.R. 680.

137 See *Four B Manufacturing v. United Garment Workers*, [1980] 1 S.C.R. 1031 (Four B Manufacturing); *YMHA v. Brown*, [1989]; and *Canada Labour Relations Board et al. v. Paul L'Anglais Inc. et al.*, [1983] 1 S.C.R. 147.

138 With regard to federal undertakings, see *Irwin Toy v. Quebec*, [1989]; with regard to "federal persons" (i.e., Aboriginals) see *Four B Manufacturing*, [1980].

139 See Leclair (2003).

and multinational models. For these groups, this centralist tendency raises questions about the neutrality of the Court and alienates these subscribers from the federal system that stems from these decisions (as it does not reflect their view of what the federation is and ought to be). However, as I have said, decision outcomes are not my main concern; equally important is the decision process.

The issue with this trend in the SCC's work, then, is not just the tendency to side with the central government, but also *the way the centralization happens* (i.e., the fact that these decisions *impose* the pan-Canadian model). The imposing nature heightens the extent to which these decisions reinforce the perception that the SCC is biased against subscribers of the provincial-equality and multinational models, while also further alienating these subscribers from the resulting federal system. This alienation can happen because the way the central government wins legitimizes the pan-Canadian model, while delegitimizing the other models. Accordingly, those imposed upon have to deal with the negative outcome of a case while being told the way they understand the federation is wrong and illegitimate. Furthermore, they have to come to terms with the fact that the result of the decision and the reasons it is based on further align the system with the pan-Canadian model.

Of course, in over 40 per cent of the above cases the provinces win and the provincial-equality model is imposed, an outcome that could be seen as close to striking a balance between these two models. In other words, the flip side of nearly 60 per cent of these decisions imposing the pan-Canadian model is that over 40 per cent impose the provincial-equality model. The argument could be made that in the absence of "balance" *within* a decision, at least there is a measure of "balance" *between* decisions. Setting aside the 20 per cent difference, this view still does not sit well with the analysis that the imposing pan-Canadian decisions tend to be more important and have further-reaching effects for the nature of the system. More importantly, the ideal that the SCC can be "balanced" in its federalism jurisprudence by seeking a rough equilibrium where the central government wins half the time and the provinces win the other half is flawed. Such an ideal misses the fact that the outcomes of federalism jurisprudence are only half the story – the way these decisions are made is equally important. The ideal of balance in federalism jurisprudence is properly understood in relation to the extent to which the Court's decisions (in both their approach and outcome) recognize and account for the legitimate views of what the federation is and ought to be. On this score, it is hard to see how there is any balance in these seventy-four decisions. Balanced federalism jurisprudence would have no imposing decisions.

The fact that the provincial-equality model is imposed in 40 per cent of cases where the central order loses also presents a fundamental issue: a lack of support for the multinational model. This lack of support is the second problematic trend I want to highlight in these imposing decisions. The model is imposed in only one case[140] and receives a measure of legitimacy through the Court's depiction of the federation in only two others.[141] In addition, the multinational model is *actively* delegitimized in ten decisions.[142] Thus, even when the provinces are the "winners," this coincides with the imposition of the provincial-equality model, which generally delegitimizes key aspects of the multinational model (i.e., by reinforcing a view of provinces as having symmetrical powers given their status as equal territorial units).

This tendency in the SCC's imposing decisions is problematic given the reality that the multinational model is a legitimate view of what the federation is and ought to be. The fact is that a significant proportion of Canadians view the state as housing multiple nations, and that the federation does and ought to accommodate these groups. One can *argue* that Canada is a single nation, but, one can hardly deny that a great many people *believe* that the Québécois and Aboriginals are nations within Canada. The multinational model is not an abstract theory. It reflects historical processes and institutional arrangements in Canada, and it continues to inform political mobilization.

The Court's failure in these decisions to recognize the legitimacy of this model may decrease support for the process of arbitrating conflict within the federation, and for the system itself, among subscribers of the multinational model. How else can someone who sees Canada as multinational, and federation as the means to accommodate this fact, react to the Court telling them they are fundamentally wrong? The

140 *Quebec v. Grondin*, [1983].

141 See *The Queen v. Sutherland et al.*, [1980] 2 S.C.R. 451; and *Moore v. Johnson et al.* [1982] 1 S.C.R. 115.

142 See *Quebec Veto*, [1982]; *Devine v. Quebec*, [1988]; *Sobeys v. Nova Scotia*, [1989]; *National Battlefields Commission*, [1990]; *Whitbread v. Walley*, [1990]; *Ontario Hydro*, [1993]; *Hunt v. T&N*, [1993]; *BC v. Canada*, [1994]; *Delgamuukw v. British Columbia*, [1997] 3 S.C.R. 1010 (*Delgamuukw v. BC*); and *BC v. Imperial Tobacco*, [2005]. This outcome happens only once for the provincial-equality model, and does not happen for the pan-Canadian model.

potential effect of these decisions is a perceived promotion of Canada as a single nation with a strong central government, or of the provinces as equal in their status as territorial units. These views of Canada do not sit well with the views of many in the state. They also fail to account for the facts on the ground (i.e., that Canada is a plurinational federation with political and institutional arrangements that seek to accommodate groups that self-identify as nations). Ultimately, the lack of recognition afforded the multinational model in these decisions can negatively affect the ability of the Court and the system in general to manage the inherent conflict that takes place over nationality and the distribution of resources and power.

Failing to recognize the legitimacy of the multinational model, and imposing either the pan-Canadian or provincial-equality model, can also lead to problematic legal reasoning in the Court's federalism jurisprudence. The flaw in the legal reasoning of these imposing decisions is the failure to recognize and account for the legal and political facts that have been established over time that support the multinational model. The result is a set of decisions that are not based on a comprehensive (or accurate) picture of the constitutional and federal system of the state.

As chapter 1 demonstrates, the constitutional, political, and institutional foundations of Canada allow supporters of the multinational model to find support for their view. From the Royal Proclamation (1763), to the Quebec Act (1774), to the provisions of the Constitution Act (1867) that guarantee Québec a certain number of seats in the House of Commons, to the recent recognition in the House of Commons of Québec's status as a distinct society (1999) and nation (2006), the federation has developed in a way that reflects key elements of the multinational model. The federation is a system that incorporates elements of asymmetry, the validity of dividing territory along ethno-cultural lines, the accommodation of ethno-cultural difference, and a view of central institutions as spaces to represent Québec as a national minority. Ignoring these elements of the constitutional and political system in a federal decision can lead to non-optimal outcomes, since the judgment would be founded on a partial (and potentially biased) picture of the constitutional foundation. And rendering decisions on such a faulty foundation can limit the ability of the Court to generate loyalty among the groups that subscribe to the key federal models in Canada.

The issue with this form of legal reasoning is a wider problem with all decisions following the imposing approach. By denying the validity of competing perspectives (be it pan-Canadian, provincial-equality, or multinational) the Court is failing to take into consideration key elements of the federal and constitutional association in reaching an outcome. But, this practice – and the issues it creates – is most starkly exemplified in these imposing decisions through the lack of support afforded the multinational model.

The third key trend is the way these imposing decisions create stark winners and losers. A shared characteristic of virtually all the imposing decisions is that they overwhelmingly resort to zero-sum outcomes. In these decisions one jurisdiction generally achieves absolute victory, and importantly this happens in a way that aligns the federation with a particular federal model. Of the seventy-four imposing decisions there are only five cases where one jurisdiction does not win outright.[143] I recognize that the adversarial nature of most legal conflicts creates a need to declare a winner and to dispose of rights accordingly. However, the process of arbitration can be done in a way that rejects stark, zero-sum outcomes. Such an approach was embraced in the *Secession Reference* and, as the next chapter demonstrates, in many of the decisions that follow its lead.

The *dispute-resolution* approach in these imposing decisions has the potential to cause a number of problems. First, similarly to the first two trends in these cases, it may erode the legitimacy of the Court as arbiter and the federation more generally. Creating stark winners and losers generates resentment towards the process of conflict resolution and the resulting system that stems from the decision. Moreover, SCC decisions have a measure of finality, with no further appeal and the permanency of law. When they are delivered in a way that reinforces this finality, as is in the cases discussed above, the effect can be to suppress the continued conflict over the federal system that is inherent in any association. As argued earlier, the suppression of conflict over the nature of the federation does little to manage it (and can actually work to exacerbate it in the long run). Also, the nature of these decisions as definitive and clearly siding with one jurisdiction while reinforcing one

143 In these five cases the outcome is positive for more than one jurisdiction (*BC Family Relations Act*, [1982]; *Exported Natural Gas Tax*, [1982]; *Quebec Sales Tax*, [1994]; *Sobeys v. Nova Scotia*, [1989]) or is ambivalent among the parties to the conflict (*Delgamuukw v. BC*, [1997]). However, in all these cases one jurisdiction tends to come out ahead and the outcomes still reinforce the legitimacy of primarily one federal model. It should also be noted that there are ten additional cases where I could identify the negative outcome for a particular jurisdiction being mitigated, to a small extent.

model creates precedents in the case law that structure and influence future decisions. Such precedents based on imposing decisions and rationalizations work to tilt the scales in favour of one particular model in future cases involving similar issues, which can negatively affect the perceived fairness of the process of solving disputes as well as leading to non-optimal outcomes.

The underlying issue with the Court's dispute-resolution approach in these imposing cases is that it is seeking to solve a problem by imposing a fixed constitutional and federal system. This tendency for the Court to eschew its proper role as facilitator of negotiation to manage conflict within and over the federal system is the fourth point I want to touch on here. While there are a few examples of the Court embracing this role in some way, as discussed above, the general tendency is for the Court to embrace a role that reinforces a particular model. In these instances the Court is cloaking itself in a false veil of impartiality (e.g., by saying it is the umpire of the federation). Such a position negatively affects the legitimacy of the institution in decisions that are anything but neutral – decisions that draw from and reinforce particular federal models. Adopting this role sets a benchmark of neutrality the Court simply cannot live up to in the eyes of the participants to the conflict. As already argued, the Court is not, and cannot be, a neutral arbiter: it is part of the field of struggle and is inherently a political institution. Accordingly, to maintain loyalty to the process of dispute arbitration within and over the federation, the Court needs to embrace and account for its nature as a political institution. I argue the best way to account for its status, as a political institution, is to first and foremost *manage* conflict by facilitating negotiation between conflicting parties in its federalism jurisprudence.

These four trends all exemplify the problem with these imposing decisions. They all show how an imposing federalism jurisprudence has the potential to negatively affect the legitimacy of the federal arbiter and the federation more generally. These trends also show how this decision approach can lead to non-optimal outcomes and imposing precedents in the constitutional law. I elaborate further on these points in the final chapter; but, first, it is prudent to look more closely at the SCC's federalism jurisprudence that recognizes the legitimacy of multiple models and the federation as the process and outcome of negotiation between the subscribers of these models.

Chapter Six

A Federalism Jurisprudence of Recognition

This chapter completes my account of the SCC's federalism jurisprudence by looking at the decisions that follow the ideal of the *Secession Reference*.[1] These decisions are markedly different from the group of imposing judgments discussed in the last chapter, as they recognize the legitimacy of multiple federal models and the federation as the process and outcome of negotiation between the subscribers of these models. Approximately 43 per cent of the SCC's federalism jurisprudence follows this approach. Moreover, this appears to be the increasingly favoured approach of the SCC: after the *Secession Reference* in 1998, some 71 per cent of the Court's federalism jurisprudence adheres to this approach of recognizing the legitimacy of multiple federal models.[2] While this number falls short of the ideal of every decision following the example of the *Secession Reference*, it is a welcome trend. These decisions seek to manage (not solve) conflict over the federal system. The shift in approach has the potential to generate loyalty to the process of conflict management and the federation itself. By reviewing these cases, the goal of this chapter is to highlight both their potential benefits as well as how federal arbiters can actually fulfil their role in line with this approach.

A decision that follows the exemplar of the *Secession Reference* is the opposite of the imposing cases discussed in the previous chapter. Like its counterpoint, however, the ideal-type has three key characteristics. The first is a depiction of the federation that recognizes it is a process

1 *Reference re Secession of Quebec*, [1998] 2 S.C.R. 217.

2 Compare this to the fact that for the period from 1980 to 1998, approximately 64% of decisions *imposed* a federal model.

and outcome of negotiation between the subscribers of legitimate federal models. This depiction is legitimized through accepted forms of legal argument that anchor it in the constitutional law. The second characteristic is a rejection of a zero-sum approach to dispute arbitration, with the outcome of a case seeking benefits for all parties and reinforcing the legitimacy of multiple federal models. Third, the Court adopts a role that seeks to manage the conflict by, first and foremost, facilitating negotiation between the conflicting parties.

It is when these three characteristics combine that a decision substantially adheres to the ideal-type. We can see this happening, for example, in a decision like *Fédération des producteurs de volailles du Québec.*[3] Here, the SCC presents the federation as the process and outcome of negotiation between the subscribers of the legitimate federal models,[4] pointing out that such a view is supported by the case law and legal doctrine.[5] Working from this understanding of the federal system, the Court decides that an agreement between the central government and the provinces is grounds to allow the provinces to regulate the production of poultry (despite the significant effect this has on the central

3 *Fédération des producteurs de volailles du Québec v. Pelland*, [2005] 1 S.C.R. 292. The issue in this case is whether an agreement between the central and provincial government that delegates control over the production of poultry to provinces (and which affects the inter-provincial and international trade of poultry, areas of central government competence) results in the provinces acting outside their legislative jurisdiction. The decision was unanimous (authored by Abella J).

4 See *Fédération des producteurs de volailles du Québec*, [2005] at 15, where the Court notes that central-provincial agreements on how to implement the division of powers "reflect and reify Canadian Federalism's constitutional creativity and cooperative flexibility"; also see at 2–3, 28, 38, and 53.

5 From the outset of *Fédération des producteurs de volailles du Québec* (at 2–3, 15) the Court says the validity of central-provincial cooperative schemes that regulate agricultural production and marketing is established by a landmark 1978 SCC decision. The Court goes on to summarize the applicability of that case to the one at bar (at 22–3): "In the *Egg Reference* … the Court reached the following relevant conclusions: although constitutional jurisdiction over marketing is divided, agricultural production is *prima facie* a local matter under provincial jurisdiction; the provincial scheme was not aimed at controlling extraprovincial trade, but was deemed to be coordinated and integrated with the regulations established under federal authority; and, most pertinently, producers could not claim exemption from provincial control over production by electing to devote their entire output to extraprovincial trade. Any effect of the provincial egg marketing and production scheme on [central competence over] extraprovincial trade was found to be incidental to the *constitutionally permissible purpose of controlling agricultural production within the context of a cooperative federal-provincial agreement*" (emphasis added).

government's exclusive jurisdiction over inter-provincial and international trade). The decision thus also provides an example of the Court adopting a role of facilitating, and deferring to, such negotiated schemes that seek flexible solutions to implement the division of powers in the federation.[6]

The basic architecture of this type of decision informs the structure of analysis below. In the first section I discuss how the federation is depicted in these fifty-six decisions to account for, and reinforce, the legitimacy of multiple federal models. The second section looks at the use of legal argument to reinforce the legitimacy of how the federation is depicted. The third section investigates the Court's rejection of a zero-sum approach in reaching outcomes in these cases. I then turn to analyse the tendency of the Court in these decisions to embrace a role as the facilitator of negotiation within a broader conflict-management approach.

In each of these sections I look at the extent to which all fifty-six decisions discussed here adhere to the ideal-type, while also exemplifying how they do this by looking at specific examples. Also, as in the last chapter, I analyse both division-of-powers cases and federal references in each section.[7]

Following this analysis, I conclude by picking up on some of the points made at the end of the last chapter that support the wider arguments of the book. I start by highlighting the fundamental differences between the fifty-six decisions discussed in this chapter and the seventy-four imposing decisions. In particular, I focus on four trends in these fifty-six decisions: (1) the inclusive nature of the Court's understanding and presentation of the federation; (2) the (increasing) tendency to recognize the legitimacy of the multinational model; (3) the rejection of zero-sum outcomes; and (4) the Court's (increasing) willingness to adopt a role of facilitator of negotiation and to promote political processes to manage conflict. I argue that the fundamental benefit of a federalism jurisprudence that exhibits these qualities is that it can generate legitimacy for the federal arbiter and the federation more generally.

---

6 See *Fédération des producteurs de volailles du Québec* in addition to the above (at 38): "With respect, I see no principled basis for disentangling what has proven to be a successful federal-provincial merger."

7 As discussed in chapters 3 and 5, while I recognize the differences between these two streams of federalism jurisprudence, they share fundamental similarities that justify considering them together.

Table 6.1. Issues in "recognizing" federal references, 1980–2010

Reference	Primary (and related) area of jurisdiction	Issue
Patriation [1981]	Constitutional amendment	Ability of centre to unilaterally seek amendment of constitution
Newfoundland Continental Shelf [1984]	Natural resources	Ownership of resources offshore of Newfoundland
Education Act [1987]	Education	Funding for denominational schools
Young Offenders Act [1991]	Courts (s. 96)	Validity of youth criminal courts
Same-Sex Marriage [2004]	Marriage	Central ability to change definition and administration of marriage
Employment Insurance Act [2005]	Employment insurance (property and civil rights)	Maternity benefits under central employment insurance scheme
Assisted Human Reproduction Act [2010]	Criminal law (health)	Central law regulating assisted human reproduction

Context

The fifty-six decisions discussed in this chapter include forty-nine division-of-powers decisions and seven federal references between 1980 and 2010. As in the previous two chapters, these decisions are classified as recognizing the legitimacy of multiple models by applying the framework introduced in the third chapter (which facilitates analysis of the extent to which decisions draw from and reinforce the pan-Canadian, provincial-equality, multinational, and/or dynamic federal models in their approach and outcome).

As tables 6.1 and 6.2 indicate, the issues that arise in these fifty-six decisions span a range of matters. Among the division-of-powers decisions, there are a number of cases where the primary issue is the criminal law (10), Aboriginals (8), federal works and undertakings (7),[8] conflicting central and provincial laws (4), the role and scope of the judiciary's power in the federation (3), taxation (3), the provinces'

8 As explained earlier, the centre's "works and undertakings" are those matters that fall under exclusive central control as a result of s. 92(10) of the Constitution Act, 1867. This generally includes enterprises such as inter-provincial transportation (like railways, steamships, and aviation) and telecommunications, as well as things declared by the central government to be for the general advantage of Canada, like atomic energy.

Table 6.2. Issues in "recognizing" division-of-powers cases, 1980–2010

Case	Primary (and related) area of jurisdiction	Issue
Canadian Pioneer Management [1980]	Banking (labour)	Labour relations for a trust company
Dominion Stores v. R. [1980]	Trade (agriculture)	Central law regulating quality of produce
BC v. Canada Trust [1980]	Tax	If provincial tax direct and within the province
Covert v. NS [1980]	Tax	If provincial tax direct and within the province
Fulton v. ERCB [1981]	Federal undertaking	If undertaking federal or local
Schneider v. The Queen [1982]	Health (criminal law)	Provincial law relating to heroin treatment
Multiple Access v. McCutcheon [1982]	Paramountcy (trade, property, and civil rights)	Conflicting insider trading laws
Deloitte v. WCB [1985]	Paramountcy (bankruptcy)	Provincial law relating to bankruptcy
Dick v. La Reine [1985]	Aboriginals (91.24)	Application of provincial hunting law to Aboriginals
Derrickson v. Derrickson [1986]	Aboriginals (91.24)	Application of provincial divorce law to Aboriginals
R. v. Edwards Books [1986]	Property and civil rights	Sunday shopping prohibition
ON v. OPSEU [1987]	Labour	Regulation of provincial officials in federal elections
Rio Hotel v. NB [1987]	Criminal law (property and civil rights)	Regulation of adult entertainment
O'Hara v. BC [1987]	Criminal law (admin. of justice)	Provincial investigation of police and prison officials
Bell Canada v. QC [1988]	Federal undertaking (labour)	Application of provincial health and safety law
Canadian National Railway [1988]	Federal undertaking (labour)	Application of provincial health and safety law
Alltrans Express v. BC [1988]	Federal undertaking (labour)	Application of provincial health and safety law
R. v. Francis [1988]	Aboriginals (91.24, paramountcy)	Application of provincial traffic law to Aboriginals
ON v. Pembina [1989]	Maritime Law (courts)	Province granting inferior court maritime jurisdiction
Alberta Government Telephones [1989]	Federal undertaking (telecoms.)	If provincial crown corp. is federal undertaking
IBEW v. Alberta Government Telephones [1989]	Federal undertaking (labour)	If provincial crown corp. is federal undertaking
Starr v. Houlden [1990]	Criminal law	Provincial investigation of criminal activity

Table 6.2. Issues in "recognizing" division-of-powers cases, 1980–2010 (Continued)

Case	Primary (and related) area of jurisdiction	Issue
R. v. S. (S.) [1990]	Criminal law	Delegation of youth sentencing to provinces
R. v. F.(J.T.) [1991]	Courts (s. 96)	Validity of youth criminal courts
R. v. W.(D.A.) [1991]	Courts (s. 96)	Validity of youth criminal courts
R. v. Furtney [1991]	Criminal law	Delegation of lottery regulation to provinces
R. v. Jones [1991]	Criminal law	Delegation of lottery regulation to provinces
Friends of the Oldman River Society [1992]	Environment	Application of central environmental regulations
R. v. Colarusso [1994]	Criminal law	Provincial power to conduct criminal investigation
MacMillan Bloedel v. Simpson [1995]	Courts (s. 96)	Powers conferred on youth courts by centre
R. v. Pamajewon [1996]	Aboriginals (self-government)	If Aboriginal band has right to self-regulate gambling
Ontario Home Builders' Association [1996]	Tax (licensing)	If provincial tax direct
Westbank First Nation v. BC Hydro [1999]	Aboriginals (91.24)	If Aboriginal band can tax provincial corp.
Global Securities v. BC [2000]	Property and civil rights	Extraterritorial effect of provincial securities law
Lovelace v. ON [2000]	Aboriginals (91.24)	Provincial law allowing Aboriginal gambling
Public School Boards of Alberta [2000]	Education	Provincial law relating to denominational schools
Law Society of BC v. Mangat [2001]	Paramountcy (immigration, property, and civil rights)	Conflicting laws relating to immigration tribunals
Ward v. Canada [2002]	Fisheries (property and civil rights, criminal law)	Central law prohibiting sale of young seals
Kitkatla v. BC [2002]	Aboriginals (91.24, property and civil rights)	Provincial law relating to cultural heritage
Krieger v. Law Society of Alberta [2002]	Criminal law (admin. of justice)	Regulation and discipline of crown prosecutors
Siemens v. MB [2003]	Criminal law (property and civil rights)	Provincial law allowing local prohibition of gambling
Paul v. BC [2003]	Aboriginals (91.24, courts)	Powers conferred on tribunal by province
Rothmans v. SK [2005]	Paramountcy	Conflicting tobacco advertising laws

(*Continued*)

Table 6.2. Issues in "recognizing" division-of-powers cases, 1980–2010 (Continued)

Case	Primary (and related) area of jurisdiction	Issue
Fédération des producteurs de volailles du Québec [2005]	Trade (Agriculture)	Delegation to regulate poultry production to provinces
Isen v. Simms [2006]	Maritime law (property and civil rights)	Regulation of civil actions relating to maritime events
Canadian Western Bank [2007]	Banking (property and civil rights, paramountcy)	Regulation of insurance sold by banks
BC v. Lafarge Canada [2007]	Federal undertaking (paramountcy)	Application of provincial laws to building of ship yard
Confédération des syndicats nationaux [2008]	Labour (employment insurance)	Central employment insurance scheme
Chatterjee v. ON [2009]	Criminal law (property and civil rights, paramountcy)	Provincial law relating to the proceeds of crime

power over property and civil rights (2), trade (2), and labour (2), among other issues. A number of federal references mirror division-of-powers cases, in that the jurisdiction of a government to pass economic or social legislation is challenged (4); but, there is also the important *Patriation Reference*[9] (which deals with constitutional amendment), as well as a reference relating to natural resources and one on the role and scope of the judiciary's power in the federation.

There is little difference between the issues covered in these fifty-six cases and the imposing decisions discussed in the last chapter. Both deal with highly contentious matters like constitutional-amendment procedures, the scope of the criminal law or ownership of strategic natural resources. Similar conflicts also take place over the scope of the various areas of jurisdiction laid out in sections 91 and 92 of the constitution (e.g., the power to regulate trade). The outcomes of these cases, which cover a wide range of issues, establish the very nature of the federation.

9 *Re: Resolution to Amend the Constitution*, [1981] 1 S.C.R. 753. The issue in this reference, as discussed in detail in previous chapters, is the constitutionality of the central order to unilaterally seek approval for a domestic constitutional amending formula from the UK. The case raises issues of both constitutional legality and constitutional conventions.

The fact that both types of cases deal with similar issues raises an interesting preliminary point. It appears that the substantive issue in a case does not drive the Court to either impose a particular federal model or recognize the legitimacy of multiple models. The structuring variables associated with a specific issue area (case law, doctrine, the framers' intent, and constitutional text) do not seem to lead the Court to impose a particular federal model. What we see, rather, is the Court interpreting these structuring variables in a way that either imposes a particular model or supports the legitimacy of multiple models.

There is one "structural" difference between the imposing decisions and those discussed here that should be mentioned at the outset: the dynamic of conflict between the orders of government. I noted in the last chapter that in many imposing decisions (58%) the orders of government are in conflict.[10] In contrast, there is a higher tendency for governments to cooperate in the cases discussed in this chapter. In 45 per cent of the cases discussed below, an order of government intervenes to support the other order of government, turning the conflict into one between a private actor, on one side, and cooperating governments, on the other. This cooperation only happens 16 per cent of the time in cases where the decision imposes a particular federal model. At the same time, in the cases discussed in this chapter the orders of government still conflict in some 38 per cent of cases. More importantly, though, the different dynamics of intergovernmental conflict do not change the fact that the cases discussed below represent conflicts between competing conceptions of the federal system. Private actors subscribe to the federal models and can argue just as forcefully as governments for a particular perspective on the nature of the federal system. Nevertheless, in cases where the orders of government are cooperating, the Court seems more likely to recognize the legitimacy of multiple models. This is both an interesting and welcome trend (as I argue below when discussing the role of the Court in these fifty-six decisions).

An Inclusive Understanding of the Federation

As explained earlier, conflict over the federation generally focuses on a number of key aspects, for example: the balance and distribution

10 This includes cases where orders of government are in direct conflict and where one order of government supports a private actor in their case against an opposing order of government.

of powers, the relationship between the orders of government, and the nature of the provinces.[11] The way the Court understands and depicts the federation in relation to these "points of conflict" is an essential element of the decision either recognizing the legitimacy of multiple federal models or imposing a particular model. The way the federation is understood and presented – the way the Court explains what the federation *is* – drives the outcome of the decision, while also working to reinforce the validity of either multiple models or a single model.

As table 6.3 indicates, in all of the fifty-six decisions discussed here, the federation is depicted in a way that reinforces the legitimacy of multiple federal models (or the dynamic model explicitly) in one of two ways: the decision *balances models off one another* when depicting the federation; and/or the decision *explicitly recognizes the federation as a process and outcome* of negotiation between the subscribers of competing federal models.[12]

Depicting the federation in a way that balances the competing models is the most prominent approach in these fifty-six decisions. We see this balancing happening in thirty-nine of the forty-nine division-of-powers cases and in four of the seven federal references. Generally, the Court adopts this approach by presenting the federation as granting both orders of government broad powers. For example, in *Ward v. Canada*[13] the central order's jurisdiction is presented as broad and validly affecting areas of provincial competence. At the same time, the Court elaborates the broad scope of provincial powers and the need

11 As outlined in previous chapters, the focal points of conflict over what the federation is generally include the way the constitution is represented; the nature of the federation; the purpose of the federation; the distribution of powers; the balance of powers; the nature of the provinces; the nature of central institutions; the relationship between the orders of government; and the national composition of the country.

12 Note that multiple approaches can be adopted within one decision (i.e., while a depiction balances federal models, it can also explicitly recognize the federation as the process and outcome of negotiation between the subscribers of these models). Table 6.3 notes when a decision has only a minimal depiction of the federation. In these cases the Court still adopts a counterbalancing method of depicting the federation, as discussed below.

13 *Ward v. Canada (Attorney General)*, [2002] 1 S.C.R. 569. The issue in this case is whether a central prohibition on the sale of young hooded and harp seals falls under its fisheries and criminal-law power (or if it infringes on provincial jurisdiction over property and civil rights). The unanimous decision was authored by Wilson CJ.

Table 6.3. Summary of "recognizing" SCC decisions, 1980–2010

Rank	Case	Depiction			Outcome		Court's role
		Primary (secondary) model recognized	Approach	Primary modality	Primary (secondary) winners	Primary (secondary) model reinforced	
High	Patriation [1981]	Pan-Can, Provincial (Multinat., Dynamic)	Balance	Text, Progress, Structure	Centre, Provinces, Particular	Pan-Can, Provincial, Multinat., Dynamic	Facilitator (Umpire, Branch)
	Multiple Access [1982]	Pan-Can, Provincial, Dynamic	Balance	Doctrine	Provinces, Centre	Provincial, Pan-Can, Dynamic	—
	R. v. S. (S.) [1990]	Pan-Can, Multinat., Provincial, Dynamic	Balance	Doctrine	Centre (Provinces, Particular)	Pan-Can, Multinat., Provincial	—
	R. v. Furtney [1991]	Dynamic, Pan-Can, Provincial	Balance	Doctrine, Text	Centre, Provinces	Dynamic, Pan-Can, Provincial	Facilitator
	R. v. Jones [1991]	Dynamic, Pan-Can, Provincial	Balance	Doctrine, Text	Centre, Provinces	Dynamic, Pan-Can, Provincial	Facilitator
	Lovelace v. ON [2000]	Pan-Can, Multinat.	Balance	Doctrine	Provinces, Centre, Particular	Pan-Can, Provincial, Multinat.	—
	Siemens v. MB [2003]	Provincial, Pan-Can, Dynamic	Balance	Doctrine	Provinces, Centre	Provincial, Pan-Can, Dynamic	Facilitator
	Fédération des producteurs de volailles du Québec [2005]	Dynamic (Pan-Can, Provincial)	Explicit	Doctrine	Centre, Provinces	Dynamic	Facilitator
	Canadian Western Bank [2007]	Dynamic, Provincial, Pan-Can, Multinat.	Balance	Doctrine	Provinces (Centre)	Dynamic, Provincial, Multinat. (Pan-Can)	Facilitator
	BC v. Lafarge Canada [2007]	Dynamic, Pan-Can, Provincial	Balance	Doctrine	Centre (Provinces)	Pan-Can, Dynamic (Provincial)	Facilitator

(*Continued*)

Table 6.3. Summary of "recognizing" SCC decisions, 1980–2010 (Continued)

Rank	Case	Depiction			Outcome		Court's role
		Primary (secondary) model recognized	Approach	Primary modality	Primary (secondary) winners	Primary (secondary) model reinforced	
High	Confédération des syndicats nationaux [2008]	Dynamic, Pan-Can, Provincial	Balance	Doctrine	Centre (Provinces)	Pan-Can, Dynamic (Provincial)	—
High	Chatterjee v. ON [2009]	Dynamic, Pan-Can, Provincial	Explicit	Doctrine	Provinces (Centre)	Provincial, Dynamic (Pan-Can)	Facilitator
High	Assisted Human Reproduction Act [2010]	Provincial, Pan-Can (Dynamic)	Balance	Doctrine	Provinces, Centre	Provincial, Pan-Can	Facilitator, Umpire (Guard)
Medium	Canadian Pioneer Management [1980]	Provincial, Pan-Can	Balance	Doctrine	Provinces (Centre)	Provincial, Pan-Can	Facilitator
Medium	BC v. Canada Trust [1980]	Pan-Can, Provincial, Dynamic	Balance	Doctrine, Progress	Provinces (Centre)	Pan-Can, Provincial, Dynamic	Facilitator
Medium	Covert v. NS [1980]		Minimal	Doctrine	Provinces (Centre)	Pan-Can, Provincial, Dynamic	—
Medium	Fulton v. ERCB [1981]	Pan-Can, Provincial (Dynamic)	Balance	Doctrine, Text	Centre, Provinces	Pan-Can, Provincial, Dynamic	Facilitator
Medium	Schneider v. The Queen [1982]	Pan-Can, Provincial (Dynamic)	Balance	Doctrine	Provinces, Centre	Provincial, Pan-Can, Dynamic	Facilitator
Medium	Deloitte v. WCB [1985]	Pan-Can, Provincial	Balance	Doctrine	Centre, Provinces	Pan-Can, Provincial	—
Medium	Dick v. La Reine [1985]	Pan-Can, Provincial, Multinat.	Balance	Doctrine	Provinces, Centre (Particular)	Provincial, Pan-Can, Multinat.	—
Medium	R. v. Edwards Books [1986]	Provincial (Pan-Can, Dynamic)	Balance	Doctrine	Provinces (Centre)	Provincial (Pan-Can)	Facilitator

Medium	Education Act [1987]	Multinat., Provincial	Balance	Text, Doctrine	Particular, Provinces	Multinat., Provincial, Dynamic	Guard (Facilitator)
	ON v. OPSEU [1987]	Provincial, Pan-Can, Dynamic	Balance	Doctrine, Structure	Provinces, Centre	Provincial, Pan-Can, Dynamic	Umpire, Branch, Guard, Facilitator
	ON v. Pembina [1989]	Provincial, Pan-Can	Balance	Structure, Text, Doctrine	Provinces, Centre	Provincial, Pan-Can	Branch
	R. v. Colarusso [1994]	Pan-Can, Provincial	Minimal	Doctrine, Prudent	Provinces, Centre	Pan-Can, Provincial	Facilitator
	R. v. Pamajewon [1996]	Multinat. (Provincial, Pan-Can)	Balance	Doctrine	(Centre, Provinces, Particular)	Multinat. (Pan-Can, Provincial)	—
	Ontario Home Builders [1996]	Provincial (Pan-Can, Multinat., Dynamic)	Balance	Doctrine, History, Structure	Provinces (Centre)	Provincial (Pan-Can, Multinat.)	(Branch)
	Law Society of BC v. Mangat [2001]	Pan-Can, Provincial, Dynamic	Balance	Doctrine	Centre (Provinces, Particular)	Pan-Can, Provincial, Dynamic	—
	Ward v. Canada [2002]	Dynamic, Pan-Can, Provincial	Balance	Doctrine	Centre	Pan-Can, Provincial	Umpire, Guard
	Paul v. BC [2003]	Provincial, Pan-Can, Multinat.	Balance	Doctrine	Provinces (Centre, Particular)	Provincial, Pan-Can, Multinat.	Branch (Umpire, Facilitator)
	Same-Sex Marriage [2004]	Pan-Can, Provincial (Dynamic)	Balance	Doctrine	Centre, Provinces	Pan-Can, Provincial, Dynamic	Facilitator (Umpire, Guard)
	Rothmans v. Sask. [2005]	Provincial, Pan-Can (Dynamic)	Balance	Doctrine	Provinces, Centre	Provincial, Pan-Can	Facilitator

(*Continued*)

Table 6.3. Summary of “recognizing” SCC decisions, 1980–2010 (Continued)

		Depiction			Outcome		Court’s role
Rank	Case	Primary (secondary) model recognized	Approach	Primary modality	Primary (secondary) winners	Primary (secondary) model reinforced	
Medium	Employment Insurance Act [2005]	Dynamic	Explicit	Doctrine, Progress	Centre	Pan-Can, Dynamic	Facilitator
	Isen v. Simms [2006]	Provincial, Pan-Can	Balance	Doctrine, Structure, Prudent	Provinces	Provincial (Pan-Can)	—
Low	Dominion Stores v. R. [1980]	Provincial, Dynamic	Balance	Doctrine	Provinces (Centre)	Provincial, Dynamic (Pan-Can)	Facilitator, Umpire
	Newfoundland Continental Shelf [1984]	Pan-Can (Provincial, Multinat.)	Balance	Doctrine	Centre	Pan-Can, Dynamic	Facilitator
	Derrickson v. Derrickson [1986]	Pan-Can, Provincial	Balance	Doctrine	Centre, Provinces	Pan-Can, Provincial	Branch (Umpire)
	Rio Hotel v. NB [1987]	Provincial, Pan-Can, Dynamic	Balance	Doctrine	Provinces, Centre	Provincial, Pan-Can	—
	O’Hara v. BC [1987]	Provincial, Pan-Can, Dynamic	Balance	Doctrine	Provinces, Centre	Provincial, Pan-Can	—
	Bell Canada v. QC [1988]	Pan-Can, Provincial, Dynamic	Balance	Text, Doctrine	Centre, Provinces	Pan-Can, Provincial	Umpire, Guard
	Canadian National Railway [1988]	Pan-Can, Provincial, Dynamic	Balance	Text, Doctrine	Centre, Provinces	Pan-Can, Provincial	Umpire, Guard
	Alltrans Express v. BC [1988]	Pan-Can, Provincial, Dynamic	Balance	Text, Doctrine	Centre, Provinces	Pan-Can, Provincial	Umpire, Guard
	R. v. Francis [1988]	Provincial, Pan-Can	Balance	Doctrine	Provinces (Centre)	Provincial, Pan-Can	—
	Alberta Government Telephones [1989]	Provincial, Pan-Can	Minimal	Doctrine	Centre, Provinces	Ambivalent	—

Low	Ibew v. Alberta Government Telephones [1989]	Provincial, Pan-Can	Minimal	Doctrine	Centre, Provinces	Ambivalent	—
	Starr v. Houlden [1990]	Pan-Can, Provincial	Balance	Doctrine	Centre	Pan-Can, Provincial	—
	Young Offenders Act [1991]	Pan-Can, Provincial (Multinat., Dynamic)	Minimal	Doctrine	Centre, Provinces, Particular	Provincial	Branch (Guard)
	R. v. F.(J.T.) [1991]	Pan-Can, Provincial (Multinat., Dynamic)	Minimal	Doctrine	Centre, Provinces, Particular	Provincial	Branch (Guard)
	R. v. W.(D.A.) [1991]	Pan-Can, Provincial (Multinat., Dynamic)	Minimal	Doctrine	Centre, Provinces, Particular	Provincial	Branch (Guard)
	Friends of the Oldman River Society [1992]	Pan-Can, Dynamic, Provincial	Balance	Doctrine, Text, Prudent, Structure	Centre, Provinces	Pan-Can, Provincial, Dynamic	Umpire
	MacMillan Bloedel v. Simpson [1995]	(Pan-Can, Provincial)	Minimal	Doctrine, Prudent	Ambivalent	Pan-Can, Provincial	Branch
	Westbank First Nations v. BC Hydro [1999]	Provincial, Pan-Can, Dynamic	Balance	Doctrine	Provinces	Provincial, Pan-Can, Multinat.	—
	Global Securities v. BC [2000]	Provincial, Pan-Can	Balance	Doctrine, Prudent	Provinces (Centre)	Provincial (Pan-Can)	(Branch)
	Public School Boards of Alberta [2000]	Provincial (Multinat.)	Balance	Doctrine	Provinces	Provincial (Multinat.)	—
	Kitkatla Band v. BC [2002]	Provincial, Pan-Can (Multinat., Dynamic)	Balance	Doctrine, Prudent	Provinces, Centre	Provincial, Pan-Can	Facilitator
	Krieger v. Law Society of Alberta [2002]	Provincial, Pan-Can (Dynamic)	Minimal	Doctrine	Ambivalent	Provincial, Pan-Can	—

to respect provincial autonomy.[14] A similar depiction that supports elements of both the pan-Canadian and provincial-equality models is evident in *O'Hara v. BC.*[15] Here, the Court offsets a liberal view of the provinces' power to administer justice in the province with a broad central power over criminal law and procedure.[16]

This balancing approach is also employed by highlighting how various aspects of each model are reflected in the federal system. For example, in *Dick v. La Reine*[17] the three main models are afforded legitimacy

14 See *Ward v. Canada* at 42–3: "Although broad, the [central] fisheries power is not unlimited. The same cases that establish its broad parameters also hold that the fisheries power must be construed to respect the provinces' power over property and civil rights under s. 92(13) of the *Constitution Act, 1867*. This too is a broad, multi-faceted power ... Thus we have before us two broad powers, one federal, one provincial. In such cases, bright jurisdictional lines are elusive." Similarly, the Court goes on to note (at 52) that "although the criminal-law power is broad, it is not unlimited." There are further examples of this method of depicting the federation that balances elements of the pan-Canadian model with elements of the provincial-equality model; see in particular at 30 and also 47–8. A similar depiction that balances broad central powers (over maritime matters) with broad provincial powers (over property and civil rights and local matters) is found in *Isen v. Simms*, [2006] 2 S.C.R. 349 at 20, 24–6.

15 *O'Hara v. British Columbia*, [1987] 2 S.C.R. 591. The issue in this case is whether the mandate of a provincially established commission to investigate actions of a provincial police force is invalid (because it infringes on the central order's powers over the criminal law and procedure). The majority decision was authored by Dickson CJ.

16 See *O'Hara v. BC* at 605: "[I]t is well established that pursuant to s. 92(14) a province may create a commission or inquiry and, in certain circumstances at least, arm such a body with coercive investigatory powers." The Court goes on to add (at 606) that "the boundaries of the 'administration of justice' do not include the discipline, organization and management of the R.C.M.P. ... [H]owever, ... the 'administration of justice' does include the organization and management of police forces created by provincial legislation." Moreover, (at 607) the Court says that "the authority to establish such an inquiry is not without limits. A province must respect federal jurisdiction over criminal law and criminal procedure," and (at 610) that "a certain degree of overlapping is implicit in the grant to the provinces of legislative authority in respect of the administration of justice and in the grant to Parliament of legislative authority in respect of criminal law and criminal procedure." In sum, (at 611–12) the Court's understanding of the division of powers in relation to the administration of justice and the criminal law seeks to convey the view that, despite considerable provincial powers, "there are limits to a province's jurisdiction to establish an inquiry and equip it with coercive investigatory authority ... [and] this limitation on provincial jurisdiction is an acknowledgement of the federal nature of our system of self-government."

17 *Dick v. La Reine*, [1985] 2 S.C.R. 309. The issue in this case is whether a provincial law restricting hunting of deer to certain times applies to an Aboriginal person (or if the law infringes on the central government's jurisdiction to exclusively legislate with regard to Aboriginals under s. 91.24). The unanimous judgment was authored by Beetz J.

in the way the federation is depicted: the multinational model by presenting the state as housing multiple national groups (with Aboriginals seen as a legitimately distinct cultural group with attendant rights);[18] the provincial-equality model with the autonomy and broad jurisdiction afforded the provinces to pass laws of general application;[19] and the pan-Canadian model by saying the central government has exclusive and paramount control over its areas of jurisdiction (like Aboriginals).[20] Similarly, in *Westbank First Nation v. BC Hydro*[21] an understanding of the federation in line with aspects of the multinational model (where Aboriginal bands represent a de facto level of government)[22] is offset by reaffirming the central government's power over Aboriginals[23] and

18 See *Dick v. La Reine* at 320, where the Court accepts that distinct social, cultural, and institutional practices form a basis for Aboriginal identity, giving rise to a core "Indianness," which provincial laws cannot fundamentally affect.

19 See *Dick v. La Reine* at 322, where the Court notes that, even though provincial laws cannot interfere with the fundamental core of a central area of jurisdiction, "it has never been suggested, so far as I know, that, by the same token, those provincial ... laws cease to be laws of general application"; see also at 325–6.

20 See *Dick v. La Reine* at 324, where the Court notes that Aboriginals are the exclusive legislative jurisdiction of the central order, and (here and at 322 and 325–6) notes that such exclusive jurisdiction is to be free of interference from provincial laws that affect the core of this jurisdiction.

21 *Westbank First Nation v. British Columbia Hydro and Power Authority*, [1999] 3 S.C.R. 134. The issue in this case is if an Aboriginal band can tax a provincial utility through a delegated power from the central government. The case thus involves issues of immunity from taxation under s. 125 of the Constitution Act, 1867, which prohibits one order of government from taxing the other's revenues. The unanimous judgment was authored by Gonthier J.

22 See *Westbank First Nation v. BC Hydro* at 20, where the Court implies this: "These principles [of immunity from taxation by other governments], and the guiding structure of the Constitution, are as applicable to Indian Band Councils exercising the right of taxation authorized by s. 83 of the *Indian Act* as they are to the federal and provincial levels of government. *The exercise of governmental powers in Canada, by any level of government,* must be done in accordance with the constitutional framework of the country" (emphasis added).

23 See *Westbank First Nation v. BC Hydro* at 37: "[T]he purposes of these [impugned] taxes are 'to promote the interests of Aboriginal peoples and to further the aims of self-government.' Thus, as the Chief Justice pointed out (at para. 43), the taxes here are 'more ambitious' than simple taxation. However, the existence of this secondary purpose does not remove these taxes from the head of power under which s. 83 is founded – s. 91(3) [the central power over Aboriginals]. Indeed, while the intention of Parliament in enacting s. 83 may have been to advance self-government, that does not mean that this is the specific purpose of the taxes themselves."

equality between the central and provincial orders of government in the federation.[24]

This same pattern of balancing models when depicting the federation takes place in the *Education Act* reference.[25] Here, the SCC presents the nature of the federation, the distribution of powers, and the balance of powers in a way that legitimizes the multinational[26] and provincial-equality models.[27] We can also see the Court highlighting aspects of the federal system that lend legitimacy to different models in *Patriation*, where the balance of powers, the relation between

24 See *Westbank First Nation v. BC Hydro* at 16–17, where the Court highlights how the constitutional immunity each order of government enjoys from taxation by another government is afforded to the central and provincial governments: "[T]he final text of s. 125 read: 'No Lands or Property belonging to *Canada or any Province* shall be liable to Taxation.' The section is one of the tools found in the Constitution that ensures the proper functioning of Canada's federal system. It grants *to each level of government* sufficient operational space to govern without interference" (emphasis added).

25 *Reference re Bill 30, An Act to Amend the Education Act (Ont.)*, [1987] 1 S.C.R. 1148. The issue in this case is whether Ontario can fully fund Catholic secondary schools (i.e., if this action is within the province's power over education and consistent with denominational school rights laid out in s. 93 of the constitution). The unanimous opinion was authored by Wilson J (with Beetz, Estey, and Lamer JJ concurring).

26 See *Education Act* at 9, 27–8, 63, and particularly 27–8, where the Court says that "the protection of minority religious [qua national minority] rights was a major preoccupation during the negotiations leading to Confederation because of the perceived danger of leaving the religious minorities in both Canada East and Canada West at the mercy of overwhelming majorities … [The resulting protections in] s. 93 was part of a solemn pact resulting from the bargaining which made Confederation possible … [It is part of the] the basic compact of Confederation." Additionally, in line with the multinational model, the Court (at 21, 23, 24, 26, 28–9, 61–3) notes that the federal and constitutional system allows for a decentralized and asymmetrical distribution of powers with regard to education via the ability of provinces (particularly Ontario and Québec) to establish denominational school systems and to augment these systems as they see fit.

27 See *Education Act* at 78, where the Court presents the compact as taking place between the provinces, not nations, a process that was about "the sharing of sovereign power between the two plenary authorities created at Confederation." This shift in focus to depict the federation in line with the provincial-equality model is buttressed by the Court (at 62, 69, 71, 79) referring to the provinces en masse as a level of government, with all provinces sharing this power equally (i.e., despite the fact that policy asymmetry may occur in response to local conditions, the power is available to all provinces to establish denominational school systems under their common head of power over education).

orders, and even the nature of the federal and constitutional association is presented in line with both the pan-Canadian[28] and provincial-equality models.[29] At the same time, there is some implied support for the multinational model.[30]

The approach of balancing models of the federation is also evident in the eight division-of-powers decisions and one federal reference where the Court dedicates a minimal amount of effort and space to explaining the nature of the federal system. For example, in *Krieger v. Law Society of Alberta*[31] the single paragraph dedicated to explaining the nature of the federal system counterbalances provincial powers to regulate professions (including the legal profession, under their property and civil rights power) with the central powers over criminal law

---

28 See *Patriation*, [1981] at 801–2, and particularly 806, where the Court states that "federal paramountcy is ... the general rule in the actual exercise of [legislative] powers," while also noting the many "unitary features" of the federal system. And, this unitary federal system mandated by the text of the constitution cannot be affected by any political conventions that may support competing federal models (see 774–5, 778–9, 784, 788); the Court (at 803) goes as far as to say that competing models to the pan-Canadian model, such as the "compact theory," are just that, theories, and "do not engage the law," which mandates a centralized federation with a superior central order.

29 See *Patriation* at 904–6, 909, where the Court (at 905) says that "the object of the [*Constitution Act, 1867*] was neither to weld the provinces into one, nor to subordinate provincial governments to a central authority, but to create a federal government in which they should all be represented, entrusted with the exclusive administration of affairs in which they had a common interest, each province retaining its independence and autonomy." And, this view of the federation – supported as it is by convention – is seen to be an integral part of the constitution, as conventions "ensure that the legal framework of the constitution will be operated in accordance with the prevailing constitutional values or principles," which leads to "conventional rules of the constitution" (at 880) – rules that often support a provincial-equality model by limiting the superior position of the central order (at 879–80, 893).

30 See *Patriation* at 893–4, where the Court, despite depicting the federation as a compact among equal provinces, does imply a special status for Québec by pointing to the ability of Québec *alone* to halt amendment negotiations and thereby implying a veto in line with its distinct status as a nation. For a similar interpretation on this aspect of the decision see Russell (1983: 225–6).

31 *Krieger v. Law Society of Alberta*, [2002] 3 S.C.R. 372. The issue in this case is whether a province can regulate and sanction the actions of a provincial crown prosecutor through their civil rights jurisdiction (or if, since the prosecutor oversees criminal proceedings, this infringes on the criminal-law and procedure jurisdiction of the central order). The unanimous decision was authored by Major J.

and procedure.[32] Similarly, in *Young Offenders Act*,[33] the Court dedicates very little space to reflecting on the federal system, spending one paragraph describing it in such a way that could support any of the three key models.[34]

The counterbalancing approach is often coupled with a more explicit recognition of the federation as a process and outcome of negotiation. This coupling happens in some thirty division-of-powers decisions and five of the seven federal references. For example, in *BC v. Lafarge Canada*[35] the Court depicts the federation in a way that draws

32 See *Krieger v. Law Society of Alberta* at 33: "Section 91(27) of the *Constitution Act, 1867* grants jurisdiction over criminal law and criminal procedure to the Federal Government. Federal jurisdiction over criminal law and criminal procedure includes the authority to determine the procedures that govern criminal trials. Sections 92(13) and (14) grant jurisdiction over property and civil rights and the administration of justice, both criminal and civil, to the Provinces. Provincial jurisdiction over property and civil rights and the administration of justice includes licensing and regulation of lawyers, including reviews of alleged breaches of ethics ... It would thus appear that there is a strong possibility of overlap between the provincial and federal spheres." The result is that the Court accepts this overlapping area of jurisdiction and goes on to determine if the rules and regulations are valid by looking at the extent to which they target the prosecutor as professional discipline or as criminal law and procedure (at 34, 38).

33 *Reference re Young Offenders Act (P.E.I.)* [1991] 1 S.C.R. 252. The issue in this case is whether s. 96 of the *Constitution Act 1867* allows Youth Courts (as established under the *Young Offenders Act*) to be presided over by judges appointed by the provinces rather than the central government. Essentially, the case deals with the scope of Superior Court jurisdiction as protected via the judicature sections of the constitution and the ability of governments to establish inferior courts. The unanimous decision (authored by Lamer CJ, with Wilson, McLachlin, La Forest and L'Heureux-Dubé JJ concurring) was delivered in tandem with *R. v. F.(J.T.)* [1991] 1 S.C.R. 285 and *R. v. W.(D.A.)* [1991] 1 S.C.R. 291.

34 See *Young Offenders Act*, [1991], where over and above one line (at 277) that implies support for the provincial-equality model by referring to the "four original confederating provinces," the only paragraph that depicts the federation (at 296) highlights the central level's broad criminal-law powers and the autonomy both orders equally share in the administration of justice, while implying that the system allows for asymmetry in the administration of justice in response to particular circumstances.

35 *British Columbia (Attorney General) v. Lafarge Canada Inc.*, [2007] 2 S.C.R. 86. The issue in this case is whether provincial laws apply to the construction of a ship offloading facility (or if this undertaking falls under the exclusive jurisdiction of the central government under its navigation and shipping jurisdiction). Essentially, the case deals with the scope and applicability of the interjurisdictional immunity doctrine. The unanimous decision was authored by Binnie and LaBel JJ (with Bastarache J concurring).

from elements of the pan-Canadian and provincial-equality models,[36] while also recognizing that it is a process and outcome of negotiation between the subscribers of these legitimate views.[37] Similarly in *R v. Furtney*[38] the Court says that the federation is flexible enough to accommodate the oft-required central-provincial agreements to implement programs and policies in areas of overlapping jurisdiction;[39] in other words, the federal system is the outcome of negotiation over how it can be implemented.

In two division-of-powers cases explicit support for a more dynamic understanding of the federation is particularly evident, as it is the primary way the federation is depicted. In addition to *Fédération des producteurs de volailles du Québec*, discussed above, we see this explicit support happening in *Chatterjee v. Ontario*.[40] Here, a view of the federal and constitutional system as a fixed set of jurisdictional enclaves

36 See *BC v. Lafarge Canada* at 36, where the Court notes the central government's broad powers over its own public property and shipping and navigation, while also (at 37) recognizing that such lands and ports have a double aspect and fall under the provinces' control under their broad jurisdiction over property and civil rights.

37 See *BC v. Lafarge Canada* at 37–8, where the Court says that the fluid and dynamic nature of the division of powers, which creates areas of overlapping jurisdiction, necessitates cooperation because the "potential for conflict" in these areas is "considerable," and accordingly "federal-provincial-municipal cooperation in such matters is not unconstitutional. It is essential." The Court goes on to reject a view of the division of powers as fixed and creating enclaves of jurisdiction (at 42–3), reinforcing the need for dialogue and negotiation between the orders of government to both implement the system and to manage conflict.

38 *R. v. Furtney*, [1991] 3 S.C.R. 89. The issue in this case is the validity of a criminal-code provision that delegates regulatory authority for lotteries from the central government to a provincial body. The unanimous decision was authored by Stevenson J.

39 See *R. v. Futney* at 102: "[I]n the exercise of its powers generally, and the criminal law specifically, Parliament is free to define the area in which it chooses to act and, in so doing, may leave other areas open to valid provincial legislation." Here, instead of focusing on the constitutional prohibition on delegating legislative powers between levels of government, the Court views the system as flexible enough to allow the levels of government to bypass the rigidity of the division of powers to negotiate and cooperate to delegate the administration and regulation of issue areas (here lotteries) through agreement.

40 *Chatterjee v. Ontario (Attorney General)*, [2009] 1 S.C.R. 624. The issue in this case is whether a provincial law relating to the seizure of proceeds of crime infringes on the central government's criminal-law power. The unanimous decision was authored by Binnie J.

is rejected, with the nature of the federation being presented as flexible and having overlapping jurisdictions that require negotiation and cooperation.[41]

This second approach to depicting the federation is also evident in the SCC's federal references. In *Assisted Human Reproduction Act*,[42] a view of the federation that supports both the pan-Canadian[43] and the provincial-equality[44] models is augmented by highlighting the federation as a normative system which creates areas of shared jurisdiction that require cooperation and compromise to implement.[45] In *Employment*

41 See *Chatterjee v. Ontario* at 2: "[R]esort to a federalist concept of proliferating jurisdictional enclaves (or 'interjurisdictional immunities') was discouraged by this Court's decisions in *Canadian Western Bank v. Alberta*, 2007 SCC 22, [2007] 2 S.C.R. 3, and *British Columbia (Attorney General) v. Lafarge Canada Inc.*, 2007 SCC 23, [2007] 2 S.C.R. 86, and should not now be given a new lease on life. As stated in *Canadian Western Bank*, 'a court should favour, where possible, the ordinary operation of statutes enacted by *both* levels of government' (para. 37 (emphasis in original))." The Court goes on (at 32) to say that "co-operative federalism recognizes that overlaps between provincial and federal laws are inevitable: 'Matters, however, which in one aspect and for one purpose fall within the jurisdiction of a province over the subjects designated by one or more of the heads of s. 92, may in another aspect and for another purpose, be proper subjects of legislation under s. 91, and in particular under head 27'"; see also at 24, 29–30, 33–5, 40.

42 Reference re *Assisted Human Reproduction Act*, [2010] 3 S.C.R. 457. The issue in this reference is whether a central law prohibiting and controlling certain acts related to assisted human reproduction falls within the central order's criminal-law power (or infringes on provincial jurisdiction relating to healthcare and the regulation of medical practices). The unanimous opinion was authored by McLauchlin CJ (with LeBel, Deschamps, Abella and Rothstein, and Cromwell JJ concurring).

43 Through a broad and exclusive scope afforded the central government's criminal-law power; see *Assisted Human Reproduction Act* at 77 and 30, 48–51, 53, 56.

44 Through broad and autonomous powers afforded the provinces over healthcare and local matters and a view of the federation as generally decentralized; see *Assisted Human Reproduction Act* at 182–3, 262–4, 287.

45 See *Assisted Human Reproduction Act* at 268, where the Court says that the "double aspect" of many matters of jurisdiction is a reflection of the "different normative perspectives that make it possible to understand certain corresponding facts" as falling under either central or provincial jurisdiction, "regardless of their legal characterization." In other words, the competing understandings of the federation are all implicitly legitimate, given the flexibility of the federal structure and the competing ways it is understood. And, this dynamic nature of the system both allows and necessitates cooperation between the orders to govern (see at 184 and 139).

Insurance Act[46] the Court explicitly recognizes the contested nature of the federal system: "[T]o derive the evolution of constitutional powers from the structure of Canada is delicate, as what that structure is will often depend on a given court's view of what federalism is. What are regarded as the characteristic features of federalism may vary from one judge to another."[47] In line with this view, the Court depicts the scope and balance of powers in the federation as legitimately shifting in response to negotiations between actors over the system.[48] Elements of this understanding of the constitutional and federal association as a contested normative framework are also observable in both *Same-Sex Marriage*[49] and *Patriation*.[50]

What the examples highlight is the tendency of the Court in these fifty-six decisions to present the federation in an inclusive manner. In these decisions the Court presents the federal system in a way that reinforces the legitimacy of multiple models, including the dynamic

46 *Reference re Employment Insurance Act (Can.), ss. 22 and 23*, [2005] 2 S.C.R. 669. The issue in this reference is whether the central government can grant parental benefits to individuals who take time off work to care for a child under its unemployment insurance jurisdiction (or if this infringes on provincial competence over property and civil rights and matters of a local or private nature). The unanimous opinion was authored by Deschamps J.

47 *Employment Insurance Act* at 10.

48 When read in tandem, aspects of *Employment Insurance Act* (at 8–10, 37, 39, 45) demonstrate this view, with the Court presenting the federation as the outcome of negotiations between the actors over which order has the right to legislate with regard to employment insurance and what the scope of that right is (the Court holding that the scope changes over time in response to conflict and negotiation over the right). The SCC nicely summarizes this aspect of the ruling (at 45): "On the one hand, no constitutional head of power is static. On the other hand, the evolution of society cannot justify changing the nature of a power assigned by the Constitution to either level of government." And so the Court turns to the negotiations between the parties over the applicable heads of power to inform its opinion on its scope, while facilitating continued negotiation over time.

49 See *Reference re Same-Sex Marriage*, [2004] 3 S.C.R. 698, at 21–30; the subtitle of the section ("The Meaning of Marriage Is Not Constitutionally Fixed") sums up the point that the constitutional and federal system should be understood as shifting in response to conflict so as to "ensure the continued relevance and, indeed, legitimacy of Canada's constituting document."

50 See *Patriation*, [1981] at 874, where the Court depicts the constitution as "the global system of rules and principles which govern the exercise of constitutional authority in the whole and in every part of the Canadian state," a view of the constitution as a normative framework where conventions play a key role (providing, as noted at 831, "constitutional constraints" that are followed by the actors in the association).

model. It adopts this inclusive understanding by recognizing aspects of Canada's political and institutional structures that support the various perspectives on what the federation is, lending legitimacy to the views of those who subscribe to different federal models. At the same time, a number of these decisions explicitly recognize the federation as a dynamic normative system – as the process and outcome of negotiation between the subscribers of legitimate perspectives on what the federation is and ought to be. It is these two elements (a balanced recognition of the key federal models and explicit support for the dynamic model) that demonstrate how these decisions follow the approach to understanding and presenting the federation displayed in the *Secession Reference*.

Framing the Inclusive Understanding through Legal Argument

This leads to the Court's use of legal argument in these fifty-six decisions, and how it buttresses a depiction of the federation as more than a mere theory. There is thus a similarity between these decisions and the imposing cases in the way accepted forms of legal argument and methods of constitutional interpretation are used to support a depiction of the federation. Both anchor perspectives on the federation in the constitutional law – reinforcing the validity of that understanding as legal fact. The difference is that in these fifty-six decisions the Court accounts for the various federal models, affording legitimacy to each (rather than legitimizing one over the others).

Table 6.3 indicates the particular forms of legal argument relied upon in these fifty-six decisions.[51] In each of the forty-nine division-of-powers decisions, and in almost all of the seven references, the Court employs doctrinal analysis as a primary means of supporting its depiction of the federation. Moreover, just as in the impositions, the textual modality plays an important role as both a primary and secondary way of anchoring the depictions of the federation in the constitutional law (as do the prudential and structural forms of reasoning).[52] While

51 The various forms of legal argument are defined and explained in chapter 3.

52 Textual analysis is employed as the primary modality to support a depiction in 10 decisions, and as a secondary mode of interpretation in an additional 17 cases. Prudential and structural analysis are both employed in support of a depiction as a primary form of legal argument in 6 decisions and as a secondary form of argument in 9 decisions.

interesting, as already argued, these figures are of secondary importance to *how* the Court employs these modes of legal argument to reinforce its depiction.[53] It is on this front that the clear difference between an imposing decision and one that recognizes the legitimacy of multiple models is found. In these fifty-six decisions we see in each case the Court employing accepted forms of legal argument to reinforce the legitimacy of multiple models and the federation as the process and outcome of negotiation.

There are numerous examples in the forty-nine division-of-powers decisions where the Court employs doctrinal reasoning to support an inclusive depiction. For example, *Schneider v. The Queen*[54] is indicative of the way support for multiple models can be pulled from the case law, with the Court saying precedent supports both a decentralized and centralized federation.[55] By contrast, in *Multiple Access*[56] an essentially novel element of the division-of-powers doctrine relating to paramountcy is established and applied along with a crystallizing double-aspect doctrine.[57] In this case, the Court raises the threshold at which central-government legislation supplants conflicting provincial laws, saying that the constitution dictates this threshold is only reached when there is an "actual conflict" and not simply parallel legislative schemes. The Court goes on to praise such parallel schemes

53 This is because the Court employs a range of modalities, adapting them to reinforce particular depictions of the federation. As explained in chapter 3, the various modes of legal argument can be shifted to support any model.

54 *Schneider v. The Queen*, [1982] 2 S.C.R. 112. The issue in this case is whether a provincial law relating to the treatment and detention of heroin addicts infringes on central jurisdiction over the criminal law. The unanimous decision was authored by Dickson J (with Laskin CJ and Estey J concurring).

55 See *Schneider v. The Queen* [1982] (at 130–3) where the Court draws on precedent to support a wide scope and autonomy for the provincial powers over healthcare issues (and issues of a local nature), and (at 126, 130–2) where the Court also draws from the case law support for the central government as ultimately superior and having broad powers via its criminal law jurisdiction.

56 *Multiple Access Ltd. v. McCutcheon*, [1982] 2 S.C.R. 161. The issue in this case is the validity of provincial and central insider-trading legislation. The case is essentially about the doctrine of central paramountcy: the key issue being if there is a conflict between provincial and central laws, and if so, do central laws take precedence. The unanimous decision was authored by Dickson J (with Beetz, Estey, and Chouinard JJ concurring).

57 The double-aspect doctrine holds that some laws can fall under both central and provincial jurisdiction and are therefore within the competency of both governments; see Hogg (2009: 375–7).

as a reflection of the dynamic nature of the division of powers, which creates overlapping jurisdictions and a necessity for cooperation.[58] The use of doctrine in the decision thus reaffirms three competing perspectives: (1) that central government's jurisdiction is broad and ultimately paramount; (2) that there is a need to protect provincial autonomy; and (3) that the federal division of powers results from, and necessitates, cooperation and negotiation. In *Canadian Western Bank*[59] the Court applies the paramountcy and double-aspect doctrine, while significantly limiting the interjurisdictional-immunity doctrine.[60] Through this combination of doctrinal reasoning the Court reinforces that the constitutional law supports the view of the division of powers as inherently dynamic and as creating overlapping jurisdictions that require negotiation to implement,[61] while also rejecting the view that the constitution fixes a centralized system with the central government's jurisdiction over matters being completely protected from provincial laws.[62]

---

58 See *Multiple Access* at 181–3, 186–91. The sum of this reasoning is expressed at 190, where the Court applies the essence of the narrowed paramountcy doctrine with the essence of the double-aspect doctrine to say that the constitutional law of Canada holds that "duplication is … 'the ultimate in harmony.' The resulting 'untidiness' or 'diseconomy' of duplication is the price we pay for a federal system in which economy 'often has to be subordinated to […] provincial autonomy.' Mere duplication without actual conflict or contradiction is not sufficient to invoke the doctrine of paramountcy and render otherwise valid provincial legislation inoperative." Compare this to the stricter test of paramountcy employed by a lower court in this case (laid out at 171), which is rejected by the SCC: "[T]he constitutional doctrine of paramountcy operates so as to invalidate provincial legislation where it duplicates valid federal legislation in such a way that the two provisions cannot live together and operate concurrently."

59 *Canadian Western Bank v. Alberta*, [2007] 2 S.C.R. 3. The issue in this case is the extent to which banks, as federally regulated institutions, must comply with provincial laws regulating the promotion and sale of insurance. The unanimous decision was authored by Binnie and LeBel JJ (with Bastarache J concurring).

60 The interjurisdictional-immunity doctrine holds that there are core areas of central jurisdiction to which provincial laws shall not apply (even laws validly enacted within areas of provincial competence); see Hogg (2009: 392–405).

61 See *Canadian Western Bank*, [2007] at 30, where the Court links this view to the double-aspect doctrine, going on (at 69–75) to employ this view with the narrowed paramountcy doctrine established in *Multiple Access* [1982] to present the law as balancing the overlapping nature of the division of powers with a recognition of the centre's ultimately paramount jurisdiction and the need to protect provincial autonomy.

62 See *Canadian Western Bank* at 35, where the Court recognizes that "the application of interjurisdictional immunity has given rise to concerns by reason of its potential impact on Canadian constitutional arrangements. In theory, the doctrine is

In cases since *Canadian Western Bank*, the Court has applied these legal principles to reinforce the position that the law recognizes the dynamic nature of the division of powers and the necessity of federal-provincial cooperation.[63] This example, and the others discussed in this section, demonstrates how the Court uses doctrinal reasoning by drawing from the case law, developing legal principles and applying established doctrine. This doctrinal approach is used to reinforce the claim that the constitutional law supports a view of the various federal models as legitimate and the federation itself as the process and outcome of negotiation.

Of course, the Court often combines doctrinal analysis with other forms of legal argument to reinforce the validity of its depiction of the federation. This layering of various modalities is exemplified well in the division-of-power case *Bell Canada v. Quebec*.[64] Here, a doctrine that seeks to balance the ultimate superiority of the central government's jurisdiction over its works and undertakings with the provinces' broad and autonomous jurisdiction over matters that touch on these works and

---

reciprocal ... However, it would appear that the jurisprudential application of the doctrine has produced somewhat 'asymmetrical' results." Going on (at 36), the Court endorses "a view of federalism that puts greater emphasis on the legitimate interplay between federal and provincial powers" and (at 40) highlights that where this doctrine has been applied it is "to protect 'essential' parts of federal 'undertakings.'" The crux of the Court's reflection on the doctrine (at 45) is that "a broad use of the doctrine of interjurisdictional immunity runs the risk of creating an unintentional centralizing tendency in constitutional interpretation. As stated, this doctrine has in the past most often protected federal heads of power from incidental intrusion by provincial legislatures. The 'asymmetrical' application of interjurisdictional immunity is incompatible with the flexibility and co-ordination required by contemporary Canadian federalism." Accordingly, the Court says (at 47) that it "does not favour an intensive reliance on the doctrine."

63 As Wright (2010, 2014) argues, this case informed a subsequent facilitative turn in the SCC's federalism jurisprudence. See *BC v. Lafarge Canada*, [2007], for example at 4, 41–2, 77; *Confédération des syndicats nationaux v. Canada (Attorney General)*, [2008] 3 S.C.R. 511, for example at 32; *Chatterjee v. Ontario (Attorney General)*, [2009] 1 S.C.R. 624, for example at 2, 42; *Assisted Human Reproduction Act*, [2010], for example at 139, 183, 188. I discuss this trend post-2010 in the conclusion.

64 *Bell Canada v. Quebec (CSST)*, [1988] 1 S.C.R. 749. The issue in this case is whether provincial health and safety legislation is constitutionally applicable to a federal undertaking. The unanimous decision (authored by Beetz J) is part of a trilogy of cases delivered together, the other two being *Canadian National Railway Co. v. Courtois*, [1988] 1 S.C.R. 868 and *Alltrans Express Ltd. v. British Columbia (Workers' Compensation Board)*, [1988] 1 S.C.R. 897.

undertakings is crystallized.[65] In developing the doctrine that the central government does have immunity from provincial laws, but only for a narrow set of activities deemed to be essential to the work or undertaking, the Court draws on the related case law, but also on the text of the constitution to justify the rule as valid constitutional law.[66] Similarly, in *Ontario v. OPSEU*[67] we see the structural modality employed (in conjunction with doctrinal and textual analysis) to reinforce the legality of a depiction of the federation as a political system in which broad central and provincial powers are counterbalanced; here, the Court says this balance is the essence of the "federal principle" and is part of "the basic structure of [the] Constitution."[68] By contrast, in *Kitkatla v. BC*[69] a depiction of the federation that grants a measure of legitimacy to the multinational, pan-Canadian, and provincial-equality models[70] is reinforced as legitimate by balancing the interests of Aboriginal groups with others in the province.[71] The Court reverts to prudential reasoning in this decision

65 See *Bell Canada v. Quebec* at 761–2, where the general doctrine is summarized: "Parliament is vested with exclusive legislative jurisdiction over labour relations and working conditions when that jurisdiction is an integral part of its primary and exclusive jurisdiction over another class of subjects, as is the case with labour relations and working conditions in the federal undertakings ... [But] works, such as federal railways, things, such as land reserved for Indians, and persons, such as Indians, who are within the special and exclusive jurisdiction of Parliament, are still subject to provincial statutes that are general in their application, whether municipal legislation, legislation on adoption, hunting or the distribution of family property, provided however that the application of these provincial laws does not bear upon those subjects in what makes them specifically of federal jurisdiction."

66 On the use of case law, in addition to *Bell Canada v. Quebec* at 761–3, see also at 815–45. Throughout the decision, though, textual analysis is continually employed to anchor the "balanced" depiction of the federation in the constitutional law (see, for example, at 815–16, 819, 828–30 and 839–40).

67 *Ontario (Attorney General) v. OPSEU*, [1987] 2 S.C.R. 2. The main issue is the validity of a provincial law limiting the participation of provincial civil servants in central elections. The unanimous decision was authored by Beetz J (with Dickson CJ and Lamer JJ concurring).

68 See *Ontario v. OPSEU* at 45–7, 57.

69 *Kitkatla Band v. British Columbia (Minister of Small Business, Tourism and Culture)*, [2002] 2 S.C.R. 146. The issue in this case is whether a provincial act relating to the protection, alteration, and destruction of cultural heritage objects is outside the province's jurisdiction over property and civil rights to the extent it applies to Aboriginals and culturally modified trees. The unanimous decision was authored by LeBel J.

70 See *Kitkatla v. BC* at 31, 43–6, 65–9, 70–5.

71 See *Kitkatla v. BC* at 62: "No heritage conservation scheme can provide absolute protection to all objects or sites that possess some historical, archaeological or cultural value

to augment the doctrinal support afforded its depiction of the federation, while also employing prudential reasoning in a way that reinforces the legitimacy of multiple models (i.e., by balancing the interests of Aboriginals as a group with those of other provincial inhabitants and the broad powers of the two orders of government vis-à-vis Aboriginals).

The use of legal argument to reinforce the legitimacy of depictions as law is also observable in all seven of the federal references noted in table 6.3. For example, in *Education Act* we can see how multiple modalities of constitutional interpretation are used to support the various federal models. Doctrine is employed to lend credence to a view of a province as a national-based unit in line with the multinational model,[72] while the text is relied upon to present provinces as equal juridical units in line with the provincial-equality model.[73] In *Newfoundland*

---

to a society. To grant such an absolute protection would be to freeze a society at a particular moment in time. It would make impossible the need to remove, for example, buildings or artifacts of heritage value which, nevertheless, create a public health hazard or otherwise endanger lives. In other cases, the value of preserving an object may be greatly outweighed by the benefit that could accrue from allowing it to be removed or destroyed in order to accomplish a goal deemed by society to be of greater value. It cannot be denied that … [the impugned provincial legislation] … could sometimes affect aboriginal interests. As will be seen below, these provisions form part of a carefully balanced scheme. As recommended by the Court in *Delgamuukw*, it is highly sensitive to native cultural interests. At the same time, it appears to strike an appropriate balance between native and non-native interests. Native interests must be carefully taken into account at every stage of a procedure under the Act. The Act clearly considers them as an essential part of the interests to be preserved and of the cultural heritage of British Columbia as well as of all First Nations." The Court goes on (at 64) to cite that the percentage of cultural artefacts to be destroyed has the effect of the "striking of a balance between the need and desire to preserve aboriginal heritage with the need and desire to promote the exploitation of British Columbia's natural resources."

72 See *Education Act*, [1987] at 23–6, 47 and particularly 28, where the Court cites a number of decisions that support its depiction, saying that "the compromise or, as Duff C.J. in the *Reference Re Adoption Act*, [1938] S.C.R. 398 at p. 402, termed it, 'the basic compact of Confederation,' was that rights and privileges already acquired by law at the time of Confederation would be preserved and provincial legislatures could bestow additional new rights and privileges in response to changing conditions."

73 See *Education Act* at 71, 75–6, 78, 79 and particularly 69, where the Court relies on the text of the constitution to demonstrate the equality of all provinces in the powers granted to them as a level of government: "[T]he opening words of s. 93 are a clear grant of legislative power to the province, providing the province with the authority to make laws in relation to education. As such, the opening words of s. 93 are similar to the various grants of provincial power found in s. 92 of the *Constitution Act, 1867* and might well have been included in s. 92."

Continental Shelf[74] the textual modality is used to reinforce the legitimacy of the pan-Canadian, provincial-equality, and multinational models.[75]

This section accentuates the difference between these fifty-six decisions and the seventy-four imposing decisions in how legal argument is used to reinforce the validity of a depiction of the federation. These examples demonstrate how the Court employs the various forms of legal argument and constitutional interpretation to present the federation as the process and outcome of negotiation between the subscribers of legitimate models. This approach is quite different than what happens in the imposing decisions, where legal argument is employed to legitimize a partial perspective of what the federation is *as the law*.

Rejecting Zero-Sum Outcomes

The way the Court understands the federation and uses legal analysis to anchor this understanding in the law is not the only important aspect of federalism jurisprudence. The outcomes are also important: they have practical political effects, aligning the constitutional and federal association with the way it is depicted, while also establishing precedents that influence future decisions.

As argued in the previous chapter there is a close link between the way the federation is presented and the outcome of a case. The depiction of

74 *Reference re Newfoundland Continental Shelf*, [1984] 1 S.C.R. 86. The issue in this case is which government (Canada or Newfoundland) has jurisdiction to exploit the natural resources of the continental shelf off the coast of the province and to legislate with regard to the exploitation of these resources. The unanimous opinion was issued by "The Court."

75 See *Newfoundland Continental Shelf* at 127–8, where the Court says that the text of the constitution mandates a general superiority for the central government: "There is nothing in s. 92 of the *Constitution Act, 1867* which could confer legislative jurisdiction upon Newfoundland in respect of such rights held by Canada. Legislative jurisdiction falls to Canada under the peace, order, and good government power in its residual capacity. Newfoundland's legislative competence, like that of all the other provinces, is confined to legislation operating within the provinces" (see also 108, 111, 115). In the same decision, the SCC (at 104–5) lends credence to the provincial-equality and multinational models by citing the text of key constitutional documents that could be taken to support a view of the federation as a compact between either provinces or nations (i.e., the Court notes the status of Newfoundland before joining the state as an autonomous political community equal to that of Canada in the Balfour Declaration).

the federation establishes what it is, while the outcome draws from that understanding and reinforces the legitimacy of that depiction as legal fact. Decisions that follow the example of the *Secession Reference* reach outcomes that mitigate the creation of stark winners and losers while also reinforcing the legitimacy of multiple federal models (and/or the dynamic model explicitly). The hallmarks of a decision that rejects an imposing approach are thus: (1) a depiction that recognizes the legitimacy of multiple federal models and the system as the process and outcome of negotiation; and (2) an outcome that is positive for multiple jurisdictions and reinforces the legitimacy of multiple models (and/or the dynamic model explicitly). We see these two elements in a significant percentage of the fifty-six decisions discussed in this chapter.

With regard to selecting winners and losers in these cases, we see a clear trend of rejecting zero-sum outcomes. There are only seven decisions where one jurisdiction wins and the others lose outright. In many decisions (34) the outcome is positive for more than one jurisdiction (i.e., both the central and provincial governments receive a beneficial outcome).[76] In the remaining fifteen decisions the Court still rejects a zero-sum approach to managing the dispute, as the negative outcome for the "losing" jurisdiction is significantly mitigated.[77]

In a high proportion of these fifty-six decisions the outcomes also reinforce the legitimacy of multiple models, and/or the dynamic model explicitly: in fifty-three decisions the outcome draws from, and works to reinforce the legitimacy of, more than one federal model; in twenty-one cases the outcome explicitly reinforces the legitimacy of the dynamic model.

Disposing of the appeal so that multiple jurisdictions "win" and multiple models are reinforced is exemplified well in a number of division-of-powers decisions. For example, in *Lovelace v. Ontario*[78] a provincial

76 Included in these 34 decisions are 5 division-of-powers decisions where the outcome was ambivalent between the central and provincial government.

77 This represents a significantly higher percentage of decisions that mitigate the negative outcome for a losing party than in the imposing decisions: 68% of these decisions that have a negative outcome for a party seek to mitigate this in some way, compared to only 15% of imposing decisions.

78 *Lovelace v. Ontario*, [2000] 1 S.C.R. 950. The division-of-powers issue in this case is the validity of a provincial law that allows Aboriginal communities to establish casinos on their reserves and mandates that all proceeds go to registered band councils (thereby excluding non-status Aboriginals and bands from accessing the proceeds). The case is thus about whether this law infringes on the central government's jurisdiction over Aboriginals. The unanimous decision was authored by Iacobucci J.

law allowing Aboriginal groups in the province to establish casinos on their reserves and mandating the proceeds to registered bands is found valid. In upholding the law, provincial autonomy to pass laws of general application within an area of competence is reinforced.[79] However, this provincial power is subject to a substantial caveat: provincial laws are valid only if they do not touch on the "Indianness" of an Aboriginal group or infringe upon Aboriginal rights (neither of which applies in this case).[80] The ruling thus also reinforces both exclusive powers for the central government over Aboriginals qua Aboriginals, *and* the distinctiveness of Aboriginals as a community that bears rights to things such as self-government (and the ability to raise revenue to fund self-government). In a similar fashion, in *Siemens v. Manitoba*[81] a provincial law allowing local communities to prohibit gambling via video lottery terminals is found valid (and as not infringing upon the central government's criminal-law jurisdiction). This outcome is positive to both the provinces (and provincial-equality model) and the central government (and the pan-Canadian model). It clearly reinforces a broad scope to the provinces' powers over property and civil rights and local commerce (allowing the prohibition of an activity with sanctions).[82] However, the

79 See *Lovelace v. Ontario* esp. at 111.

80 See *Lovelace v. Ontario* esp. at 110–11.

81 *Siemens v. Manitoba (Attorney General)*, [2003] 1 S.C.R. 6. The issue in this case is whether provincial legislation that enables local communities to hold binding referendums on whether to allow video lottery terminals in local establishments is within the province's power or if it infringes on the central order's jurisdiction over criminal law. The unanimous decision was authored by Major J.

82 See *Siemens v. Manitoba* at 22–3, 30, where the Court says: "[T]he regulation of gaming activities has a clear provincial aspect under s. 92 of the *Constitution Act, 1867* subject to Parliamentary paramountcy in the case of a clash between federal and provincial legislation … Altogether apart from features of gaming which attract criminal prohibition, lottery activities are subject to the legislative authority of the province under various heads of s. 92, including, I suggest, property and civil rights (13), licensing (9), and maintenance of charitable institutions (7)," adding that "the *VLT Act* is not, as the appellants have submitted, a colourable attempt to legislate criminal law … The respondents conceded that the *VLT Act* contains a prohibition, namely, s. 3(1) prohibits the operation of VLTs in municipalities that have banned them as the result of a binding plebiscite. Nevertheless, this alone is insufficient to establish that the *VLT Act* is, in pith and substance, criminal law. The Act does not create penal consequences, and was not enacted for a criminal law purpose … [T]he presence of moral considerations does not *per se* render a law *ultra vires* the provincial legislature. In giving Parliament exclusive jurisdiction over criminal law, the *Constitution Act, 1867* did not intend to remove all morality from provincial legislation."

central government argued in favour of this outcome, and the decision reinforces broad and ultimately superior criminal-law powers for the central government (because the Court explicitly says it can pass legislation under its criminal-law power that will take precedence and supplant provincial laws in this area if it so chooses).[83]

Siemens v. Manitoba also exemplifies how a decision can reinforce the legitimacy of the dynamic model explicitly. In the decision, the Court states that the outcome reached is informed by the fact that the central and provincial governments struck an agreement on how to operationalize the division of powers in relation to lotteries and gambling.[84] We see a similar outcome that reinforces a view of the federation as the process and outcome of discussing the specifics of the distribution of power and responsibility in *R v. Furtney*. Here, the Court finds valid a scheme that was negotiated between the central and provincial government to regulate lotteries (importantly, saying that the provincial regulation of the matter is not seen to be an unconstitutional delegation of power from the central government).[85] This case, and others

83 See *Siemens v. Manitoba* at 22; note the important caveat added to the ruling that the law is within the province's ability to regulate gambling: "In my view, the regulation of gaming activities has a clear provincial aspect under s. 92 of the *Constitution Act, 1867 subject to Parliamentary paramountcy in the case of a clash between federal and provincial legislation*" (emphasis added).

84 See *Siemens v. Manitoba* at 34: "The Attorney General of Canada's intervention in support of the provincial government creates a situation of attempted federal-provincial cooperation. The governments, in the absence of jurisdiction, cannot by simple agreement lend legitimacy to a claim that the *VLT Act* is *intra vires*. However, given that both federal and provincial governments guard their legislative powers carefully, when they do agree to shared jurisdiction, that fact should be given careful consideration by the courts."

85 See *R v. Furtney*, [1991] at 105, where the Court, speaking about the criminal code provisions that allow the provinces to regulate lotteries, says they do not "impose any right or duty on a provincial legislature … [R]egardless of the nature of the delegation, it is not a prohibited inter-delegation," going on to say that these provisions "may be read as incorporating by reference provincial legislation authorizing the Lieutenant Governor in Council to issue licences containing relevant terms and conditions or as excluding from the reach of the criminal law prohibition, lotteries licensed under provincial law so long as that licensing is by or under the authority of the Lieutenant Governor in Council. Dreidger, in the article to which I have referred, notes that the *Criminal Code* exemption for lotteries conducted in accordance with a provincial statute is not a delegation. I agree." The Court adds (at 107) that "much was made of the fact that the provinces and the federal government reached an agreement in 1985 under which the federal government agreed that it would not conduct lotteries, but rather leave the conduct of lotteries to the provinces. I am

like it,[86] shows how the Court can reach decisions that support and validate the dynamic nature of the federation (i.e., that a federation is a normative system that is defined through negotiation and cooperation among key political actors).

There are also those decisions that reject the zero-sum approach to disposing of an appeal by denying either party absolute victory, and/or mitigating the loss for a jurisdiction. *Alberta Government Telephones v. Canada*[87] exemplifies this approach. The decision in this case simultaneously finds that a provincially owned telecommunications company comes under the legislative jurisdiction of the central government (as a federal work and undertaking), but, because of provincial crown immunity, the company falls outside the reach of central telecommunications legislation (as it stood at the time).[88] The resulting regulatory vacuum denies either side a clear win (and forces more explicit legislation, as well as negotiation and coordination, to regulate the company in question).[89] A different perspective is presented in *Law Society*

---

unable to discern any grounds upon which this agreement can be said to be unconstitutional let alone have any unconstitutional effects on the provisions of the *Code*. Parliament, in the exercise of the criminal-law power, may define those agencies or instrumentalities exempt from the prohibition."

86 See, in particular, *Fédération des producteurs de volailles du Québec* [2005], *Canadian Western Bank* [2007] and *Confédération des syndicats nationaux* [2008].

87 *Alberta Government Telephones v. Canada (Canadian Radio-television and Telecommunications Commission)*, [1989] 2 S.C.R. 225. The issue in this case is whether the business of a provincial crown company brings it under the legislative jurisdiction of the central government as a federal work and undertaking pursuant to section 92.10.A of the constitution. The majority decision was authored by Dickson CJ.

88 See *Alberta Government Telephones v. Canada* at 257: "The case law clearly establishes that if a work or undertaking falls within s. 92(10)(*a*) it is removed from the jurisdiction of the provinces and exclusive jurisdiction lies with the federal Parliament." The Court goes on (at 268) to find that "AGT is an interprovincial undertaking within the meaning of s. 92(10)(*a*) of the *Constitution Act, 1867*." However, later in the decision (at 301) the Court finds that, "on the basis of the legislation as presently drafted, AGT is immune from [central] jurisdiction exercised under s. 320 of the *Railway Act*."

89 See *Alberta Government Telephones v. Canada* at 283, where the Court explicitly states that "the fact that granting immunity will produce a regulatory vacuum with respect to AGT is insufficient and does not amount to a frustration of the *Railway Act* as a whole. While granting immunity unless and until Parliament chooses to amend the legislation will produce a gap in potential coverage of the *Railway Act*, the Act can continue to function just as it did prior to this court's finding that AGT is a federal undertaking."

of British Columbia v. Mangat,[90] where we can see how an outcome that is mainly positive for the central government can still mitigate the loss for the provinces. In this case, a central-government law allowing non-lawyers to represent clients at immigration tribunals is deemed valid and applicable, despite provincial laws prohibiting non-lawyers from representing anyone at judicial proceedings. However, this provincial loss is mitigated on a number of fronts. First, the Court reinforces broad provincial powers to regulate professional activities (like the practice of lawyers), even while establishing that provinces can regulate the activity of lawyers at immigration tribunals (up to the point of conflict with central-government legislation).[91] Second, the Court applies a narrow paramountcy doctrine, which protects a measure of provincial autonomy; accordingly, it does not strike down the provincial law in question, but rather, simply "reads down" the relevant provisions so that they do not prohibit representation by non-lawyers at immigration tribunals.[92]

This same tendency to reject zero-sum outcomes is evident in the federal references noted in table 6.3. For example, in *Patriation* the opinion that it is technically legal for the central government to unilaterally seek an amendment to the constitution that affects provincial autonomy, but it must conventionally secure a measure of consent from the provinces for such an amendment, is beneficial to: the central government (as it grants the then-central government's plan legitimacy); all provinces (as it mandates, according to constitutional convention, a substantial measure of provincial consent before amending the constitution when their autonomy is affected); and a particular province (as the ambiguity on the amount of provincial consent required leaves the door open to a Québec

90 *Law Society of British Columbia v. Mangat*, [2001] 3 S.C.R. 113. The issue in this case is whether a provincial law prohibiting non-lawyers from representing clients at any judicial proceeding in the province is in conflict with a central law that allows non-lawyers to represent clients at immigration tribunal hearings. The unanimous decision was authored by Gonthier J.

91 See *Law Society of BC v. Mangat* at 38–47.

92 See *Law Society of BC v. Mangat* at 72–4. The point is that the provincial law still applies to all other judicial proceedings that are not immigration-tribunal hearings, and that it also still applies generally to immigration tribunal proceedings, with the exception of the inapplicable provisions. On the approach of reading down legislation so that it does not apply to a matter within another order's jurisdiction, see Hogg (2009: 390–2).

veto over the negotiations).[93] In *Same-Sex Marriage,*[94] the central government's legislation that changes the definition of marriage is determined to be within its power (despite impacting areas of provincial jurisdiction).[95] Nevertheless, provincial autonomy is protected in the ruling that an operational clause guiding how provinces administer marriage is invalid because it infringes upon exclusive provincial jurisdiction. Finally, *Employment Insurance Act* exemplifies both how a negative outcome can be mitigated and how the dynamic model can be explicitly reinforced.[96]

What these examples demonstrate is how the Court can, and does, manage disputes in a way that rejects a zero-sum approach. There are decisions that reach a positive outcome for multiple jurisdictions and reinforce the legitimacy of multiple models. There are also decisions that explicitly reinforce the validity of the dynamic model. And there are decisions that deny either side absolute victory or mitigate the negative

93 As noted in previous chapters, this outcome led to negotiations that resulted (without the consent of Québec) in the Constitution Act, 1982. The legality of adopting this constitution without Québec's signature and the issue of what constituted a substantial measure of provincial consent – and if this included a veto for Québec – was taken up in *Quebec Veto,* [1982] (discussed in the previous chapter), where the legality of the constitution was affirmed and a veto for Québec rejected.

94 *Reference re Same-Sex Marriage,* [2004] 3 S.C.R. 698. The issue in this reference is the ability of the central government to unilaterally change the definition of marriage to allow for same-sex marriage and exempt religious officials from necessarily performing same-sex unions. The central division-of-powers issue is whether this legislation falls within the central head of power relating to "Marriage and Divorce" or if this infringes on the provincial head of power relating to the "Solemnization of Marriage." The unanimous opinion was issued by "The Court."

95 See *Same-Sex Marriage* at 19, 31–2.

96 The decision supports the pan-Canadian model as it reinforces the legitimacy of the central government's ability to affect areas of provincial jurisdiction through an expanding power over employment insurance; see *Employment Insurance Act,* [2005] at 36–8, 67–8. However, allowing the central government to expand employment insurance to provide maternity benefits also reinforces the dynamic model, because it recognizes that the constitutional division of powers adapts in response to conflicts and negotiations over the system (see at 8–10, 39–40, 45, 67). Moreover, the loss for Québec in this case is mitigated by the Court highlighting how previously negotiated agreements between the orders of government remain open to challenge in the courts. The case itself exemplifies this point, as Québec is challenging the scope of the central government's authority to legislate with regard to employment insurance (a power divested to it via a constitutional amendment in 1940 wherein the provinces carved this right out of their own s. 92 powers over property and civil rights). A similar tempering of support for the pan-Canadian model by reinforcing the dynamic model can be seen in *Newfoundland Continental Shelf,* [1984].

outcome for one order of government in some substantial way. Each of these approaches reinforces the legitimacy of multiple federal models and the federal system as the process and outcome of negotiation, rather than aligning the federation with one particular perspective.

A Positive Role Model

The Court's adopted role can be an integral part of a decision recognizing the legitimacy of multiple models and the federation as a process and outcome of negotiation. There is a link between the conceptualization of the ideal role for the federal arbiter, how it carries out the activity of judicial review, and the understanding of the constitutional and federal system. And, in those decisions that follow the exemplar of the *Secession Reference*, ideally, an understanding of the federation as the process and outcome of negotiation between the subscribers of legitimate federal models is paired with a role for the Court as a broad facilitator of this negotiation, either explicitly or more indirectly.

The more explicit facilitator role is marked by an attempt to manage conflict by promoting negotiation and cooperation between conflicting parties through political processes. It is in assuming this role that the Court ideally seeks to reinforce the legitimacy of the various parties' perspectives, to affirm the legitimacy of the political and institutional processes that allow negotiation and cooperation, and to induce the parties to use these processes. In instances where negotiation and cooperation are unlikely (which is not uncommon, given the inherently adversarial nature of conflict) the Court can and does still indirectly facilitate negotiation by adopting a fair approach to arbitration. Here the ideal is to avoid imposing a particular party's perspective on another party, to reaffirm the legitimacy of the losing party's perspective, and to mitigate the loss for a party to the extent possible, while also seeking to emphasize that continued disagreement is reasonable and that the federal system can account for this situation as a flexible and dynamic association.

As table 6.3 indicates, I was able to determine the Court's self-selected role in thirty-seven of these fifty-six decisions.[97] The ideal role of facilitator was adopted in some twenty-four decisions. In the remaining thirteen

97 While this is a higher percentage of cases where I was able to determine the Court's role than in the imposing decisions, the same reason applies for the lack of information in some decisions: the SCC's tendency to avoid theoretical discussions on points such as the role of the judiciary in the federation, unless the issue is raised by a party.

cases one or more of the three traditional roles was adopted (i.e., the umpire, branch of government, and guardian roles).[98] Interestingly in a high percentage (79%) of cases where the facilitator role is employed, it is paired with a depiction of the federation in line with the dynamic model. This tendency indicates a strong link between the Court endorsing an understanding of the federation as the process and outcome of negotiation and approaching its role as a facilitator of that negotiation.

The ideal role of facilitator is exemplified in *Canadian Western Bank*. In this decision the Court shows deference to, and reinforces the legitimacy of, a central-provincial scheme to regulate insurance provided by banks.[99] The Court, in reaffirming the validity of the scheme and the political process that establishes it, explicitly recognizes that its role in the federation is to "facilitate, not undermine … co-operative federalism."[100] In this decision the Court even explicitly links this ideal role to a dynamic understanding of the constitution and federation: "[T]he Constitution, though a legal document, serves as a framework for life and for political action within a federal state, in which the courts have rightly observed the importance of co-operation among government actors to ensure that federalism operates flexibly."[101] The explicit

98 While this falls short of the ideal that in every case the Court recognizes its role as the facilitator of negotiation between conflicting parties as laid out in the *Secession Reference*, these 13 cases tend to follow the example of the *Secession Reference* in other ways (i.e., in the depiction of the federation and the outcomes). Accordingly, they are still considered to meet the threshold of a decision that recognizes the federation as the process and outcome of negotiation between the subscribers of legitimate models. Still, as a result, these cases do tend to fall on the lower end of the spectrum of adherence to this ideal-type. In addition, it is interesting to note that in many of these decisions the traditional roles are employed in a way that still reinforces the legitimacy of multiple federal models (for example, by employing one or more models to justify and reinforce aspects of a depiction that counterbalances competing models).

99 See *Canadian Western Bank*, [2007] at 20.

100 See *Canadian Western Bank* at 24: "As the final arbiters of the division of powers, the courts have developed certain constitutional doctrines, which, like the interpretations of the powers to which they apply, are based on the guiding principles of our constitutional order. The constitutional doctrines permit an appropriate balance to be struck in the recognition and management of the inevitable overlaps in rules made at the two levels of legislative power, while recognizing the need to preserve sufficient predictability in the operation of the division of powers. The doctrines must also be designed to reconcile the legitimate diversity of regional experimentation with the need for national unity. *Finally, they must include a recognition that the task of maintaining the balance of powers in practice falls primarily to governments, and constitutional doctrine must facilitate, not undermine what this Court has called 'co-operative federalism'*" (emphasis added).

101 *Canadian Western Bank* at 42.

promotion of, and deference to, the political processes that manage conflict through negotiation and cooperation is clearly evident in a number of other decisions.[102] The important point is that this tendency grants legitimacy to these processes and pushes governments to use them.

This role of facilitator of negotiation and cooperation is also embraced in *BC v. Lafarge*.[103] However, here, the secondary role of fair arbiter is also explicitly embraced. In this decision, the Court says that where parties "are in disagreement, of course, the courts will have to resolve the difference."[104] This statement needs to be understood in the context of what the Court says about the nature of the federation in this decision (i.e., that it is a process and outcome of negotiation between the subscribers of legitimate models). From all of this, it can safely be implied that here the Court is promoting an arbiter role that reaches a decision that properly accounts for the competing ways the federation is understood.[105]

The same tendency to adopt a role of facilitator and fair arbiter is also evident in the federal references that follow the lead of the *Secession Reference*. For example, in *Employment Insurance Act* the SCC explicitly recognizes a connection between the federation as a normative system and its ideal role of facilitating negotiation and cooperation through political processes, saying: "[W]hat are regarded as the characteristic features of federalism may vary from one judge to another, and will be based on political rather than legal notions ... [and so] the task of maintaining the balance between federal and provincial powers falls primarily to governments."[106] Similarly, in *Assisted Human Reproduction*

102 See, for example, *Chatterjee v. Ontario*, [2009] at 2, 29–30; *Siemens v. Manitoba*, [2003] at 33–4; *Ontario v. OPSEU*, [1987] at 19–20.

103 See *BC v. Lafarge* [2007] at 3, 38–9.

104 See *BC v. Lafarge* at 90.

105 See the comments above on the way the federation is depicted in *BC v. Lafarge*.

106 *Employment Insurance Act*, [2005] at 10; in other words, the Court ought not simply be an umpire of the federation and impose the rules on the actors, nor act as a branch of government and have a role in shaping them, nor act as a guardian to protect the federal system – it is the role of the Court to facilitate the management of issues by the governments themselves. Related to this, and in line with the role of facilitator first and fair arbiter second, the Court says (at 8) that given the propensity of governments to conflict over the division of powers, and "because a decision regarding the scope of the powers assigned by the *Constitution Act, 1867* has undeniable social and political consequences," when negotiation cannot resolve the issue it falls to the Court to step in as a fair arbiter – to "approach the task assigned to it by the law with considerable circumspection."

Act the Court says that "flexible, cooperative" federalism "should be encouraged" by the courts.[107] In *Newfoundland Continental Shelf* the facilitator and fair-arbiter roles are implicitly merged and applied. In this decision, which grants the central government rights over natural resources sought by the province,[108] a seemingly one-sided outcome plays a crucial role in managing a decades-long dispute between governments through a political process. The Court's ruling is delivered in the context of a heated political negotiation, and the ruling in favour of the central government offsets an earlier ruling by the Newfoundland Court of Appeal strengthening the province's position vis-à-vis ownership of the resources. The Court thus plays a crucial role in the resulting intergovernmental agreement on offshore resource management between Canada and Newfoundland, ensuring that both parties' perspectives are granted a measure of legitimacy and facilitating fruitful and fair negotiations.[109]

These examples demonstrate how the Court, at times, embraces a role as a facilitator and fair arbiter within a comprehensive conflict-management approach that follows that laid out in the *Secession Reference*. This role and approach works from, and reinforces, an understanding of the federation as the process and outcome of negotiation between the subscribers of legitimate federal models. These examples illuminate the links the Court makes between this understanding and a role for itself as the facilitator of negotiation over the federation. They show how the Court can understand the federation as a contested normative system, with the federal arbiter's role being one of managing the conflict over the federation by promoting cooperation through political processes. This role is thus informed by an understanding that the judiciary – in its role as federal arbiter – is an inherently political position. These decisions reflect an acceptance by the Court that it is part of the field of struggle over the nature and ideal direction of the federation. The importance of the SCC embracing such a view of the federation and its role within the system, as I am about to elaborate on, is that it allows the Court to implement a conflict-management approach that

107 See *Assisted Human Reproduction Act*, [2010] at 139: "The Court's endorsement of a flexible, cooperative approach to federalism suggests that this kind of pragmatic lawmaking should be encouraged."

108 For a summary of the decision see *Newfoundland Continental Shelf*, [1984] at 128–9.

109 For a similar view, see Swinton (1992: 139) and Monahan (1987: 9).

can build support for the process of managing disputes and generate loyalty to the resulting federal system.

A Turn towards Conflict Management

The above analysis demonstrates the fundamental difference between the fifty-six decisions discussed here and the seventy-four imposing decisions covered in the previous chapter. In the decisions discussed above, the approach of presenting the federation in line with only one model is rejected. Instead, the Court depicts the federation in a way that draws from, and reinforces the legitimacy of, multiple federal models, including the dynamic model. And, this comprehensive depiction is anchored in the constitutional law through the use of legal argument, while in the imposing cases legal argument is used selectively to highlight aspects of the law that reinforce the legitimacy of a particular depiction. Similarly, the approach of declaring stark winners and losers, and reaching outcomes that align the federal system with a particular model is rejected. What we see in the decisions above is an attempt to find benefits for all parties to the conflict (or at least mitigate the loss for a party), while also reinforcing the notion that the federation is dynamic and incorporates elements of many federal models. In line with this approach, we also see in these decisions a tendency for the Court to adopt a role as the facilitator of negotiation and cooperation between the orders of government to manage conflict over the system. This approach and role is in contrast to the tendency in the imposing decisions for the Court to employ a role (as umpire, branch of government, or guardian) that reinforces key aspects of a specific federal model's depiction of the federation and which justifies outcomes that reinforce that model.

This chapter thus provides the final element in this study of how the SCC accounts for (or fails to account for) the inherent contestation over nationality and the federation in its role as federal arbiter. The analysis highlights the positive aspects of the SCC's federal work: those decisions that follow the lead of the *Secession Reference* and recognize the federation as the process and outcome of negotiation between the subscribers of legitimate federal models.

Completing this picture shows that the *Secession Reference* is not an aberration. This decision marks a significant turn in how the Court understands the federation, how it manages conflict and how it views its own role within the process. As this chapter shows, the *Secession*

Reference built upon elements from decisions that preceded it; but the approach outlined in the reference has also increasingly been followed in subsequent jurisprudence: 71 per cent of SCC decisions from 1999 forward follow the approach outlined in the *Secession Reference.* Indeed, the majority of cases with substantial adherence to the ideal-type come *after* the *Secession Reference.*

As I argued in chapter 4,[110] this change in approach can be seen as an attempt by the Court to maintain the legitimacy of the federal arbiter and the entire system in the face of considerable challenges. The issues presented in the *Secession Reference* (the legality of a unilateral secession by Québec) and the political context surrounding it (being so close to a nearly successful secession referendum) directly challenged the very existence of the federation. The most pressing political issue of the time was the unity of the state and the perceived need to find a way to save the federation. Given this context, I argue that to understand the shift in approach with the *Secession Reference* we need to accept the idea that when a political and legal system is facing its disintegration or destruction the "tendency of judges may be to struggle to save the system from collapse."[111] In this case, then, the Court was forced to demonstrate how the federal system was able to deal with the challenge to its legitimacy and come out the stronger for it.

This argument – that the Court, as federal arbiter, needs to generate legitimacy in how it deals with conflict over the system – is built on the idea that in all conflicts over the federal system the courts are indeed part of the field of struggle.[112] The SCC cannot remove itself from these struggles because, as federal arbiter, it is part of the entire system of government: it is the institution that oversees and arbitrates conflict over the distribution of power and resources within the federation. Accordingly, challenges to the existing constitutional and federal association also challenge the Court's legitimacy and place within it. It has even been argued that a primary strategic motivation for the Court's actions in the *Secession Reference* was to cultivate its own institutional legitimacy.[113] Building on this explanation of the Court's motivation, if we also take into consideration the SCC's often self-promoted role

110 And elsewhere; see Schertzer (2008: 117–19), from which the following two paragraphs are largely drawn.

111 Walters (1999: 371); see also Hart (1961: 114).

112 See Tully (2004: 86).

113 Radmilovic (2010).

as guardian of the constitution, it is logical to argue that the SCC uses its place in the system to ensure that the legal continuity, stability, and, above all, legitimacy of the federal political system are maintained.

The significant turn with the *Secession Reference*, then, comes in shifting from an imposing and assimilative approach to maintaining stability to one that recognizes the inherently dynamic nature of the system. In line with this turn, the Court used the tools it had at hand to achieve the goal of generating and maintaining legitimacy: the law, as it interpreted it. On this rendering, the *Secession Reference* does not represent a mere rhetorical turn, or *just* a self-centred attempt to "define its place" within the political system as legitimate.[114] Rather, the decision approach can be seen as a fundamental shift in how to legitimize both the federal arbiter and the entire federation.

Given the potential benefits, it should be clear why the SCC has largely followed the recognizing approach in its federalism jurisprudence after the *Secession Reference*. If, as others and I have argued, a principal concern of the Court is to generate and maintain legitimacy for the institution and for the system as a whole, then the SCC should seek out the optimal way to achieve this objective. The approach of recognizing the competing perspectives on the national and federal character of the country is an important element of generating and maintaining legitimacy for the system when managing conflicts over the distribution of power and resources. This stance holds true for all federalism jurisprudence, not just the extraordinary case of the *Secession Reference*. As I argued earlier, all of the 131 decisions reviewed in this study deal with conflicts over the very nature of the federal system (in how identities are recognized and power and resources are accordingly distributed). So, once the SCC explicitly made the shift towards generating legitimacy in line with a recognizing approach in the *Secession Reference*, it is logical that it would largely transition to this approach in its future decisions.

This is not to say that in the real world I would expect each and every decision after the *Secession Reference* to follow its lead perfectly. The SCC has to deal with a number of factors that influence its judgments: preceding decisions, doctrine, and precedent; the particular bias and understanding of the federation each justice holds as an individual; the fact situations of particular cases; and the broader political context

114 See McHugh (2000: 461).

within which decisions are reached, among other things. The point, though, is that with the *Secession Reference* we can see and expect a general shift in the approach of the SCC, and this is something we should note in thinking about the Court's role as federal arbiter.

Highlighting this positive turn in the Court's work, though, should not overshadow the problematic elements noted in the preceding chapter. The fact remains that a significant proportion of the SCC's federalism jurisprudence over the past three decades imposes a particular federal model in both its approach and outcome. The 57 per cent of cases between 1980 and 2010, and even the 25 per cent following the *Secession Reference*, that impose a federal model fall well short of the ideal of zero. I have already discussed the problematic nature of these decisions – the fact that they can negatively affect the legitimacy of the federal arbiter and the federation more generally. In so doing, I have also made the case for why this situation needs to be addressed (both in Canada and as part of broader federal theory).

If anything, what this chapter highlights is the problematic nature of the SCC's imposing decisions. It shows that an alternative approach to managing conflict is possible. It demonstrates that the Court can and does embrace an inclusive understanding of the federation, while reaching decisions that reject zero-sum outcomes and facilitating negotiation and cooperation among conflicting parties. Reflecting on these points clarifies why an approach to solving conflict that imposes fixed rules in line with a particular federal model can negatively affect the legitimacy of the arbiter and the federation. And it is the contrast between the problematic decisions in the last chapter and the positive ones in this chapter that illuminates the path to a welcome new approach in federalism jurisprudence.

It should be evident why I see the decisions that follow the lead of the *Secession References* as a positive turn in federalism jurisprudence: they account for the contestation that takes place over nationality and the federation in Canada by recognizing, and reinforcing the legitimacy of, the federation as a process and outcome of negotiation between the subscribers of legitimate perspectives on what the system is and ought to be. This approach to managing the inherent conflict over the system in plurinational federations is central to the federal arbiter, and the federation itself, remaining legitimate (given the arbiter's critical role in managing the regular conflict that manifests in such states).

Elaborating on this positive element of the SCC's federalism jurisprudence – explaining further what the benefits are – is best achieved by referring back to some of the key trends that emerge from the above analysis. There are four trends in particular that warrant discussion.

First is the Court's understanding of the federation as an inclusive association that takes place in virtually every one of the fifty-six decisions noted in this chapter. In the previous chapter, I made the point that a significant percentage of the SCC's federal decisions impose the pan-Canadian model and centralize the federation. I argued that this tendency raises questions about the Court's neutrality among the subscribers of other federal models, and ultimately works to alienate these groups. What we see in the above decisions is the opposite: the Court understanding and presenting the federation as one where the subscribers of each federal model can find recognition. In other words, the Court consistently depicts the federation in a way that reflects elements of what each model says it is.

This inclusive view of the federation, which simultaneously affords legitimacy to an understanding of the system as centralized *and* decentralized, as granting symmetrical *and* asymmetrical powers to the provinces, may seem incoherent. However, as I argued when discussing the *Secession Reference*, these decisions properly recognize there are competing understandings of the federation, while also accounting for the reality that the constitution has evolved in a way that reflects this competition. This perspective stands in contrast to the approach discussed in the previous chapter, where the federation is depicted in line with only one perspective.

The difference between these two ways of presenting the federation is that one can create problems for the federation, while the other has potential benefits. Most notably, presenting the federation in an inclusive manner can potentially generate legitimacy for the federation and the way it handles conflict. By demonstrating that the views of all parties on the nature of the federation are taken seriously and accounted for in arbitrating disputes, the Court can generate loyalty to the conflict-management process. Simply telling the subscribers of a federal model they are wrong, or imposing a view of what the federation is on these groups, is not a sound conflict-management approach. It can actually destabilize the association, and lead to more, and increasingly intense, conflict in the future. The flip side is that recognizing, and accounting for, all parties' perspectives in arbitrating a conflict works to create buy-in to the process and the outcome. Accordingly, reinforcing the notion that the constitutional law supports and reflects the various perspectives on what the federation is and ought to be also generates and maintains loyalty to the federation itself.

The SCC is an important institution. How it presents the federation matters. When it affords legitimacy to the subscribers of the various models – and employs legal argument to anchor these perspectives in the constitutional law – it is demonstrating to actors that the federation is an inclusive association. In rejecting the approach of simply ignoring a particular perspective – or saying that one is right and the others are wrong – the Court is helping to reinforce the view that the federation is, in fact, a dynamic and contested normative system to which the subscribers of each model can be loyal. This approach thus provides rhetorical tools, which carry the legitimacy of SCC decisions, for each party to wield in future political and legal conflicts.[115] At the same time, inclusive depictions of the federation reflect the view that the Court is subject to, and affected by, the prevailing dynamics of the federal system, which helps to show how it is part of a fair and representative federal system.

Closely linked to this inclusivity is the second important trend stemming from the above analysis: the increasing tendency of the Court to recognize the legitimacy of the multinational model in its decisions. In the previous chapter I discussed how the multinational model is granted a measure of legitimacy in only three of the seventy-four imposing decisions. In contrast, as table 6.3 indicates, in these fifty-six cases the multinational model is drawn from and reinforced in the approach and outcome of some sixteen decisions. Moreover, twelve of these decisions were delivered after 1990, indicating an increasing willingness of the Court to embrace the legitimacy of this model in recent years.

The recognition of the multinational model is a positive development in the SCC's federalism jurisprudence, given the fact that there is a significant population within Canada that believe it is a multinational state. Canada is a plurinational federation, with groups holding conflicting views on the national character of the state. One of these fundamental views is that Canada contains multiple nations, including the Québécois and Aboriginals. Moreover, this view finds support in a number of institutional and political processes that accommodate groups as nations via the federation. To deny these things – to pretend that the federation is only a centralized system representing a pan-state nation or an association of provinces that are equal territorial

115 The point is that all sides are given such tools, rather than just one side; this mitigates the ability for one party to use an SCC decision in a coercive way in future negotiations or court cases.

units – fails to account for these fundamental aspects of the Canadian political landscape.

This reality is why granting the multinational model its due as a legitimate perspective is so welcome. In doing so, the Court avoids serious legitimacy issues. Ignoring, or actively delegitimizing, the multinational model alienates a significant population of Canadians. As argued in the last chapter, the paucity of support afforded this model in imposing decisions is one of the central failures. In contrast, the tendency for the Court to afford the multinational model legitimacy in the decisions discussed above provides two distinct benefits.

First, it generates loyalty among the subscribers of the multinational model to the conflict-management process and to the federation itself. Recognizing the legitimacy of the multinational model when arbitrating disputes eases the fears of subscribers that the system is biased against their perspective. It also reduces the ability of nationalist entrepreneurs to use this claim as evidence of disenfranchisement. By accounting for this perspective in the conflict-management process, the Court ensures that the federation is understood and implemented in a way that reflects elements of the multinational model, which helps to generate loyalty among subscribers to the federal system itself. This recognition is particularly important given that the subscribers of the multinational model tend to be national minorities (i.e., Québécois and Aboriginals). Generating loyalty among these groups to the conflict-management process and the federal system – establishing that the federation reflects their perspectives on what it is and ought to be – is an important step in alleviating destabilizing political mobilization and managing conflict within and over the federation in Canada.

Second, recognizing the legitimacy of the multinational model should lead to sounder federalism jurisprudence. As argued in the last chapter, the imposing decisions fail to recognize and account for the legal and political facts that have been established over time and that support the multinational model. The issue with failing to account for the multinational model is that the Court's imposing federalism jurisprudence is based on a partial, potentially biased, picture of the constitutional and federal system. The implication, then, is that the resulting legal reasoning and precedent established from these decisions rests on a faulty foundation, one that ignores important elements of the constitutional and political structure of the state. In contrast, the decisions discussed in this chapter that do account for the multinational model provide a much more comprehensive view of the association.

This more comprehensive, accurate, understanding of the constitutional and federal structure should be the basis from which the Court makes decisions that inform the development and application of constitutional law. As I argued in chapters 1 and 2, each federal model is reflected in the institutional and legal structures of the federation. Ignoring these elements of the constitutional system when ruling on pertinent questions about the nature of the system invites criticism of the Court's method of legal reasoning and federalism jurisprudence. In contrast, a comprehensive account of the institutional and political landscape should lead to better decisions, which take into consideration the full breadth of institutional and legal structures that support the various parties' perspectives. And, a comprehensive approach should lead to more optimal outcomes in reaching decisions: by taking into account the breadth of perspectives on the federal association, the judgments are more likely to find a basis that reflects the constitutional and political landscape, while being acceptable to the parties in conflict and rejecting zero-sum outcomes. Such decisions that are built on the strength of a plurality of perspectives have the associated benefit of generating loyalty to the outcomes, rather than alienating a particular party by imposing an opposing view of what the federal system is and ought to be.

An important related point to make is that the support afforded the multinational model in the above decisions does not come at the expense of the other models. I am not saying that *imposing* the multinational model would be beneficial: that would lead to the subscribers of the other models feeling alienated from the conflict-arbitration process and the resulting federal system. There is a need to ensure that other groups, particularly pan-Canadianists inside and outside Québec, do not feel slighted by a perceived over-recognition of the multinational character of the state (or a perceived over-accommodation of national minorities by the Court). Such sentiments about the conflict-management process and the federation are detrimental to its legitimacy and ultimately threaten unity and order. The support for the multinational model comes in the context of an approach to managing conflict over the federation that sees it as the process and outcome of negotiation between the subscribers of *multiple legitimate* models. In these decisions the Court is rejecting the approach that legitimizes one view of the federation over others, seeking instead to generate legitimacy for an inclusive federation and to the way it manages conflict.

This brings us to the third trend I want to highlight: the rejection of a zero-sum approach to resolving disputes. As I highlighted above, in these decisions there is a tendency for the Court to either seek positive outcomes for all parties, to deny any party an absolute victory, or to substantially mitigate the loss for a party. This approach can be contrasted with the way appeals are disposed of in the seventy-four imposing decisions. In those cases, the outcomes generally create stark winners and losers. As I argued in the previous chapter, such an approach is problematic in federalism jurisprudence, because it can negatively affect the loyalty of losing parties towards the conflict-management process and the resulting federal system. The flip side is that the approach to managing conflict adopted by the Court in these fifty-six decisions can actually benefit the association.

By rejecting a zero-sum approach, as is done in the above decisions, the Court can protect the legitimacy of the conflict-management process and the federal system. In decisions that follow this approach, subscribers to the various federal models are able to find an aspect of the outcome that supports their particular view of what the federation is and ought to be. In this way, even when parties "lose" a case, this is mitigated, as their perspective is legitimized in the way the federation is presented and/or because the negative outcome is offset by some positive element. Accordingly, the subscribers of the various models are not alienated from the resulting federal system (they do not see the system as inherently biased against their position); rather, they see the decision as reaffirming that elements of the federal system reflect their view. The conflicting parties see the conflict-management process as fair, because their perspective on what the federation is and ought to be is afforded legitimacy in the outcome of a decision. They also see the result as acceptable, because it does not align the federal system with any one perspective over their own (allowing all parties a leg to stand on in future conflicts).

In other words, this revised approach creates legitimacy (1) by affording the subscribers of each model recognition through decision outcomes; (2) where this is not possible, by mitigating and offsetting the negatives of a decision for the losing parties; and (3) by demonstrating through outcomes how the constitutional law incorporates elements of each federal model. Moreover, these three factors combine to show that parties can affect the way the Court makes decisions, even if they do not win. This efficacy means that court-decided outcomes can be seen as more than merely in-built and imposed; rather, each party can see how it directly and indirectly shapes the federal system that stems from the judicial process, which means the subscribers of each model see elements of the federal system as "theirs." The potential effect of the approach is that loyalty to the method of conflict management, and to the federal system that stems from that management, can be generated and maintained.

I recognize that not every judgment can be structured in a way that affords all parties a positive outcome. The nature of some cases requires a winner and loser to be declared and for the disposition of rights and privileges to be ordered. The adversarial nature of law makes this a reality. I am not promoting an ideal where everyone wins all the time. Rather, I am arguing for a conflict-management approach that avoids creating resentment towards the process of dispute arbitration and the resulting federal system. The above analysis demonstrates that this approach *can be followed*, that federalism jurisprudence can be undertaken in a way that rejects a complete zero-sum approach to arbitrating disputes. There are many cases where the outcome can be positive to multiple parties, and almost always a negative outcome can be mitigated. Even in those cases where a positive outcome for all cannot be manufactured, presenting the federation in a way that supports a conflicting party's perspective can help to generate loyalty to the process and the system.

Arguing that one of the key goals of the SCC's federalism jurisprudence should be generating loyalty to the system stems from an appreciation that the Court occupies a unique role when it acts as the federal arbiter. As already argued, federalism jurisprudence is a rather exceptional stream of constitutional law. It is not simply about determining which side is right. It involves struggles over the very nature of the constitutional association, how it recognizes identities, and accordingly how power and resources are distributed. Similar dynamics are also at play in Charter jurisprudence, where there are often clashes between different conceptions of the nature of the constitutional association, with the Court occupying a political role in arbitrating these disputes. However, in federalism jurisprudence, the selection of particular positions on the link between identity recognition and the distribution of resources and power via federal institutions is an explicitly political exercise (i.e., it is a decision about "what" order of government should be responsible for an activity, not "if" government should be undertaking the activity at all). The inherently political nature of these cases, where the Court and its role within the federation are part of the field of struggle, means there is no neutral ground to which it can retreat. In such cases, simply choosing winners and losers (especially when this is accompanied by imposing a federal model) jeopardizes the legitimacy of the federation. What we see in the above decisions is how the Court can avoid this problem by adopting a conflict-management approach that works from, and reinforces, an understanding of the federation as the process and outcome of negotiation between the subscribers of legitimate models.

The final trend I want to highlight here is the tendency of the Court to adopt a broad role-perception as a facilitator of negotiation to manage conflict. This role, which in its explicit form pushes parties to use the political process to manage their conflict via negotiation and cooperation, both reflects, and is part of, the broader conflict-management approach adopted by the Court in these decisions. Such a facilitator approach is increasingly the favoured role of the SCC: in eight of the last eleven division-of-powers decisions examined in this study the Court has adopted this role. Accordingly, we may be seeing a transition, where the vestiges of an outmoded role that seeks to impose fixed rules to solve problems is giving way to a role that seeks to facilitate negotiation and cooperation to manage conflict.[116]

The problematic nature of these outmoded roles was discussed in the previous chapter. In the imposing decisions the Court acts under a false veil of neutrality to impose a fixed set of rules that favours particular understandings of the federation. The potential effect of this approach is that inappropriate expectations of neutrality are established that cannot be met, and decisions are rendered that are at odds with the political and institutional landscape. This ideal of neutrality, which cannot be achieved, can thus create resentment towards the arbiter and generate feelings that the federation is biased.

A broad facilitator role is the preferable approach because it can avoid these negative effects, while potentially generating legitimacy for the Court and the federation. It achieves this outcome by rejecting the view that it sits above the political system and hands down final judgments. Working from a view that the federation is a contested normative system, and that the arbiter is part of this system, the Court seeks to act in a way that reinforces the legitimacy of this system and its place within it. It strives for transparency in how it reaches its decisions, while also working to have the parties negotiate and cooperate to manage the dispute (by granting each of these parties a measure of

116 Of course, the outmoded roles, anchored as they are in the constitutional law and given their pedigree in federalism jurisprudence, will likely continue to be employed.

equality at the negotiating table). In this way, those within the association see the Court as part of the system, but they see the system as fair and unbiased towards their perspective. They see how they can work within the federation to raise their concerns and work to negotiate mutually agreeable outcomes. This role clearly has benefits for the legitimacy of the federal arbiter, but it can also help to generate legitimacy for the federation more generally.

The inherent aspect of the facilitator role that pushes parties to use political processes to manage conflict works to legitimize those processes, which are the heart of the federation. At the core of the facilitator role is the recognition that the federal system is the process and outcome of negotiation. By showing deference to the outcome of negotiations over the way to implement the federal system, and pushing parties to use these processes to manage disputes, the Court reinforces their validity and usefulness. It generates loyalty not only to the way conflict is managed through the courts, but also to how it is dealt with through other forums (like intergovernmental relations). The Court thus demonstrates that the federation is a fair process which leads to collaborative outcomes that incorporate participants' perspectives.

The increasing adoption of the facilitator role, and the other three trends, exemplify the potential benefits of a federalism jurisprudence that follows the lead of the *Secession Reference*. They show, among other things, the potential ways the SCC can generate and maintain legitimacy for itself and the federation more generally.

Conclusion

This book has two related lines of analysis. The first looks at the management of diversity and conflict through federal systems and the role of the federal arbiter (focusing on both Canada and broader theory and policy). The second looks at the work of Canada's federal arbiter, the Supreme Court of Canada, arguing that it exercises its duties in a way that has the potential to either negatively or positively affect the legitimacy of the federation. In this concluding chapter, I discuss how these two lines of analysis support the central argument of the book, while also reflecting on some of the potential issues with applying this argument to Canada and beyond.

The Argument, Revisited

Federal arbiters matter in the management of diversity and conflict via federal systems, particularly in plurinational federations like Canada, where the recognition of national identities and the distribution of resources and power via the federation are continually contested by those subject to the system. In such states, the federal arbiter is important because it plays a key role in the development of the association and in maintaining its legitimacy (and thus unity). As the review of SCC federalism jurisprudence demonstrates, the arbiter can exercise this role in potentially problematic or beneficial ways. The key difference between the former and the latter is the extent to which the Court imposes a particular understanding of the federation or recognizes it as the process and outcome of negotiation between the subscribers of competing perspectives. I argue the second approach, where the Court adopts a broad role as a facilitator of this negotiation, is preferable because it has the potential to generate and maintain legitimacy for the federation and the way it manages conflict.

As I said in the introduction, this argument has a number of layers. It rests on an examination of the Canadian case and general theory. In addition, the argument builds on both theoretical and empirical analysis. Revisiting and reflecting on these layers here, by tracing the two lines of analysis in the book, is prudent before turning to discuss the potential limitations of the argument.

The first and second chapters focused on the first line of analysis: the use of federal systems to manage diversity and conflict and the role of the federal arbiter. Both chapters engaged general theory and the case of Canada. In this way, they treated Canada as a *particular type* of case within the *broader category* of plurinational federations. By looking at this case, the analysis in these chapters can thus inform and advance theory on the use of federal systems to manage diversity in Canada and other similar cases.

The first chapter examined the context and theory related to the management of diversity through federalism. It started by discussing why national minorities are generally viewed as a "problem" to be "solved": they challenge the legitimacy (and thus unity) of the state in the modern period by questioning the way sovereign power is legitimized via the doctrine of national self-determination. I then looked at the compromise of federalism, which is popular given its perceived ability to protect the territorial integrity of a state while providing sub-state groups with autonomy. I identified three federal approaches to manage diversity and conflict: trimming, trading, or segregating away the offending diversity via institutional structures. I argued the foundational element of each of these approaches is to contain conflict within nations by eliminating diversity and creating homogeneous political communities (the first two through assimilation and the latter through segregation).

Turning to Canada, I demonstrated how the trimming, trading, and segregating approaches are expressed as the pan-Canadian, provincial-equality, and multinational federal models, respectively. Highlighting this link illuminates the fact that the federal models represent particular perspectives of both what the Canadian federation *is* and what it *ought* to be. At the same time, the models are not just abstract theories. They have driven (and continue to drive) political mobilization. Their subscribers see them as valid perspectives and have mobilized accordingly, which has informed the development of the federation in Canada. And so, the subscribers of each model can point to aspects of the political and institutional structures of Canada to support their view (as my review of Canada's constitutions showed). This *combination* of continued *adherence* by groups of people and the *institutionalization* of elements of each perspective is why each federal model is legitimate.

Examining the use of the federation to manage diversity and conflict in Canada, and in broader theory and policy, was the necessary starting point for the book. It established the foundation to discuss the problems with the broader approaches, while also facilitating a reinterpretation of the key case of Canada from outside the paradigms of the pan-Canadian, provincial-equality, and multinational models. This examination, in turn, allowed me to build a contrasting federal model for Canada in the second chapter.

Reinterpreting this key case also contributes to general theory.[1] Understanding the case from outside the paradigms of these approaches illuminates the potential shortfalls of exporting a particular understanding of Canada as *the* Canadian model. It shows there are different understandings of what the federation is and ought to be (and that in reality each is valid, to an extent). Analysis and prescriptions that work from only one of these understandings can miss important ways in which the Canadian federation actually operates to help maintain stability in the face of considerable diversity. This understanding also facilitates comparative analysis. While the pan-Canadian, provincial-equality, and multinational federal models are Canadian-specific views of the federation, their theoretical underpinnings have links to wider approaches to managing diversity via federalism applied to other states. As I point out below, looking at the conflict between the subscribers of competing federal models, and particularly at how the federal arbiter in Canada manages this conflict, is a solid base for subsequent comparative research.

The second chapter picked up on this point, making the related argument that the federal arbiter is important in the management of diversity and conflict, especially in plurinational federations like Canada.

---

1 As argued in the introduction (and elsewhere in the book), Canada is a key case within the field of federal theory and policy. Models building on analysis of Canada have informed theories and policy for other states, especially over the last 20 years in the area of managing diversity and conflict via territorial self-government. Accordingly, analysis that illuminates shortfalls in how the case tends to be understood, and drawing links to how these understandings drive aspects of broader theory and policy, can help to inform that broader theory and policy.

This argument stems from an appreciation of the dynamics of conflict in Canada over both national identity and the federation. Chapter 2 elaborated on this point by arguing that Canada, in reality, *is* a plurinational state – not uninational or multinational, as the subscribers of the competing federal models attest. The chapter also pointed out that the federation's status as a normative framework means it is continually contested by some group subject to the association. It is the combination of these two characteristics – Canada's status as both *plurinational* and a *federation* – that drives the indeterminate conflict over the federal system (as potent views related to the recognition of identities explicitly combine with views about the proper distribution of resources and power). The chapter also examined the main forums that manage these conflict dynamics in federations. I focused on the federal arbiter as a particularly important forum since it is the final domestic institutional mechanism to manage conflict over the nature of a federation within the political process. Because of this status, federal arbiters can have a significant effect on the development of a federation and the maintenance of legitimacy (and thus unity) for the system. As explained in the chapter, I focused on the apex court model of federal arbitration because it is the most prominent approach across federations, and because it is the model in Canada. The chapter also reflected on the three main roles often promoted for the judiciary as federal arbiter: an umpire of the federation, an independent branch of government, or a guardian of the federal system. I discussed how these three roles are linked to the wider approaches of managing diversity through federalism and the shared issue, which is that each ideal role for the federal arbiter fails to adequately account for the contestation that takes place in plurinational federations over the nature of nationality and the federation.

The second chapter concluded by sketching a federal model that seeks to address the identified problems with the three main federal approaches and their related roles for the federal arbiter. Building on my analysis of the Canadian case, this contrasting federal model seeks to account for the dynamics of conflict over nationality and the federation in plurinational states, focusing in particular on the role of the federal arbiter in the development and maintenance of legitimacy for the federal system. In this regard, it represents an attempt to better integrate federal and judicial theory as they relate to diverse states. The model I developed promotes federal systems as the process and outcome of negotiation over the way identities are recognized and power and resources are distributed via the institutional structures of a federation. In other words, a federal model that seeks to *manage* diversity and conflict by institutionalizing processes of free and fair negotiation and dialogue, rather than *solving* the *problem* through institutional structures above politics (that seek to trim, trade, or segregate away diversity). As I argued in the chapter, a central component of this model is a role for the federal arbiter as a facilitator of negotiation between those who conflict because they hold competing perspectives on the nature of the federation. The key aspect of this role is that when the courts are called upon to interpret the constitution or mediate a dispute they should work to reinforce the dynamic elements of the federal system. The ultimate objective of this approach is to facilitate ongoing negotiation to manage conflict, either by explicitly pushing parties to use political processes or, where this is not possible, more indirectly by arbitrating the dispute fairly, recognizing and accounting for the different legitimate perspectives on the nature of the federation. The second chapter thus laid out the initial case for why federal arbiters matter and how they ought to fulfil their role in the management of diversity and conflict via federalism.

The chapter sought to make a contribution to federal theory in two related areas. First, working from the proper understanding of the dynamics of conflict over national identity and the federation in Canada, it constructed and promoted a federal model for that country that can account for (and manage) these dynamics. Second, again building on this understanding of the key case of Canada, it sought to inform broader federal theory applicable to states *with similar dynamics of conflict*. It made the case that there is a need to account for the contestation that takes place in plurinational federations over both national identity and the federation. The main approaches generally fail to account for these dynamics, which is particularly evident with their under-conceptualized and problematic roles for the federal arbiter.

Chapters 1 and 2 are thus about more than stage setting, or contextualizing my argument to facilitate later analysis of the SCC's work; together, the two chapters made linkages between general theory and the case of Canada to advance federal theory designed to manage diversity and conflict in that state and beyond. Together, they analysed and applied general theory to inform an understanding of the Canadian case as a state with conflict between the subscribers of competing, partial perspectives on the nature of national identity and the federation. This understanding allows for reflection back on the general theory of federalism as a means to manage diversity in states with similar dynamics of conflict, particularly the need to account for the contested nature of nationality and the federation and the important role the federal arbiter plays in managing this conflict.

This line of analysis raises a number of questions. First and foremost, is how these dynamics of conflict play out in the plurinational federation of Canada and how the SCC has exercised its role as federal arbiter to manage them. There is also the related question of the effect the Court has when exercising its duties as federal arbiter (i.e., on the legitimacy of the federation). Finally, there are questions about the extent to which the SCC can live up to the role set out in chapter 2 of a facilitator of negotiation and fair arbiter.

The second part of the book sought to answer these questions by investigating the SCC's work arbitrating conflict within and over the nature of the federation between the subscribers of competing federal models. This part argued that how the SCC fulfils its role has the potential to either negatively affect the legitimacy of the association (by imposing a particular understanding) or generate legitimacy for the system (by recognizing and accounting for the competing perspectives on the federation and facilitating negotiation between the subscribers of these perspectives). This line of analysis thus also highlighted the practices that should be avoided, and promoted, in the arbitration of conflict over the federal system by the SCC and, to an extent, other federal arbiters.

The third chapter introduced this second line of analysis. It explained why I looked at *the SCC, in particular,* and why I focused on the last thirty years of its work. As I pointed out, the SCC has always played an important part in the development of the federation and managing conflict over its nature (and increasingly so, since 1980). The chapter also explained how I analysed the SCC's work as federal arbiter over this period. It presented the framework and indicators used to assess the extent to which the Court either imposes a particular federal model or recognizes the legitimacy of multiple models in the 131 decisions reviewed in the study.

The fourth chapter examined the *Secession Reference*. There are two reasons I began my empirical research by looking in depth at this case: it helps the reader understand how I conducted my analysis of a decision (which is important given the number of cases dealt with in the book); and the decision is an exemplar of the way a federal arbiter can (in practice) work from an understanding of the federation as the process and outcome of negotiation and recognize the legitimacy of competing perspectives on the nature of the federation, while also acting as the facilitator of this negotiation. In this way, the *Secession Reference* is a useful benchmark against which other decisions can be compared.

The decision is significant for two reasons. First, it is (by some measure) the decision that most closely adheres to the ideal-type of a decision that works from, and reinforces, an understanding of the federation as the process and outcome of negotiation between legitimate competing perspectives on the system, with an associated role for the Court as a facilitator of this negotiation. I highlighted how the decision adheres to this approach through an inclusive depiction of the federation, the rejection of zero-sum outcomes, and the facilitation of negotiation to manage future related conflict. Second, the *Secession Reference* marks a shift in the SCC's approach to its role as federal arbiter. Prior to the decision, 64 per cent of the SCC's decisions *impose* one federal model; after the decision, 71 per cent of the Court's decisions *recognize* the legitimacy of multiple federal models and the federation as the process and outcome of negotiation, with the SCC's role being to facilitate such negotiation. As discussed in the chapter, this turn comes in response to the direct challenge to the legitimacy of the system posed by the potential unilateral secession of Québec. Accordingly, the reference can be seen as an example of how a federal arbiter can react to conflict over the nature of the federation and seek to generate legitimacy in the way it presents the system and manages the conflict.

In chapter 5, I turned to look at those decisions that do not adhere to the benchmark of the *Secession Reference* – decisions that impose a particular federal model. The chapter thus discussed the decisions that have the potential to negatively affect the legitimacy of the federation and the conflict-management process. I identified seventy-four decisions that impose a particular federal model in their approach and outcome (which represents 57% of federal decisions analysed between 1980 and 2010).

I argued that this stream of federalism jurisprudence is problematic because it can negatively affect the legitimacy of the federation and the Court's standing as federal arbiter. This argument rests on four related points made in the chapter. First is the fact that the seventy-four decisions tend to impose the pan-Canadian model, with outcomes that favour the central government to the detriment of the other jurisdictions. This tendency to side with one jurisdiction is problematic because it can instigate mobilization among subscribers of competing models in the other jurisdictions, while also calling into question the fairness of the conflict-management process. Second is the lack of legitimacy afforded the multinational model in the seventy-four imposing decisions. This lack of support is something that does not sit well with the reality of Canada as a plurinational federation where a significant percentage of the population views Canada as containing multiple nations (and so, again, is something that can lead to mobilization in defence of the multinational perspective and perceptions that the Court is biased). Third is the tendency of the Court to create stark winners and losers in its imposing decisions. This approach is problematic because it can foster resentment towards the conflict-management process and the system that stems from that process. Finally, there is the tendency for the SCC to reject a facilitative role in these decisions, adopting instead the role of umpire, branch of government, or guardian. As explained in the chapter, this approach can create expectations of neutrality that cannot be met, while also reinforcing a sense that the system is not operating fairly for all participants.

The fifth chapter thus does two things for my argument. First, it demonstrates that the Court has imposed particular federal models in a significant proportion of its work as federal arbiter. Second, it makes the case for why this approach is problematic. The chapter advances the argument that the activity (and potential) of a federal arbiter imposing a particular perspective on the nature of the federation should be accounted for and addressed in federal theory and policy applicable to Canada (and to other plurinational federations).

The sixth chapter discussed the decisions that follow the lead of the *Secession Reference* and recognize that the federation is the process and outcome of negotiation between the subscribers of competing perspectives on the system, with the role of the Court being to facilitate this negotiation. I identified fifty-six such decisions (which represents 43% of federal decisions between 1980 and 2010).

The chapter argues that these decisions are a welcome turn in the Court's approach as federal arbiter because their underlying approach has the potential to positively affect the legitimacy of the federation through its conflict-management process. As in chapter 5, this argument relies on four related points. First is the fact that virtually all of the fifty-six decisions discussed in chapter 6 depict the federation in an inclusive manner. This approach is beneficial to the (legitimacy and unity of the) federation because it can generate loyalty to the system among the subscribers of each federal model (by showing them the federation recognizes their views). Second is the SCC's increasing tendency to recognize the legitimacy of the multinational model in these decisions. This recognition is something that can mitigate the potential mobilization among national minorities (i.e., Québécois and Aboriginals) against the association.[2] Third is the consistent rejection of a zero-sum approach to resolve disputes, which can help parties see that the conflict-management process is fair and balanced, while also generating loyalty to the resulting federal system as one that recognizes and accounts for their perspective. Finally, in these decisions, the SCC tends to explicitly adopt the role of facilitator between the subscribers of the conflicting perspectives, rather than relying on the outmoded roles of umpire, branch of government, or guardian. The benefit of the Court embracing this approach is that it can generate loyalty to the federation *in the way it goes about fairly managing conflict* (by pushing parties to use the political process, acting with transparency and accepting that it is part of the field of struggle).

The sixth chapter thus rounds out the argument of the book by making two related points. The first is that the Court can exercise its duties in a way that accounts for, and manages, the dynamics of conflict over national identity and the federation in Canada. Second, discussing how the Court has exercised its duties helps bring to light an approach that can be promoted for the federal arbiter in Canada (and beyond), along with the potential benefits for plurinational federations.

The second part, as a whole, demonstrates how Canada's federal arbiter manages conflict over national identity and the federation, and how it can do this in potentially problematic or beneficial ways. This line of analysis lays out what activities I argue should be avoided (and followed) by the federal arbiter (both in Canada and, to an extent, in other plurinational federations). The second part of the book, much the same as the first, therefore seeks to reflect on the particular case of Canada (and how the federation manages diversity and conflict, with a particular focus on the federal arbiter) to both understand that case and help advance general theory. However, just as the first part of the book raised a number of questions that were taken up in the second, this line of analysis raises a number of additional questions, particularly related to the defensibility and applicability of my arguments within and beyond Canada.

2 As discussed in the chapter (and also below), recognition of the multinational model comes in tandem with recognition of the legitimacy of the pan-Canadian and provincial-equality views. In these decisions the Court does not impose the multinational model. This is an important distinction, because imposing the multinational model could push the dominant majority of pan-Canadianists to mobilize in defence of their perspective.

Considering the Argument in the Canadian Context

Reflecting on my argument in the Canadian context raises a number of considerations. Discussing these here both buttresses my argument and helps to explain it further.

First and foremost is the question of whether my approach and argument falls prey to one of the main criticisms I levy at the promoters of the three federal models in Canada: whether I work from a *partial* understanding of Canada to derive a normative federal model. Put another way, does my preferred method of managing diversity via the federation and the SCC's role collapse the categories of "is" and "ought" (which is what the three Canadian federal models do)?

From the outset, the book makes the point that each of the three federal models work from a misunderstanding of the Canadian case. The subscribers of the pan-Canadian, provincial-equality, and multinational models *assume* that Canada is either uninational or multinational, while seeking to promote and reinforce this understanding through the federation. In other words, they think Canada *is* uninational or multinational and say that the federation *ought* to reflect and protect this "reality." I have made the case that, in reality, Canada *is* plurinational (that the concept of nationality in Canada is contested between the subscribers of these competing understandings).

Accordingly, I work from an understanding that accounts for the sociological reality of the state. Seeing Canada as a plurinational case – outside the paradigms of the competing nationalist narratives – helps to show how the federation can account for the conflict taking place between the subscribers of these competing understandings of the state. Admittedly, I work from an understanding of Canada; however, it is one that is more comprehensive than that of the promoters of the main federal models.[3] I have also tried to avoid the problems associated with promoting a federal model based on a partial understanding of Canada by recognizing and accounting for the continual conflict that

---

3 This understanding focuses on the *main* competing perspectives on the national character of Canada – there are more narratives than the three discussed in the book. I focused on the pan-Canadian, provincial-equality, and multinational perspectives, however, as they are the key ones competing to define and influence the federation in Canada and to inform broader federal theory and policy. For reasons of simplicity, I also sought to distil these positions to their core; however, within the groups subscribing to these perspectives there are also competing narratives.

takes place over the nature of the federation itself. The failure to adequately account for this dynamic of conflict is one of the central issues with the main Canadian models, as each seeks to fix, largely above political contestation, a particular institutional structure.

I recognize that such a claim is open to criticism that I have made "straw men" out of the models: each model is not entirely fixed and each does allow for adaption of the federal structure (i.e., through amendment).[4] At the same time, these models, at their core, are about institutionalizing a particular federal approach to managing diversity based on (and seeking to bring about) a particular understanding of the state. My analysis in this study works from a distillation of these models to facilitate comparison between them (and with my own approach) to advance theory and policy. As with any such categorization and comparison, nuance is lost. At the same time, focusing on the core of an approach allows for useful reflection on its utility and applicability. An approach's assumptions and starting point matter: the three main federal models in Canada are flawed because they start from flawed understandings of the social underpinnings of the state and go on to promote fixed institutional structures based on that partial understanding.[5]

Turning to the role of the federal arbiter, there are a number of issues that arise in relation to my analysis of the SCC. In particular, questions arise about the argument that the Court either negatively affects the legitimacy of the federation by imposing a particular model or positively affects the legitimacy of the system by recognizing the legitimacy of multiple models.

One of the central issues with this argument is whether the Court actually "chooses" to impose (or recognize) a particular model in any

---

4 Each model also promotes mechanisms that seek to recognize and account for elements of competing perspectives. For example, the pan-Canadian model is a centripetalist-inspired *federal* model (i.e., it still promotes shared and self-rule through a federal institutional structure). Similarly, the promotion of the multinational model is generally accompanied by the promotion of "intra-state" federal measures (like representation in the central legislature and executive) designed to offset centrifugal forces created by the granting of territorial autonomy.

5 It is prudent for me to say that my analysis tends to focus on the model promoted by the multinational federalists of the Canada School as an essentialist, consociational model, rather than liberal-consociationalist. The latter tends to recognize the fluidity of identity and the ability of groups to define their own identity more than the former; on this distinction, see Wolff (2011: 166–8); on the Canada School of multinational federalists as more essentialist, see Schertzer and Woods (2011).

given case. There are legitimate questions to ask about the agency of the SCC to either impose or recognize federal models in its decisions. These questions stem from the perspective that doctrine (or other structural factors like the text of the constitution) leads the Court to rule in a particular manner,[6] or that the fact situation of a case requires the Court to impose a federal model and side with a jurisdiction. The implication of such a view is that my argument that the Court is *imposing* a particular federal model may be incorrect because what the SCC may actually be doing is properly applying judicial doctrine to interpret the constitution. And, since the text of the division of powers is drafted in some respects quite clearly, some fact situations may necessitate an outcome that either centralizes or decentralizes the federal system.

I have already addressed this positivist perspective that doctrine and other factors like the text structure the SCC's federalism jurisprudence. As argued in the third chapter, and demonstrated in the second part of the book, judicial doctrine, precedent, and the methods of constitutional interpretation can all be used in a way that justifies and validates competing understandings of the nature of the constitution. Constitutions, even when they appear to be quite clear, are inherently ambiguous and are ultimately given meaning through the act of judicial interpretation and enforcement. And, while the doctrine and precedent that builds up over time certainly structures decision making, we need to ask what *initially* informed the development of doctrine around the scope of the heads of power or issues such as the effect of one order of government's legislation on the other order. My response to this question, which is upheld through the empirical analysis of this book, is that underlying theories of federalism structure judicial decision making. Similarly, this view helps to explain the shifts that do take place over time in how the federal system is conceptualized and the constitution accordingly interpreted by the Court to either impose a particular view or recognize the competing views.

The activity of reinforcing particular perspectives through creative legal reasoning also helps address critiques that would argue that the fact situation of a case leads to a particular outcome. Demonstrating that the SCC can support particular depictions of the federation by shifting its interpretation of the case law and constitution through the various modes of legal analysis shows the Court has the agency

6 For an argument in this vein, see Baier (2006).

to either impose or recognize particular federal models in any given case. In other words, my analysis shows that the SCC is able to use the various modes of legal analysis to anchor any of the competing understandings of the federation in the constitutional law. This agency means that even where the particular fact situation of a case pushes the Court to impose a particular federal model, this can be overcome by highlighting how the constitution can support an inclusive depiction of the federation and an outcome that reinforces the legitimacy of the various models. At the same time, the particular fact situations in a case may favour an outcome for a particular jurisdiction. In some cases it is quite clear who is going to win. What matters in these situations, though, is how the Court reaches its decision and the extent to which it accounts for, and recognizes, the competing federal models in its depiction of the federation and in reaching the outcome. My argument is that this is where the Court has agency, and it can make its decision in a way that either imposes a particular federal model or recognizes the legitimacy of competing models.

A brief look at how the SCC *could* have rendered a decision in one of its (more significant) impositions helps to support this claim. As I explained in chapter 5, in *Canada Assistance Plan*[7] the Court imposes the pan-Canadian model by depicting the federation as centralized with a central government that is superior to the provinces (through the principle of parliamentary sovereignty, which cannot be hindered by agreements with the provinces). This understanding of the federation is presented as a legal fact supported by the text of the constitution, which the Court says it is bound to enforce as an umpire. And through this line of reasoning the Court grants the central government the power to unilaterally amend funding agreements negotiated with the provinces that help them deliver services in their areas of competence.

In contrast to this imposing approach and outcome, the Court *could* have embraced a more inclusive understanding of the federation and a broad role of facilitator to arbitrate the dispute in this case. It could have noted that the central government has autonomy to control its spending (as per section 91 of the constitution and the supremacy of Parliament). At the same time, it should have recognized that the federation grants the provinces considerable autonomy in their own areas

7 *Reference re Canada Assistance Plan (B.C.)*, [1991] 2 S.C.R. 525. The issue in this case is whether the central government can unilaterally amend funding agreements with the provinces. It was a unanimous decision (authored by Sopinka J).

of competence. Moreover, it should have accounted for the fact that the division of powers contemplates coordinate action and negotiation between the orders of government (especially where one's actions touch on the others' areas of jurisdiction). In this way, while the text of the constitution does not limit the central government's ability to control its spending, political actions and conventions show that where this power concerns spending in areas of provincial competence it should be exercised in consultation and cooperation with the provinces. From this understanding of the federation (which balances central superiority with provincial autonomy and also recognizes that the federation necessitates negotiation and coordination) the Court could have reached an alternative outcome that did not *impose* the pan-Canadian model. Following this depiction of the federation, the Court could have said that while technically, under the letter of the law, the central order has the ability to control its resources and spending, when it enters into an agreement to fund services in provincial areas of competence it is under a duty to negotiate changes to that agreement (in line with the principle of federalism that necessitates such negotiation when actions are coordinated).[8] While the central government would still "win" the case, this win would be offset by the Court providing a normative check on its ability to unilaterally alter such agreements (thereby rejecting a zero-sum approach). Moreover, in such a decision the Court would be abandoning the umpire role (which simply enforces the rules of the constitution), as it would be pushing parties to negotiate an agreement that deals with the conflict, similar to the way it did in *Patriation* and *Secession Reference.*

This exercise shows that while the central government would still win the case, the *way* it wins could be significantly altered. The facts did not preclude the above from happening; the approach and outcome reflect the agency of the SCC to choose the path it took. And, as I argue, this choice has repercussions, as the approach adopted by the Court imposed a particular federal model that has the potential to negatively affect the legitimacy of the federation and the conflict-management process (both in the instance of the *Canada Assistance Plan* reference, but

---

8 Such an opinion would thus mimic the logic in *Reference re Resolution to Amend the Constitution*, [1981] 1 S.C.R. 753 [*Patriation*] and *Secession Reference* [1998]. On this aspect of the principle of federalism, as explained in that opinion, see *Secession Reference* at 55–60.

also as a basis to validate future unilateral action with regard to federal-provincial agreements).

There are those who would certainly question the wisdom of the approach to judicial review I am arguing for here, notably because it does envision a role for conventions in judicial decision making. Adam Dodek has presented a forceful case against the reliance on conventions in Canadian constitutional law, arguing that courts are ill suited to properly identify the shifting nature of political conventions and that the potential for errors in this high-stakes area may threaten the legitimacy of the institution and the wider system.[9] Ultimately, Dodek and others who share this view are concerned that relying on conventions blurs the line between law and politics as autonomous spheres. The SCC understandably shares this concern – even where it embraces and identifies conventions, it limits its role to the recognition of conventions (stopping short of their enforcement). In my view, integrating the recognition of conventions into judicial decision making, paired with an account of the text of the constitution and related legal doctrine and precedent, provides a more inclusive approach that is likely to recognize the inherently contested nature of the federal system. The argument here is that conventions can act as waypoints that help guide the Court's understanding of the constitutional framework in a much more transparent (and inclusive) manner than creative legal reasoning that applies doctrine under a veil of supposed legal neutrality. Importantly, the approach I am arguing for here does not require the Court to turn away from traditional forms of legal reasoning and embrace a purely political role; rather, it calls for an acknowledgment in decision making of the competing perspectives on the nature of the federal system which are contained in both more formal structures (the text of the constitution, precedent, and doctrine) and more informal ones (political and constitutional conventions).

There are other related questions about the perceived effect of imposing decisions. First is whether decisions that impose a federal model actually have a negative affect on legitimacy (and, conversely, whether those that recognize multiple models and facilitate negotiation between the subscribers of these models positively affect legitimacy). As I said at the outset, an empirical proof of this point is beyond the scope of the project. To prove such an argument (i.e., by looking at nationalist

9 See Dodek (2011).

sentiment and mobilization or public opinion polls following either imposing or recognizing decisions) requires the analysis conducted here first.[10] Before quantifying the effect, it is necessary to identify what constitutes an imposing or recognizing decision. This analysis is clearly the next stage of research stemming from this project. At the same time, I have made a case for why such decisions may affect legitimacy and the importance of accounting for this activity.

The second question is whether imposing a particular federal model, at a particular time, may actually help to manage the conflict over nationality and the federation in Canada. An argument could be made that the Court is actually managing conflict undercover by handing a particular jurisdiction or model a victory in a case (and in so doing, even generating legitimacy for the federation by acting in line with broader sociopolitical sentiments). There is a line of argument that at times it is necessary to reinforce pan-state identity to hold a diverse federation together and maintain order, with some even saying this is a role the judiciary can (and does) help fulfil through its jurisprudence.[11]

The problem with this view is that it fails to account for the argument that impositions are problematic, not just because one side wins, but also in *how* the party wins. While, at first blush, granting one party in the federation a victory might seem to help keep the association together (e.g., by strengthening pan-state identities and institutions), doing this by *delegitimizing* the other parties' perspectives is not a sound conflict-management strategy. Such an approach can foster resentment towards the arbitration process and the resulting system among those being imposed upon, thereby fuelling mobilization. As I argued in chapters 5 and 6, recognizing the validity of multiple models and facilitating negotiation to manage conflict is a preferable approach to conflict resolution because it can generate legitimacy for the system by generating loyalty among multiple groups. In other words, in a plurinational federation like Canada, failing to recognize and account for the competing perspectives on the nature of national identity and the federation only pushes the subscribers of these views to mobilize outside the political process.

10 For an example of a foundational study that does consider diffuse and specific support for the institutional legitimacy of apex courts among the population in 18 countries through survey methods, see Gibson, Caldeira, and Baird (1998).

11 See Hirschl (2013).

At the same time, there is the related question of whether recognizing the legitimacy of competing perspectives jeopardizes stability and unity in Canada by eroding the status and importance of pan-state identity. In other words, will following the dynamic model and facilitative approach to federal arbitration exacerbate conflict by either eroding pan-state identity (thus allowing centrifugal forces to pull the federation apart) or threatening pan-state nationalists (thereby pushing them to assert their dominance)? This line of argument rests on the view that strong pan-state identity is necessary for unity in states like Canada.[12] Pan-state identity is *one* of the important mechanisms that help to maintain unity in diverse states and federations. We see the importance of this identity in Canada, particularly given the fact that pan-state nationalists within Québec and Aboriginal groups help to offset the centrifugal forces of national minority mobilization.

At the same time, a focus on the value of pan-state identity as the main mechanism of maintaining unity fails to account for the need and benefit of recognizing the various competing perspectives on the nature of nationality in a plurinational state like Canada. The institutions that recognize and account for the dynamics of conflict over nationality and the federation are better equipped to manage diversity and conflict than those that work from only one of the competing perspectives. In other words, in a plurinational federation like Canada, seeking unity and order via pan-state identity and institutions *alone* will likely exacerbate conflict, because it will lead those who subscribe to other perspectives on the nature of the state's institutions and national character to mobilize in defence of their perspective. Accordingly, the critique that my approach fails to foster the necessary pan-state identity would be valid if I were arguing that the Court recognize and impose *only* a multinational understanding of the federation. However, as pointed out in chapter 6, my argument is that the Court should recognize and account for the legitimacy of the pan-Canadian, provincial-equality, *and* multinational perspectives (not to impose one over the others). This is one of the reasons I focus on the SCC, as I argue it can play an important role in generating and maintaining unity in the plurinational federation of Canada *outside the paradigm of pan-state nationalism* at times

12 As Brendan O'Leary has argued, stability in diverse federations can be linked to the presence of a large, dominant *Staatsvolk* (i.e., a group that adheres to a pan-state identity and identifies with pan-state institutions); see O'Leary (2001).

of heightened conflict where arbitration is needed.[13] This recognition does not have to come at the expense of pan-state identity and institutions; rather, it is about granting these identities and institutions legitimacy in *conjunction with competing identities and (ways of understanding) institutions.*

The ability of the SCC to help generate and maintain legitimacy for the federation rests on a view that it is an important institution in the system. Chapter 3 already raised and addressed the counter-point to this perspective. It is not necessary to discuss it again here. It suffices to say that there is an argument that the SCC is ultimately not that important in the federation, mainly because actors can work around negative decisions if they so choose (and so its actual effect on the development of the federation is questionable). There is also a line of argument that says the public is largely unaware of the SCC's decisions, even if they do support the institution.[14] However, scepticism about the importance of the SCC fails to fully account for the fact that, for the elite actors in the system, it is not just the outcome of a case that matters, but also how that outcome is reached. What the SCC says in a decision about a group has ramifications for that group's political (and material) standing in the system. Moreover, the potential for elite actors and governments to "work around" decisions does not mean they are unimportant (it simply means the decision is part of the process of managing certain conflicts, and the fact that the route of federal arbitration is taken speaks to its perceived importance by the actors participating).

Finally, my analysis of the Court's imposing decisions raises questions related to the frequency with which this happens and the continued need to address this activity. In other words, the fact that the Court imposes a model in a bare majority of cases (57%), and seems to be doing this less since 1998, calls into question the need to promote an alternative approach.

In response, as I argued previously, seventy-four impositions since 1980 is a significant number. The goal is zero impositions, not 50 per cent.

---

13 In other words, it is one of the institutional mechanisms that can help to keep Canada together by generating support for the way the state manages conflict over the recognition of identity and distribution of power and resources. This is part of a wider argument that part of the "glue" that holds Canada together is political and institutional mechanisms that manage conflict between groups over how the state recognizes identity and distributes power and resources.

14 See Goodyear-Grant et al. (2013).

In other words, in more than half of the cases over the thirty years studied the Court has exercised its duties in a way that has the potential to damage the legitimacy of the federation. The tendency of the Court post-1998 to impose models less often is, as I have already said, a welcome trend. However, this also means that in roughly 25 per cent of cases between 1998 and 2010 the SCC acted in a possibly detrimental fashion.

In the years since 2010 the Court has largely followed the approach of recognizing and reinforcing the dynamic nature of the federal system. From 2010 through July 2015 there have been nineteen decisions by the SCC that have a significant federalism component. These cases have dealt with a wide breadth of issues, including constitutional amendment, the scope of the criminal-law power, the intersection of Aboriginal rights and federal-provincial powers, financial regulation, labour relations, healthcare, and aeronautics, among others. Federalism conflicts are clearly still an important part of the Court's work.

Two elements of federalism jurisprudence have been particularly evident in these nineteen cases, determining the validity of unilateral action by the central government and assessing whether an order of government's legislation interfered with the core of the other order's jurisdiction (notably involving a consideration of the interjurisdictional immunity doctrine).[15] The trend when dealing with these two areas of federalism jurisprudence over this five-year period has been to work from, and reinforce, a dynamic understanding of the federal system.

The recognition and reinforcement of this understanding of the federation is most clearly expressed through the Court's consistent rejection of unilateral action by the central government to alter key elements of the federal system. For example, in the *Senate Reform Reference*, the SCC blocked a set of changes proposed by the central government to the tenure and appointment processes for senators.[16] At the heart of this decision was an appreciation of the federal system as necessarily based upon intergovernmental negotiation and cooperation,[17] with the

15 In this second stream of decisions the federal-paramountcy, double-aspect, and ancillary-powers doctrines were also often engaged. For an explanation of these doctrines, see my discussion of them in chapter 3.

16 *Reference re Senate Reform*, [2014].

17 See *Reference re Senate Reform* at 67, 97, 110.

Court's role being to facilitate this activity.[18] Similarly, in the *Nadon Reference*, the SCC stopped a unilateral attempt by the central government to change the rules related to the composition of the Court, in large part to maintain the legitimacy of the institution and the wider federal system.[19] These two cases built upon an earlier decision in 2011 on a central-government initiative to establish a pan-state securities regulator, a function that has traditionally been fulfilled by provinces. In this case the Court also rejected the ability of the central government to go it alone, calling for negotiation and cooperation to find a mutually agreeable solution in line with the principles of a dynamic, collaborative federal system.[20]

A continued narrow and restrained application of the interjurisdictional immunity doctrine has also been a clear development over this five-year period. As explained in chapter 3, this doctrine holds that

---

18 See *Reference re Senate Reform* at 4, where the Court says, "Our role is not to speculate on the full range of possible changes to the Senate. Rather, the proper role of this Court in the ongoing debate regarding the future of the Senate is to determine the legal framework for implementing the specific changes contemplated in the questions put to us. The desirability of these changes is not a question for the Court; it is an issue for Canadians and their legislatures."

19 See *Reference re Supreme Court Act, ss. 5 and 6*, [2014], particularly at 82 and 93, where the Court says: "The fact that the composition of the Supreme Court of Canada was singled out for special protection in s. 41(*d*) is unsurprising, since the Court's composition has been long recognized as crucial to its ability to function effectively and with sufficient institutional legitimacy as the final court of appeal for Canada. As explained above, the central bargain that led to the creation of the Supreme Court in the first place was the guarantee that a significant proportion of the judges would be drawn from institutions linked to Quebec civil law and culture. The objective of ensuring representation from Quebec's distinct juridical tradition remains no less compelling today, and implicates the competence, legitimacy, and integrity of the Court. Requiring unanimity for changes to the composition of the Court gave Quebec constitutional assurance that changes to its representation on the Court would not be effected without its consent."

20 See *Reference re Securities Act*, [2011], particularly at 7 and 9, where the Court says: "It is open to the federal government and the provinces to exercise their respective powers over securities harmoniously, in the spirit of cooperative federalism. The experience of other federations in the field of securities regulation, while a function of their own constitutional requirements, suggests that a cooperative approach might usefully be explored, should our legislators so choose, to ensure that each level of government properly discharges its responsibility to the public in a coordinated fashion." Interestingly, unwritten constitutional principles play an important role in this decision (see at 57).

each order of government's jurisdiction has a "basic, minimum and unassailable" core that is immune from the application of another government's legislation.[21] As discussed in chapter 6, *Canadian Western Bank* in 2007 signalled a shift in how the Court approached this doctrine in the light of a more dynamic understanding of the system.[22] Recent decisions have further restricted the application of this idea and narrowed the test of immunity to better account for the dynamic and inherently contested nature of the federal system, as well as its ability to adapt through intergovernmental negotiation and cooperation. A trilogy of cases that upheld the validity of provincial consumer-protection legislation relating to credit cards exemplifies the restrained application of the interjurisdictional immunity rule.[23] As the Court said in *Bank of Montreal v. Marcottee*, the limited application of the interjurisdictional-immunity doctrine is directly related to a view of the federation as a dynamic system: "A broad application of the doctrine is in tension with the modern cooperative approach to federalism which favours, where possible, the application of statutes enacted by both levels of government."[24] The narrowing of the actual test to strike down a law that does touch on the core of another order's area of responsibility is also exemplified in *Marine Services International*.[25]

While these two developments in the jurisprudence reinforce the overlapping and dynamic nature of the federal system where intergovernmental negotiations are vital, the Court has also started to grapple with the limits of this understanding of the association. There are still examples of cases that depict the central government's power as

21 See *Bell Canada v. Quebec*, [1988] at 839; *Canadian Western Bank v. Alberta*, [2007] at 33; Hogg (2009: 392–404).

22 Wright (2010, 2014) also explores the related jurisprudence and explains the link between this case and the Court's shift towards a more facilitative approach.

23 See *Bank of Montreal v. Marcotte*, [2014] 2 S.C.R. 725; *Marcotte v. Fédération des caisses Desjardins du Québec*, [2014] 2 S.C.R. 805; *Amex Bank of Canada v. Adams*, [2014] 2 S.C.R. 787. Also see *Tsilhqot'in Nation v. British Columbia*, [2014] 2 S.C.R. 256, where the Court rejected using interjurisdictional immunity to protect a broad central government power over Aboriginals.

24 *Bank of Montreal v. Marcotte* at 63.

25 *Marine Services International Ltd. v. Ryan Estate*, [2013] 3 S.C.R. 53 at 56: "[W]e must determine whether the encroachment is sufficiently serious. Rather than just 'affect' the core, the impugned legislation must 'impair' it for interjurisdictional immunity to apply."

broad and superior in areas like the criminal law.[26] In addition, in a recent case where Québec challenged the destruction of information held in a central government database after it cancelled a firearms registry, the SCC held that the broad principle of collaborative federalism developed in the jurisprudence could not erase the essential core of the division of powers and responsibilities between the orders of government. The majority in this case clearly indicated that there has to be some level of autonomy and exclusivity between the separate areas of responsibility for the federation to function.[27] The desire to avoid completely collapsing central and provincial areas of responsibility into one category is also evident in other post-2010 decisions.[28] Thus, while the trend from 2010 to 2015 has been for the SCC to continue on with – and even advance – a dynamic understanding of the federation, there are still areas where the Court is working out the boundaries and limits of this approach.

---

26 See, for example, *Carter v Canada*, [2015] SCC 5, where the Court said that the regulation of doctor-assisted dying is a valid exercise of the central power over the criminal law, even if it does touch on provincial responsibility over healthcare. However, even in this situation the Court explicitly recognized the concurrent and dynamic nature of the field of health in Canada (at 53) and in this case the federal legislation prohibiting doctor-assisted dying was ultimately overturned on Charter grounds. Similarly, in *Canada v. PHS Community Services Society*, [2011] 3 S.C.R. 134 the Court ruled the central government could regulate drug injection sites through the criminal law despite the impact on provincial responsibility over healthcare (while also reinforcing a narrow understanding of interjurisdictional immunity); however, again the central legislation was struck down on Charter grounds.

27 See *Quebec v. Canada*, [2015] SCC 14, particularly at 19, where the Court says: "The principle of cooperative federalism … cannot be seen as imposing limits on the otherwise valid exercise of legislative competence." Although, it warrants saying that the minority decision in this case was more open to the limits that a dynamic understanding of the federation should impose on government action. This indicates the Court is still wrestling with the extent to which it will rely on unwritten constitutional principles in its judicial decision-making. For example, the majority position adopted in *Quebec v. Canada* can also be contrasted with *Trial Lawyers Association of British Columbia v. British Columbia*, [2014] 3 S.C.R. 31, where the SCC explicitly relied upon the rule-of-law principle to limit provincial fees in the name of protecting access to justice.

28 See *Quebec v. Lacombe*, [2010] 2 S.C.R. 453 and *Quebec v. Canadian Owners and Pilots Association*, [2010] 2 S.C.R. 536, where the Court accepted and protected the central power over aeronautics from encroachment by municipal by-laws limiting the location of aerodromes. However, in both cases, the SCC's decision was constructed to recognize the need to protect this traditional area of central-government responsibility within a more dynamic understanding of the system.

Considering the Argument beyond Canada

Looking beyond Canada, there are also broader questions related to the argument. These questions stem from one of my stated aims, which is to inform general theory on the management of diversity and conflict via federalism.

The most pertinent of these questions is the extent to which I can generalize my argument about (or export my preferred approach for) federal systems and the role of the federal arbiter in the management of diversity and conflict. Generalizability is a problem common to all case studies. Each state is unique, having its own mix of characteristics (from institutional, to geopolitical, to economic, to demographic, to historical, to political factors). These factors limit the generation and application of general theories. Building a theory from one unique case runs into problems when you try to apply that theory to other cases that are unique in their own right.

Within the field of ethno-national conflict management – that is, among those that seek to manage conflict framed in ethno-national terms through institutional mechanisms like federal systems – comparability is a particularly important issue. When thinking about the applicability or potential success of any theory or policy related to the management of conflict in a diverse state, there are myriad factors to consider, including the particular nature of the conflict; the commitment of the participants to find mutually acceptable outcomes for their conflict; the preferences of the actors for a predetermined set of solutions or institutions; the current institutional makeup of the state; the territorial patterns of ethnic demography; the relative significance (in material, strategic, or symbolic terms) of contested or important territories to the groups in conflict; the distribution of resources within and across groups; the geopolitical significance of the state; and the presence of external states or groups with an interest in the conflict (be it material or symbolic), among others.[29] These factors – the context of a case – clearly matter to the applicability of any proposed approach;[30] they are vital considerations when thinking about how institutions can manage

29 On these factors, and their relative importance in the application of theories and approaches to managing ethno-national conflict and diversity, see Wolff (2011: 176–84). Also, on the importance of the distribution of resources within and between groups (particularly the unequal distribution of capital), see Green (2011).

30 See the analytic framework developed by Wolff (2011: 180), which shows how the content of institutional design can account for the context of a case.

diversity and conflict. In other words, "cookie-cutter" solutions from the various (consociationalist or centripetalist) handbooks are unlikely to succeed in managing diversity and conflict without adaptations that take into account the context of a particular case.

At the same time, the importance of context does not preclude the generation of (or mitigate the value of) general theory. It simply means that we need to think carefully about how to *apply* general theories as specific policies. The observation that context matters in how particular institutional approaches are applied (and the analysis of how they are applied, and should be applied) necessarily follows the development of those general approaches themselves. And in a related turn, general theory is often (and properly) generated by analysing and reflecting on how diversity and conflict are managed in particular cases.

As explained earlier, one of my aims here is to inform broader theory and policy through such case-specific analysis. In particular, the book seeks to advance thinking about one of the central factors just mentioned that relate to the applicability and success of ethno-national conflict-management theory and policy in any given case: *the nature of conflict*. The basis of comparability in this study comes down to the particular dynamics of conflict over national identity and the federation in plurinational federations. This study has focused on these two dynamics in Canada, while examining how the federal arbiter has managed them (both successfully and problematically). By focusing on these dynamics, I have sought to explicitly frame Canada as a plurinational federation (set against other views of it as a multinational federation, for example). It is from this analytical perspective that a number of claims can be derived to inform aspects of theory and policy for that state and others, specifically in relation to the management of conflict over nationality and the federation through the federal arbiter.

In addition, Canada represents a key case within the literature on the use of federalism to manage diversity. As noted in the introduction, this is true both of the comparative study of federations[31] and among those who promote federal systems (particularly the multinational federal model).[32] Accordingly, there is value in examining this key case to

31 See, for example, Hueglin and Fenna (2006), Burgess (2006), Erk (2008), Baier (2006).

32 For a review of the "Canada School" of multinational federalists, exemplified by the work of Will Kymlicka, see Schertzer and Woods (2011). A recent example of the prominence of Canada in the promotion of the promise of federalism to manage diversity can be seen in Skogstad et al. (2013).

help inform the body of theory that is, in large part, built upon examinations of Canada. At the same time, there is a valid concern that my own study, focused on federal judicial review, may be limited by the particularities of constitutional law in Canada and the functioning of the judicial system. In response to such a view, first and foremost, it is worth stating that the study of any jurisdiction's constitutional law is inherently comparable. There are key similarities in the very nature of public law as a practice endemic to the modern state system that lend themselves to general and comparative analysis. I thus align myself with the emerging practice of comparative constitutional law.[33] There is a pedigree of work that helps show how analysis of Canadian federalism jurisprudence can inform both comparative analysis and general theory building.[34] In addition, my discussion in chapter 2 on the different forms of federal arbitration identified the similarities and links between the apex-court approach used in Canada and the general approach of relying upon courts of law as the federal arbiter in twenty-five of the twenty-six current federations across the globe. In other words, a study of how the SCC fulfils its role when it is called upon to arbitrate disputes over the federation can inform reflection on the role of other federal arbiters (given their broadly shared place in federal systems of government). This is a case study; but it has been designed to investigate aspects of a key case that can advance general theory and provide a basis for future comparative analysis.

At the same time, my focus on conflict dynamics and the mechanisms to manage them means that careful consideration of the context of a given case is needed when thinking about the application of my analysis beyond Canada. My aim is thus not to argue for *a particular federal model* to manage diversity and conflict (it is, in fact, quite the opposite); nor is it to say that federal arbiters *must* act as explicit facilitators of negotiation *in all cases and all contexts*. At the same time, outside the Canadian context, there are elements of my analysis and argument that can inform federal theory when thinking about how to manage particular dynamics of conflict in diverse states.

First, federal arbiters matter because they are important in the development of a federal system over time and in maintaining its legitimacy. In dealing with conflicts between parties over the nature of the

33 For an overview of the key issues in comparative constitutional law see Choudhry (2006).

34 See Baier (2003, 2006); Choudhry (2008b); Walters (1999); McHugh (2000).

federation they shape the process and outcome of federation. And, among the forums that manage conflicts over identity and the distribution of power and resources through federal institutions, federal arbiters represent one of the last lines of defence to keep these within the domestic political process (i.e., to stop them from spilling over into violence). Accordingly, federal theorists and policymakers should account for this important role when analysing federations and when designing institutions in diverse states.

Second, courts are particularly important in *plurinational* federations. This book has focused on the importance of the arbiter by showing how the SCC has managed conflict over national identity and its link to the division of powers in Canada. The importance of the federal arbiter in managing this particular dynamic of conflict is an observation applicable beyond this case: plurinational federal systems,[35] by definition, have some measure of conflict over identities and the way those identities are recognized in the distribution of resources and power between orders of government. Accordingly, analysis of how the federal arbiter in Canada has managed this conflict, and my arguments about how this activity can potentially affect the legitimacy of the federation, are broadly applicable to this category of states (within the confines of the qualifications noted at the outset of this section). Some brief reflection on the key characteristics of different plurinational federal systems helps to identify the *categories of cases* where *elements* of my analysis and argument may be applicable.

India represents such a case, given its nature as an established federation with considerable ethno-national diversity and a pedigree of judicial review by an apex court.[36] Following independence from British rule, India instituted a constitution in 1950 that (following Canada) enshrined a federal system with a strong central government to help offset the

35 I am purposely using the moniker of federal system here (rather than federation) to indicate that the analysis is applicable to states with forms of government that follow the broader model (such as unions, decentralized unions/quasi-federations, confederations, etc.), of which federation is a type. On this distinction and system of classification see my discussion in chapter 1, and Watts (2008: 8–19; 1998).

36 Support for this claim of comparability builds upon the work of Stepan, Linz, and Yadav (2011: 1), which presents India and Canada as similar cases with "deep cultural diversity, some of which is territorially based and political articulated by significant groups that, in the name of nationalism and self-determination advance claims of independence" (so-called state-nations; what I would call plurinational states). For an example of explicit comparison between Canadian and Indian federalism, see the contributions to Saxena (2002).

centrifugal forces of a vast, diverse population.[37] The markers of diversity in India are largely ethno-linguistic, religious, and caste-based; but ethno-linguistic diversity is the primary form of identity that is territorially concentrated, with the federal system reflecting this through a redesign along ethno-linguistic lines in the mid-1950s.[38] In addition, the special powers (relative to the other states) granted to Jammu and Kashmir by article 370 of the constitution are often cited as evidence that India has an asymmetrical federal system that accommodates territorially concentrated diversity.[39] Finally, the Supreme Court of India has a long history of practising judicial review of legislation on constitutional grounds.[40] One of the clearest examples of the Supreme Court's influence on the development of the Indian federation is the line of decisions that limit the central government's ability to use its "emergency powers" (under article 356) to take control of state governance.[41] In this federalism jurisprudence, we can see how actors within India contest the nature of the federal system (and how it recognizes identities and distributes power and resources), calling upon the federal arbiter to mediate the disputes.

Spain represents another comparable case. While not a federation in name, there is general acceptance that following its 1978 constitution Spain has progressed through a process of decentralization to the point where it can be considered a federal state in practice.[42] The foundation for the federal institutional structure in Spain is article 137 of the constitution, which allows for the creation of municipal, provincial, and *autonomous communities* of self-government.[43] In practice,

37 See Watts (2008: 36).

38 See Varshney (2013: 49–50); Watts (2008: 36–7). It should be noted that in the case of Punjab, the ethno-linguistic and religious forms of identity are aligned.

39 For an overview (and critical commentary of this view), see Tillin (2007).

40 The tradition (and protection) of judicial review is exemplified by the battle between the Court and Indian Parliament over article 368 of the constitution, which relates to the power of Parliament to amend the constitution; for an overview, see Chopra (2006); Reede (2006).

41 See Tummala (2007). For a broader discussion of judicial review and federalism in Canada and India, see Green (2002).

42 See, for example, Watts (2008: 12–13, 41–2); Harty (2005); Agranoff and Ramos Gallarín (1997).

43 From this basis, a number of routes to attaining autonomy can be followed, including the recognition of historic plebiscites (used for Basque Country, Catalonia, and Galicia), a slower process applied to most other territories through the related article 148, and an exceptional route used for Andalucía (requiring multiple referenda); see Harty (2005: 327–8).

the process and powers granted the seventeen autonomous communities of Spain have resulted in an asymmetrical (and dynamic) federal system.[44] This process of decentralization is driven in large part by the competing perspectives on the national character of the country as both a pan-state community and one that contains multiple minority nations.[45] This tension results in considerable conflict (both political and violent), marked by consistent mobilization in support of increased autonomy or independence for self-identified nations (notably, among the Basques, Catalans, and Galicians). A key institution in the management of this conflict over the recognition of national identity and the federal system has been Spain's Constitutional Court. In general, the Constitutional Court is presented as protecting the interests and powers of the autonomous communities, most notably through a landmark decision in 1983 that reinforced the jurisdiction of sub-state governments over their areas of competence (by rejecting large portions of the central Organic Law on the Harmonization of the Autonomous Process).[46] The continued importance of the Court as a player in the conflict over the very nature of the federal system was reinforced by its role in the central government's (largely unsuccessful) attempts to stop an independence referendum from taking place in Catalonia in November 2014.[47] In any event, Spain stands as an example of a state with a federal system of government, significant groups of territorially concentrated

44 The process of negotiations between the autonomous communities and the central government means that the list of competencies and how they are implemented regularly changes; however, in general, Basque, Catalonia, Galicia, and Andalucía exercise the highest level of autonomy; for an overview that still provides a sense of the variation and current status, see Agranoff and Ramos Gallarín (1997: 8–11). For an overview of change as it relates to Catalonia (and the role the Constitutional Court plays in this process), see Colino (2009).

45 This tension is even explicitly captured in Article 2 of the Constitution, which recognizes "the indissoluble unity of the Spanish Nation…[and]…the right to autonomy of the nationalities and regions of which it is composed." On this tension and its link to territorial autonomy in Spain, see Moreno (2002: 400–2).

46 For an overview of this decision and the Constitutional Court's role in the federation, see Agranoff and Ramos Gallarín (1997: 12–19); Lopez (2008); Vale (2013).

47 The Constitutional Court agreed to hear a central-government challenge to the referendum and ordered a halt to the vote; however, the Catalan government proceeded with a "symbolic vote" disobeying the Court's order. Roughly 80% of participants voted in favour of independence (with two million of Catalonia's approximately seven and a half million people voting). The extent to which this vote, the Court's ruling, and the continuing political conflict will impact the legitimacy of the federal arbiter and political system are important questions that remain unanswered.

individuals that share common ethno-national identities who mobilize in defence of their autonomy, and a tradition of the federal arbiter managing the related conflict dynamics over the recognition of identities and the distribution of power via federal institutions.

In addition to these two examples, many other states share the same basic characteristics of a federal system of government, ethno-national diversity, and a tradition of judicial review to manage the resulting dynamics of conflict over the recognition of identity and distribution of power. Notably, South Africa, a diverse federal system with a strong Constitutional Court, marks a possible avenue to explore the application of my analysis and argument. At the same time, the boundaries of the provincial units in South Africa are explicitly designed to not coincide with the territorial concentration of ethno-national diversity, and the system is quite centralized (with extensive concurrent jurisdiction between the spheres of government and ultimate federal paramountcy).[48] In addition, while the South African Constitutional Court is largely viewed as a strong, independent institution, its jurisprudence has tended to focus on civil rights protections (not federal arbitration).[49] This focus on civil rights is likely because South Africa is a relatively new democracy (where rights protections are a particularly important concern) and the fact that the federal system is designed to facilitate a collaborative approach to intergovernmental relations (with the constitution requiring the spheres of government to exhaust negotiations before calling on the arbiter for intervention).[50]

With some conceptual stretching, elements of my study may also be applicable to inform analysis of the European Union (EU) and the role of the European Court of Justice (ECJ). The ECJ is the apex court within the EU and so is comparable to apex courts in other federal systems. And similar to other apex courts, the ECJ has been singled out by many as a key integrating force in the rise of the EU as a quasi-federal system.[51] There are clear limitations to applying my argument to the ECJ and its line of jurisprudence related to the centralization of power in the EU (notably the considerably different conflict and negotiation dynamics created by member states' willingness to recognize

48 See Watts (2008: 49); van der Westhuizen (2005: 313–14).

49 For an overview, see Roux (2008); Mohallem (2011); Corder (2004).

50 See Watts (2008: 49–50).

51 For an overview, see Josselin and Marciano (2007); Vaubel (2009); Burley and Mattli (1993).

and abide by the Court's rulings in a situation where alternatives are present).[52] However, in line with the scholarship that does focus on the ECJ as a form of federal arbiter, within a community that has conflicting notions of identity (as a pan-European community and a community of nations), there are avenues to explore my argument in this context.

Of course, further research is required to explore the conflict dynamics in these and other plurinational federal states. This research marks a future direction of study. The presence of conflict dynamics over national identity and the federal system (and the fact that they are linked to political and violent conflict as competing conceptions of identity mix with competing conceptions of the way power and resources should be distributed) points to the importance of the mechanisms by which they are managed – and, among these mechanisms, the federal arbiter can play a critical role. Given that my research has explored these dynamics in a case study of Canada, it bears repeating that the applicability of my analysis is inherently limited by context (even in the most similar cases). But, the counter-point to the limitations is that since we can see similar core characteristics in this *type* of case (plurinational federations), elements of my analysis and argument can inform the study of these cases.

My argument with regard to the importance of the federal arbiter does go beyond the sub-set of states that are plurinational and have federal systems of government; aspects of my argument apply to all states with a federal character. Contestation over the distribution of power and resources is something that is a common feature of all federal states by virtue of the fact that they are federal states. As I argued earlier, federal systems are normative frameworks. They are always contested by some group in the way the association recognizes identities and distributes power and resources. Accordingly, in such states the federation, and related institutions (like the federal arbiter), should be designed to manage this conflict. Many of my earlier points on the value of the federation being open to adaption over time in response to such conflict, and the benefits of the federal arbiter acting as a broad facilitator of negotiation between those with competing perspectives on the nature of the association, apply in this vein.

---

52 Within a traditional federal system, sub-state governments that disagree with an apex-court ruling have little alternative but to accept the judgment, while, as Garrett (1995) argues, this is not the case in the EU (where he argues member states have largely *chosen* to follow the Court of Justice's rulings, even when they lead to the centralization of power in the EU).

There are also aspects of my argument that may be applicable to inform theory and policy related to (non-federal) plurinational states. Specifically, accounting for the conflict over the nature of nationality in designing and reforming institutions can have positive benefits for loyalty to the state (and thus order) in plurinational states. For example, in the decentralized union of the United Kingdom, there are those who stress a pan-British identity and those who see the state as comprising multiple nations (i.e., the English, Scots, and Welsh). The competing conceptions of the state and its national composition within and between these groups motivates ongoing political (and at times violent) conflict in the UK over the distribution of resources and power through devolution, with the 2014 Scottish referendum on independence, and the resulting negotiations and agreement to devolve additional powers to Scotland following the (unsuccessful) vote, being a case in point. This line of analysis could also apply to Turkey, where there is (political and violent) conflict within and between pan-state nationalists, the dominant ethno-national group of Turks and the minority ethno-national group of Kurds. In this case, looking at methods of institutional design that can recognize and account for the competing conceptions of identity and competing arguments about how power and resources should be distributed may help to manage the long-running conflict through political processes. The point is that in plurinational states, institutions should be designed to mitigate the imposition of particular views on nationality to avoid a loss of loyalty and legitimacy to the way the state recognizes the views of its citizens. However, such specific analysis and prescription is well beyond the scope of this book (though it represents a future line of research that could build on the work here).

Turning back to plurinational federal systems, my argument about the potentially negative or positive effects stemming from the way a federal arbiter exercises its duties may also have applicability beyond Canada. Again, the broader implications of my analysis in this regard relate to how the arbiter manages the dynamics of conflict over nationality and the federation present in a plurinational federal state. My analysis can draw attention to the potential benefits that can arise from a federal arbiter recognizing and accounting for the various legitimate perspectives on the nature of the association. It also draws attention to the potential legitimacy costs of (1) a federal arbiter favouring a particular view of the nation and the federation when exercising its role in such states; and (2) promoting an ideal of simple neutrality and independence for the federal arbiter, given the potential for this to create expectations that cannot be reached (or because it can allow the arbiter to impose a particular perspective on the nature of a federation under the veil of neutrality). Both of these problems could increase the likelihood of mobilization by disaffected groups against the federation as an unfair system.

While the more specific arguments with regard to the way the SCC can generate legitimacy in exercising its duties made at the end of chapters 5 and 6 may seem context-specific, underlying them is a set of claims that could inform theory applicable to federal arbiters in other plurinational federal systems. That is, while it is context-specific to say the SCC should not impose the pan-Canadian model, or should recognize the legitimacy of the multinational model, underlying these arguments are more broadly applicable points.

Looking back to the arguments made at the end of chapters 5 and 6, three lessons can inform how federal arbiters in plurinational federal systems should exercise their duties to avoid eroding legitimacy for the system and its conflict-management process. These lessons are applicable to the broader form of federal political systems, as well as to the broader classification of federal arbiters. In other words, as discussed in chapter 1, my analysis here is not limited to the apex-court model used in federations proper; rather, it applies to the institutional body (whether it is a court of law or constitutional court) charged with mediating disputes between orders of government over the distribution of power and resources within a federal political system (whether it is a decentralized union, a federation, a confederation, etc.). The focus is thus on the role federal arbiters play as institutional mechanisms in states where there are similar conflict dynamics to those in Canada. Because of this focus on conflict dynamics, the potentially generalizable lessons for federal arbiters are directed towards institutions operating in plurinational states where there are competing perspectives on the national and federal character of the state.

The first lesson stems from my focus on a particular type of state: in fulfilling their role, federal arbiters should recognize and account for the plurinational character of a country and how this drives conflict over the federation. The objective should be to take into account the inherent conflict that takes place in plurinational states over the recognition of identities and the subsequent distribution of power and resources. In other words, federal arbiters should not impose only one particular perspective on a state's national character and a related view of how the federation should distribute power and resources. This claim seeks to take into account the fact that plurinational states have – as a matter of definition – competing perspectives over the very nature of the state as uni-national or multinational.

Second, federal arbiters should avoid a zero-sum approach to managing disputes over the nature of the federation. Rather than creating stark winners and losers, they should work to find mutually agreeable outcomes for conflicting parties, or at least mitigate losses by reinforcing the validity of a losing party's perspective. The rejection of zero-sum outcomes as an advisable approach stems in large part from the first lesson: if there are multiple, competing, well-established perspectives on the nature of a state's national and federal character that enjoy broad support and have been expressed in the political, institutional, and constitutional foundations of the state, imposing one on a consistent basis will impact the legitimacy of the arbiter and the system. The alternative approach – reaching outcomes that reinforce how the conflict-management process and federal system incorporate elements of each established perspective – is better suited to generating and maintaining the legitimacy of the association over time.

Finally, building on these two lessons, arbiters should avoid the outmoded approach of being an umpire, branch of government, or guardian and embrace a role and approach to judicial review focused on reinforcing the dynamic nature of federal systems with a view to broadly facilitating negotiation between conflicting parties. The point here is to avoid the problematic approach of sitting above a conflict as an independent body; by embracing a role as part of the system and field of struggle, federal arbiters can facilitate the management of conflict through negotiation and the political process, or at least render decisions that recognize and account for the validity of the competing perspectives of the parties. Thus, the lesson here, ideally, is to follow the general principles exemplified in the *Secession Reference* for how arbiters can manage a conflict by pushing the parties to deal with their issues through negotiation and political processes, while also rendering a decision that builds on an inclusive depiction of the federal system, uses the applicable forms of legal reasoning to reinforce this depiction, and reaches an outcome that avoids a zero-sum nature.

The applicability of my argument beyond Canada relies on the presence of the conflict dynamics present in Canada and the shared institutional elements of federal political systems; however, there are other factors that also play into the exportability and generalizability of my analysis. As I noted above, these include geopolitical, economic, and other broad factors that are part of any comparative analysis. Setting these general issues aside, there are two additional factors that are important to consider when thinking about how my analysis can inform broader theory.

The first is another aspect related to the nature of the conflict taking place in any given state: in general, my analysis is most applicable to states with long-running (mainly) political conflict. The approach and arguments are generally of limited application when thinking about how to manage "hot" conflicts (i.e., those instances where violence is widespread and conflict is taking place primarily outside the political process). In such situations, the focus is necessarily on the cessation of violence, restoring order, and bringing parties back into the political process to manage their differences. The argument of this book offers little that can be applied in such instances and processes. Nevertheless, at the juncture where discussions turn towards institutional design to manage conflict and diversity within the political process, some of the above analysis may be informative. That is, when thinking about institutional design in post-conflict states that have territorialized groups that identify as nations, some of the above points (on the importance of designing federal systems that are open to continued contestation and the important role the federal arbiter plays in managing this contestation) may be broadly applicable.[53]

The second limiting factor is the extent to which the participants of a conflict recognize the legitimacy of competing groups, *as groups*, within a broader context of accepting the rule of law. The applicability of my argument rests on there being a measure of mutual recognition between the parties in conflict (which generally takes place where there is commitment to liberal values of autonomy and equality).[54] The ability to manage conflict (successfully) through processes of negotiation and dialogue is necessarily reliant on such recognition among parties

53 Again, while specific prescriptions beyond Canada are outside the scope of the book, mechanisms such as interpretative clauses in the constitution that direct the federal arbiter to recognize and account for the competing conceptions of the state's national and federal character, along with ways of privileging intergovernmental relations as a means to manage disputes and the ability to adapt the constitutional system over time, are what I have in mind here.

54 Related to this point is the importance of adherence to the rule of law for the applicability of my argument. For example, the ability of the judiciary or federal arbiter to manage diversity and conflict within the political process is linked to broader adherence to the rule of law, which is not always the case in post-conflict states.

about the status of the other.[55] Such mutual recognition is clearly not always present in states marked by ethno-national conflict. We see this conflict and lack of mutual recognition and broad respect for liberal values, for example, in the Russian Federation. Here, there is an oft-made distinction between the two competing concepts of Russian: "rossiyki" (referring to pan-state Russian identity) and "russkiy" (referring to the dominant, ethnic nation of Russians, which constitute over 80 per cent of the population of the state).[56] In addition to this pan-state identity, there are numerous groups within the remaining 20 per cent that self-identify as ethnic groups or nations (and which mobilize in defence of this identity), notably the Chechens. The tension between and within these groups (i.e., the pan-state nationalists, dominant ethno-national Russians, and minority ethno-national groups) over the nature of national identity and the related distribution of power and resources has been a central component of contemporary politics and conflict in Russia. In situations such as this (where there is a lack of mutual recognition among groups), promoting bilateral negotiations to manage conflict can actually be counter-productive, as it can allow those with material or power advantages to dominate and oppress other groups free of legal or institutional checks that may take place under more structured conflict-management mechanisms.

At the same time, as institutional and liberal rights protections take hold in post-conflict states, and a sense of mutual recognition develops, some of my analysis could be helpful in thinking about specific institutional and policy choices. For example, a focus on keeping conflict over national identity and the associated distribution of resources and power via institutions within the political process can be an important element in mitigating the outbreak of violence (and, again, the domestic arbiter or judiciary can play a role in this process).

Given the above considerations, one of the overall contributions of the book to broader federal theory and the management of diversity

---

55 Such recognition does not mean there is agreement between the parties on their actual status as groups, something that the conflict over nationality in Canada demonstrates. For example, while pan-Canadianists and multinationalists disagree about the status of Québec as a nation, neither group denies the other the ability to make its claims. In this way, while the groups conflict about the nature of the state's national character, the fact that each group recognizes the existence of the other and enters into debate and dialogue with them demonstrates a basic level of mutual recognition.

56 On this distinction, see Simonsen (1996).

and conflict is to draw attention to one of the important factors in thinking about the applicability of such theory and policy (the nature or dynamics of conflict), linking this to the mechanisms that manage the conflict (particularly focusing on the role of the federal arbiter). My overall argument with regard to the applicability of my analysis beyond Canada is that it can *inform aspects* of federal theory and policy in this area. Specifically, my analysis draws attention to particular dynamics of conflict that should be accounted for when thinking about how to employ federal systems to manage diversity and conflict. The most applicable point for broader theory and policy stemming from this is that federal arbiters matter because how they fulfil their role can have the potential to negatively or positively affect the legitimacy of an association.

Bibliography

Acton, J. 1985. "Nationality." In *Selected Writings of Lord Acton*, ed. J. Fears. 409–33. Indianapolis: Liberty Classics.

Agranoff, R., and J. Ramos Gallarín. 1997. "Toward Federal Democracy in Spain: An Examination of Intergovernmental Relations." *Publius* 27 (4): 1–38. http://dx.doi.org/10.1093/oxfordjournals.pubjof.a029931.

Almond, G., and S. Verba. 1963. *The Civic Culture: Political Attitudes and Democracy in Five Nations*. Princeton: Princeton University Press.

Anderson, B. 1991. *Imagined Communities: Reflections on the Origins and Spread of Nationalism*. London: Verso.

Archibugi, D. 2003. "A Critical Analysis of the Self-determination of Peoples: A Cosmopolitan Perspective." *Constellations* (Oxford, England) 10 (4): 488–505. http://dx.doi.org/10.1046/j.1351-0487.2003.00349.x.

Arendt, H. 1958. *The Human Condition*. Chicago: University of Chicago Press.

Arendt, H. 1973. *On Revolution*. Harmondsworth: Penguin.

Baier, G. 2003. "The Law of Federalism: Judicial Review and the Division of Powers." In *New Trends in Canadian Federalism*, ed. F. Rocher and M. Smith. 111–33. Peterborough, ON: Broadview Press.

Baier, G. 2006. *Courts and Federalism: Judicial Doctrine in the United States, Australia, and Canada*. Vancouver: UBC Press.

Baier, G. 2012. "The Courts, the Constitution, and Dispute Resolution." In *Canadian Federalism: Performance, Effectiveness and Legitimacy*, ed. H. Bakvis and G. Skogstad. 79–95. Don Mills: Oxford University Press.

Baier, B., and H. Bakvis. 2007. "Federalism and the Reform of Central Institutions: Dealing with Asymmetry and the Democratic Deficit." In *Constructing Tomorrow's Federalism: New Perspectives on Canadian Governance*, ed. I. Peach. 89–114. Winnipeg: University of Manitoba Press.

Bellamy, R. 1999. *Liberalism and Pluralism: Towards a Politics of Compromise*. London: Routledge.

Bellamy, R. 2000. "Dealing with Difference: Four Models of Pluralist Politics." *Parliamentary Affairs* 53 (1): 198–217. http://dx.doi.org/10.1093/pa/53.1.198.

Bellamy, R. 2007. *Political Constitutionalism: A Republican Defence of the Constitutionality of Democracy*. Cambridge: Cambridge University Press. http://dx.doi.org/10.1017/CBO9780511490187.

Benner, E. 2012. "The Nation State." In *Cambridge History of Philosophy in the Nineteenth Century*, ed. A. Wood. 699–730. Cambridge: Cambridge University Press. http://dx.doi.org/10.1017/CHO9780511975257.032.

Benz, A., and J. Broschek, eds. 2013. *Federal Dynamics: Continuity, Change, and the Varieties of Federalism*. Oxford: Oxford University Press.

Bilodeau, R. 2010. "Supreme Court of Canada – Structure, Status and Challenges." *Commonwealth Law Bulletin* 36 (3): 421–41. http://dx.doi.org/10.1080/03050718.2010.500831.

Black, E. 1975. *Divided Loyalties: Canadian Concepts of Federalism*. Montreal: McGill-Queen's University Press.

Bobbitt, P. 1982. *Constitutional Fate: Theory of the Constitution*. Oxford: Oxford University Press.

Bobbitt, P. 1991. *Constitutional Interpretation*. Oxford: Blackwell.

Breuilly, J. 1993. *Nationalism and the State*. Manchester: Manchester University Press.

Breuilly, J. 2011. "On the Principle of Nationality." In *The Cambridge History of Nineteenth-Century Political Thought*, ed. G. Stedman and G. Claeys. 77–109. Cambridge: Cambridge University Press. http://dx.doi.org/10.1017/CHOL9780521430562.005.

Brown, C. 2002. *Sovereignty, Rights and Justice*. Cambridge: Polity.

Brubaker, R. 1996. *Nationalism Reframed: Nationhood and the National Question in the New Europe*. Cambridge: Cambridge University Press. http://dx.doi.org/10.1017/CBO9780511558764.

Brubaker, R. 2004. *Ethnicity without Groups*. Cambridge, MA: Harvard University Press. http://dx.doi.org/10.1017/CBO9780511489235.004.

Burgess, M. 2006. *Comparative Federalism: Theory and Practice*. London: Routledge.

Burley, A., and W. Mattli. 1993. "Europe before the Court: A Political Theory of Legal Integration." *International Organization* 47 (1): 41–76. http://dx.doi.org/10.1017/S0020818300004707.

Butler, J. 1997. *The Psychic Life of Power: Theories in Subjection*. Stanford: Stanford University Press.

Bzdera, A. 1993. "Comparative Analysis of Federal High Courts: A Political Theory of Judicial Review." *Canadian Journal of Political Science* 26 (1): 3–29. http://dx.doi.org/10.1017/S0008423900002420.

Cairns, A. 1971. "The Judicial Committee and Its Critics." *Canadian Journal of Political Science* 4 (3): 301–45. http://dx.doi.org/10.1017/S0008423900026809.

Cairns, A. 1994. "The Charlottetown Accord: Multinational Canada v. Federalism." In *Constitutional Predicament*, ed. C. Cook. 25–63. Montreal: McGill-Queen's University Press.

Cameron, D., and R. Simeon. 2002. "Intergovernmental Relations in Canada: The Emergence of Collaborative Federalism." *Publius* 32 (2): 49–72. http://dx.doi.org/10.1093/oxfordjournals.pubjof.a004947.

Cassese, A. 2005. *International Law*. Oxford: Oxford University Press.

Chambers, S. 2004. "Democracy, Popular Sovereignty and Constitutional Legitimacy." *Constellations* (Oxford, England) 11 (2): 153–73. http://dx.doi.org/10.1111/j.1351-0487.2004.0370.x.

Chopra, P., ed. 2006. *The Supreme Court versus the Constitution: A Challenge to Federalism*. New Delhi: Sage Publications.

Choudhry, S., ed. 2006. *The Migration of Constitutional Ideas*. Cambridge: Cambridge University Press.

Choudhry, S., ed. 2008a. *Constitutional Design for Divided Societies: Integration or Accommodation*. Oxford: Oxford University Press.

Choudhry, S. 2008b. "Ackerman's Higher Lawmaking in Comparative Constitutional Perspective: Constitutional Moments as Constitutional Failures?" *International Journal of Constitutional Law* 6 (2): 193–230. http://dx.doi.org/10.1093/icon/mon002.

Choudhry, S., and J. Gaudreault-DesBiens. 2007. "Frank Iacobucci as Constitution Maker: From the Quebec Veto Reference to the Meech Lake Accord and the Quebec Secession Reference." *University of Toronto Law Journal* 57 (2): 165–93. http://dx.doi.org/10.1353/tlj.2007.0010.

Choudhry, S., and R. Howse. 2000. "Constitutional Theory and the Quebec Secession Reference." *Canadian Journal of Law and Jurisprudence* 13 (2): 143–70.

Clarke, J. 2006. "Beyond the Democratic Dialogue, and Towards a Federalist One: Provincial Arguments and Supreme Court Responses in Charter Litigation." *Canadian Journal of Political Science* 39 (2): 293–314. http://dx.doi.org/10.1017/S0008423906060112.

Claude, I. 1955. *National Minorities: An International Problem*. Cambridge, MA: Harvard University Press. http://dx.doi.org/10.4159/harvard.9780674494275.

Colino, C. 2009. "Constitutional Change without Constitutional Reform: Spanish Federalism and the Revision of Catalonia's Statute of Autonomy." *Publius* 39 (2): 262–88. http://dx.doi.org/10.1093/publius/pjn037.

Cooper, B. 1994. "Looking Eastward, Looking Backward: A Western Reading of the Never-Ending Story." In *Constitutional Predicament*, ed. C. Cook. 89–107. Montreal: McGill-Queen's University Press.

Corder, H. 2004. "Judicial Authority in a Changing South Africa." *Legal Studies* 24 (1–2): 253–74. http://dx.doi.org/10.1111/j.1748-121X.2004.tb00250.x.

Crawford, J. 2007. *The Creation of States in International Law*. Oxford: Oxford University Press.

Dahl, R. 1956. *A Preface to Democratic Theory*. Chicago: University of Chicago Press.

Dahl, R. 1989. *Democracy and Its Critics*. New Haven: Yale University Press.

Des Rosiers, N. 2000. "From Quebec Veto to Quebec Secession: The Evolution of the Supreme Court of Canada on Quebec-Canada Disputes." *Canadian Journal of Law and Jurisprudence* 39 (2): 171–84.

Dicey, A. 1982. *An Introduction to the Study of the Law and Constitution*. Indianapolis: Liberty Classics.

Dion, S. 1999. *Straight Talk: Speeches and Writings on Canadian Unity*. Montreal: McGill-Queen's University Press.

Dodek, A. 2011. "Courting Constitutional Danger: Constitutional Conventions and the Legacy of the Patriation Reference." *Supreme Court Review* 54 (2): 117–42.

Dowd, K., and A. Sayeed. 1985. "Federal–Provincial Fiscal Relations: Some Background." In *Ottawa and the Provinces: The Distribution of Money and Power*, ed. T. Courchene, D. Conklin, and G. Cook. 253–75. Toronto: Ontario Economic Council.

Drache, D., and P. Monahan. 1999. "In Search of Plan A" *Canada Watch* 7 (1–2): 1–2, 29–32.

Eckstein, H. 1966. *Division and Cohesion in Democracy: A Study of Norway*. Princeton: Princeton University Press.

Eckstein, H., and T. Gurr. 1975. *Patterns of Authority: A Structural Basis for Political Inquiry*. London: Wiley-Interscience.

Elazar, D. 1987. *Exploring Federalism*. Tuscaloosa: University of Alabama Press.

Elliot, R. 2001. "References, Structural Argumentation and the Organizing Principles of Canada's Constitution." *Canadian Bar Review* 80 (1): 67–142.

Emerson, R. 1971. "Self-Determination." *American Journal of International Law* 65 (3): 459–75. http://dx.doi.org/10.2307/2198970.

Epstein, L., and J. Kobylka. 1992. *The Supreme Court and Legal Change: Abortion and the Death Penalty*. Chapel Hill: University of North Carolina Press.

Erk, J. 2008. *Explaining Federalism: State, Society and Congruence in Austria, Belgium, Canada, Germany and Switzerland*. London: Routledge.

Fearon, J., and D. Laitin. 2003. "Ethnicity, Insurgency, and Civil War." *American Political Science Review* 97 (1): 75–90. http://dx.doi.org/10.1017/S0003055403000534.

Fink, C. 2000. "Minority Rights as an International Question." *Contemporary European History* 9 (3): 385–400. http://dx.doi.org/10.1017/S0960777300003052.

Finkelstein, N. 1986. *Laskin's Canadian Constitutional Law*. Toronto: Carswell.

Fitzgerald, P., and B. Wright. 2000. *Looking at Law: Canada's Legal System*. Toronto: Butterworths.

Friedrich, C.J. 1968. *Trends of Federalism in Theory and Practice*. New York: Praeger.

Gagnon, A. 2007. "Democratic Multinational Federalism under Scrutiny: Healthy Tensions and Unresolved Issues in Canada." In *Multinational Federations*, ed. M. Burgess and J. Pinder. 17–30. London: Routledge.

Garrett, G. 1995. "The Politics of Legal Integration in the European Union." *International Organization* 49 (1): 171–81. http://dx.doi.org/10.1017/S0020818300001612.

Gaudreault-DesBiens, J. 1999. "The Quebec-Secession Reference and the Judicial Arbitration of Conflicting Narratives about Law, Democracy, and Identity." *Vermont Law Review* 23 (4): 793–843.

Geertz, C. 1973. *The Interpretation of Cultures*. London: Fontana.

Gellner, E. 1983. *Nations and Nationalism*. Oxford: Blackwell.

Gibson, G. 1999. "A Court for All Seasons" *Canada Watch* 7 (1–2): 23, 35.

Gibson, J., G. Caldeira, and V. Baird. 1998. "On the Legitimacy of National High Courts." *American Political Science Review* 92 (2): 343–58. http://dx.doi.org/10.2307/2585668.

Goodyear-Grant, E., J.S. Matthews, and J. Hiebert. 2013. "The Courts/Parliament Trade-off: Canadian Attitudes on Judicial Influence in Public Policy." *Commonwealth and Comparative Politics* 51 (3): 377–97. http://dx.doi.org/10.1080/14662043.2013.805540.

Green, E. 2011. "The Political Economy of Nation Formation in Modern Tanzania: Explaining Stability in the Face of Diversity." *Commonwealth and Comparative Politics* 49 (2): 223–44.

Green, I. 2002. "The Judicial Dimension of Federalism in India and Canada: A Comparative Analysis." In *Mapping Canadian Federalism for India*, ed. R. Saxena. 258–78. Delhi: Konark Publishers.

Greschner, D. 1999. "What Can Small Provinces Do?" *Canada Watch* 7 (1–2): 24, 37.

Greschner, D. 2000. "The Supreme Court, Federalism, and Metaphors of Moderation." *Canadian Bar Review* 79 (2): 47–76.

Grosby, S. 1994. "Debate: The Verdict of History: The Inexpungeable Tie of Primordiality – A Response to Eller and Coughlan." *Ethnic and Racial Studies* 17 (1): 164–71. http://dx.doi.org/10.1080/01419870.1994.9993817.

Gurr, T. 1993. *Minorities at Risk: A Global View of Ethnopolitical Conflicts*. Washington: United States Institute of Peace Press.

Gurr, T., J. Hewitt, and J. Wilkenfeld. 2008. "Introduction." In *Peace and Conflict 2008*, ed. J. Hewitt, J. Wilkenfeld, and T. Gurr. 1–4. Boulder: Paradigm Publishers. http://dx.doi.org/10.1017/CBO9780511754326.002.

Habermas, J. 1995. *Moral Consciousness and Communicative Action*. Cambridge: Cambridge University Press.

Habermas, J. 2001. "Constitutional Democracy: A Paradoxical Union of Contradictory Principles?" *Political Theory* 29 (6): 766–81.

Halberstam, D. 2008. "Comparative Federalism and the Role of the Judiciary." In *The Oxford Handbook of Law and Politics*, ed. G. Calderia, R. Kelemen, and K. Whittington. 142–64. Oxford: Oxford University Press. http://dx.doi.org/10.1093/oxfordhb/9780199208425.003.0009.

Hart, H. 1961. *The Concept of Law*. Oxford: Oxford University Press.

Harty, S. 2005. "Spain." In *Handbook of Federal Countries, 2005*, ed. A. Grffiths. 325–42. Montreal, Kingston: McGill-Queen's Press.

Hausegger, L., and T. Riddell. 2004. "The Changing Nature of Public Support for the Supreme Court of Canada." *Canadian Journal of Political Science* 37 (1): 23–50. http://dx.doi.org/10.1017/S000842390404003X.

Hayek, F. 1960. *The Constitution of Liberty*. London: Routledge and Kegan Paul.

Hayek, F. 1973. *Law, Legislation and Liberty: Volume One, Rules and Order*. Chicago: University of Chicago Press.

Hewitt, J. 2008. "Trends in Global Conflict: 1946–2005." In *Peace and Conflict 2008*, ed. J. Hewitt, J. Wilkenfeld, and T. Gurr. 21–6. Boulder: Paradigm Publishers.

Higgins, R. 1994. *Problems & Process: International Law and How We Use It*. Oxford: Oxford University Press.

Hirschl, R. 2004. *Towards Juristocracy: The Origins and Consequences of the New Constitutionalism*. Cambridge, MA: Harvard University Press.

Hirschl, R. 2008. "The Judicialization of Mega-Politics and the Rise of the Political Courts." *Annual Review of Political Science* 11 (1): 93–118. http://dx.doi.org/10.1146/annurev.polisci.11.053006.183906.

Hirschl, R. 2013. "The Constitutional Jurisprudence of Federalism and the Theocratic Challenge." In *The Global Promise of Federalism*, ed. G. Skogstad et al. 139–64. Toronto: University of Toronto Press.

Hobsbawm, E. 1990. *Nations and Nationalism since 1780: Programme, Myth, Reality*. Cambridge: Cambridge University Press.

Hogg, P. 1979. "Is the Supreme Court of Canada Biased in Constitutional Cases?" *Canadian Bar Review* 57 (4): 721–39.

Hogg, P. 1999. "The Duty to Negotiate" *Canada Watch* 7 (1–2): 1, 33–5.

Hogg, P. 2007. "Canada: From Privy Council to Supreme Court." In *Interpreting Constitutions*, ed. J. Goldsworthy. 55–105. Oxford: Oxford University Press. http://dx.doi.org/10.1093/acprof:oso/9780199226474.003.0003.

Hogg, P. 2009. *Constitutional Law of Canada (Student Edition)*. Toronto: Carswell.

Hogg, P., and A. Bushell. 1997. "The *Charter* Dialogue between Courts and Legislatures (Or Perhaps the *Charter of Rights* Isn't Such a Bad Thing After All)." *Osgoode Hall Law Journal* 35 (1): 75–124.

Horowitz, D. 2000. *Ethnic Groups in Conflict*. Berkeley: University of California Press.

Horowitz, D. 2003. "A Right to Secede?" In *Secession and Self-Determination*, ed. S. Macedo and A. Buchanan. 84–131. London: New York University Press.

Horowitz, D. 2007. "The Many Uses of Federalism." *Drake Law Review* 55 (4): 953–66.

Hubbard, R., and G. Paquet. 2007. *Gomery's Blinders and Canadian Federalism*. Ottawa: University of Ottawa Press.

Hueglin, T. 2013. "Federalism and Democracy: A Critical Reassessment." In *The Global Promise of Federalism*, ed. G. Skogstad et al. 17–42. Toronto: University of Toronto Press.

Hueglin, T., and A. Fenna. 2006. *Comparative Federalism: A Systematic Inquiry*. Peterborough, ON: Broadview Press.

Hutchinson, J. 2005. *Nations as Zones of Conflict*. London: Sage.

Iacobucci, F. 2002. "The Supreme Court of Canada: Its History, Powers and Responsibilities." *Journal of Appellate Practice and Process* 4 (2): 27–40.

Jackson, R. 2003. *The Global Covenant: Human Conduct in a World of States*. Oxford: Oxford University Press. http://dx.doi.org/10.1093/0199262012.001.0001.

Jackson, R. 2005. *Classic and Modern Thought on International Relations*. New York: Palgrave Macmillian. http://dx.doi.org/10.1057/9781403979520.

Jackson, R. 2007. "Sovereignty and Its Presuppositions: Before 9/11 and after." *Political Studies* 55 (2): 297–317. http://dx.doi.org/10.1111/j.1467-9248.2007.00668.x.

Jackson Preece, J. 1998. *National Minorities and the European Nation-States System*. New York: Clarendon Press.

Jackson Preece, J. 2005. *Minority Rights*. Cambridge: Polity Press.

Jackson Preece, J. 2008. "Democracy, Minority Rights and Plural Societies: Plus ça Change?" *Sociology Compass* 2 (2): 609–24. http://dx.doi.org/10.1111/j.1751-9020.2007.00070.x.

Jennings, I. 1956. *The Approach to Self-Government*. Cambridge: Cambridge University Press.

Joffe, P. 1999. "Quebec's Sovereignty Project and Aboriginal Rights." *Canada Watch* 7 (1–2): 6–7, 13.

Josselin, J., and A. Marciano. 2007. "How the Court Made a Federation of the EU." *Review of International Organizations* 2 (1): 59–75. http://dx.doi.org/10.1007/s11558-006-9001-y.

Kaufmann, E. 2008. "The Lenses of Nationhood: An Optical Model of Identity." *Nations and Nationalism* 14 (3): 449–77. http://dx.doi.org/10.1111/j.1469-8129.2008.00357.x.

Kaufmann, E. 2009. "Dominant Ethnicity and Dominant Nationhood: Empirical and Normative Aspects." In *Dominant Nationalism, Dominant Ethnicity: Identity, Federalism and Democracy*, ed. A. Lecours and G. Nootens. 35–56. Brussels: PEI Peter Lang.

Kaufmann, E. 2011. "Demographic Change and Conflict in Northern Ireland: Reconciling Qualitative and Quantitative Evidence." *Ethnopolitics* 10 (3–4): 369–89. http://dx.doi.org/10.1080/17449057.2011.596117.

Keating, M. 2001. *Plurinational Democracy: Stateless Nations in a Post-Sovereignty Era*. Oxford: Oxford University Press. http://dx.doi.org/10.1093/0199240760.001.0001.

Keating, M. 2002. "Plurinational Democracy in a Post-Sovereign Order." *Northern Ireland Legal Quarterly* 53: 351–65.

Kelly, J. 2001. "Reconciling Rights and Federalism during Review of the Charter of Rights and Freedoms: The Supreme Court of Canada and the Centralization Thesis." *Canadian Journal of Political Science* 34 (2): 321–55. http://dx.doi.org/10.1017/S000842390177792X.

Kelly, J., and M. Murphy. 2005. "Shaping the Constitutional Dialogue on Federalism: Canada's Supreme Court as Meta-Political Actor." *Publius* 35 (2): 217–43. http://dx.doi.org/10.1093/publius/pji010.

King, P. 1982. *Federalism and Federation*. London: Croom Helm.

Kymlicka, W. 1995. *Multicultural Citizenship: a Liberal Theory of Minority Rights*. Oxford: Oxford University Press.

Kymlicka, W. 1998. *Finding Our Way: Rethinking Ethnocultural Relations in Canada*. Oxford: Oxford University Press.

Kymlicka, W. 2000. "Federalism and Secession: At Home and Abroad." *Canadian Journal of Law and Jurisprudence* 13 (2): 207–24.

Kymlicka, W. 2001. *Politics in the Vernacular: Nationalism, Multiculturalism and Citizenship*. Oxford: Oxford University Press. http://dx.doi.org/10.1093/0199240981.001.0001.

Kymlicka, W. 2002. "Multiculturalism and Minority Rights: West and East." *Journal of Ethnopolitics and Minority Issues in Europe* 3 (4): 1–25.

Kymlicka, W. 2005. "National Minorities in Post-Communist Europe: The Role of International Norms and European Integration." In *Ethnic Politics after Communism*, ed. Z. Barany and R. Moser. 191–217. Ithaca: Cornell University Press.

Kymlicka, W. 2006. "Emerging Western Models of Multination Federalism: Are They Relevant to Africa?" In *Ethnic Federalism: The Ethiopian Experience in Comparative Perspective*, ed. D. Turton. 32–64. Addis Ababa: Addis Ababa University Press and James Currey Publishers.

Kymlicka, W. 2007. "Multi-nation Federalism." In *Federalism in Asia*, ed. B. He, B. Galligan, and T. Inoguchi. 33–56. Cheltenham: Edward Elgar Publishing.

L'Heureux-Dubé, C. 1990. "The Length and Plurality of Supreme Court of Canada Decisions." *Alberta Law Review* 28 (3): 581–8.

Lamer, A. 2000. "A Brief History of the Court." In Supreme Court of Canada, *The Supreme Court of Canada and Its Justices*. Ottawa: Public Works and Government Services.

Laponce, J. 1960. *The Protection of Minorities*. London: Cambridge University Press.

Laskin, B. 1955. "Tests for Validity of Legislation: What's the 'Matter'?" *University of Toronto Law Journal* 11 (1): 114–27. http://dx.doi.org/10.2307/824140.

Laitin, D. 2007. *Nations States and Violence*. Oxford: Oxford University Press. http://dx.doi.org/10.1093/acprof:oso/9780199228232.001.0001.

Lawson, George. 1992. *Politica Sacra et Civilis or, A Modell of Civil and Ecclesiasticall Government* (1660). Ed. C. Condren. Cambridge: Cambridge University Press.

Leclair, J. 1999. "A Ruling in Search of a Nation" *Canada Watch* 7 (1–2): 22, 36.

Leclair, J. 2002. "Canada's Unfathomable Unwritten Constitutional Principles." *Queen's Law Journal* 27 (2): 389–444.

Leclair, J. 2003. "The Supreme Court of Canada's Understanding of Federalism: Efficiency at the Expense of Diversity." *Queen's Law Journal* 28 (2): 411–53.

Lederman, W. 1964. "Classifications of Laws and the British North America Act." In *The Courts and the Canadian Constitution*, ed. W. Lederman. 177–99. Ottawa: Carleton University Press.

Lederman, W. 1975. "Unity and Diversity in Canadian Federalism: Ideals and Methods of Moderation." *Canadian Bar Review* 53 (3): 595–620.

Lederman, W. 1981. *Continuing Canadian Constitutional Dilemmas*. Toronto: Butterworths.

Lederman, W. 1983. "The Supreme Court of Canada and Basic Constitutional Amendment." In *And No One Cheered: Federalism, Democracy and the Constitution Act*, ed. K. Banting and R. Simeon. 176–88. Toronto: Methuen.

Leerssen, J. 2006. *National Thought in Europe: A Cultural History*. Amsterdam: Amsterdam University Press.

Levy, J. 2007. "Federalism, Liberalism, and the Separation of Loyalties." *American Political Science Review* 101 (3): 459–77. http://dx.doi.org/10.1017/S0003055407070268.

Lijphart, A. 2008. *Thinking about Democracy: Power Sharing and Majority Rule in Theory and Practice*. Abingdon: Routledge.

Livingston, W. 1952. "A Note on the Nature of Federalism." *Political Science Quarterly* 67 (1): 81–95. http://dx.doi.org/10.2307/2145299.

Locke, J. 1982. *Second Treatise of Government* (1690). Arlington Heights: H. Davidson.

Lopez, E. 2008. "Judicial Review in Spain: The Constitutional Court." *Loyola of Los Angeles Law Review* 41: 529–62.

Loughlin, M. 2003. *The Idea of Public Law*. Oxford: Oxford University Press.

Luhmann, N. 1996. "Quod Omnes Tangit: Remarks on Jurgen Habermas's Legal Theory." *Cardozo Law Review* 17 (4–5): 883–900.

Macartney, C. 1934. *Nation States and National Minorities*. London: Oxford University Press.

Macfarlane, E. 2010. "Consensus and Unanimity at the Supreme Court of Canada." *Supreme Court Review* 52: 379–410.

Macfarlane, E. 2013. *Governing from the Bench: The Supreme Court of Canada and the Judicial Role*. Vancouver: UBC Press.

MacKay, A. 2001. "The Supreme Court of Canada and Federalism: Does/Should Anyone Care Anymore?" *Canadian Bar Review* 80 (1–2): 241–80.

Mahler, G. 1987. *New Demensions of Canadian Federalism: Canada in a Comparative Perspective*. Mississauga, ON: Associated University Presses.

Makin, K. (2011) "Justice Ian Binnie's Exit Interview" *Globe and Mail*, 23 September 2011.

Mallory, J. 1977. "Five Faces of Federalism." In *Canadian Federalism: Myth or Reality?* ed. P. Meekison. 19–30. Toronto: Methuen.

Mandel, M. 1994. *The Charter of Rights and the Legalization of Politics in Canada*. Toronto: Thompson Educational Publishers.

Mandel, M. 1999. "A Solomonic Judgment" *Canada Watch* 7 (1–2): 20–1.

Manfredi, C. 2001. *Judicial Power and the Charter: Canada and the Paradox of Liberal Constitutionalism*. Toronto: Oxford University Press.

Manfredi, C. 2002. "Strategic Behaviour and the Canadian Charter of Rights and Freedoms." In *The Myth of the Sacred: The Charter, the Courts, and the Politics of the Constitution of Canada*, ed. P. James, D. Abelson, and M. Lusztig. 147–70. Montreal: McGill-Queen's University Press.

Mann, M. 1986. *The Sources of Social Power*. Vol. 1. Cambridge: Cambridge University Press. http://dx.doi.org/10.1017/CBO9780511570896.
Mann, M. 1993. *The Sources of Social Power*. Vol. 2. Cambridge: Cambridge University Press. http://dx.doi.org/10.1017/CBO9780511570902.
Marchildon, G. 2009. "Postmodern Federalism and Sub-State Nationalism." In *The Ashgate Research Companion to Federalism*, ed. A. Ward and L. Ward. 441–58. Surrey: Ashgate.
Mayall, J. 1990. *Nationalism and International Society*. Cambridge: Cambridge University Press. http://dx.doi.org/10.1017/CBO9780511559099.
McCormick, P. 2000. *Supreme at Last: The Evolution of the Supreme Court of Canada*. Toronto: James Lorimer and Company Ltd.
McCormick, P. 2004. "Blocs, Swarms, and Outliers: Conceptualizing Disagreement on the Modern Supreme Court of Canada." *Osgoode Hall Law Journal* 42 (1): 99–138.
McCormick, P. 2008. "Standing Apart: Separate Concurrence and the Modern Supreme Court of Canada, 1984–2006." *McGill Law Journal / Revue de Droit de McGill* 53 (1): 137–66.
McCormick, P. 2009. "Structures of Judgment: How the Modern Supreme Court of Canada Organizes Its Reasons." *Dalhousie Law Journal* 32 (1): 35–67.
McCrudden, C., and B. O'Leary. 2013. *Courts and Consociations: Human Rights versus Power-Sharing*. Oxford: Oxford University Press. http://dx.doi.org/10.1093/acprof:oso/9780199676842.001.0001.
McGarry, J. 2007. "Asymmetry in Federations, Federacies and Unitary States." *Ethnopolitics* 6 (1): 105–16. http://dx.doi.org/10.1080/17449050701232983.
McGarry, J. 2013. "Designing a Durable Federation: The Case of Cyprus." In *The Global Promise of Federalism*, ed. G. Skogstad et al. 99–138. Toronto: University of Toronto Press.
McGarry, J., and B. O'Leary. 1993. "Introduction: The Macro-Political Regulation of Ethnic Conflict." In *The Politics of Ethnic Conflict Regulation*, ed. J. McGarry and B. O'Leary. 1–40. London: Routledge.
McGarry, J., and B. O'Leary. 2007. "Federation and Managing Nations." In *Multinational Federations*, ed. M. Burgess and J. Pinder. 180–211. London: Routledge.
McGarry, J., and B. O'Leary. 2009. "Must Pluri-National Federations Fail?" *Ethnopolitics* 8 (1): 5–25. http://dx.doi.org/10.1080/17449050902738838.
McHugh, J. 2000. "Making Public Law, Public: An Analysis of the Quebec Reference Case and Its Significance for Comparative Constitutional Analysis." *International and Comparative Law Quarterly* 49 (2): 445–62. http://dx.doi.org/10.1017/S0020589300064228.

McIlwain, C. 1947. *Constitutionalism: Ancient and Modern*. Ithaca: Cornell University Press.

McLachlin, B. 2006. "Unwritten Constitutional Principles: What Is Going On?" *New Zealand Journal of Public and International Law* 4 (2): 147–64.

McRoberts, K. 1999. "In the Best Canadian Tradition" *Canada Watch* 7 (1–2): 11–13.

McRoberts, K. 2001. "Canada and the Multinational State." *Canadian Journal of Political Science* 34 (4): 683–713. http://dx.doi.org/10.1017/S0008423901778055.

McRoberts, K. 2003. "Conceiving Diversity: Dualism, Multiculturalism, and Multinationalism." In *New Trends in Canadian Federalism*, ed. F. Rocher and M. Smith. 85–109. Peterborough, ON: Broadview Press.

Mill, J. 1991. *Considerations on Representative Government* (1862). Buffalo: Prometheus Books.

Mohallem, M. 2011. "Immutable Clauses and Judicial Review in India, Brazil and South Africa: Expanding Constitutional Courts' Authority." *International Journal of Human Rights* 15 (5): 765–86. http://dx.doi.org/10.1080/13642987.2011.572703.

Monahan, P. 1984. "At Doctrine's Twilight: The Structure of Canadian Federalism." *University of Toronto Law Journal* 34 (1): 47–99. http://dx.doi.org/10.2307/825449.

Monahan, P. 1987. *Politics and the Constitution: The Charter, Federalism and the Supreme Court of Canada*. Toronto: Carswell.

Montalvo, J.G., and M. Reynal-Querol. 2005. "Ethnic Polarization, Potential Conflict, and Civil Wars." *American Economic Review* 95 (3): 796–816. http://dx.doi.org/10.1257/0002828054201468.

Moreno, L. 2002. "Decentralization in Spain." *Regional Studies* 36 (4): 399–408. http://dx.doi.org/10.1080/00343400220131160.

Morton, F.L. 2002. *Law, Politics and the Judicial Process in Canada*. Calgary: University of Calgary Press.

Morton, F.L., and R. Knopff. 2000. *The Charter Revolution and the Court Party*. Toronto: University of Toronto Press.

Noel, A. 1994. "The Charlottetown Accord: Multinational Canada v. Federalism." In *Constitutional Predicament*, ed. C. Cook. 25–63. Montreal: McGill-Queen's University Press.

Norman, W. 2006. *Negotiating Nationalism: Nation-building, Federalism and Secession in the Multinational State*. Oxford: Oxford University Press. http://dx.doi.org/10.1093/0198293356.001.0001.

O'Leary, B. 2001. "An Iron Law of Nationalism and Federation?" *Nations and Nationalism* 7 (3): 273–96. http://dx.doi.org/10.1111/1469-8219.00017.

O'Leary, B. 2005. "Power-Sharing, Pluralist Federation, and Federacy." In *The Future of Kurdistan in Iraq*, eds. B. O'Leary, J. McGarry, and K. Salih. 47–91. Philadelphia: University of Pennsylvania Press.

Osainder, A. 1994. *The States System of Europe, 1640–1990*. Oxford: Clarendon Press.

Ostberg, C., and M. Wetstein. 2007. *Attitudinal Decision Making in the Supreme Court of Canada*. Vancouver: UBC Press.

Ostberg, C., M. Wetstein, and C. Ducat. 2004. "Leaders, Followers, and Outsiders: Task and Social Leadership on the Canadian Supreme Court in the Early 'Nineties." *Polity* 36 (3): 505–28.

Petite, P. 1997. *Republicanism: A Theory of Freedom and Government*. Oxford: Oxford University Press.

Quinn, D. 2008. "Self-Determination Movements and Their Outcomes." In *Peace and Conflict 2008*, ed. J. Hewitt, J. Wilkenfeld, and T. Gurr. 33–8. Boulder: Paradigm Publishers.

Radmilovic, V. 2010. "Strategic Legitimacy Cultivation at the Supreme Court of Canada: Quebec *Secession Reference* and Beyond." *Canadian Journal of Political Science* 43 (4): 843–69. http://dx.doi.org/10.1017/S0008423910000764.

Radmilovic, V. 2011. "*Between Activism and Restraint: Institutional Legitimacy, Strategic Decision Making and the Supreme Court of Canada*." PhD thesis, University of Toronto.

Rawls, J. 1993. *Political Liberalism*. New York: Columbia University Press.

Reede, J. 2006. "Protection of Basic Constitutional Features in India and Europe." *European Constitutional Law Review* 2: 476–82.

Reilly, B. 2001. *Democracy and Divided Societies*. Cambridge: Cambridge University Press. http://dx.doi.org/10.1017/CBO9780511491108.

Requejo, F. 2005. *Multinational Federalism and Value Pluralism*. Abingdon: Routledge. http://dx.doi.org/10.4324/9780203329627.

Resnick, P. 1994. *Thinking English Canada*. Toronto: Stoddart.

Riddell, T., and F.L. Morton. 2004. "Government Use of Strategic Litigation: The Alberta Exported Gas Tax Reference." *American Review of Canadian Studies* 34 (3): 485–509. http://dx.doi.org/10.1080/02722010409481209.

Rocher, F., and M. Smith. 2003. "The Four Dimensions of Canadian Federalism." In *New Trends in Canadian Federalism*, ed. F. Rocher and M. Smith. 21–44. Peterborough, ON: Broadview.

Rocher, F., and N. Verrelli. 2003. "Questioning Constitutional Democracy in Canada: From the Canadian Supreme Court Reference on Secession to the Clarity Act." In *The Conditions of Diversity in Multinational Democracies*, ed. A. Gagnon, M. Guibernau, and F. Rocher. 207–40. Montreal: Institute for Research on Public Policy.

Romney, P. 1999. "Provincial Equality, Special Status and the Compact Theory of Canadian Confederation." *Canadian Journal of Political Science* 32 (1): 21–39. http://dx.doi.org/10.1017/S0008423900010088.

Rousseau, J.-J. 1993. *The Social Contract and Discourses* (1762). London: Dent.

Roux, T. 2008. "Principle and Pragmatism on the Constitutional Court of South Africa." *International Journal of Constitutional Law* 7 (1): 106–38. http://dx.doi.org/10.1093/icon/mon029.

Russell, P. 1969. "Constitutional Reform of the Canadian Judiciary." *Alberta Law Review* 7 (1): 103–29.

Russell, P. 1983. "Bold Statescraft, Questionable Jurisprudence." In *And No One Cheered: Federalism, Democracy and the Constitution Act*, ed. K. Banting and R. Simeon. 210–38. Toronto: Methuen.

Russell, P. 1987. *The Judiciary in Canada: The Third Branch of Government*. Toronto: McGraw-Hill Ryerson.

Russell, P. 2004. *Constitutional Odyssey: Can Canadians Become a Sovereign People?* Toronto: University of Toronto Press.

Ryan, C. 2000. "Consequences of the Quebec Secession Reference: The Clarity Bill and Beyond." *C.D. Howe Institute Commentary* 139: 1–32.

Sabetti, F. 1982. "The Historical Context of Constitutional Change in Canada." *Law and Contemporary Problems* 45 (4): 11–32. http://dx.doi.org/10.2307/1191542.

Saunders, C. 2006. "Comparative Conclusions." In *Legislative, Executive, and Judicial Governance in Federal Countries*, ed. J. Kincaid, K. Le Roy, and C. Saunders, 344–84. Montreal: McGill-Queen's University Press.

Saxena, R., ed. 2002. *Mapping Canadian Federalism for India*. Delhi: Konark Publishers.

Saywell, J. 2002. *The Lawmakers: Judicial Power and the Shaping of Canadian Federalism*. Toronto: University of Toronto Press.

Schertzer, R. 2008. "Recognition or Imposition? Federalism, National Minorities, and the Supreme Court of Canada." *Nations and Nationalism* 14 (1): 105–26. http://dx.doi.org/10.1111/j.1469-8129.2008.00324.x.

Schertzer, R., and E. Woods. 2011. "Beyond Multinational Canada." *Commonwealth and Comparative Politics* 49 (2): 196–222. http://dx.doi.org/10.1080/14662043.2011.564473.

Schneiderman, D. 1999. "Introduction." In *The Quebec Decision: Perspectives on the Supreme Court Ruling on Secession*, ed. D. Schneiderman. 1–13. Toronto: James Lorimer and Co. Ltd.

Segal, J.A., and H.J. Spaeth. 1993. *The Supreme Court and the Attitudinal Model*. Cambridge: Cambridge University Press.

Segal, J., and H. Spaeth. 2002. *The Supreme Court and the Attitudinal Model Revisited*. New York: Cambridge University Press. http://dx.doi.org/10.1017/CBO9780511615696.

Sharpe, R. 2000. "The Constitutional Legacy of Chief Justice Brian Dickson." *Osgoode Hall Law Journal* 38 (1): 189–220.

Sieyès, E.J. 1963. *What Is the Third Estate?* (1789). Trans. M. Blondel. Ed. S. Finer. London: Pall Mall.

Simeon, R. 1984. "Criteria for Choice in Federal Systems." *Queen's Law Journal* 8 (1–2): 131–57.

Simeon, R. 2006. *Federal-Provincial Diplomacy: The Making of Recent Policy in Canada*. Toronto: University of Toronto Press.

Simeon, R. 2009. "Constitutional Design and Change in Federal Systems: Issues and Questions." *Publius* 39 (2): 241–61. http://dx.doi.org/10.1093/publius/pjp001.

Simeon, R. 2011. "Preconditions and Prerequisites: Can Anyone Make Federalism Work?" In *The Federal Idea: Essays in Honour of Ron Watts*, ed. T. Courchene et al. 207–23. Kingston: McGill-Queen's University Press.

Simeon, R. 2013. "Reflections on a Federalist Life." In *The Global Promise of Federalism*, ed. G. Skogstad et al. 279–93. Toronto: University of Toronto Press.

Simonsen, S. 1996. "Raising 'The Russian Question': Ethnicity and Statehood – Russkie and Rossiya." *Nationalism and Ethnic Politics* 2 (1): 91–110. http://dx.doi.org/10.1080/13537119608428460.

Sisk, T. 1996. *Power Sharing and International Mediation in Ethnic Conflict*. Washington: United States Institute for Peace Press.

Skogstad, G., et al., eds. 2013. *The Global Promise of Federalism*. Toronto: University of Toronto Press.

Smiley, D. 1970. *Constitutional Adaptation and Canadian Federalism since 1945*. Ottawa: Queen's Printer.

Smiley, D. 1980. *Canada in Question: Federalism in the Eighties*. Toronto: McGraw-Hill Ryerson.

Smiley, D., and R. Watts. 1985. *Intrastate Federalism in Canada*. Toronto: University of Toronto Press.

Smiley, D. 1987. *The Federal Condition in Canada*. Toronto: McGraw-Hill Ryerson.

Smith, A. 1998. *Nationalism and Modernism: A Critical Survey of Recent Theories of Nations and Nationalism*. London: Routledge. http://dx.doi.org/10.4324/9780203167960.

Smith, A. 2003. *Chosen Peoples: Sacred Sources of National Identity*. Oxford: Oxford University Press.

Smith, A. 2009. *Ethnosymbolism and Nationalism: A Cultural Approach*. London: Routledge.

Smith, J. 2003. "The Constitutional Debate and Beyond." In *New Trends in Canadian Federalism*, ed. F. Rocher and M. Smith. 45–65. Peterborough, ON: Broadview Press.

Songer, D., et al. 2012. *Law, Ideology and Collegiality: Judicial Behaviour in the Supreme Court of Canada*. Montreal, Kingston: McGill-Queen's University Press.

Songer, D., and S. Johnson. 2007. "Judicial Decision Making in the Supreme Court of Canada: Updating the Personal Attribute Model." *Canadian Journal of Political Science* 40 (4): 911–34. http://dx.doi.org/10.1017/S0008423907071156.

Songer, D., and J. Siripurapu. 2009. "The Unanimous Decisions of the Supreme Court of Canada as a Test of the Attitudinal Model." *Canadian Journal of Political Science* 42 (1): 65–92. http://dx.doi.org/10.1017/S0008423909090039.

Stepan, A., J. Linz, and Y. Yadav. 2011. *Crafting State-Nations: India and Other Multinational Democracies*. Baltimore: Johns Hopkins University Press.

Strayer, B. 1988. *The Canadian Constitution and the Courts: The Function and Scope of Judicial Review*. Toronto: Butterworths.

Swinton, K. 1990. *The Supreme Court of Canada and Canadian Federalism: The Laskin-Dickson Years*. Toronto: Carswell.

Swinton, K. 1991. "Dickson and Federalism: In Search of the Right Balance." *Manitoba Law Journal* 20 (2): 483–518.

Swinton, K. 1992. "Federalism under Fire: The Role of the Supreme Court of Canada." *Law and Contemporary Problems* 55 (1): 121–65. http://dx.doi.org/10.2307/1191760.

Swinton, K., and C. Rogerson. 1988. *Competing Constitutional Visions: The Meech Lake Accord*. Toronto: Carswell.

Teschke, B. 1998. "Geopolitical Relations in the European Middle Ages: History and Theory." *International Organization* 52 (2): 325–58. http://dx.doi.org/10.1162/002081898753162848.

Tiebout, C. 1956. "A Pure Theory of Local Expenditures." *Journal of Political Economy* 64 (5): 416–24. http://dx.doi.org/10.1086/257839.

Tierney, S. 2003. "The Constitutional Accommodation of National Minorities in the UK and Canada: Judicial Approaches to Diversity." In *The Conditions of Diversity in Multinational Democracies*, ed. A. Gagnon, M. Guibernau, and F. Rocher. 169–206. Montreal: Institute for Research on Public Policy.

Tierney, S. 2009. "Crystallizing Dominance: Majority Nationalism, Constitutionalism and the Courts." In *Dominant Nationalism, Dominant*

Ethnicity: Identity, Federalism and Democracy, ed. A. Lecours and G. Nootens. 87–109. Brussels: PEI Peter Lang.

Tillin, L. 2007. "United in Diversity? Asymmetry in Indian Federalism." *Publius* 37 (1): 45–67. http://dx.doi.org/10.1093/publius/pjl017.

Tilly, C. 1994. "States and Nationalism in Europe 1492–1992." *Theory and Society* 23 (1): 131–46. http://dx.doi.org/10.1007/BF00993675.

Toft, M. 2003. *The Geography of Ethnic Violence: Identity, Interests, and the Indivisibility of Territory*. Princeton: Princeton University Press.

Tremblay, G. 1991. "Judicial Interpretation and the Canadian Constitutional Reform Dilemma." *National Journal of Constitutional Law* 1: 163–78.

Trudeau, P.E. 1998. *The Essential Trudeau*. Ed. R. Graham. Toronto: McClelland & Stewart.

Tully, J. 1994. "Diversity's Gambit Declined." In *Constitutional Predicament*, ed. C. Cook. 149–98. Montreal: McGill-Queen's University Press.

Tully, J. 1995. *Strange Multiplicity: Constitutionalism in an Age of Diversity*. Cambridge: Cambridge University Press. http://dx.doi.org/10.1017/CBO9781139170888.

Tully, J. 2000a. *The Unattained Yet Attainable Democracy: Canada and Quebec Face the New Century*. Montreal: Programme d'études sur le Québec de l'Université McGill.

Tully, J. 2000b. "Struggles over Recognition and Distribution." *Constellations* 7 (4): 469–82. http://dx.doi.org/10.1111/1467-8675.00203.

Tully, J. 2001. "Introduction." In *Multinational Democracies*, ed. A. Gagnon and J. Tully. 1–34. Cambridge: Cambridge University Press. http://dx.doi.org/10.1017/CBO9780511521577.003.

Tully, J. 2004. "Recognition and Dialogue: The Emergence of a New Field." *Critical Review of International Social and Political Philosophy* 7 (3): 84–106. http://dx.doi.org/10.1080/1369823042000269401.

Tummala, K. 2007. "Developments in Indian Federalism: 2005–2007." *Asian Journal of Political Science* 15 (2): 139–60. http://dx.doi.org/10.1080/02185370701511313.

Turp, D. 1999. "Globalizing Sovereignty." *Canada Watch* 7 (1–2): 4–5.

Vale, H. 2013. "The Judicialization of Territorial Politics in Brazil, Colombia and Spain." *Brazilian Political Science Review* 7 (2): 88–113. http://dx.doi.org/10.1590/S1981-38212013000200004.

van den Berghe, P. 1978. "Race and Ethnicity: A Sociobiological Perspective." *Ethnic and Racial Studies* 1 (4): 401–11. http://dx.doi.org/10.1080/01419870.1978.9993241.

van den Berghe, P. 1995. "Does Race Matter?" *Nations and Nationalism* 1 (3): 357–68. http://dx.doi.org/10.1111/j.1354-5078.1995.00357.x.

van der Westhuizen, J. 2005. "South Africa." In *Handbook of Federal Countries, 2005*, ed. A. Griffiths. 309–23. Montreal, Kingston: McGill-Queen's University Press.

Varshney, A. 2013. "How Has Indian Federalism Done?" *Studies in Indian Politics* 1 (1): 43–63. http://dx.doi.org/10.1177/2321023013482787.

Vaubel, R. 2009. "Constitutional Courts as Promoters of Political Centralization: Lessons for the European Court of Justice." *European Journal of Law and Economics* 28 (3): 203–22. http://dx.doi.org/10.1007/s10657-009-9108-8.

Vaughan, F. 1986. "Critics of the Judicial Committee of the Privy Council: The New Orthodoxy and an Alternative Explanation." *Canadian Journal of Political Science* 19 (3): 495–519. http://dx.doi.org/10.1017/S0008423900054536.

Verelli, N. 2008. "*The Supreme Court of Canada: Reaffirming the Norm through the Veil of Constitutional Neutrality*." PhD thesis, Carleton University, Ottawa.

Walters, M. 1999. "Nationalism and the Pathology of Legal Systems: Considering the Quebec Secession Reference and Its Lessons for the United Kingdom." *Modern Law Review* 62 (3): 371–96. http://dx.doi.org/10.1111/1468-2230.00212.

Walzer, M. 1983. *Spheres of Justice: A Defence of Pluralism and Equality*. New York: Basic Books.

Watts, R. 1994. "Contemporary Views on Federalism." In *Evaluating Federal Systems*, ed. B. de Villiers. 1–29. Dordrecht: Martinus Nijhoff Publishers.

Watts, R. 1998. "Federalism, Federal Political Systems, and Federations." *Annual Review of Political Science* 1 (1): 117–37. http://dx.doi.org/10.1146/annurev.polisci.1.1.117.

Watts, R. 1999. *Comparing Federal Systems*. 2nd ed. Kingston: McGill-Queen's University Press.

Watts, R. 2007. "Multinational Federations in Comparative Perspective." In *Multinational Federations*, ed. M. Burgess and J. Pinder. 225–47. London: Routledge.

Watts, R. 2008. *Comparing Federal Systems*. 3rd ed. Kingston: McGill-Queen's University Press.

Webber, J. 1994. *Reimagining Canada: Language, Culture, Community and the Canadian Constitution*. Kingston: McGill-Queen's University Press.

Weber, M. 1968. *Economy and Society*. New York: Bedminster Press.

Weiler, P. 1974. *In the Last Resort: A Critical Study of the Supreme Court of Canada*. Toronto: Carswell-Methuen.

Weinstock, D. 2001. "Towards a Normative Theory of Federalism." *International Social Science Journal* 53 (167): 75–83. http://dx.doi.org/10.1111/1468-2451.00295.

Weller, M. 2005. "The Self-determination Trap." *Ethnopolitics* 4 (1): 3–28. http://dx.doi.org/10.1080/17449050500072796.
Wheare, K.C. 1963. *Federal Government*. London: Oxford University Press.
Wight, M. 1977. *Systems of States*. Leicester: Leicester University Press.
Wimmer, A. 2008. "The Left-Herderian Ontology of Multiculturalism." *Ethnicities* 8 (2): 254–60. http://dx.doi.org/10.1177/14687968080080020102.
Wittgenstein, L. 1967. *Philosophical Investigations*. Oxford: Blackwell.
Wolff, S. 2009. "Complex Power Sharing and the Centrality of Territorial Self-governance in Contemporary Conflict Settlements." *Ethnopolitics* 8 (1): 27–45. http://dx.doi.org/10.1080/17449050902738853.
Wolff, S. 2011. "Managing Ethno-National Conflict: Towards an Analytical Framework." *Commonwealth and Comparative Politics* 49 (2): 162–95. http://dx.doi.org/10.1080/14662043.2011.564471.
Woods, E.T., R. Schertzer, and E. Kaufmann. 2011. "Ethno-National Conflict and Its Management." *Commonwealth and Comparative Politics* 49 (2): 153–61. http://dx.doi.org/10.1080/14662043.2011.564469.
Woods, E.T. 2012. "Beyond Multination Federalism: Reflections on Nations and Nationalism in Canada." *Ethnicities* 12 (3): 270–92. http://dx.doi.org/10.1177/1468796811432684.
Wright, W. 2010. "Facilitating Intergovernmental Dialogue: Judicial Review of the Division of Powers in the Supreme Court of Canada." *Supreme Court Review* 51 (2): 625–93.
Wright, W. 2014. "*Beyond Umpire and Arbiter: Courts as Facilitators of Intergovernmental Dialogue in Division of Powers Cases in Canada.*" PhD thesis, Columbia University, New York.
Yack, B. 2001. "Popular Sovereignty and Nationalism." *Political Theory* 29 (4): 517–36. http://dx.doi.org/10.1177/0090591701029004003.
Zahar, M. 2013. "A Problem of Trust: Can Federalism Silence the Guns?" In *The Global Promise of Federalism*, ed. G. Skogstad et al. 69–98. Toronto: University of Toronto Press.
Zimmer, O. 2003. "Boundary Mechanisms and Symbolic Resources: Towards a Process-Oriented Approach to National Identity." *Nations and Nationalism* 9 (2): 173–93. http://dx.doi.org/10.1111/1469-8219.00081.

Cases

Marbury v. Madison [1803] 5 US 137
Re the Initiative and Referendum Act [1919] A.C. 935
Edwards v. Attorney General for Canada [1930] A.C. 124
Reference re Anti-Inflation Act [1976] 2 S.C.R. 373

Re: Authority of Parliament in Relation to the Upper House [1980] 1 S.C.R. 54
Canadian Pioneer Management Ltd. v. Labour Relations Board of Saskatchewan [1980] 1 S.C.R. 433
Dominion Stores Ltd. v. R. [1980] 1 S.C.R. 844
Labatt Breweries of Canada Ltd. v. Attorney General of Canada [1980] 1 S.C.R. 914
Four B Manufacturing v. United Garmet Workers [1980] 1 S.C.R. 1031
Ritcey et al. v. The Queen [1980] 1 S.C.R. 1077
Fowler v. The Queen [1980] 2 S.C.R. 213
Northwest Falling Contractors Ltd. v. The Queen [1980] 2 S.C.R. 292
The Queen v. Sutherland et al. [1980] 2 S.C.R. 451
Attorney General of British Columbia v. Canada Trust Co. et al. [1980] 2 S.C.R. 466
Covert et al. v. Minister of Finance of Nova Scotia [1980] 2 S.C.R. 774
Boggs v. R. [1981] 1 S.C.R. 49
Fulton et al. v. Energy Resources Conservation Board et al. [1981] 1 S.C.R. 153
Re: Residential Tenancies Act, 1979 [1981] 1 S.C.R. 714
Re: Resolution to Amend the Constitution [1981] 1 S.C.R. 753
Crevier v. A.G. (Québec) et al. [1981] 2 S.C.R. 220
Attorney General of Alberta et al. v. Putnam et al. [1981] 2 S.C.R. 267
Massey-Ferguson Industries Ltd. et al. v. Government of Saskatchewan et al. [1981] 2 S.C.R. 413
Re: B.C. Family Relations Act [1982] 1 S.C.R. 62
Moore v. Johnson et al. [1982] 1 S.C.R. 115
Minister of Finance of New Brunswick et al. v. Simpsons-Sears Ltd. [1982] 1 S.C.R. 144
Re: Exported Natural Gas Tax [1982] 1 S.C.R. 1004
Regional Municipality of Peel v. Mackenzie et al. [1982] 2 S.C.R. 9
Schneider v. The Queen [1982] 2 S.C.R. 112
Multiple Access Ltd. v. McCutcheon [1982] 2 S.C.R. 161
A.G. Can. v. Law Society of B.C. [1982] 2 S.C.R. 307
Robar v. The Queen [1982] 2 S.C.R. 532
Re: Objection by Quebec to a Resolution to Amend the Constitution [1982] 2 S.C.R. 793
Capital Regional District v. Concerned Citizens of British Columbia et al. [1982] 2 S.C.R. 842
Westendorp v. the Queen [1983] 1 S.C.R. 43
Canada Labour Relations Board et al. v. Paul L'Anglais Inc. et al. [1983] 1 S.C.R. 147
Zavarovalna Skupnost (Insurance Community Triglav Ltd.) v. Terrasses Jewellers Inc. [1983] 1 S.C.R. 283
McEvoy v. Attorney General for New Brunswick et al. [1983] 1 S.C.R. 704
Northern Telecom v. Communication Workers [1983] 1 S.C.R. 733

Bisaillon v. Keable [1983] 2 S.C.R. 60
A.G. (Can.) v. Can. Nat. Transportation, Ltd. [1983] 2 S.C.R. 206
R. v. Wetmore [1983] 2 S.C.R. 284
Attorney General of Quebec v. Grondin [1983] 2 S.C.R. 364
Reference re Newfoundland Continental Shelf [1984] 1 S.C.R. 86
Reference re Upper Churchill Water Rights Reversion Act [1984] 1 S.C.R. 297
Reference re: Ownership of the Bed of the Strait of Georgia and Related Areas [1984] 1 S.C.R. 388
Goldwax v. Montreal [1984] 2 S.C.R. 525
Skoke-Graham v. The Queen [1985] 1 S.C.R. 106
R. v. Big M Drug Mart Ltd. [1985] 1 S.C.R. 295
Re: Manitoba Language Rights [1985] 1 S.C.R. 721
Deloitte Haskins & Sells v. Workers' Comp. Board [1985] 1 S.C.R. 785
Dick v. La Reine [1985] 2 S.C.R. 309
Derrickson v. Derrickson [1986] 1 S.C.R. 285
Scowby v. Glendinning [1986] 2 S.C.R. 226
R. v. Edwards Books and Art Ltd. [1986] 2 S.C.R. 713
Reference re Bill 30, An Act to Amend the Education Act (Ont.) [1987] 1 S.C.R. 1148
Ontario (Attorney General) v. OPSEU [1987] 2 S.C.R. 2
Rio Hotel Ltd. v. New Brunswick (Liquor Licensing Board) [1987] 2 S.C.R. 59
O'Hara v. British Columbia [1987] 2 S.C.R. 591
R. v. Crown Zellerbach Canada Ltd. [1988] 1 S.C.R. 401
Bell Canada v. Quebec (Commission de la santé et de la sécurité du travail) [1988] 1 S.C.R. 749
Canadian National Railway Co. v. Courtois [1988] 1 S.C.R. 868
Alltrans Express Ltd. v. British Columbia (Workers' Compensation Board) [1988] 1 S.C.R. 897
R. v. Francis [1988] 1 S.C.R. 1025
Clark v. Canadian National Railway Co. [1988] 2 S.C.R. 680
Devine v. Quebec (Attorney General) [1988] 2 S.C.R. 790
Ontario (Attorney General) v. Pembina Exploration Canada Ltd. [1989] 1 S.C.R. 206
Sobeys Stores Ltd. v. Yeomans and Labour Standards Tribunal (N.S.) [1989] 1 S.C.R. 238
General Motors of Canada Ltd. v. City National Leasing [1989] 1 S.C.R. 641
Québec Ready Mix Inc. v. Rocois Construction Inc. [1989] 1 S.C.R. 695
Irwin Toy Ltd. v. Quebec (Attorney General) [1989] 1 S.C.R. 927
YMHA Jewish Community Centre of Winnipeg Inc. v. Brown [1989] 1 S.C.R. 1532
Alberta Government Telephones v. (Canada) Canadian Radio-Television and Telecommunications Commission [1989] 2 S.C.R. 225
IBEW v. Alberta Government Telephones [1989] 2 S.C.R. 318

MacKeigan v. Hickman [1989] 2 S.C.R. 796
Bank of Montreal v. Hall [1990] 1 S.C.R. 121
Starr v. Houlden [1990] 1 S.C.R. 1366
R. v. S. (S.) [1990] 2 S.C.R. 254
Knox Contracting Ltd. v. Canada [1990] 2 S.C.R. 338
Commission de Transport de la Communauté Urbaine de Québec v. Canada (National Battlefields Commission) [1990] 2 S.C.R. 838
United Transportation Union v. Central Western Railway Corp. [1990] 3 S.C.R. 1112
Whitbread v. Walley [1990] 3 S.C.R. 1273
Reference re Young Offenders Act (P.E.I.) [1991] 1 S.C.R. 252
R. v. F.(J.T.) [1991] 1 S.C.R. 285
R. v. W.(D.A.) [1991] 1 S.C.R. 291
Monk Corp. v. Island Fertilizers Ltd. [1991] 1 S.C.R. 779
R. v. Swain [1991] 1 S.C.R. 933
Reference re Canada Assistance Plan (B.C.) [1991] 2 S.C.R. 525
R. v. Furtney [1991] 3 S.C.R. 89
R. v. Jones [1991] 3 S.C.R. 110
Friends of the Oldman River Society v. Canada (Minister of Transport) [1992] 1 S.C.R. 3
Reference re Goods and Services Tax [1992] 2 S.C.R. 445
Ontario Hydro v. Ontario (Labour Relations Board) [1993] 3 S.C.R. 327
R. v. Morgentaler [1993] 3 S.C.R. 463
Hunt v. T&N plc [1993] 4 S.C.R. 289
Allard Contractors Ltd. v. Coquitlam (District) [1993] 4 S.C.R. 371
R. v. Colarusso [1994] 1 S.C.R. 20
British Columbia (Attorney General) v. Canada (Attorney General); An Act Respecting the Vancouver Island Railway (Re) [1994] 2 S.C.R. 41
Reference re Quebec Sales Tax [1994] 2 S.C.R. 715
RJR-MacDonald Inc. v. Canada (Attorney General) [1995] 3 S.C.R. 199
Husky Oil Operations Ltd. v. Minister of National Revenue [1995] 3 S.C.R. 453
MacMillan Bloedel Ltd. v. Simpson [1995] 4 S.C.R. 725
Reference re Amendments to the Residential Tenancies Act (N.S.) [1996] 1 S.C.R. 186
R. v. Pamajewon [1996] 2 S.C.R. 821
Ontario Home Builders' Association v. York Region Board of Education [1996] 2 S.C.R. 929
Reference re Remuneration of Judges of the Provincial Court of Prince Edward Island [1997] 3 S.C.R. 3
R. v. Hydro-Québec [1997] 3 S.C.R. 213
Delgamuukw v. British Columbia [1997] 3 S.C.R. 1010
Westcoast Energy Inc. v. Canada (National Energy Board) [1998] 1 S.C.R. 322

Reference re Secession of Quebec [1998] 2 S.C.R. 217
Consortium Developments (Clearwater) Ltd. v. Sarnia (City) [1998] 3 S.C.R. 3
Ordon Estate v. Grail [1998] 3 S.C.R. 437
M & D Farm Ltd. v. Manitoba Agricultural Credit Corp. [1999] 2 S.C.R. 961
Westbank First Nation v. British Columbia Hydro and Power Authority [1999] 3 S.C.R. 134
Global Securities Corp. v. British Columbia (Securities Commission) [2000] 1 S.C.R. 494
Reference re Firearms Act (Can.) [2000] 1 S.C.R. 783
Lovelace v. Ontario [2000] 1 S.C.R. 950
Public School Boards' Assn. of Alberta v. Alberta (Attorney General) [2000] 2 S.C.R. 409
Mitchell v. M.N.R. [2001] 1 S.C.R. 911
Law Society of British Columbia v. Mangat [2001] 3 S.C.R. 113
Ward v. Canada (Attorney General) [2002] 1 S.C.R. 569
Kitkatla Band v. British Columbia (Minister of Small Business, Tourism and Culture) [2002] 2 S.C.R. 146
Krieger v. Law Society of Alberta [2002] 3 S.C.R. 372
Siemens v. Manitoba (Attorney General) [2003] 1 S.C.R. 6
Unifund Assurance Co. v. Insurance Corp. of British Columbia [2003] 2 S.C.R. 63
Paul v. British Columbia (Forest Appeals Commission) [2003] 2 S.C.R. 585
R. v. Malmo-Levine; R. v. Caine [2003] 3 S.C.R. 571
R. v. Demers [2004] 2 S.C.R. 489
Reference re Same-Sex Marriage [2004] 3 S.C.R. 698
Rothmans, Benson & Hedges Inc. v. Saskatchewan [2005] 1 S.C.R. 188
Fédération des producteurs de volailles du Québec v. Pelland [2005] 1 S.C.R. 292
British Columbia v. Imperial Tobacco Canada Ltd. [2005] 2 S.C.R. 473
Reference re Employment Insurance Act (Can.), ss. 22 and 23 [2005] 2 S.C.R. 669
Kirkbi AG v. Ritvik Holdings Inc. [2005] 3 S.C.R. 302
Isen v. Simms [2006] 2 S.C.R. 349
Dunne v. Quebec (Deputy Minister of Revenue) [2007] 1 S.C.R. 853
Canadian Western Bank v. Alberta [2007] 2 S.C.R. 3
British Columbia (Attorney General) v. Lafarge Canada Inc. [2007] 2 S.C.R. 86
Confédération des syndicats nationaux v. Canada (Attorney General) [2008] 3 S.C.R. 511
Quebec v. Lacombe [2010] 2 S.C.R. 453
Quebec v. Canadian Owners and Pilots Association [2010] 2 S.C.R. 536
Reference re Assisted Human Reproduction Act [2010] 3 S.C.R. 457
Canada v. PHS Community Services Society [2011] 3 S.C.R. 134
Reference re Securities Act [2011] 3 S.C.R. 837

Marine Services International Ltd. v. Ryan Estate [2013] 3 S.C.R. 53
Reference re Supreme Court Act, ss. 5 and 6 [2014] 1 S.C.R. 433
Reference re Senate Reform [2014] 1 S.C.R. 704
Tsilhqot'in Nation v. British Columbia [2014] 2 S.C.R. 256
Bank of Montreal v. Marcotte [2014] 2 S.C.R. 725
Amex Bank of Canada v. Adams [2014] 2 S.C.R. 787
Marcotte v. Fédération des caisses Desjardins du Québec [2014] 2 S.C.R. 805
Trial Lawyers Association of British Columbia v. British Columbia [2014] 3 S.C.R. 31
Carter v. Canada [2015] SCC 5
Quebec v. Canada [2015] SCC 14

Legislation

Constitution Act, 1867
Constitution Act, 1982
Supreme Court Act, RSC, 1985, C S-26
Clarity Act, SC, 2000, C 26

Index

www.ingramcontent.com/pod-product-compliance
Lightning Source LLC
LaVergne TN
LVHW040152080826
844660LV00014B/937/J

* 9 7 8 1 4 8 7 5 0 0 2 8 3 *